Quantifying Consciousness

An Empirical Approach

EMOTIONS, PERSONALITY, AND PSYCHOTHERAPY

Series Editors:
Carroll E. Izard, *University of Delaware, Newark, Delaware*
and
Jerome L. Singer, *Yale University, New Haven, Connecticut*

A Continuation Order Plan is available for this series. A continuation order will bring delivery of each new volume immediately upon publication. Volumes are billed only upon actual shipment. For further information please contact the publisher.

Quantifying Consciousness

An Empirical Approach

Ronald J. Pekala
West Chester, Pennsylvania

Plenum Press • New York and London

Library of Congress Cataloging-in-Publication Data

Pekala, Ronald J.
    Quantifying consciousness : an empirical approach / Ronald J.
  Pekala.
        p.   cm. -- (Emotions, personality, and psychotherapy)
    Includes bibliographical references and index.
    ISBN 0-306-43750-3 (hardbound)
    1. Consciousness--Testing. 2. Self-report inventories.
  3. Phenomenological psychology--Methodology.   I. Title.
  II. Series.
    [DNLM: 1. Consciousness. 2. Psychometrics--methods.   BF 311
  P379q]
  BF311.P319   1991
  126--dc20
  DNLM/DLC
  for Library of Congress   91-24226
                                                                  CIP

ISBN 0-306-43750-3

© 1991 Plenum Press, New York
A Division of Plenum Publishing Corporation
233 Spring Street, New York, N.Y. 10013

Printed in the United States of America

To my parents,
John and Susan Pekala

Preface

This book presents an approach to quantifying consciousness and its various states. It represents over ten years of work in developing, testing, and researching the use of relatively simple self-report questionnaires in the retrospective assessment of subjective or phenomenological experience. While the simplicity of the method allows for subjective experience to be reliably and validly assessed across various short stimulus conditions, the flexibility of the approach allows the cognitive psychologist, consciousness researcher, and mental health professional to quantify and statistically assess the phenomenological variables associated with various stimulus conditions, altered-state induction techniques, and clinical procedures.

The methodology allows the cognitive psychologist and mental health professional to comprehensively quantify the structures and patterns of subjective experience dealing with imagery, attention, affect, volitional control, internal dialogue, and so forth to determine how these phenomenological structures might covary during such stimulus conditions as free association, a sexual fantasy, creative problem solving, or a panic attack. It allows for various phenomenological processes to be reported, quantified, and statistically assessed in a rather comprehensive fashion that should help shed greater understanding on the nature of mind or consciousness.

The methodology also allows for states of consciousness associated with hypnosis, progressive relaxation, biofeedback, drug-intoxicated states, shamanistic trances, psi-related experiences, and various other altered-state induction procedures to be not only accurately measured, but also statistically assessed and visually displayed. Hence, it provides a heretofore unavailable phenomenological methodology for mapping and diagraming the structures and patterns of consciousness and identity, discrete, and altered states of consciousness (Tart, 1975).

The approach espoused in this book can be useful not only to those individuals interested in quantifying and mapping the terrain of inner space, but to psychologists, psychiatrists, other mental health professionals, artificial intelligence researchers, computer scientists, anthropologists, and related individuals interested in how the mind processes, stores, and retrieves phenomenological data and organizes and structures those data into states and altered states of consciousness. By asking subjects what they experience during various stimulus conditions, the researcher or clinician can determine how the mind processes phenomenological information and compare this information with neurological, psychological, electrophysiological, and/or clinical data.

The book is divided into four parts: Background, Instruments, Methodology, and Applications. Hence, the reader is led from theoretical background material to the actual instruments and methodology, to conclude with various applications of this methodology for understanding hypnosis, stress management strategies, and even an out-of-the-body experience.

In this volume, the foundation is laid for the assessment and quantification of phenomenological or subjective data through sophisticated psychological and statistical methodologies. I hope that the information and data contained in this book will provide an understandable theoretical and empirical foundation for beginning to use self-report, retrospective inventories in psychophenomenological research.

I would like to thank several colleagues, notably V. K. Kumar (Department of Psychology, West Chester University), Ralph L. Levine (Department of Psychology, Michigan State University), and Elizabeth Forbes (Department of Nursing, College of Allied Health Sciences, Thomas Jefferson University), for their support, discussions, and hard work in collaborating with me on the many research studies on which this book draws.

I would also like to thank Drs. Charles Wilson and Steven Cavicchia, respectively former Chief and Chief of Psychology, Coatesville VA Medical Center. Their encouragement and support in allowing me to conduct the pure and applied clinical research on consciousness, phenomenological experience, hypnosis, and stress management techniques were partly responsible for several of the 20-plus professional articles that I have published in the last ten years and which I have been able to draw upon in writing this book. In addition, I would like to thank the staff of the Medical Media Department of the Coatesville VA Medical Center for their time and effort concerning the construction of the many figures that needed to be completed for those articles and associated professional presentations, several of which were subsequently used in this book.

It is important to also acknowledge and extend my appreciation to the Departments of Psychology at Michigan State University and West Chester University, and to the Department of Nursing at Thomas Jefferson University, for the opportunity to gain access to their students. Many of the research findings presented in these chapters are based on student participation from these departments.

Finally, I must thank the many reviewers—anonymous and otherwise—who have reviewed the published papers upon which this book draws, and the many colleagues and acquaintances who attended seminars wherein some of the material cited in this book was discussed, and whose suggestions and comments were graciously presented. Without their helpful suggestions, critiques, and encouragement, this book would have remained only a noetic reality.

Although many others have made significant contributions to my thinking concerning the methodology presented in this book, I must acknowledge total responsibility and culpability for the opinions, data, and theoretical and empirical material cited in this book. My hope is that other researchers can critique, build, modify, and enlarge upon what I have tried to do here. For this purpose I have recently established an institute, one purpose of which is to unravel the structures and patterns of consciousness in ways that I hope will expand on what I have written. Interested parties are encouraged to contact me at the Mid-Atlantic Educational Institute, 309 North Franklin Street, West Chester, Pennsylvania 19380–2765.

Acknowledgments

This book is based, in part, on the following articles written by colleagues and me within the past ten years. I thank the publishers for allowing me to use the material from those articles, in modified form, in this book.

Kumar, V. K., & Pekala, R. J. (1988). Hypnotizability, absorption, and individual differences in phenomenological experience. *International Journal of Clinical and Experimental Hypnosis, 36,* 80–88.

Kumar, V. K., & Pekala, R. J. (1989). Variations in phenomenological experience as a function of hypnotic susceptibility: A replication. *British Journal of Experimental and Clinical Hypnosis, 6,* 17–22.

Maitz, E., & Pekala, R. J. (1991). Phenomenological quantification of an out-of-the-body experience associated with a near-death event. *OMEGA, 22,* 199–214.

Pekala, R. J. (1980). *An empirical-phenomenological approach for mapping consciousness and its various "states."* (Doctoral dissertation, Michigan State University, 1980.) *44* (University Microfilm No. 82–02, 489.)

Pekala, R. J., (1985). A psychophenomenological approach to mapping and diagraming states of consciousness. *Journal of Religion and Psychical Research, 8,* 199–214.

Pekala, R. J. (in press). Hypnotic types: Evidence from a cluster analysis of phenomenal experience. *Contemporary Hypnosis.*

Pekala, R. J., & Bieber, S. L. (1990). Operationalizing pattern approaches to consciousness: An analysis of phenomenological patterns of consciousness among individuals of differing susceptibility. *Imagination, Cognition, and Personality, 9,* 303–320.

Pekala, R. J., & Forbes, E. J. (1988). Hypnoidal effects associated with several stress management strategies. *Australian Journal of Clinical and Experimental Hypnosis, 16,* 121–132.

Pekala, R. J., & Forbes, E. J. (1989). Phenomenological effects associated with several stress management strategies. *Imagination, Cognition, and Personality, 8,* 265–281.

Pekala, R. J., & Forbes, E. J. (1990). Subjective effects associated with several stress management strategies: With reference to attention. *Journal of Behavioral Medicine, 16,* 39–44.

Pekala, R. J., & Kumar, V. K. (1984). Predicting hypnotic susceptibility by a self-report phenomenological state instrument. *American Journal of Clinical Hypnosis, 27,* 114–121.

Pekala, R. J., & Kumar, V. K. (1985). A short program for assessing the equality of two independent correlation matrices. *Educational and Psychological Measurement, 45,* 175–177.

Pekala, R. J., & Kumar, V. K. (1986). The differential organization of the structures of consciousness during hypnosis and a baseline condition. *Journal of Mind and Behavior, 7,* 515–539.

Pekala, R. J., & Kumar, V. K. (1987). Predicting hypnotic susceptibility via a self-report instrument: A replication. *American Journal of Clinical Hypnosis, 30,* 57–65.

Pekala, R. J., & Kumar, V. K. (1988). Phenomenological variations in attention across low, medium, and high hypnotically susceptible individuals. *Imagination, Cognition, and Personality, 7,* 303–314.

Pekala, R. J., & Kumar, V. K. (1989). Patterns of consciousness during hypnosis: Relevance to cognition and individual differences. *Australian Journal of Clinical and Experimental Hypnosis, 17,* 1–20.

Pekala, R. J., & Levine, R. L. (1981). Mapping consciousness: Development of an empirical-phenomenological approach. *Imagination, Cognition, and Personality, 1,* 29–47.

Pekala, R. J., & Levine, R. L. (1982). Quantifying states of consciousness via an empirical-phenomenological approach. *Imagination, Cognition, and Personality, 2,* 51–71.

Pekala, R. J., & Nagler, R. (1989). The assessment of hypnoidal states: Rationale and clinical application. *American Journal of Clinical Hypnosis, 31,* 231–236.

Pekala, R. J., & Wenger, C. F. (1983). Retrospective phenomenological assessment: Mapping consciousness in reference to specific stimulus conditions. *Journal of Mind and Behavior, 4,* 247–274.

Pekala, R. J., Wenger, C. F., & Levine, R. L. (1985). Individual differences in phenomenological experience: States of consciousness as a function of absorption. *Journal of Personality and Social Psychology, 48,* 125–132.

Pekala, R. J., Steinberg, J., & Kumar, V. K. (1986). Measurement of phenomenological experience: Phenomenology of Consciousness Inventory. *Perceptual and Motor Skills, 63,* 983–989.

Acknowledgment is made to the publishers listed below for permission to quote from the following sources:

Izard, C. E. (1977). *Human emotions.* New York: Plenum Press, p. 155.

James, W. (1902/58). *The varieties of religious experience.* New York: New American Library, p. 298.

Kukla, A. (1983). Toward a science of experience. *Journal of Mind and Behavior, 4,* pp. 235, 243, 244–245.

Contents

I. THE BACKGROUND

II. THE INSTRUMENTS

III. THE METHODOLOGY

IV. APPLICATIONS

Introduction

In this book, I have tried to present an empirical-phenomenological approach for mapping the structures and patterns of consciousness. By consciousness I mean one's awareness of one's subjective experience, including both the processes of being aware and the various contents of that awareness. This includes both the *noeses* and the *noema* of phenomenological consciousness (Kockelsman, 1967) and also one's "state of consciousness" (Tart, 1975), as one's stream of subjective experience is apprehended over a period of time.

The approach is called *retrospective phenomenological assessment* (RPA) and involves the retrospective completion of a self-report, phenomenological state instrument in reference to a preceding stimulus condition. It is thus a relatively simple approach in that subjects retrospectively rate the intensity of various aspects of their subjective or phenomenological experience by means of a self-report inventory. Although this initial procedure is relatively uncomplicated, the methodological presuppositions underlying the use of such instruments are more involved, as are the procedures for diagraming the phenomenological intensity and pattern effects obtained from these instruments.

The use of retrospective phenomenological assessment in assessing phenomenological experience gives the researcher and clinician a means to not only describe and evaluate subjective experience, but to quantify and statistically assess variations in subjective experience across various stimulus conditions, altered-state induction techniques, and clinical procedures. The variations in subjective experience are quantified by means

1

of the dimensions and subdimensions of consciousness (or attention) mapped by the questionnaires.

By means of *psygrams* (graphs of the pattern structures among dimensions of consciousness), *pips* [phenomenological intensity profiles or profiles of (sub)dimension intensity effects], *icons* [two-dimensional representations of (sub)dimension intensity effects], and *hypnographs* (graphs of the hypnoidal effects associated with a given stimulus condition), the researcher has a means to diagram the intensity and pattern parameters of the state of consciousness associated with a particular stimulus condition. Thus, this approach presents a methodology for quantifying, diagraming, and statistically assessing: (1) various schemas (Singer & Kolligian, 1987), processing units (Rumelhart, Hinton, & McClelland, 1986) or subsystems of consciousness (Tart, 1977); (2) states and altered states of consciousness (Tart, 1975); and also (3) hypnoidal states of consciousness (Pekala & Nagler, 1989).

Abraham Maslow, one of the founders of humanistic psychology, once said that if all you have is a hammer, you treat everything as a nail. If psychologists are going to attempt to understand and explore mind or consciousness, methodologies must be developed to adequately assess the domain of mind or consciousness. (I will use these two terms synonymously.) The self-report questionnaires and the devices used to illustrate the results obtained from those instruments represent such a methodology.

WHY AN EMPIRICAL PHENOMENOLOGY?

I have always been intrigued by those neuroscientists who said they went into neuroscience to "find" mind or consciousness. Just as a hammer will treat everything as a nail, a scalpel will treat everything as flesh. And in the tradition of Descartes, mind is not flesh!

Although consciousness is grounded in the brain and its neurophysiology, this does not mean that it is *completely reducible* to that level of analysis. Different levels of analysis must be developed to assess the different aspects of consciousness, be it psychological (Ornstein, 1972), psychobiological (Davidson & Davidson, 1980), or social-ecological (Feuerstein, 1987; Gebser, 1986). Hence, methodologies must be developed to map, assess, and quantify mind if psychology is to understand mind or consciousness. In particular, empirical *phenomenological* or *noetic* (from *nous*, Greek for "mind"; *Webster*, 1970) methodologies must be developed and implemented to understand mind, since mind is phenomenological or noetic (of or relating to various aspects of mind, i.e., cognition, volition, affect, memory, perception, etc.) à la Husserl (1913/72).

I believe psychology has been successful in understanding human behavior because it has attempted to *quantify* and *statistically assess* that behavior. Just as psychology has moved from a behavioral to a cognitive perspective, I believe it will move from a cognitive-behavioral to a noetic-behavioral perspective in its attempt to understand human behavior and experience. And just as psychology has tried to quantify human behavior, it will need to quantify and statistically assess human phenomenology. An understanding of the nature of the human mind will be found, I believe, in an understanding of the phenomenology of mind, in addition to psychological, biological, and neurochemical explanations.

This is not to say that neuroscience is not useful in understanding human consciousness; on the contrary, without the gains made by neuroscience, I believe I would not now be able to talk about human phenomenology. Rather, what I want to say is that neuroscience does not go far enough in understanding the human mind. Just as the psychology of learning is based on the physiology of learning, but yet is not completely reducible to physiology (and hence the need for a psychology of learning), a phenomenology of consciousness is not *completely* reducible to human neuroanatomy, neurophysiology, and so forth. Consciousness needs to be conceptualized on many levels; the phenomenological level is one of these, as are the neurophysiological and the neurochemical levels.

Psychology needs to develop a phenomenology of consciousness, a phenomenology of mind, where it attempts to map, quantify, and statistically assess the phenomenology of mind just as neurophysiology has attempted to define a neurophysiology of mind. This phenomenology will need to go beyond the descriptive phenomenology of Husserl (1913/72) and the phenomenological psychologists (Valle & King, 1978). Whereas descriptive phenomenology seeks a "detailed description of [the phenomena of] consciousness as they appear in consciousness" (Ashworth, 1976, p. 364), a methodology is needed to not only describe but to empirically quantify and statistically assess the phenomena of consciousness.

Thus a major difference between the approach presented in this book and that of historical phenomenology (Kockelsman, 1967) is the presupposition that mind or consciousness can be quantified and statistically assessed. To many this may seem implausible, and yet the chapters to follow will not only show that this is possible, but quite desirable, if one wants to understand and predict particular aspects of human behavior and experience.

In order to quantify human consciousness or mind, one must have something to measure and hence the need to have "structures" or "subsystems" of consciousness. It is here that I may be accused of "reifying" consciousness. I do not believe, however, that one can quantify consciousness unless one has "something" of consciousness to quantify; hence the need for structures or subsystems. What has been done in this book, in attempting to quantify mind, is no different than what physicists have done is attempting to quantify and measure "charm." The concept of, let us say, "rationality" is no more a reification than is the concept of "charm." Both are concepts used to describe a process that has been defined in a particular way. We can no more easily see or taste "charm" than we can "rationality," and yet I believe we understand the concept of "rationality" better than we do that of "charm," at least if we are not nuclear physicists!

The explosion of research in cognitive psychology (Neisser, 1967), artificial intelligence (Newell & Simon, 1972), and parallel distributed processing (PDP) models of consciousness (McClelland & Rumelhart, 1988) draws heavily on the use of such structures, schemas, or processing units, and the present approach is consistent with the above. The "proof of the pudding" concerning any scientific approach lies in what that approach can yield us in terms of "understanding and predicting human behavior" and experience, to paraphrase J. B. Watson (1913). I believe this book yields a quite interesting methodology on human consciousness and presents an approach that is quite pregnant with possibilities.

The psygrams, pips, icons, and hypnographs are examples of such possibilities. In charting an unknown area, one must at times create new devices for measuring and understanding the data of the domain being charted. The aforementioned devices, although rather simple, allow the structures and patterns of human consciousness to be more easily illustrated and, I believe, understood. It might be argued, however, that these devices are somewhat arbitrary. To this I would agree. Psygrams and pips could have been constructed differently, possibly utilizing different structures or subsystems of consciousness and expressed in different formats. The fact, however, that a particular graphing device is constructed in a particular manner does not detract, however, from the usefulness of that device. Rather it depends on what that device can do to help us better understand and conceptualize the phenomena of interest. What has been constructed I think will be quite useful, especially since there is very little else available for phenomenologically diagraming and statistically assessing the patterns and structures of mind.

I have labeled the approach presented in this book *psychophenomenological* (Pekala, 1980, 1985a,c) to distinguish it from the approaches of classical introspectionism, the phenomenological psychologists, and the phenomenological approach that Shor (1979) has described concerning hypnosis. It is *phenomenological* in the sense that it seeks to describe the phenomenological contents of consciousness as do the phenomenologists and the phenomenological psychologists and *psychological* in the sense of using traditional psychological and statistical approaches to do this (i.e., a self-report questionnaire to arrive at a quantification of the phenomena of interest and *t*-tests, analyses of variance, and so on to statistically evaluate the psychological data that are obtained from this quantification).

There is also a philosophical presupposition that underlies this approach, as I conceive it, that necessitates using a new term to define it. In contrast to cognitive-behavioral approaches, which tend to emphasize the primal data of psychology as cognitive and behavioral (which, incidentally, necessarily follows from psychology's historical past and in no way is meant to debase that approach), is the philosophical presupposition of the present approach, which is also common to the phenomenological approach of Husserl (1913/72). This presupposition is that *all* the phenomena of consciousness or mind, regardless of whether they can be independently verified by an "outside" observer, are legitimate objects of scientific investigation. Such nonpublicly verifiable data [or phenomenological data, as it is currently called (Hilgard, 1980)] need not be relegated to second- or third-class scientific citizenship because validity/verification cannot be achieved to the same *degree* that most behavioral data can.

As Kukla (1983) has argued, introspective or phenomenological reports require no new departure from the established natural science approach:

> (P)hysical and experiential reports must be assigned the same scientific status . . . I do not mean to suggest that the enterprise of introspective psychology is free from either practical or logical difficulties. But I do not see any *new* difficulties that do not already have their exact counterpart in physical science. The same problems arise, with the same severity, whether we talk to each other about the motion of particles and the behavior of organisms, or about our feelings, images, and thoughts. (p. 244)

Although the reliability and validity of phenomenological data may be harder to establish in comparison to overt behavioral data, I am in complete agreement with   linger's (1978) statement that the validity of introspective data, or any type of data for that matter, will finally reside "in ruling out artifacts, in replications, and ultimately, in the usefulness of data or theory for making possible other forms of prediction and perhaps control" (p. 227).

In a way, the approach espoused in this book is somewhat similar to what Wundt (1897) and Titchener (1898) tried to do at the turn of the century in the then "structural" attempt to understand human consciousness. The present approach is different, however, in that no claim is made that the various (sub)dimensions of consciousness (or attention) mapped by the self-report inventories are "fundamental" structures of consciousness in the Wundtian sense. Rather they are (sub)dimensions of subjective experience found to be relatively stable and reliable structures of consciousness across the stimulus conditions that they have been used to assess.

Although much more research yet needs to be done to replicate, validate, and extend the findings reported here, the research to date suggests that this approach can be a useful means for understanding, predicting, and possibly controlling human behavior and experience.

I feel that the psychophenomenological approach offered in this book is only an initial and somewhat incomplete attempt to try to quantify human consciousness. Given such a grandiose goal, I feel this approach is neither comprehensive nor complete, but rather represents a *beginning* attempt to try to map and decipher the workings of the human mind. Hopefully, it will lay the foundation for more complex methodologies for an understanding and analysis of human consciousness.

On the other hand, with all its limitations, I feel this approach can greatly add in a significant way to our understanding of human consciousness, for it delineates a methodology, heretofore unavailable, for mapping, quantifying, statistically assessing, and diagraming the structures and patterns of mind.

ORGANIZATIONAL FORMAT

This book is organized into four main sections: background, instruments, methodology, and applications. The first four chapters concern historical background material and the theoretical rationale for mapping the structures and patterns of consciousness and states of consciousness. Chapter 1 traces the development of man's understanding of "consciousness" from Descartes (1641/1969) to Kukla (1983) and argues for the return of introspection as a legitimate psychological methodology. The second chapter discusses contemporary introspective perspectives on consciousness. Phenomenological theorizing and research into the stream of consciousness and states of consciousness are discussed. This is followed by Chapter 3, which reviews the recent cognitive revolution in psychology with particular reference to Singer, Mandler, Anderson, Baars, Izard, the PDP researchers, and psychologists interested in the conscious-unconscious domain.

After reviewing reasons for the lack of phenomenological research methods, Chapter 4 discusses a rationale for operationalizing and quantifying a state of consciousness. Retrospective phenomenological assessment and stimulus-state specificity, terms used to describe the methodology and principle for the assessment of states of consciousness, are then introduced. Chapter 4 ends with a brief introduction to psygrams, pips, icons, and hypnographs, devices for diagraming the data obtained from using self-report phenomenological instruments in retrospective phenomenological assessment.

The next four chapters describe several self-report instruments that have been developed to map the structures and patterns of consciousness phenomenologically. Thus, Chapters 5 and 6, respectively, describe the development, reliability, and validity of the Phenomenology of Consciousness Questionnaire (PCQ) and the (Abbreviated) Dimensions of Consciousness Questionnaire [(A)DCQ], predecessor instruments to the current instrument for mapping the structures of consciousness, the Phenomenology of Consciousness Inventory (PCI).[1] Chapter 7 reviews the PCI, along with data on its development, reliability, and validity. This is followed by a chapter on the development and use of the Dimensions of Attention Questionnaire (DAQ), a more recently developed instrument for mapping various facets of attention.

The next section of the book describes the charting devices and the methodology for using self-report phenomenological state instruments in retrospective phenomenological assessment. Chapter 9 defines and illustrates various graphing devices, that is, psygrams, pips, icons, and hypnographs; instruments for graphing the results obtained from the PCI or the DAQ. This chapter is followed by a chapter on the methodological and statistical limits for using the PCI or the DAQ in retrospective phenomenological assessment.

The last major section of the book is addressed to demonstrating

---

[1]The researcher or clinician interested in using the Phenomenology of Consciousness Inventory (PCI) (Pekala, 1982, 1991b) or the Dimensions of Attention Questionnaire (DAQ) (Pekala, 1985d, 1991a) can procure the inventory, manual scoring sheets, and supporting materials from the Mid-Atlantic Educational Institute, Inc., 309 North Franklin Street, West Chester, Pennsylvania 19380–2765.

how the PCI, the DAQ, and their use in retrospective phenomenological assessment, in conjunction with psygrams, pips, and hypnographs, can be used to understand and predict human behavior and experience. Watson (1913) defined psychology's goal as the prediction and control of human behavior. It seemed quite apropos to demonstrate how self-report instruments such as the PCI and the DAQ can be used to understand and predict human phenomenological experience and, additionally, human behavior as assessed by the Harvard Group Scale of Hypnotic Susceptibility (Shor & Orne, 1962) in particular. By providing not only experimental but also clinical data, this section demonstrates what may be accomplished when using the PCI and the DAQ to map the structures and patterns of consciousness associated with hypnosis, stress management conditions, and even an out-of-the-body experience.

A final section summarizes the material in the book and intimates what future uses may evolve for this psychophenomenological approach to understanding the human mind.

I

The Background

1

Consciousness and Introspection
Historical Developments

INTRODUCTION

In 1879 the father of experimental psychology, Wilhelm Wundt (1832–1920), founded the first psychological laboratory of the world. This laboratory was established to investigate *Erfahrungswissenschaften*, the science of experience. Since the data of such a science were *anschaulich*, or phenomenal, the methodology of psychology was introspection, the process of engaging in and examining one's own thought processes and sensory experiences. Such a methodology sought, in short, to understand consciousness and its component processes.

As outlined by Wundt, the problems of psychology as the science of experience were:

> (1) the *analysis* of conscious processes into *elements*, (2) the determination of the manner of connection of these elements, and (3) the determination of their laws of connection. (cited in Boring, 1929/50, p. 333)

It is now over a century since the founding of Wundt's psychological laboratory, dedicated to exploring the structures and nature of consciousness. One hundred years later, it can justifiably be said that the scientists of the 1990s are not much further ahead than Wilhelm Wundt was in explaining and understanding the nature and operations of consciousness.

The number of neurons in the brain, over 10 billion, is similar to the number of stars in the Milky Way, our home galaxy (Wilson, 1978), and yet the science of consciousness is at about the same place as astronomy was in the 17th century when Galileo turned his telescope on the moons of Jupiter.

Whereas modern psychology began its existence with the study of consciousness under such brilliant scientists as Wundt, Titchener, and James, after a few short decades the interest in consciousness waned. By 1930 it was hard to find even a reference to the word "consciousness" in the popular textbooks and journals of America. Consciousness and introspection had been exorcised from the mainstream of American psychology. But just as what has been repressed continues to haunt the repressor, ever remaining beneath the surface ready to erupt when the defenses have weakened, consciousness and the study of its processes erupted to gain in scientific importance with the cognitive revolution of the 1970s and 1980s (Baars, 1986).

It will be the purpose of this chapter to explore the rise, fall, and resurrection of consciousness as a legitimate area of psychological research. The emergence of psychology from philosophy as a separate discipline in the late 1800s, its rise to prominence as the science of consciousness, and its slide into oblivion only a few decades later will form the first half of the following chapter. The second half will then focus on: (1) the resurrection of the study of consciousness that began in the second half of the 20th century, and (2) the arguments used to defend introspection, or phenomenological assessment as contemporary introspection is now called, as a legitimate scientific methodology.

CONSCIOUSNESS AND PHILOSOPHY

The word "consciousness" comes from the Latin compound *conscius*, which means to "know with," or "know together" (*Webster*, 1970). It was first used in the English-speaking world by Francis Bacon (1561–1629) in the early 17th century (Marsh, 1977), although its primacy in experience can be traced back at least to Descartes's (1596–1650) *Cogito, ergo sum*: I think, therefore, I am.

In attempting to break away from medieval scholasticism, Descartes wanted to find something of which he would be indubitably certain. Such a certainty would serve as a foundation for erecting a theory of knowledge divorced from theological speculations. In attempting to doubt everything conceivable, in hopes of finding something of which he could not doubt, Descartes realized that his awareness of himself was indubitable. Even if God were an evil genius deceiving him, this evil genius could not deceive Descartes as to his own existence.

Descartes realized that awareness is necessarily experienced as part of the experience of existence, and being deceived presupposes an existent being who is aware of the possibility of deception:

> Doubtless then, I exist, since I am deceived; and let him deceive me as he may, he can never bring it about that I am nothing, so long as I shall be conscious that I am something. So that it must, in fine, be maintained, all things being maturely and carefully considered, that this proposition, I am, I exist, is necessarily true each time it is expressed by me, or conceived in my mind. (Descartes, 1641/1969, pp. 126–127)

Descartes's *I think, therefore, I am* implicates *thinking*, however, and not consciousness as the indubitable basis of knowledge. But he later defines thought as

> all that we are conscious as operating in us. And that is why not only understanding, willing, and imagining, but also feelings are here the same thing as thought. (Descartes, 1644, cited in Copleston, 1963, p. 102)

Thus, thinking for Descartes corresponds to what we would today characterize as consciousness. The *cogito* thus brought thinking, and hence consciousness, to the center of philosophy, and it has remained there ever since.

Descartes's *Meditations* (1641/1969) marks a turning point in Western philosophy and science. Besides finding an indubitable basis for man's knowledge, Descartes went on in his *Meditations* to separate the spiritual and mental domains from that of the material. Since Descartes defined the mind in terms of an immaterial, unextended substance and the body in terms of a material, extended thing, each "substance" now had its own characteristics and separate domains; one amenable to the spiritual/religious and one to the empirical spheres of influence. Philosophy and science were now free to explore and understand the nature of material reality without irking the wrath of religious dignitaries in the process. This, in turn, helped set the stage for the split between man's mind and his body, and his science and his religion, for the coming centuries.

The British empiricists, Locke (1632–1704), Berkeley (1685–1753), and Hume (1711–1776), took up where Descartes left off. They continued the dualism advocated by Descartes but they also became interested in how the mind attempts to bridge the gulf between mind and body when coming to know the external world.

Locke, the father of British empiricism, held that all ideas, which he defined as "whatever is meant by phantasm, notion, species, or whatever it is which the mind can be employed about in thinking" (Locke, 1690/1959, p. 8), were either simple or complex and were grounded in experience. In his system, the mind was a *tabula rasa*, or blank tablet, upon which the ideas were impressed. He defined consciousness as "the perception of what passes in a man's own mind" (p. 138), and it included the changing panorama of ideas.

Hume, like Locke, derived all mental events from experience, but did so by using the word "perceptions" for Locke's "ideas." He also divided perceptions into impressions and ideas. Impressions were the immediate data of experience, or what we would today call sensations, while ideas were the faint images of impressions used in thinking and reasoning. Ideas came from impressions and were less vivid and lively.

Another Englishman, David Hartley (1705–1755), took Locke's ideas on association and came up with the doctrine or principle of association. Hartley hypothesized that man's complex mental life is constructed by simple ideas becoming associated, via contiguity, with other ideas, so that complex mental ideas were produced from and ultimately traceable to simpler ideas.

CONSCIOUSNESS AND PSYCHOLOGY

Structural Psychology

The work of these Englishmen was used by Wilhelm Wundt (1832–1920) to inaugurate scientific psychology in Germany. Drawing upon the British empiricists' ideas on sensations, thinking, and association, Wundt attempted to make psychology as scientific as physics. Physics, for Wundt, dealt with experience mediately, for its elements, that is, force, gravity, and so on, were inferred and not given immediately in experience. Psychology, on the other hand, dealt with experience immediately, as subjectively perceived. For Wundt, then, both physics and psychology dealt with experience. But the difference between them lay in the point of view with which experience was to be regarded.

To inaugurate psychology as a scientific discipline dealing with immediate experience, Wundt turned to chemistry for his model. Wundt looked for the psychological atoms of experience and used the principle of association to build up the molecules, compounds, and higher levels of mental activity. Sensations, and perhaps feelings and images, were the psychological atoms that could be combined to form perceptions, ideas, and higher mental processes. To deal with the fact that the mind is in constant flux, Wundt emphasized that an element, such as a sensation, was a "mental process" that was not substantial and thus not an "element" in the traditional sense of chemistry.

The fact that later psychological introspectionists tended to treat mental processes, such as sensations, images, and feelings, as static bits of consciousness was a perversion of the meaning intended by Wundt. Nevertheless, Wundt was not completely innocent, however, for to hold that an element is also a process is to invite ambiguity as to exactly what meaning is to be attached to the *structural approach* to consciousness that Wundt advocated.

At the heart of Wundt's structural approach to psychology was his methodology, now termed *classical introspection*. Wundt distinguished between inner perception and introspection. Inner perception was basically introspection by untrained observers. In contrast, introspection per se was introspection by trained observers. These observers were so trained that it was said that a introspectionist had to perform 10,000 introspective judgments before he could provide data for a publishable report from Wundt's laboratory (Boring, 1953). After having been trained as to the nature of the elements and their sensory nature, such introspection consisted of being aware of what was occurring in consciousness during a given interval of time and then retrospectively reporting on that awareness.

A student of Wundt's, E. B. Titchener (1867–1927), brought the structural approach of introspection to America. Titchener regarded structural psychology as analogous to the discipline of anatomy in biology. Just as an anatomical description of the structures of the organism are necessary before an adequate understanding of the functioning of the organism can be grasped, so likewise an analysis of the structure or morphology of consciousness was necessary before one could truly begin to understand its nature and operations.

In his classic paper of 1898, Titchener defined the "structural elements of mind," their number, and their nature. *Sensations* were designated the elementary mental processes as were the *affective* processes, and they were the only elements of mind:

> It seems safe, then, to conclude that the ultimate processes are two, and two only, sensations and affections, though we must not forget that the first class, that of sensations, includes the two well-defined subspecies, "sensation" and "idea." (1898, p. 459)

Whereas sensation referred to percepts from the external world, ideas referred to internal processes less clear and vivid than that derived from sensations.

Any mental element for Titchener had at least two attributes or determinants: quality and intensity. Quality made an element specific and individual, as a red or yellow, sweet or sour, or pleasant or unpleasant sensation, whereas intensity referred to the gradient or intenseness with which the sensation or affection was experienced. Along with these attributes, affective elements also had a duration, and sense elements had duration, clearness, and in some instances extent.

Titchener came to these conclusions, as did Wundt, through introspection on himself and by others who worked as students in his laboratory. However, Titchener placed much greater restraints on introspection than did Wundt or other introspectionists. Titchener maintained the requirement that the description of conscious experience should exclude statements of meaning. Titchener originally coined the concept of *stimulus error* as the reporting of meanings about the independent existence of stimulus objects, something an introspectionist should not do. When Kulpe claimed to find imageless thought in "the consciousness of judgment, action, and other thought processes" (Boring, 1953, p. 173), Titchener broadened his definition to include any meanings at all in the data of introspection. He felt that such stimulus-error inferences about conscious data did not exist in the same way as did the elemental processes of sensation and affection.

Titchener's methodology, while purporting to exclude meaning, seemed to let it in by the back door; for introspection as practiced under Titchener was greatly dependent upon retrospection. For example, an observation that took only a second or two to complete might take 20 minutes to describe completely, during which time "the introspectionist racked his brain to recall what happened 1000 seconds ago" (Boring, 1953, p. 174). Such retrospection would seem to have to rely heavily on the role of memory and inference.

As a reaction against such rigid and pedantic constraints on introspectionism, Kulpe (1862–1915) developed *systematic experimental introspection*, also known as the Wurzburg school of introspection. Whereas Wundt had said that thoughts could not be studied experimentally, Kulpe thought they could and set out to do just that. He had observers think under specific controlled conditions and then let the observers introspect about the thought processes taking place. His students' results indicated that observers could not determine how a particular solution to a cognitive process was found; that is, how thought was directed toward a particular goal. To address the question of what the observers were experiencing when problem solving was not associated with images or sensations, one of Kulpe's students, Ach, coined the term, *unanschauliche Bewusstheiten* (impalpable awarenesses), to describe the vague and evanescent contents of consciousness evident during problem solving.

Whereas the Wurzbergers thought they had discovered a new kind of mental element, Titchener suggested that this was nothing but "vague evanescent patterns of sensations and images, and, in part, meanings and inferences which ought to be kept out of psychology" (Boring, 1953, p. 174). Thus began the controversy over imageless thought that helped to initiate the downfall of structuralism.

Functional Psychology

Besides this controversy, another reason why structuralism never really caught on in America was due to the practical nature of Americans, who looked for practical and functional solutions to problems. Those Americans besides Titchener who were interested in introspection espoused a functional instead of a structural approach to consciousness.

The two most famous proponents of *functionalism* in America were William James (1842–1910) and James Angell (1869–1949). William James, the father of American psychology, can be said to be the main American proponent of functionalism. He enunciated his position in his tour de force, *The Principles of Psychology* (1890/1950). James began his book by defining the scope of psychology:

> Psychology is the Science of Mental Life, both of its phenomena and their connections. The phenomena are such things as we call feelings, desires, cognitions, reasonings, decisions, and the like. (1890/1950, p. 1)

Like the Wundtians, psychology for James was concerned with the nature of mental life. But whereas the structuralists attempted to "freeze" a single moment of consciousness and then analyze that moment for its elemental structures and contents, James conceived the study of consciousness in terms of process. It is he who is credited with popularizing the term *stream of consciousness* (or the stream of thought) to refer to the fleeting and changing character of consciousness over time.

James characterized consciousness by five attributes: personal, always in flux, continuous, intentional, and selectional. Every thought is part of a personal consciousness and thought is always changing and never the same. As with Heraclitus's stream, one cannot step into the stream of thought twice, for each moment it changes and varies. Similarly, like a stream or river, the stream of consciousness is continuous and "without breach, crack, or division." The fourth characteristic of thought, its intentionality, refers to the fact that consciousness deals with objects independent of itself; that is, consciousness is always consciousness of something.

Lastly, consciousness "is always interested in more than one part of its object rather than in another, and welcomes and rejects, or chooses, all the while it thinks" (p. 284). These last two characteristics of thought deal with attention; the fact that attention is always an aspect of consciousness that is directed toward something and that attention is selectional, choosing one particular thing to attend to at a time. These five characteristics of consciousness epitomize the functionalist approach to consciousness and are contrasted with the elementary processes of sensations and affections and their corresponding attributes of intensity, quality, and so forth of the structuralists.

In a paper by the other major American functionalist, James Angell (1907), the opposition between structuralism and functionalism was more fully delineated. Angell wrote that functional psychology was concerned "with the effect to discern and portray the typical *operations* of consciousness under actual life conditions, as over against the attempt to analyze and describe its elementary and complex contents" (p. 63). Whereas a structural psychology of sensation would undertake to determine the number and attributes of the elements of the various sensory modalities, a functional psychology of sensation would concentrate on determining the characteristics of the various sensory *capabilities* and how they differ from one another.

Angell argued that mental events are evanescent, fleeting, and at times vague. To characterize them as elements, as an anatomist would the organs of a body, is to give to such mental contents a durability that they do not possess. According to Angell:

> In the measure in which consciousness is immanently unstable and variable, one might anticipate that a functional classification would be more significant and penetrating than one based upon any supposedly structural foundation. (1907, p. 75)

Angell also objected to the structuralist's use of the "state of consciousness" concept. When analyzing any particular state of consciousness for the elements that compose it, what the observer notices depends on the particular stimulus condition and setting that call them forth. Since one cannot get a fixed and specific color sensation without keeping constant the internal and external conditions in which it appears, the particular sensation experienced is a function of the multitude of variables that may have influenced consciousness at the particular moment of observation. Thus, the structural approach, in analyzing the elements of consciousness, may yield different results in different environments; and more so, whatever it does find may be more a function of the method used than the actual state of consciousness experienced.

Angell argued that functionalism, on the other hand, is not liable to the above criticism when investigating the psychology of mental operations, since the function and not the content of consciousness is being investigated. A functionalistic approach also addressed itself to how the mind mediates between the environment and the needs of the organism. This allows for the determination of the functional utility of consciousness. Angell suggested that his functional approach to consciousness is thus more appropriate to the process nature of consciousness and can yield more reliable and useful results than the structural approach.

Phenomenological Approaches

Besides the structuralist and functionalist approaches to consciousness, another approach to consciousness, much more evident in Europe than America, was the phenomenological approach espoused by the Gestalt psychologists. When Wundt in 1874 was busy completing his handbook, Brentano wrote his *Psychologie vom Empirischen Standpunkt* (1874/1925). Thus, while Wundt was busy analyzing consciousness in terms of content, Brentano was involved in defining consciousness in terms of *acts*.

Brentano thought that psychical acts, in contrast to physical phenomena, possess immanent objectivity. Psychical acts are directed toward an object and "have the object 'inexisting intentionally' within them" (Boring, 1929/50, p. 360). An act of consciousness always implies an object or refers to a content, whereas physical phenomena are self-contained and do not refer beyond themselves. This doctrine of intentionality was taken up by Brentano's pupil, Husserl, and became the foundation for his philosophical system of pure phenomenology.

For Husserl, consciousness is "consciousness of something" (1913/72, p. 223) and phenomenology is the methodology used to elucidate consciousness. Through the *epoche*, a suspension of judgment, the existence of the external world is "bracketed" or suspended, and the phenomenologist is now free to describe the basic data of experience as they present themselves. By means of the epoche and the phenomenological method, the psychologist now has at his disposal "the only secure basis upon which a strong empirical psychology can be built" (1913/72, p. 62). By distinguishing *noeses* (intentional acts of consciousness, i.e., perceiving, thinking, and so on) from *noema* (the objects of consciousness), Husserl attempted to define and understand consciousness from his "pure phenomenology" perspective.

It is from this phenomenological foundation that the Gestaltists came to speak of the data of direct experience as *phenomena*. This phenomenological approach generated a great deal of good research through Gestalt approaches to perception. Gestalt psychology became a legitimate school of psychology with the works of Katz, Wertheimer, and Kohler.

In contrast to the elementalism of the structuralists, the Gestaltists asserted that the whole is greater than the sum of its parts and protested against the analysis of an experience into a predetermined list of elements. They argued that since a person can see a whole object without knowing what conscious elements it is composed of or can see movement without being able to specify the "quality" of the movement, such enumeration of elements is futile and not necessary for an understanding of the phenomena being studied. They were also not afraid to include meaning in their analyses, something that a classical introspectionist like Titchener would never do. In 1929 Kohler published his *Gestalt Psychology*, and with the death of Titchener two years earlier, phenomenological observation had won out over classical introspection.

Besides Gestalt psychology, phenomenology continued to be further defined in the works of Heidegger (1927/62) and Sartre (1943/71). The work of Jean Paul Sartre (1943/71) is especially important in understanding the phenomenology of consciousness. Drawing upon Husserl's methodology of pure phenomenology, Sartre objected to the simplicity of Descartes's formula: "I think, therefore, I am." By positing that the consciousness that says "I am" is not actually the consciousness that thinks but secondary to it, Sartre attempted to demonstrate that pure awareness or "consciousness of" was the basis of subjective experience, and when it reflected on itself or the object of consciousness, the reflexivity of the Cartesian *cogito* was born.

Hence, prior to the cogito of Descartes is Sartre's *pre-reflective cogito*. The pre-reflective cogito "is the condition of the Cartesian cogito" (Sartre, 1943/71, p. 13). For Sartre the pre-reflective cogito is pure awareness, pure intentionality (in the Husserlian sense), or "nonpositional self-consciousness." When this pre-reflective cogito reflects upon itself or the object of its awareness, positional self-consciousness is born:

> consciousness deliberately reflects upon its own acts and states and in so far as possible posits itself as an object. The Cartesian cogito, of course, belongs to the second order. (Sartre, 1943/71, p. xii)

Sartre's nonpositional and positional self-consciousness anticipate the latter distinctions made by Natsoulas (1978) and Baruss (1987) on the different definitions and conceptions of consciousness.

The Rise of Behaviorism

Although it was the phenomenological observations of the Gestalt psychologists that triumphed over classical introspection in Europe, in America it was behaviorism that dealt the final blow to classical introspection and with it the study of consciousness. The beginning of the end was foreshadowed in J. B. Watson's (1878–1958) classic paper of 1913 entitled "Psychology as the Behaviorist Views It." With this paper, not only did Watson derogate introspection and its disciplines of structuralism and functionalism, but Watson also founded *behaviorism* as the new psychology, a psychological paradigm still very much in influence today. The first paragraph of this seminal paper sums up Watson's attitude and approach to psychology:

> Psychology as the behaviorist views it is a purely objective, experimental branch of natural science. Its theoretical goal is the prediction and control of behavior. Introspection forms no essential part of its method, nor is the scientific value of its data dependent upon the readiness with which they lend themselves to interpretation in terms of consciousness. (1913, p. 158)

Watson suggested that by making consciousness the primary subject matter of psychology, behavioral data were reduced to having no value. Since 50 years of experimental introspection had failed to make psychology an undisputed natural science, it was time for psychology to discard all reference to consciousness. Watson argued that the presence or absence of consciousness anywhere in the phylogenetic scale had made no impact on the problems of behavior. He suggested that neither structural nor functional psychology had allowed for adequate experimental treatment of the facts. These disciplines had rather enmeshed themselves in a series of speculative questions not amenable to experimental verification.

Behaviorism, on the other hand, allowed for the adequate testing of psychological problems. In support, Watson reviewed those fields of psychological endeavor where the behavioristic approach was already yielding promising results. In such an approach, introspection had no place, except perhaps to the extent of using verbal report to assess "thought processes (that) are really motor habits in the larynx" (Watson, 1913, p. 174).

Watson's protest against consciousness fit well with America's *Zeitgeist*. America's practical spirit was well-suited for a functional and practical approach to psychology and behaviorism offered the American psychologist a paradigm that was both functional and extremely practical. According to Boring (1929/50), by "the 1920s it seemed as if all

America had gone behaviorist" (p. 645). During the behavioristic hegemony, Watson was not the only proponent of behaviorism lighting the way for a functional and behavioral psychology that shunned consciousness.

With men like E. B. Holt (1873–1946), A. P. Weiss (1879–1931), E. C. Tolman (1886–1961), and B. F. Skinner (1904–1990), behaviorism retained its hold over American experimental psychology and did not deviate much from Watson's initial ostracism of consciousness. Although Tolman was one of the few behaviorists to even attempt a definition of consciousness (Tolman, 1927), his behavioristic approach gave consciousness little more than nominal status. He did, nevertheless, espouse a system called *purposive behaviorism*, in which purpose, if not consciousness, was given a prominent place in his theoretical account of behavior.

The most recent leader and philosopher of behaviorism was B. F. Skinner. In clarifying his views about the relationship between behaviorism and consciousness, Skinner (1974) neither denied the existence of mental events (as Watson did at one time) nor did he hold to their inaccessibility to scientific analysis because they are private: "Radical behaviorism . . . does not call these (private) events unobservable, and it does not dismiss them as subjective" (p. 116).

Rather, Skinner regarded mental events, such as tasting an apple, as just another form of behavior, that is, a particular class of responses governed by the same behavioral principles as overt events. However, he did not hold to the view that they should be used in explaining other behavior. According to him, mental events are not necessary for a functional analysis of behavior and can, for all practical purposes, be ignored.

Fifty years of behaviorism, in contrast to the previous 50 years of introspection, has allowed psychology to make tremendous strides in becoming a scientific and legitimate science with voluminous applications. Behaviorism was a necessary and needed change to the pedantic and controversial researches of the introspectionists. It has also produced much of the desired results that Watson so prophesied. Just as introspection was superseded after 50 years by behaviorism, however, so behaviorism began to be superseded by cognitive psychology.

A MODERN RETURN TO CONSCIOUSNESS

An already classic paper published just 51 years after Watson's paper on behaviorism was the essay by R. R. Holt (1964) entitled "Imagery:

The Return of the Ostracized." In this paper Holt explored the banishment of imagery by psychology at the hands of the behaviorists and its return through interest in sensory deprivation, attention, dreaming, and so on to the laboratories of psychologists. Whereas "controversy over imageless thought became a death struggle of introspectionism, and imagery was one of the main foci of Watson's attack in the polemic that founded behaviorism" (1964, p. 263), it was the recent interest in imagery that brought consciousness, introspection, and subjective experience back to the scientific forum. Holt suggested that the study of imagery could help psychologists understand behavior. Besides helping to construct a "detailed working model of the behaving organism," such an approach could take into account the operations inside the famous black box of the mind.

Whereas Holt's article reviewed how imagery was making a comeback since the turn of the century, a more recent article that defended the use of introspection in psychology was D. A. Lieberman's (1979) article entitled "Behaviorism and the Mind: A (Limited) Call for a Return to Introspection." Lieberman's article cites evidence for the return of introspection as a legitimate adjunctive methodology for use with behavioral observation.

Lieberman argued that although many experimental psychologists have abandoned the language of behaviorism, many still continue to be influenced by its methodological and philosophical assumptions and constraints. Yet the dangers of introspection are not nearly quite so detrimental as has been painted by the behaviorists. Lieberman then systematically explores these dangers and determines why they are somewhat, although not completely, unfounded, provided the requisite restraints are used. The following subsection will review Lieberman's polemics.

For and Against Introspection

Three general arguments have been advanced by the behaviorists against the use of introspection as a scientific technique. The first concerns the argument that mental events do not exist, an argument that was once used by Watson himself (Watson & McDougall, 1929). Lieberman dismisses their argument without discussion since virtually no contemporary psychologists, in their right mind, have chosen to attack mental events by denying their existence.

A more subtle argument consists in saying that the mind exists but denies that it is involved in the causality of behavior. Such an epiphenomenal version of mind suggests that consciousness is but an "incidental by-product" of the electrical activity of the neural elements and so does not play a causal role in influencing behavior. Besides suggesting that such an epiphenomenalist position is empirically untestable and hence no scientific position at all, Lieberman argues that since mental and neural events are correlated, an analysis of mental events can lead to an understanding, and possibly prediction, of neural events.

The ultimate argument of whether or not introspective data are useful in psychology is the extent to which such data can help lead to the "prediction and control of behavior," to cite Watson (1913) himself. Whether the mind is or is not causal for behavior is not a valid argument against introspection, especially since the evidence suggests "that mental and neural states are, at least, correlated" (Lieberman, 1979, p, 321).

A third argument, the most persuasive, is that introspection, by its very nature, is the observation of internal events that are not accessible to outside observation. Without a means of confirming observations, arguments over the reliability and validity of such observations will doom introspective accounts to futile and needless controversy, just as it did the early structural and functional introspectionists.

Lieberman acknowledged that there is some validity to this argument, but also suggests that reports from others are not the only means of validating introspective data. The repeatability or reliability of an observation is one measure of its validity and the methods and data of modern psychophysics show that scientific, empirical data can be procured from introspective reports that are reliable and valid. Moreover, subjective events reported by introspection can be correlated with other data, such as neurological events like EEG potentials, to check on the validity of the self-report. Although there is room for error while confirming subjective reports, the lack of perfect accuracy must be weighed against the empirical usefulness of such reports in predicting and controlling behavior.

Lieberman also addressed the objections of the behaviorist B. F. Skinner (1974) against using introspection. (Although they are basically variations of the above three arguments, they will also be reviewed here.) Skinner's main objection is that introspective reports are "inherently inaccurate." Lieberman admits that much of our internal subjective experience is inaccessible and the correlation between verbal reports and observable states is unlikely to be perfect. Nevertheless, as long as some correlation exists, introspective reports can be useful, especially when the correlations are high, as is the case in some experiments (Kroll & Kellicut, 1972).

A second objection of Skinner is that mental events are not necessary for a functional analysis of behavior. Lieberman argues that if behavior were fully predictable from observable environmental events, there would be no need to bother with the murkiness of mental events. But all behavior cannot be predicted by behaviorists from the current conditions of the environment and the individual's past behavior.

Moreover, sometimes merely asking the subject his intentions can yield better results than an exhaustive analysis of environmental and historical variables. As an example, public opinion polls can now usually predict election results to within 1 or 2% by merely asking voters of their intentions. Would a knowledge of environmental conditions and historical variables that presumably lead to voter behavior do the same?

A final main objection raised by Skinner is that introspection can too easily lead to such a preoccupation of mind so as to ultimately neglect environmental factors that control behavior. But Lieberman contends that just because a methodology may lead to dangers is not sufficient reason for not studying and using it.

Lieberman summarizes by suggesting that instead of trying to force behavior and methodology into the "procrustean bed prescribed by (behavior) theory, . . . it would be far less taxing, as well as more honest, to accept what we so clearly believe in covertly" (1979, p. 330).

The Legitimacy of Introspective Observation

Whereas Lieberman argues for the adjunctive use of introspection, the case has been made by Kukla (1983) for the use of introspection as a legitimate psychological investigative technique in its own right. Since his approach and that advocated in this book are very similar, the next subsection will present his arguments for the legitimacy of introspective or phenomenological observation.

Kukla (1983) rebukes Lieberman for conceding too much to the methodological behaviorists and attempts in his "science of experience" to show that introspective and behavioral data play identical roles in the scientific enterprise. The distinction between "public" and "private" events, which Kukla claims is the only basis for differential treatment of these two types of evidence, is logically incoherent.

Kukla's thesis is that experiential data derived from introspective observation are entirely equal to behavioral data and no basis exists for ascribing different roles to them in the scientific enterprise. Although introspection is not problem free, "introspection raises no *unique* problems that are not already encountered in the enterprise of behavioral psychology" (p. 233). Kukla's thesis is quite germane to the central thesis of this book: phenomenological observations are amenable to assessment, evaluation, and statistical control according to the scientific method just as are behavioral observations. For this reason they will be reviewed in some detail.

Kukla's major defense of introspective accounts hinges on the only criteria ever suggested for supposing that experiential events are different from behavioral events; that is, that the former are *private* events while the latter are *public* events. He then discusses the two different criteria of publicity and privacy employed to exclude private (subjective) events from scientific investigation, which he classifies under the *traditional* and *consensual* views.

The traditional view on publicity avers that any event is public if it can, at least in principle, be observed by any properly situated person. Whereas behavioral events meet this criteria, introspective events do not. Kukla argues that this traditional methodological rejection of experiential (private) reports undermines the behaviorist's own concept of publicity. Thus the traditional arguments say that I can establish that physical events are public by ascertaining that another person can also observe them. But this other person's observation of the physical event is as hidden from me as this other person's own feelings, thoughts, and images. Although I can observe the physical event myself, I cannot observe that the other person observed it. As an example, someone may observe my little boy playing, just as I can observe him playing, but they cannot experience my visual perceptions of him playing, just as they cannot experience that sense of fatherly love that I feel as I see him playing.

Just as another person cannot observe me experiencing the color red, or love, or a sweet taste, another person cannot observe my perceptions of a pigeon pirouetting or my perception of a thermometer reading 98.6°F. Although I can attempt to consensually validate the perception of a pigeon pirouetting by using my visual apparatus, I can also attempt to consensually validate the taste of a dry wine, feelings of love toward one's country, or the color red (provided I'm not color blind)). But I cannot consensually validate the perception of a pigeon pirouetting if I am congenitally blind, just as I cannot validate the experience of orgasm if I am impotent.

Kukla argues:

> In summary, traditional methodological behaviorists wield an inconsistently selective skepticism. When they are told that someone has an (subjective) experience, they reject this claim because they cannot independently verify it. But they are evidently prepared to accept another's claim to have observed a physical event, for otherwise they could not conclude that physical events are publicly observable. Yet the one claim is no less problematic than the other. (1983, p. 235)

Thus the traditional argument is fallacious due to a biased understanding of publicity which selectively includes (visual) perception, but not emotions, images, and so forth. Dismissing this biased perspective then leads Kukla to the consensualist argument.

According to Kukla, consensualists concede the above argument against the traditional behaviorist: we can no more verify that others observe a physical event than we can verify that they have an "itch or woe." Nevertheless, consensualists argue that there is a methodological distinction between physical and experiential reports: people's reports of physical events tend to be in *agreement* with one another, while introspective reports do not.

Against the consensualist's position, Kukla argues that agreement is a continuous variable that may range from 0 to 100%. Whereas behavioral reports are relatively more public than experiential reports, some behavioral observations are more public than others, for example, the reading of a digital printout from a mass spectrograph versus the color red (especially to a color-blind person). Thus, the decision to draw the public-private line where behavioral reports leave off and experiential reports begin is an arbitrary one. Implicit in the consensualist argument is the thesis that "all physical events elicit greater conformity of report than all experiential events" (p. 239). Yet this assumption is also false, as shown by Kimble and Garmezy's (1968) afterimage experiments vis-à-vis Skinner's (1974) behavioral observations of a pigeon, where the former elicited a much higher percentage of agreement than the latter.

Kukla argues that if the scientist is to be really comprehensive, both public and private aspects of the data assessment must be taken into account. Thus, the consensualist goes astray when he stipulates "that publicity requires only 'conformity of report' from observer to observer, and high intercorrelated changes in the reported observations with experimental manipulation of the environment" (Spence, 1957, cited in Kukla, 1983, p. 241). To be comprehensive the word "environment" must include not only the relevant environmental conditions, but also the relevant personal conditions of observation. Thus, not only must the experimenter control for environmental variables, he must also control for the "state the observer is in." This includes such things as the observer's perceptual apparatus, linguistic training, and motivation. Just as a blind person cannot train a pigeon to pirouette or a lay person interpret the photographic tracings of a pi meson in a bubble chamber, differences in personality characteristics and previous training will make some people's introspective reports less valid, as they will also make some people's behavioral observations less valid.

And just as we do not stop training pigeons because we cannot use blind trainers (we go out and find a sighted person) or stop nuclear fission experiments because we cannot use lay persons (we go out and find a nuclear physicist), we should not desist from introspective experiments because of the lack of high agreement. Rather, we should find ways to increase agreement of introspective reports, whether by statistical control or training.

Kukla summarizes:

> We see the complete evaporation of the public-private distinction as either the methodological or the practical behaviorist would formulate it . . . . The scientific enterprise becomes instead a search for conditions, both environmental and personal, which reliably elicit any kind of observational reports. And this will necessarily be a search which some people can take part in more than others. The blind cannot tell us anything about pointer readings; the tone-deaf cannot tell us anything about the melodic properties of music; and perhaps some people never feel nostalgic. (p. 243)

Unbiased Scientific Observation

The scientific enterprise presupposes the assumption of *determinism*. If two behaviorists obtain divergent results in a behavioral experiment, it is taken for granted that some causally significant but uncontrolled variable must have made a difference. Likewise, instead of rejecting divergent reports of introspecting subjects as unscientific, it would be far more unbiased, and scientifically more honest, to look for relevant environmental or personal conditions of observation that have not been taken into account.

To selectively exclude introspective or phenomenological observations from scientific experimentation and analysis is to logically contradict the very foundation on which the scientific enterprise and its implicit methodological assumption of determinism is based. Although private events are less publicly verifiable than most public events, they are no less eligible for scientific investigation, for the difference is one of degree and not one of kind.

Although the enterprise of phenomenological assessment is not free from either practical or logical difficulties, there are no new "difficulties that do not have their exact counterpart in physical science. The same problems arise, with the same severity, whether we talk to each other about the motion of particles and the behavior of organisms, or about our feelings, images, and thoughts" (Kukla, 1983, pp. 244–245).

Although phenomenological observations may be more difficult to verify than most behavioral observations, they are not unverifiable. Repeated observations by the same subject, observations of many subjects in reference to the phenomena of interest, observations tied to verifiable and repeatable stimulus conditions, and correlation of introspective observations with behavioral, physiological, and/or neurochemical data can all lead to increased verification, as can experimental and statistical control of subject characteristics and training.

Given the previous arguments for the legitimacy of introspective observation and its use as an appropriate psychological methodology in its own right, the next two chapters will focus on contemporary introspective approaches to understanding consciousness and the cognitive revolution in psychology. These chapters will then be followed by a chapter describing a theoretical rationale and empirical methodology for mapping, diagraming, and statistically assessing the structures and patterns of consciousness.

Phenomenological Perspectives on Consciousness

The recent literature reflects two general trends in the study of consciousness: trends that parallel the structuralist-functionalist camps of introspection during the early 20th century. Like the functionalists, one approach to consciousness attempts to investigate the stream of consciousness (Pope & Singer, 1978a,b) and its relationship to personality measures and related variables. The other approach, paralleling that of the structuralists, attempts to investigate the structure of states of consciousness; states that are hypothesized to be of different intensities (Singer, cited in Zinberg, 1977) or patterns (Tart, 1975) from other states of consciousness.

The following paragraphs will review the theorizing and empirical research into each of these two major approaches for studying the phenomenological nature of human consciousness. But first, a contemporary introduction to consciousness and its phenomenology, since we should first define what consciousness is or appears to involve before explicating the two major approaches for researching the phenomenology of consciousness.

CONSCIOUSNESS

Consciousness can mean different things to different people. Baruss (1987) did a metanalysis of the different behavioral and phenomenological definitions of consciousness as defined by Battista (1978), Bowers (1986), Helminiak (1984), Klein (1984), Merrell-Wolff (1973), Miller and Buckhout (1973), Natsoulas (1978), Pribram (1976), Savage (1976), Strange (1978), and Toulmin (1982). Baruss came up with three groups of definitions, which he defined as consciousness$_1$, consciousness$_2$, and consciousness$_3$.

Consciousness$_1$ refers to the group of definitions that define consciousness in terms of potential cognitive functions that denote being alive and refer to the "characteristics of an organism in a running state which entails the registration, processing, and acting upon information" (1987, p. 325). Consciousness$_2$, on the other hand, refers to subjective awareness that is characterized by intentionality or the fact that consciousness is consciousness *of* something.

According to Baruss, consciousness$_3$ is the most elusive of the three definitions. It represents "knowledge of one's existence as a concomitant of one's experience" and is defined as "the sense of existence of the subject of mental acts" (p. 327). A sense of "self" is implied by this definition.

That consciousness can have a variety of definitions has been well described by Natsoulas. Natsoulas has written prodigiously on consciousness, its problems, and its definitions (see Natsoulas, 1987). In 1981 he wrote about many of the basic problems that confront the scientist, researcher, or philosopher interested in learning more about consciousness. According to Natsoulas, these problems include: conscious experience, intentionality, imagination, awareness, introspection, personal unity, the subject, "consciousness," the normal waking state, conscious behavior, and explicit consciousness. In his 1981 paper Natsoulas attempted to further explicate each of these areas in terms of what they can teach us about consciousness, its functions, operations, and nature.

Natsoulas (1987), like Baruss, has also tried to elucidate the various ways in which the word "consciousness" can be used. Using the six conceptions of consciousness as defined by the *Oxford English Dictionary* (1933), Natsoulas (1978, 1987) clarified the meaning of consciousness according to these definitions. These definitions concern consciousness as: joint or mutual knowledge (consciousness$_1$), internal knowledge or conviction (consciousness$_2$), awareness (consciousness$_3$), direct (reflective) awareness (consciousness$_4$), tertiary (personal unity) consciousness which "is direct (reflective) awareness of the stream as involving reflective constituents" (1987, p. 309) (consciousness$_5$), and one's normal waking state (consciousness$_6$). These definitions concern the ways in which consciousness is phenomenologically and behaviorally experienced and indicate that this term is quite pregnant with various meanings and nuances of meanings.

Consciousness$_1$, joint or mutual knowledge, refers to a relationship between people where they share knowledge, feelings, and so forth with one another. This is a notion of consciousness, according to Natsoulas, that can be traced back to the Greeks and Romans. Citing psychoanalytic conceptions, the notion of "consciousness raising," and radical behaviorism, consciousness$_1$ refers to something one *does*. "It is *joint knowledge* that is achieved, in this view, in the first phase of becoming a conscious member of a certain verbal community" (Natsoulas, 1978, p. 910). Although we may now refer to consciousness primarily as something that is very personal and private, it is important to realize that consciousness *originates* in a community of people who discourse with one another. Hence, this early definition of consciousness reminds us of the *social* origins of consciousness.

Consciousness$_2$, internal knowledge or conviction, refers to the fact that one stands in a certain cognitive relation to oneself to the extent that one is a *witness* or *observer* of one's acts and deeds. Because one is a witness to one's deeds, one has internal knowledge and confidence of those deeds and actions.

Opposed to the previous two definitions, the following definitions are more akin to how consciousness is currently defined. Consciousness$_3$ is "the state or faculty of being mentally conscious or aware of anything" (Natsoulas, 1978, p. 910). Of consciousness$_3$, Natsoulas writes:

> It is arguably our most basic concept of consciousness, for it is implicated in all the other senses. One's being conscious, whatever more it may mean, must include one's being aware of something. What it is to be aware of something is, therefore, eminently worthy of our attention, perhaps as much as the nature of matter is worthy of the attention of other scientists. (1978, p. 910)

This definition of consciousness implicates awareness as the primary datum of consciousness and is akin to Husserl's (1913/72) doctrine of intentionality; that is, consciousness is consciousness of something or Sartre's (1943/71) *pre-reflective cogito*.

Consciousness$_4$ for Natsoulas is direct (reflective) awareness. It is an awareness of awareness:

> One exemplifies consciousness$_4$ by being aware of, or by being in a position to be aware of, one's own perception, thought, or other occurrent mental episode. It is a matter, however, of being noninferentially aware of them, or of undergoing what we may call "direct awarenesses." (1978, p. 911)

Consciousness$_4$ is an awareness of our own mental episodes in the sense that we can reflexively examine that we are aware of (being aware of) something. This is Sartre's (1943/71) reflective, thetic, or positional self-consciousness.

Consciousness$_5$, which Natsoulas labels "personal unity," refers to "the totality of the impressions, thoughts, and feelings, which make up a person's conscious being" (1978, p. 912). Consciousness$_5$ represents an *achievement* in the sense that we are not usually aware of a great many of our experiences, and hence to obtain a unified perspective on all of our conscious experiences is an achievement contingent upon the effort that we apply.

Consciousness$_6$ is the normal state of consciousness that is characteristic of an active, waking state. Altered states of consciousness (Tart, 1975) are altered in reference to Natsoulas's consciousness$_6$. Natsoulas also describes a seventh definition of consciousness, "double consciousness," which the *Oxford English Dictionary* defines as "a condition which has been described as a double personality sharing in some measure two separate and independent trains of thought and two independent mental capabilities in the same individual" (cited in Natsoulas, 1978, p. 913). In this book, we will be primarily concerned with consciousness in the sense of Natsoulas's consciousness$_5$ and consciousness$_6$, although consciousness$_3$ and consciousness$_4$ are also implicated. The word awareness will be used primarily in the sense that Natsoulas defines consciousness$_3$.

For the purpose of this book, consciousness will be defined as the sum total of one's awareness of (or attention to) one's stream of subjective experience. It includes what Husserl (1913/72) would define as the *noeses* (the subjective intentional acts of consciousness, i.e., perceiving, willing, imagining, etc.) and *noema* (the objects of consciousness, i.e., thoughts, feelings, visualizations, etc.) of that experience, including whatever awareness/attention is capable of being aware of, and also encompasses states and altered states of consciousness.

Having now come to some agreement as to how consciousness can be defined and described, we will move on to consciousness as understood from a more empirical and less philosophical perspective.

THE PHENOMENOLOGY OF CONSCIOUSNESS

According to Battista (1978), phenomenological observations about the nature of human consciousness are fraught with difficulties, owing to the nature of consciousness and the problems in observing it. Nevertheless, there are three essential points of agreement that tend to show up again and again across a variety of investigations on consciousness. These three points are: conscious experience is primary; it is a field; and it is a stream in continuous flux.

The observation that conscious experience is primary refers to the fact that consciousness forms the basis of all knowledge by transcending the split between knower and known and uniting both in the experience of consciousness. It is consciousness's intentional nature that allows this unity of experience to take place.

Battista's second point of agreement, that consciousness is a field, refers to the fact that consciousness is a Gestalt experience. The field of consciousness consists of a multitude of perceptions, emotions, thoughts, and so on that are unified into the fabric of experience such that the contents of consciousness are continuous and nondisjunctive with each other. Battista's third point, that consciousness is in continuous flux, refers to the fluid and changeable nature of consciousness, whose flow can be analogized to the flow of a stream.

Battista also distinguishes eight main content areas of conscious experience. These include: "sensations, perception, emotion, affect, cognition, intuition, self-awareness, and unition—'the experience of oneness or unification with everything'" (1978, p. 590). These content areas are defined in the following paragraphs.

Sensations are the physiological reactions to stimuli that impinge upon the nervous system. They are the "raw physical" experiences that form the foundation for perceptions. Perceptions, in turn, are our experiences of sensations, and can occur as sights, sounds, touches, smells, and so forth.

Emotions, for Battista, are the internal experiences that arise in response to sensations and consist of such experiences as hunger, grief, sexual feelings, and so on. Affects are the positive and negative reactions that are experienced in reference to emotions and refer to the pleasant and unpleasant nature of emotions. Cognition, on the other hand, is that complex "state of consciousness" that is the conceptualization, abstraction, and reflection upon experience in a logical, sequential manner.

Intuition is that means of understanding experience that is holistic and simultaneous and may correspond to the "aha" experience, as when multifarious data are seen as a whole or organized unity. Self-awareness is that unique property of consciousness that allows it to reflect upon itself. Finally, unition is the term used to denote a transcendence of subject-object dichotomies in which one is merged with the universe or surround. According to Battista, one's phenomenological experience is composed of these contents in a unity that is everflowing and continuous.

In a somewhat different perspective for describing the phenomenological attributes of consciousness, Marsh (1977) talks about consciousness is terms of four categories: focus, structure, attributes, and flow. Focus, for Marsh, means the direction of attention, whether inward or outward, its intensity, and its breath. All three can be thought of as the different aspects of attention.

Structure refers to the field of awareness as foreground, background, and aerial. The foreground of awareness is the current ideas, memories, impressions, and so on that capture one's attention at a particular moment. The background of awareness refers to the "more general, persistent awareness of time, place, social reality, and personal identity" (Marsh, 1977, p. 126) that forms the basis for the foreground of awareness. And finally, the aerial or overview perspective refers to one's self-awareness, that quality of being aware that one is aware.

Marsh's third category, attributes, are the qualities or characteristics that describe and delimit images, perceptions, feelings, and so forth as to their quality, form, and structure. Some attributes are clear/blurred, real/imagined, and like/dislike. The last of Marsh's categories, that of flow, refers to the fact that the experience of consciousness is subjectively felt as in flux and never the same.

Marsh's perspective thus describes the framework of consciousness in which the contents of consciousness, as enumerated by Battista, are organized. Both Marsh and Battista characterize consciousness as always in flux, an unending stream of thought. One of the two major contemporary perspectives for understanding phenomenological consciousness consists of tapping and assessing one's ongoing stream of thought.

THE NATURE OF THE STREAM OF CONSCIOUSNESS

Investigations into the stream of consciousness as phenomenologically experienced can be traced, in large measure, to the work of J. L. Singer and his colleagues. Singer's approach to studying the stream of consciousness has been through daydreaming. Since "daydreaming is one manifestation of an ongoing stream of relatively self-activated cognitive responses which characterize consciousness, further knowledge of its dimensions and functional implications for personality seems desirable" (Singer & Antrobus, 1963, p. 187).

Thus began an exploration into the stream of consciousness that has yielded a tremendous amount of data on the nature of daydreaming (Singer, 1966, 1975), its relationship to the ongoing stream of thought (Singer, 1977), a variety of personality variables (Rabinowitz, 1975; Singer & Schonbar, 1961), psychopathology (Starker & Singer, 1975), affect and stress (Singer & Rowe, 1962), fantasy (Singer & Singer, 1976), imagination (Singer, 1981), and many other areas.

Singer's approach to the study of daydreaming has been primarily through the use of a retrospective self-report questionnaire that consists of 400 self-descriptions. It is called the Singer-Antrobus Imaginal Process Inventory (IPI) (Singer & Antrobus, 1972) and it has been shown to be a reliable and valid questionnaire for assessing subjective daydreaming experiences. This questionnaire has succeeded in showing that daydreaming patterns can be understood as an assortment of independent factors. Three major factors have been found to characterize ongoing thought during daydreaming. These include: a Positive-Vivid daydreaming scale, a Guilty-Dysphoric daydreaming scale, and a Mindwandering-Distractible scale characterized by fleeting thoughts and the inability to focus on extended fantasy.

One of the many results that the IPI has uncovered that has been supported by interview data is the discovery that most, if not all, of us carry on complex processing of imagery sequences and moderately elaborate chains of thought that are often unrelated to some specific task or social situation in which we are involved. In other words, one's stream of thought is continually occupied with looking into the future and looking back into the past, and planning and fantasizing possible outcomes of events with concomitant imagery and affect. Singer (1978) suggests that the function of the stream of consciousness may be to provide us with the possibilities of action that we can choose from, so as to determine the most appropriate short- and long-term goals and behaviors to enact.

Another approach to studying the stream of thought that utilizes direct assessment is the research being done by E. Klinger (1978) at the University of Minnesota. In one particular study, subjects were trained to become aware of their inner experience and then participated in in-the-laboratory and out-of-the-laboratory assessment sessions. During these sessions, at each sound of the buzzer the subjects completed a thought-sampling questionnaire on the nature of their stream of consciousness. The questionnaire measured such phenomenological contents as duration of thought, vagueness of imagery, amount of direct thought, visualness of imagery, and so on.

Among the many results that were found, some of the following were:

> The five dimensions of thought: operant (directed) versus respondent (non-directed), stimulus-bound, fancifulness, degenerateness, and relation of ego to imagery—are functionally separate even though they may be statistically related. . . . Most thought in college student participants is specific, detailed,

predominantly visual, unfanciful, controlled, present tense, related to the immediate situation, and recallable within a few seconds with at least moderate confidence. (Klinger, 1978, pp. 255–256)

These results indicate that the thought-sampling method can yield intriguing and valuable data about the nature of the stream of consciousness.

In a different but related type of study (Pope, 1978), the effects of gender, solitude, and posture upon the stream of consciousness were assessed. Subjects reported on their stream of consciousness by thinking aloud into a cassette recorder. The results indicated that although the flow of consciousness is exceedingly rich and varied, it can be reliably categorized and varies with the type of stimulus condition. Pope suggested that to the extent that his particular study tapped "normal thinking," "people seem to spend a great deal of time in fantasy and long-term memory" (1978, p. 288).

STATES OF CONSCIOUSNESS

In contrast to the above studies, which attempted to investigate the nature of the stream of consciousness, are those studies and theories that investigated the nature of "states" of consciousness. In recent times, there has been an increased interest in trying to experience, categorize, and understand "states" of consciousness and "altered" (Tart, 1969, 1972, 1975, 1977) or "alternate" (Zinberg, 1977) states of consciousness, in particular.

These terms refer to the belief that besides waking consciousness there are also other, altered or alternate states of consciousness that people experience. Altered states of consciousness have received much more attention than one's ordinary waking state of consciousness for obvious reasons.

An interest in the scientific study and exploration of altered states of consciousness is not new to American psychology, however. William James, the father of American psychology, wrote in 1902:

Some years ago I myself made some observations on this aspect of nitrous oxide intoxification . . . . One conclusion was formed upon my mind at that time and my impression of its truth has ever since remained unshaken. It is that our rational consciousness, as we call it, is but one special type of consciousness, whilst all about it, parted from it by the filmiest of screens, there lie potential forms of consciousness entirely different. We may go through life without suspecting their existence, but apply the requisite stimulus, and at a touch they are there in all completeness, definite types of mentality which probably somewhere have their field of application and adaptation. No account of the universe in its totality can be final which leaves these other forms of consciousness quite disregarded. How to regard them is the question—for they are so discontinuous with ordinary consciousness. Yet they may determine attitudes though they cannot furnish formulas and open a region though they fail to give a map. (1902/58, p. 298)

By definition, altered states of consciousness would be experienced differently from a waking, baseline state. Several slightly different definitions have been provided to clarify exactly what an altered state of consciousness is. According to Krippner (1972),

an altered conscious state can be defined as a mental state which can be subjectively recognized by an individual (or by an objective observer of the individual) as representing a difference in psychological functioning from that individual's "normal, alert, waking, state." (p. 1)

Ludwig (1972), in a slightly different definition, defines an altered state of consciousness as

any mental state(s), induced by various physiological, psychological, or pharmacological maneuvers or agents, which can be recognized subjectively by the individual himself (or by an objective observer of the individual) as representing a sufficient deviation in subjective experience or psychological functioning from certain general norms for that individual during alert, waking consciousness. (p. 11)

And finally, C. T. Tart (1972), the father of altered states of consciousness (ASC) theorizing, defines an ASC as "a qualitative alteration in the overall pattern of mental functioning such that the experiencer feels his consciousness is radically different from the 'normal' way it functions" (p. 95).

An Eastern Enumeration of States of Consciousness

Although we in the West are just beginning to define and map states of consciousness and theorize about them, some of the Eastern philosophies and religions have very elaborate maps and theories about consciousness and its multifarious states (Tart, 1977). According to Goleman (1977), the Buddhist classic entitled the *Abhidhamma*, "is probably the broadest and most detailed traditional psychology of states of consciousness" (p. 1) in written existence.

The *Abhidhamma* represents an encyclopedic compilation of the discourses of the Buddha. In the fifth century A.D. that portion of the *Abhidhamma* dealing with meditation was summarized by Buddhaghosa and entitled the *Visuddhimagga*, or "the path of purification." The *Visuddhimagga* is really a recipe book for meditation and lists among other things the states of consciousness attainable by meditation. These states of consciousness are enumerated according to two general classification systems, one based on concentration and the other based on insight.

The path of concentration lists the states of consciousness the mind can experience based on the degree to which one-pointed concentration or absorption are developed. When there is full absorption, or *jhana*, upon the object of meditation, there is a total break with normal consciousness and here begins the first of eight different jhanas, each concerned with specific, yet higher, levels of consciousness.

The following are the main characteristics of the first through eighth jhanas: (1) cessation of hindering thoughts, sustained attention to the object of concentration, and feelings of rapture and bliss; (2) no primary object of concentration, feelings of rapture, bliss, and one-pointedness; (3) cessation of rapture, feelings of bliss, one-pointedness, and equanimity; (4) cessation of bodily pleasures, feelings of equanimity, one-pointedness, and bliss; (5) consciousness of infinite space, equanimity, and one-pointedness; (6) objectless infinite consciousness, equanimity, and one-pointedness; (7) awareness of nothingness, equanimity, and one-pointedness; and (8) neither perception nor nonperception, equanimity, and one-pointedness.

Paralleling the path of concentration is the path of insight. The *Visuddhimagga* enumerates the different levels of mindfulness attainable, based on the degree of insight, or the ability to "see things as they are." These stages include, from the least to the greatest insight: bare insight, mindfulness, the stage of reflections, pseudonirvana, realization, effortless insight, nirvana, and nirodh. Like the stages of concentration, each stage of insight has corresponding cognitive, affective, and noetic concomitants.

According to Goleman, at the higher stages, the paths of concentration and insight tend to merge, although subtle differences remain, based on the fact that each path uses a different methodology to achieve alteration of state. Whereas the concentration method uses absorption in the object of meditation, the insight method uses attention to, yet detachment from, the object of meditation, which may be the meditator's own stream of consciousness.

A Western Enumeration of States of Consciousness

The West has also come up with several articles reviewing and delineating states of consciousness distinct enough from each other so as to merit enumeration. Two such reviews are those of Krippner (1972) and Ludwig (1972).

Krippner lists 20 states of consciousness that need to be further mapped. These include the states of dreaming and sleeping; the hyp-nagogic and hypnopompic states; states of hyperalertness and lethargy; states of rapture, hysteria, fragmentation, and regression; meditative and trance states; reverie; the daydreaming state; internal scanning; stu-por; coma; stored memory; "expanded" consciousness; and last but not least, the normal, everyday state of consciousness.

In a seminal article on altered states, Ludwig (1972) has concep-tualized altered states of consciousness as having several common de-nominators and dimensions in contrast to ordinary, everyday waking consciousness. According to Ludwig, most of the following features, to a greater or lesser extent, tend to characterize most altered states of consciousness: alterations in thinking, disturbed time sense, loss of con-trol, changes in emotional expression, body image changes, perceptual distortions, changes in meaning or significance, a sense of the ineffable, feelings of rejuvenation, and hypersuggestibility.

Besides merely enumerating states of consciousness is a Western interest in how they come about. Several theories have been presented that attempt to determine the theoretical foundations and functions that make altered states of consciousness possible. The following subsections will review the contemporary major Western theories that attempt to account for the ability of consciousness to change and yet stabilize itself in various and sundry states.

Theories of States of Consciousness

R. Fischer (1978) has developed a cartography of conscious states based on the level of arousal of the organism. According to his mapping of consciousness, levels of arousal can be mapped along a continuum that extends from ordinary perception to hyperaroused states, and in the opposite direction from perception to hypoaroused activity levels. According to Fischer, one half of the consciousness continuum

> is along the perception-hallucination continuum of increasing ergotropic arousal—an inner excitation, called sympathetic or hyperarousal; and the second along the perception-meditation continuum of increasing tropho-tropic arousal—a tranquil relaxation, or central hypoarousal. A voyage along the path of hyperarousal is experienced by Western travelers as normal, creative, hyperphrenic (including manic and schizophrenic as well as cataleptic and ecstatic states); the voyage along the path of hypoarousal is a succession of meditative experiences referred by Eastern travelers as *zazen, dharna, dhyan, savichar,* and *nirvichar samadhi*. (Fischer, 1978, p. 25)

In accordance with Fischer's paradigm, the "perception-hallucina-tion continuum of increasing ergotropic arousal is characterized by diffuse cortical excitation, as in awakening (Gellhorn & Kiely, 1972), EEG desynchronization-hypersynchronization (Winters, *et al.*, 1972)" (Fischer, 1978, p. 30), and an augmentation in sympathetic discharge that originates in the locus coeruleus. High levels of arousal lead to hallucinatory experience, high S/M ratios (or inner sensation versus motor actions), and a (usually) desynchronized EEG. The perception-meditation continuum of increasing trophotropic arousal is characterized by an activation of the parasympathetic nervous system, a synchronized EEG, and deep, nonactive meditational states, such as are achieved from Zen, *vipassana* or insight meditation, or any number of other meditational disciplines.

Fischer's cartography is a blend of Eastern and Western psychology that is based on a neurophysiological analysis of arousal and concomitant phenomenological experiences. States of consciousness are defined and divided according to the arousal level of the organism. This arousal level seems in turn to be based on neurophysiological interactions between the reticular activating system of the brain (Lindsley, 1960), the thalamus (Andersen & Andersson, 1968), limbic structures (Thatcher & John, 1977), and cortical structures (Diamond, 1976; Pribram & McGuiness, 1975). Fischer does not discuss the exact nature of the phenomenology of these states of consciousness, but rather uses the Eastern and Western labels (such as *zazen, dhrana,* etc.) and correlates such labels with neurological substrates.

A somewhat different paradigm has been put forward by J. Silverman (1968) for understanding altered states of consciousness that is based on attention instead of arousal. According to Silverman, individuals in altered states evince behaviors that have the following characteristics:

> (1) Subjective disturbances in concentration, attention, and also memory and judgment, (2) disturbed time sense, (3) difficulty in control, (4) changes in emotional tone, (5) bodily image changes, (6) perceptual distortions, (7) and changes in meaning or significance. (pp. 1201–1202)

Such altered states are typically preceded, according to Silverman, by sensory overload or sensory underload, hyper- or hypoattentiveness to sensory or ideational stimuli, and changes in the biochemistry or neurophysiology of the body. Silverman suggests that recent advances in attention and perceptual behavior have suggested a new framework for understanding altered states of consciousness. This framework is based on the analysis of attention and its three related component factors, derived from factor analytic studies, that regulate and monitor the "reception and utilization of environmental and internal stimuli" (Silverman, 1968, pp. 1202–1203). These three factors are attention intensiveness, extensiveness (scanning), and selectiveness (field articulation).

Attention intensiveness refers to the subject's sensitivity to stimuli and how absorbed or involved he becomes in those stimuli. Whereas an ordinary state of consciousness involves a "midrange" sensitivity to stimuli, according to Silverman, "unusual hypersensitivity appears to be a precondition for an altered state of consciousness experience" (1968, p. 1208). Extensiveness of attention refers to the degree of sampling of the elements in the stimulus field. Whereas a person in an ordinary waking state is in a balanced state of scanning the environment, in an altered state of consciousness there is restricted scanning of the environment for the person is preoccupied with a very narrow circle of internal or external stimuli.

Silverman's third variable, the selectiveness of attention, "refers to responses which determine which elements in a stimulus field exert a dominant influence on the perceiver" (p. 1203). Thus, differences in selectivity of attention are represented by whether the subject responds to the discrete elements of the field or takes a more holistic and global perspective. A person in a normal waking state of consciousness generally has articulative control that is active, analytical, and segmentalizing, whereas a person in an altered state has a passive, global-relational set of attention selectivity. Silverman cites Deikman (1966) in support:

> The active, intellectual style is replaced by a receptive, perceptual mode . . . , the undoing of automatic, perceptual and cognitive structures permits a gain in sensory intensity and richness at the expense of abstract categorization and differentiation. (1966, pp. 329–331)

Thus the deployment of attention and the degree to which it is intensive, extensive, and selective will help to determine the degree to which an altered state of consciousness is experienced.

Fishkin and Jones (1978) present a model for the understanding of consciousness and altered states that also has attention in a very prominent position. In their approach, the contents of consciousness at any moment are determined by what is being attended to and how it is being attended to. Certain phenomena are *potentially available to consciousness* (PAC) and attention toward the PAC determines what will gain access to consciousness.

According to their model, attention is represented as a movable "window" between the potentially conscious and what gets into consciousness. The size of the window determines the breadth of attention, the rate of window movement determines the rate of shifts in attention, and the pattern of window movement determines the temporal sequence of attentional shifts.

Besides these parameters, four other parameters are necessary to determine a particular state of consciousness. The fluidity of the PAC and its structure determine the amount of material to enter into consciousness and the specifics of that material, respectively. The last two parameters deal with the energy state of the organism. The distribution of available energy will help to determine the intensity of consciousness, the rate of attention shifts, and the rigidity of the PAC contents, while the amount of available energy determines the total energy accessible for trade-offs in distribution of available energy.

According to Fishkin and Jones, "on the basis of these parameters a state of consciousness (SC) may be defined. Each SC is characterized by a particular set of values and/or attitudes of the eight parameters" (1978, p. 278). In terms of this conceptualization, they define the ordinary state of consciousness by the following values of the previously defined parameters: The location of the window tends to be located on perception of external or body events or verbal thinking. The rate of window movement is fast while the pattern of window movement is sufficient to maintain contact with the external environment and maintain a satisfactory self-concept. Talking to oneself (or others) and shifts between internal verbal thinking and the perception of external events and bodily events also characterize the pattern of window movement. The size of the window tends to fluctuate about midpoint. The fluidity of the PAC tends to be low to moderate while its structure is such that one's associations form at a moderate rate. Both the distribution and amount of available energy tend to be low to moderate.

Altered states of consciousness involve modulations in these eight parameters. Drug-induced altered states are characterized as involving the following features: shifts from external to internal focus, alterations of moods or feelings, changes in the breadth of attention and intensity of experience, time distortions, occurrences of strengthening of new associations, persistent or enhanced internal imagery, loss of memory, shifts from verbal to nonverbal thinking, increased availability of deep-lying memories or unconscious material, alteration of complex psychological phenomena, loss of self-concept, and the experience of unity, oneness, or connectedness.

A much different perspective on the nature of altered states is the "psychedelic model of altered states of consciousness" (Hunt & Chefurka, 1976). Hunt and Chefurka argue that since the nature of consciousness is intentional, that is, pointing "beyond itself (into the world of everyday conduct)" (p. 867), then any direct awareness of experience of one's immediate subjectivity "could be experienced as anomalous, and would be dysfunctional in terms of adaptation" (p. 867). They suggest that a psychedelic model of altered states would view altered states as the subjective reflections or by-products of general mental activity, resulting when the "known object" of focal awareness is replaced by features of the "knowing medium" (1976, p. 867).

In order to test this hypothesis, subjects, after being placed in one of four groups, sat immobile for ten minutes in a bare well-lit room. Different instructions were given to each group. Group 1 was a baseline group who were given instructions that were not to sensitize them to their subjective experience. Group 2 received instructions to pay attention to their "subjective experience." Group 3 received instructions similar to that given observers of the classic introspectionists in the tradition of Titchener (1924), James (1890/1950), and Cattell (1930). Group 4 received instructions in imaginative role-playing.

The results, according to the authors, confirmed the psychedelic model for the different conditions evoked differing degrees of unusual experiences. The main results indicated that the sensitization instruction group was associated with greater altered state reports than the baseline or subjective experience groups. Unexpectedly, however, were the findings that the group instructed to just sit (the baseline group) reported greater alterations in experience than the group told to be aware of their subjective experience.

These and other results suggested that spontaneous altered state reports can be elicited in very short periods of time without recourse to elaborate experimental manipulations. The authors concluded by suggesting that altered states are always present, but "backwardly masked" because they are microgenetically primitive processes prior to the conscious experience of perceptions, feelings, cognitions, etc. As such, Hunt and Chefurka suggest that "in a formal sense, there is no such thing as 'altered states of consciousness,' rather we find states of consciousness typically subordinated within conduct and consciousness, atypically manifested" (p. 876).

TART'S THEORETICAL APPROACH TO STATES OF CONSCIOUSNESS

In contrast to Hunt and Chefurka, a consciousness theorist who firmly espouses the existence of altered states of consciousness and who was the original popularizer of the concept is Charles T. Tart (1969). Tart is the most rigorous and systematic researcher and theorist to approach the study of altered states of consciousness and his approach will be discussed in some detail. For Tart, one's ordinary state of consciousness is a "semi-arbitrary construction," dependent on the belief systems of the culture and the personal psychological makeup of the person. As amply demonstrated by research, the act of perception is a "highly complex, automated construction" that is dependent on the physiological, psychological, and cultural needs of the organism (Tart, 1975). The emotions a person feels and the thoughts he thinks are also dependent on his enculturation by the society, the process by which a particular culture selects certain human potentialities for use. Such a viewpoint is also supported by others.

As examples, the work of Bruner (1957) has emphasized how perception is conditioned by the categories of conceptualization that we employ, and Kelly (1955) has concluded that each person tends to create his own world by means of "personal constructs" or categories. From a completely different cultural perspective, an Islamic mystic organization, the Sufis, have always maintained that ordinary consciousness is but a construction:

> The Sufis emphasize the constantly changing biases that constitute our normal awareness. "What a piece of bread looks like depends on whether you are hungry," says a Sufi poet, Jallaudin Rami. (They) quite explicitly consider the effects of our limited category system on awareness. The Sufis and other traditions contend that the selective and restricted nature of awareness is an obstacle to be overcome and that the process of meditation, among other exercises, is a way of turning down the restrictions that normally limit our awareness. (Ornstein, 1972, p. 191)

This belief is also paralleled by the Eastern tradition of labeling ordinary consciousness as one of illusion or *maya* (Ram Dass, 1974; Singh, 1973). Thus Tart's contention that ordinary consciousness is a construction is supported by contemporary research and millennia of mystical tradition. But how then is it constructed?

Like Silverman and Fishkin and Jones, Tart makes awareness/attention the basic theoretical and experiential given in the construction of consciousness. Awareness, for Tart, "refers to the basic knowledge that something is happening to perceiving or feeling or cognizing in its simplest form" (Tart, 1975, p. 27). Consciousness, on the other hand, is awareness as modulated and regulated by psychological structures, which are those relatively stable organizations or component processes that perform one or more related psychological functions.

Whereas awareness/attention constitutes the major energy source of consciousness, the *structures* are the mechanisms by which consciousness is experienced. Permanent structures, such as the nervous system, are the "hardware" of the mental system, to analogize from computer programming, whereas structures created by learning, conditioning, and enculturation are software, or less permanent structures.

The interaction of awareness/attention with psychological structures determines the *discrete state of consciousness* (d-SoC), to use Tart's terminology, of the individual at the moment. A d-SoC is defined as a specific pattern of functioning of consciousness, and although it may show a range of variations in its specifics, the d-SoC still retains the same overall pattern. Thus,

> within a d-SoC, particular parts of the pattern, particular psychological functions, may function faster or slower, more or less efficiently, or show a change in a particular content they are working with, but the overall pattern remains the same. (Tart, 1977, p. 14)

In contrast, a *discrete altered state of consciousness* (d-ASC) is a radical modification of the overall patterning and functioning of consciousness, compared to a baseline state, such as one's ordinary state of consciousness. In summary, the experiencer of the altered state "can tell that different laws are functioning and that a new, overall pattern is superimposed on his existence" (1977, p. 14). The observer thus notices a qualitative difference in his state of consciousness in which it appears there are new patterns of functioning set up between the different psychological structures.

Besides altered states, Tart has also enumerated identity states of consciousness. An identity state is a specialized version of a nonaltered state of consciousness that has an overall pattern that distinguishes it from other identity states. It is composed of psychological structures that possess unique properties not present in other identity states due to the pattern of organization between subsystems, but it is not perceived as a radically different state of consciousness.

Ten subsystems are hypothesized to make up a particular state of consciousness, besides awareness/attention. These are: exteroceptors, interoceptors, input processing, memory, sense of identity, evaluation and decision making, motor output, subconscious, emotion, and space/time. An altered state of consciousness will demonstrate changes in these subsystems such that the patterning of activity between subsystems is different from that of one's ordinary state of consciousness. This is a point that Tart finds crucial for d-SoCs and d-ASCs, since "pattern differences are the essential defining element of different d-SoC's. Particular psychological functions may be identical for several d-SoC's, but the overall system functioning is quite different" (1975, p. 57).

In order to stabilize a particular state of consciousness, Tart hypothesizes four stabilizing systems. These include: loading stabilization, negative and positive feedback stabilization, and limiting stabilization. These four stabilization processes keep a particular state of consciousness generally in the same overall pattern, and thus maintain that state of consciousness.

EXPERIMENTAL STUDIES IN THE PHENOMENOLOGY OF STATES OF CONSCIOUSNESS

As can be seen, there has been a great deal of theorizing on the nature of consciousness and the organization of its different subsystems to form particular states of consciousness. Research into the phenomenology of states of consciousness, although less than adequate, is increasing and has now been undertaken in such areas as psychedelic drugs (Pahnke, 1972), meditation (Deikman, 1972; Maupin, 1972; Osis *et al.*, 1973; Greenfield, 1977), alpha EEG biofeedback training (Kamiya, 1972; Plotkin, 1979), the smoking of cannabis (Tart, 1971), hypnosis (Aaronson, 1972; Tart, 1972), and other areas. The following paragraphs will briefly review several of these studies.

In a drug study by Pahnke (1972), 20 theological students listened to a religious ceremony. Half of the students were given psilocybin one and one-half hours before the ceremony and the other half received a placebo containing nicotinic acid. A double-blind technique for the administration was employed. Data collection afterward consisted of questionnaires and interviews.

The treatment and control groups were compared, among other things, on nine dimensions thought to be related to mystical experience: unity, transcendence of space and time, deeply felt positive mood, sacredness, objectivity and reality, paradoxicality, alleged ineffability, transiency, and persisting positive change in attitude and behavior. For seven of the nine categories, the subjects receiving the psilocybin evinced phenomenological experiences significantly different from the controls.

A study by Osis, Bokert, and Carlson (1973) investigated the phenomenological dimensions of the meditative experience. Self-selected meditators met once a week for a two-hour session over a period of six to eight months. After each meditation session they then completed a 30-item postsession questionnaire. The items were then factor analyzed trying to determine the dimensions of the meditative experience that might emerge. Six factors were found. One referred to the premeditative state that the subjects brought to the meditative session while the others differentiated five different phenomenological dimensions of the meditative experience. These included: self-transcendence and openness, intensification and change in consciousness, a meaning dimension, forceful exclusion of images, and general success in meditation. Five of these six factors were replicated thrice and were fairly stable, having core items that were the same over a period of a few years. The authors concluded that the dimensions that emerged did not seem to express everyday states of consciousness and that meditation led to altered states of consciousness (Osis *et al.*, 1973). Their data collection, however, did not allow for an adequate defining or mapping of the ordinary state of consciousness.

In an involved and elegant study, Greenfield (1977) studied individual subjective responses to three types of meditation. Forty-five females experienced meditations involving the use of a mantra, visualization, and bare attention over a ten-week period. Their subjective experiences were assessed by questionnaires; individual personality variables were also monitored.

The results indicated several significant differences in subjective experience across the three meditational techniques, although mystical experience, as assessed by the mystical experience dimension of the postmeditational questionnaire, was not significantly different across the three techniques. This mystical experience dimension indicated, however, that meditators were consistent in rating their experience along phenomenological domains that included high ratings for feelings of unity, noetic feelings of reality and truth, a sense of sacredness, deeply felt positive mood, a sense of paradoxicality, transcendence of space and time, transiency, and, to a lesser extent, ineffability.

Individual differences across meditators were also monitored and related to depth of meditation and level of mystical consciousness experienced. Individuals who scored high in a paper-and-pencil test of absorption (Tellegen, 1981), a measure correlated with hypnotic susceptibility, were found to experience a greater alteration and change of consciousness than meditators who scored low on this measure. Subjects who were highly tolerant of ambiguity were also better able to relax during meditation.

In two other meditation studies, Maupin (1972) demonstrated that strong subjective feelings could be evoked in subjects who had very little meditation training and Deikman (1972) found that subjects who meditated on a blue vase experienced subjective changes in perception that Deikman traced to a "deautomatization" of cognitive and perceptual processes.

An area of research that may be tapping similar types of phenomenological experiences as meditation is that of alpha EEG biofeed-back training. In such training the subject is given feedback as to when he is experiencing rhythmic alpha activity in certain areas of his cerebral cortex. Subjects who have undergone such training report a configuration of phenomenological experiences that have been labeled the "alpha high state" (Kamiya, 1972). Subjective experiences include such things as a general pleasantness, a relaxation of the mental apparatus, and a lack of critical or cognitive skepticism about the nature of the experience.

In a review of the relationship between the alpha experience and EEG activity (Plotkin, 1979), the alpha experience was characterized as a pleasant, relaxed, and serene state characterized by a loss of body and time awareness, an absence or diminution of thought, and a feeling of egolessness. Some research (Orne & Wilson, 1978), however, casts doubt as to whether EEG alpha activity is necessarily associated with the alpha high experience and there may be no relationship between the strength or density of EEG alpha activity and the occurrence of the alpha experience. Other researchers (Fehmi, 1978), however, suggest that it is the synchronous activation of EEG activity over the entire cerebral hemisphere, and not the density of alpha activity in a particular region, that determines the nature of the alpha experience.

Phenomenological approaches to understanding hypnosis are also becoming more acceptable. Questionnaires mailed to members of the American Society of Clinical Hypnosis and the Society of Clinical and Experimental Hypnosis indicated that research into the phenomenological parameters of hypnosis is expected to increase in the coming years (Fromm, 1979). Shor (1979) has published "a phenomenological method for the measurement of variables important to an understanding of the nature of hypnosis" and the Chicago group (Fromm et al., 1981) has described the phenomenological characteristics of self-hypnosis using the approach advocated by Shor.

Johnson (1979) has used a phenomenological approach to compare self- and heterohypnosis. Forty-eight college students were administered hetero- and self-hypnosis induction techniques in counterbalanced order during which both phenomenological and behavioral responses to the inductions were recorded. The results indicated that inexperienced subjects were as able to hypnotize themselves as to be hypnotized by another. Whereas heterohypnosis evoked more feelings of unawareness, passivity, and loss of control, self-hypnosis evoked more feelings of time distortion, disorientation, active direction, and trance variability. Nevertheless, the phenomenological experiences between the two types of inductions were deemed to be sufficiently similar that both self-hypnosis and heterohypnosis could be conceptualized with the same label.

Sheehan and McConkey (1982) have developed a phenomenological approach to understanding hypnosis that involves the retrospective assessment of the subject's own observations about their experiences of hypnosis when the events of the hypnotic experience are made available to them through videotape playback or imagery-induced recall. Their technique, called the experiential analysis technique, suggested that the experience of hypnosis is an active cognitive process that involves intervention of the subject, and that there appear to be different types of high hypnotically susceptible subjects, based on their phenomenological reports.

A more recent study (Oxman et al., 1988) compared the subjective experiences associated with different altered states of consciousness. A computerized content analysis was applied to autobiographical accounts concerning schizophrenia, mystical ecstacy, hallucinogenic drug states, and control conditions. The authors concluded by suggesting that the "findings can be used to argue against the various conceptualizations of altered states of consciousness as sharing key experiential elements such as primary process thinking" (p. 408). Oxman and co-workers suggest that the altered states that were assessed via their content analysis approach are "more different from one another than alike" (p. 408), at least in certain key respects.

Besides the above, the phenomenological experience during a profound hypnotic trance state (Tart, 1970) has also been studied, as has the subjective experience of the hypnagogic state just before sleep (Vogel et al., 1972).

CONCLUSIONS

The previous studies are just some of the phenomenological investigations that have been done to explore and understand specific stimulus conditions and altered state induction procedures. The above review has shown that there has been substantial phenomenological research into specific altered state induction procedures and associated altered states of consciousness, and that research is continuing to grow. Yet there has been relatively little *systematic* and *comprehensive* research into the structures and patterns of consciousness across various altered state induction procedures through the observation and quantification of subjective experience.

There has also been little research that compares the phenomenological parameters of altered states of consciousness against normal, nonaltered states. Such comparisons may be crucial, especially since some evidence (Hunt & Chefurka, 1976) suggests that altered states may not be that different phenomenologically from ordinary, nonaltered states of consciousness. Hence, although the phenomenological parameters associated with specific induction procedures have been investigated, a phenomenological methodology to map and assess the structures and patterns of consciousness across various conditions and altered state induction procedures and compare them to ordinary states of consciousness is needed.

This concludes the review of phenomenological approaches to consciousness. The next chapter will address the recent cognitive revolution in psychology and associated disciplines and how that revolution has placed consciousness back to center stage.

3

The Cognitive Revolution in Psychology

INFORMATION PROCESSING

No history of psychology and the role of consciousness in psychology would be complete without a review of the recent cognitive revolution in psychology (Gardner, 1985). Baars (1986) suggests that between 1955 and 1965 a quiet revolution occurred in scientific psychology that led to the cognitive revolution of the 1970s and 1980s.

The birth of contemporary cognitive psychology in the 1950s can be talked about in terms of the birth of information theory, information flow, and information processing (Knapp, 1986). Information *theory* was introduced in 1949 by Shannon and Weaver (1949). They described a model of a communication system and enumerated five basic parts: an information source, a transmitter, a channel, a receiver, and a destination. Their theory was a general statistical formulation for describing the relationships between these systems. It was Miller (1951), however, who took the statistical formulations developed by Shannon and introduced them to psychology. Miller's *Language and Communication* (1951) came to be seen as a bridge between the psychology of behaviorism and the new cognitive psychology by suggesting how information theory could be applied to problems in psychology.

Information *flow* refers to the encoding processes and how information travels through a system. Broadbent (1958) can be said to be the first person to introduce the language of information flow into psychology in an influential fashion. His *Perception and Communication* (1958) was to represent the first in a series of attempts to conceptualize traditional psychological subject areas in terms of communication theory. Broadbent has been referred to as the contemporary father of information-processing psychology (Haber, 1974). He developed a new "cybernetic" language to help fill the gap between behaviorism and neurophysiology.

Information *processing*, on the other hand, "is generally identified in psychological discussions with the formulations of Newell and Simon (1972)" (Knapp, 1986, p. 20) who described how a limited set of elementary processes can operate on a set of symbols. Newell and Simon's information-processing approach to psychology (Newell *et al.*, 1958) attempted to explain problem-solving behavior in terms of a program: "a specification of what the organism will do under varying environmental circumstances in terms of certain elementary information processing it is capable of performing" (p. 153). They then proceeded to develop programs for chess playing, theorem proving, and even paired-associate learning. With the introduction of these terms in psychology, scientific psychology ceased to be a discipline concerned only with stimulus-response associations, but, in addition, a discipline concerned with information processing.

If cognitive psychology had its birth in the 1950s, its growth into a separate discipline occurred in the 1960s as exemplified in Neisser's *Cognitive Psychology* (1967). Neisser's book gave a label to the field and he contrasted his cognitive approach against psychodynamic, behavioristic, and physiological approaches. For Neisser, one's view of the world is a mediated one and the cognitive psychologist is interested in trying to understand how a man selects, stores, recovers, combines, outputs, and manipulates information, much the way a computer program would. Neisser's *Cognitive Psychology* looked at the world from a cognitive and information-processing point of view.

If the 1960s can be said to be the adolescence of cognitive psychology, it became institutionalized in mainstream academic psychology in the 1970s (Anderson, 1976; Knapp, 1986). *Cognition* began to be published in 1972 and *Memory and Cognition* a year later.

ASSUMPTIONS AND CONCEPTS

This information-processing approach to psychological phenomena moved psychologists from a behavioristic model of man to an informational model of man. The information-processing approach to cognition can be said to be based on five assumptions (Palmer & Kimchi, 1986): informational description, recursive decomposition, flow continuity, flow dynamics, and physical embodiment. Given the importance of these assumptions, they will be briefly defined.

Information description means that *mental events can be described* (italics are mine). A mental event has input information (what it starts with), an operation (what gets done to the input), and an output (what the system ends up with).

Recursive decomposition means that "any complex informational event at one level of description can be specified more fully at a lower level by decomposing it into: (1) a number of components, each of which is itself an informational event, and (2) the temporal ordering relations among them that specify how the information 'flows' through the system of components" (Palmer & Kimchi, 1986, p. 39).

Flow continuity requires that all input information required to enact an operation must be available in the output, while *flow dynamics* means that the output cannot be produced by an operation until the input has been processed. Finally, *physical embodiment* means that information is embodied in the states of the system (the system's representations) and operations that use that information are embodied in changes of state (called processes).

Although the aforementioned assumptions are not the only assumptions underlying an information-processing approach to psychology, the five assumptions are "certainly among the most important ones and form a widely held set of 'core beliefs'" (Palmer & Kimchi, 1986, p. 39).

Certain concepts in an information-processing approach to cognition are of central importance in cognitive psychology. Two of these include: mental representations and schemas.

Representation is a central issue in cognitive psychology. "*Representational systems* are [the] theoretical constructs that are postulated as underlying (responsible for) the observable thoughts and actions of the organism" (Mandler, 1984, p. 4). Hence, the representation of knowledge is the theoretical system postulated to explain, understand, and predict behavior and experience. In the words of B. J. Baars (1988):

> a *representation* is a theoretical object that bears an abstract resemblance to something outside itself. In somewhat different terms, there is an abstract match or *isomorphism* between the representation and the thing that is represented. (pp. 44–45)

Schemas, on the other hand, are used to "construct representations" (p. 5), and processes are the transformations, operators, search and storage mechanisms, and inferential processes that operate on representations.

Representations can involve declarative or procedural knowledge.

Whereas the former is "knowledge coded essentially as a set of stored facts or declarations" (Gardner, 1985, p. 161), procedural knowledge is "knowledge coded as a set of procedures or actions to be carried out" (p. 161). There may be several modes of mental representation, each tied to a particular content, such as visualization, audition, speech production, and so forth.

Mandler (1984) defines schemas as "the basic units of the mind." A schema is a "bounded, distinct, and unitary representation" (p. 55) that one builds up in the course of interaction with the environment; they are "abstract representations of environmental regularities" (p. 55). We use schemas to organize experience. They vary from concrete to abstract representations and they organize experience from discrete features to general categories. Schemas are "the primary representations of our physical world, . . . they are the mental counterpart of all events and objects that we regularly encounter" (Mandler, 1984, p. 65).

CURRENT COGNITIVE MODELS OF MIND

An understanding of the cognitive revolution would be incomplete without some discussion of current cognitive models of consciousness in psychology and information processing. The following paragraphs will review several of these cognitive models. Although not comprehensive, the following models delineate several different yet powerful ways for conceptualizing the progress being made in cognitive psychology toward understanding consciousness.

Singer's Review into Private Experience and Personality

J. L. Singer (1978, 1984, 1985) has been instrumental in bringing to the forefront of psychological research the study of daydreaming and the stream of consciousness and their interface with personality and cognitive psychology. In his 1987 article with J. Kolligian (Singer & Kolligian, 1987) Singer reviewed the interface between personality, private experience, and cognitive psychology. Because his approach is deemed to be what scientists in the 1990s will be exploring in terms of personality and subjective experience, his article will be briefly reviewed.

Singer suggests that the 1980s have seen an increased interest in private experience as social cognition research and personality psychology converge. Social psychologists have found that extensive samplings of an individual's conscious beliefs and expectations can "lead to rather good predictions of how people will behave in specific settings or in response to naturally-occurring events" (Singer & Kolligian, 1987, p. 538). The research also suggests "that people can generally provide reasonably valid and reliable indices of their own differential patterns of ongoing inner thought through relatively short questionnaires" (p. 542). Given that subjects can be reasonably reliable and valid at introspection, Singer goes on to discuss the great body of research that has grown up around self-consciousness and its relationship to public and private self-consciousness.

Besides relating subjective experience to aspects of self-consciousness, there has been an explosion of studies relating cognition and affect to human experience and personality. "Our ways of knowing the world are intrinsically bound up with our ways of feeling (Rychlak, 1977, 1981; Tomkins, 1962, 1963; Zajonc, 1984)" (Singer & Kolligian, 1987, p. 548), and it appears impossible to separate the emotional system from the cognitive system and vice versa.

Singer highlights the importance of a cognitive-affective perspective in understanding how personality and private experience interact: "There is now ample experimental evidence that cognitions, especially in the form of ruminations about affectively-toned events, may powerfully influence mood states and overt behaviors" (Singer & Kolligian, 1987, p. 551). Not only are there robust effects of mood on cognition, but effects of mood on memory have also been amply demonstrated (Blaney, 1986; Singer & Salovey, 1985).

In an article with Pope (Pope & Singer, 1978a), Singer emphasizes the "extreme interrelatedness of the cognitive and affective processes" (p. 128) in the regulation of the stream of consciousness:

> The stream of consciousness does not flow epiphenomenally or without great efficacy in our day-to-day affairs. Among a number of influences, not only the mental work, the information processing of a wealth of stimuli, but also our feelings, in their own right or serving to amplify other systems, regulate the flow of the stream of consciousness. And this continuous flow, in turn, helps regulate our thoughts, feelings, and behavior. (p. 128)

According to Singer, the 1960s marked a paradigm shift away from the stimulus-response unit to the cognitive unit as the "basic unit" for understanding human behavior and experience. Noteworthy among the key concepts of this new psychology are schemas, scripts, and prototypes in the structure of private experience.

Schemas are relatively organized meaning structures (Bartlett, 1932; Piaget, 1962; Shower & Canter, 1985) that "provide selection criteria for regulating attention and lend a focus to the encoding, storage, and retrieval of information in a domain" (Singer & Kolligian, 1987, p. 555).

Schemas allow the person to identify stimuli, chunk stimuli into manageable units, and select appropriate strategies to solve a problem or reach a goal. According to Singer, schemas represent the starting point for theory-driven or "top-down" information processing, as opposed to data-driven or "bottom-up" processing.

Although schemas appear to be involved in information processing, errors including confirmatory biases, representativeness heuristics, and so on do occur. Schemas also appear to be quite helpful to us in everyday settings as we attempt to process millions of bits of information from the environment and also our private selves. Although schemas can be of any variety, Singer suggests that *self-schemas* may be of particular interest to psychologists. A self-schema is "a hierarchically organized body of knowledge or beliefs about one's intentions and capacities in long-term memory" (Singer & Kolligian, 1987, p. 557).

In addition to self-schemas, socially interactive schemas called scripts and prototypes have been hypothesized. Scripts are schemas that are powerful, emotionally laden events originating in childhood that are linked together and form the basis "of the dominant themes that guide cognitive processing and social behavior through life" (Singer & Kolligian, 1987, p. 560). Prototypes, on the other hand, are "relatively stable, abstract representations of a large set of more or less associated attributes, trait characteristics, characteristic behaviors performed by a type of person, and even situations commonly associated with people of that type" (Turk & Salovey, 1985, p. 8).

As can be seen from Singer's review, cognitive psychology readily embraces the use of concepts and representations concerning schemas, scripts, and cognitive-affective interactions in an attempt to understand personality from the vantage points of both behavior *and* private experience. The use of introspective questionnaires to measure schemas, moods, cognitive scripts, and the like suggests that such questionnaires can not only be reliable, but can also yield valuable data on the nature of the human personality and its interaction with the social environment.

Mandler's Structure of Mind and Consciousness

For Mandler (1984) the mind "is the complex of organizations and structures ascribed to an individual that processes information (including information from its own actions and experiences) and generates information to various subsystems" (p. 49). One inclusive subsystem of mind is the cognitive-interpretative system. It is that system concerned with knowledge (cognition) and is able to transform information into functional units (hence, interpretative).

The cognitive-interpretative system is composed of various cognitive structures that organize knowledge and information in terms of *mental representations*. Mental representations are the consciously available knowledge about the world that Mandler describes in terms of schemas: bounded, distinct, and unitary representations that are the primary representations of our physical world—they are the mental counterpart of all events and objects that we encounter.

Processes, on the other hand, are usually seen as a separate class of theoretical mechanisms that operate on representations, although processes are also representational systems that "operate directly on informational structures, creating new structures, activating other processes, and lead directly to action" (Mandler, 1984, p. 33).

For Mandler, awareness "is constructed out of activated systems" (p. 71); the contents of awareness are constructed out of "abstract schematic representations" that become less abstract and more concrete, depending on the task, the situation, and the personality of the person.

According to Mandler, all data coming into the mental system are accepted to the extent that they fit into available structures. Thus, evidence undergoes "meaning analysis," that is, a given event is "located" in terms of its particular characteristics, attributes, and features, and a particular event is processed in reference to other structures and sets of events, comparing the present event to current evidence and past experiences.

There is a "preconscious state-of-the-world" knowledge for Mandler that is a "set of schemas or representations that were recently activated and updated and that, being in some state of current activation above resting level, can be distinguished from other inactive mental contents" (1984, p. 72). This preconscious knowledge provides the "backdrop" for how we experience our world.

For Mandler, as with Tart, consciousness is a *construction*. Drawing on Marcel's (1983) perceptual work, Mandler views consciousness as "a construction of phenomenological experience out of one or more of the available preconscious events, schemas, and structures" (Mandler, 1984, p. 92), abstracting relevant information from the "preconscious state-of-the-world knowledge" to construct the conscious state. Our resulting phenomenological experience is then a constructed conscious experience dependent on activated schemas that are set in motion in response to the requirements of the moment.

Because of limited attentional capacity, consciousness is also of limited capacity and only particular schemas or structures can be activated at any particular time to occupy the attentional field. Attention is a key concept for Mandler. It is "the process whereby a specific part of the space-time continuum is automatically made available for further processing" (Mandler, 1985, p. 83). Attention partakes of both "top-down" and "bottom-up" processing using both parallel (late selection) and serial (early selection) processing modes.

Attention's limited capacity necessitates a selection process over which schemas and structures will occupy the field of attention and hence lead to the flow of consciousness states. Such states are activated by environmental requirements, specifying in rather "abstract terms of where we are and what we are doing" (Mandler, 1984, p. 104). The juxtaposition of arousal and meaning analysis on the organism's experience of the environment leads to changes in the organism's state of consciousness.

As a first approximation, Mandler defines a state of consciousness as "constructed out of the most general structures currently being activated by current concerns and environmental requirements" (1985, p. 60). States of consciousness change "whenever there is a change in the state of the world, defined as any change in the sensory evidence or in intentions, instructions, content, or situation" (p. 61).

Anderson's ACT* Model

John Anderson's (1983) ACT* (Adaptive Control of Thought—the asterisk indicates the final version) model is his general model of the "architecture of cognition." In contrast to the parallel distributed processing approach described below, Anderson's model is a "unitary" approach. This approach "holds that all higher-level cognitive functions can be explained by one set of principles" (1983, p. 2). This is in contrast· to the "faculty" approach, which holds that distinctly different cognitive principles underlie the operations of distinct cognitive functions. Anderson does not deny that there are distinct systems for vision, audition, and so forth, but rather he holds that higher-level cognition involves a unitary system.

Anderson's model makes use of *production systems*. The basis of production systems is that "underlying human cognition is a set of condition-action pairs called *productions*. The condition specifies some data patterns, and if elements matching these patterns are in working memory, then the production can apply" (p. 5). Production systems form the *procedural* component in Anderson's model. For a production to apply, the information to be acted on must be matched against information in working memory. The information active in working memory is part of the system's *declarative* component.

Hence Anderson's model consists of three types of memory: *working* memory (which consists of the information with which the system is currently working and refers to "declarative knowledge, permanent or temporary, that is in an active state", p. 20), *declarative* memory (information from long-term memory), and *production* memory.

A basic architectural assumption of ACT* is the distinction between declarative and procedural knowledge, that is, knowledge coded as a set of stored facts or declarations and knowledge coded as a set of procedures or actions to be performed. The use of both types of knowledge with separate systems eliminates the possibility of conflict between the production system and declarative memory.

Knowledge, for Anderson, is encoded in terms of *cognitive units* or chunks. Cognitive units can be abstract propositions, temporal strings, or spatial images. A cognitive unit "encodes a set of elements in a particular relationship" (p. 23) and contains no more than five elements. More complex structures are created hierarchically, by having particular units embedded in other units. Knowledge units in a simple network are defined as *nodes* and the connections between nodes as *links*. The concept of *activation* is used to measure "how closely associated a piece of information is to information currently used" and this concept is a "heuristic assumption that associated information is mostly likely to be needed to guide processing" (p. 27).

John Anderson's architectural system of cognition, briefly defined above, allows for different types of representational knowledge, that is, procedural versus declarative, to be integrated into a system that allows for propositional units, strings, and images to be unified in a single cognitive system.

Parallel Distributed Processing (PDP) Models of Consciousness

In contrast to a serial view of information processing (like John Anderson's model), parallel distributed processing (PDP) models of consciousness are neurally based rather than computer-based, taking the actual structures and connections among the neurons of the brain as the basis for a parallel processing model (McClelland & Rumelhart, 1985; McClelland *et al.*, 1986; Rumelhart *et al.*, 1986b). This model posits thousands to billions of "connections" among hundreds to millions of "units."

It is the "strengths" of these connections, in terms of inhibitions and excitations, that determine the "state" of the system, which, in turn, activates various structures and schemas to generate the organism's current state of consciousness. In a parallel distributed processing model, the human brain is conceptualized as a variety of different modules or processors (Arbib, 1980; Geschwind, 1979; Mountcastle, 1978). These processors are connected in parallel with one another. " 'Perception,' 'action,' or 'thought' occur as a consequence of the altering of the strengths (or weights) of connections among these units" (Gardner, 1987, p. 394).

Thus, instead of memory being viewed as a set of facts or events that are stored in the brain, "memory is viewed as the set of relationships that obtain among various aspects of facts or events as they are encoded in groupings or patterns of units. What is stored are the connections and strengths among units which allow the patterns to be subsequently recreated" (Gardner, 1987, p. 395).

Parallel distributed processing models can be described in terms of eight components (Rumelhart *et al.*, 1986a). These include: a set of processing units, a state of activation, an output function for each unit, a pattern of connectivity among units, a propagation rule for propagating patterns of activity through the connective networks, an activation rule for combining inputs to produce a new level of activation, a learning rule whereby patterns of connectivity are experience-modified, and an environment.

A *set of processing units* represent the first step in delineating a PDP model. These units may represent particular conceptual objects; more generally, they are "simply abstract elements over which meaningful patterns can be defined" (Rumelhart *et al.*, 1986a, p. 47). Individual units *are not* the meaningful level of analysis; rather, it is the pattern as a whole (among the units) that represent the meaningful level of analysis. Units can be labeled as input, output, or hidden, depending on whether they receive or send inputs to or from the environment, or if they are hidden within the system being modeled.

The *state of activation* is the representation of the state of the system at a particular time. It is this pattern of activation across the units that determines what the system is representing at a particular moment. The *output of the units* is an output function which "maps the current state of activation to an output signal" (pp. 48–49).

The *pattern of connectivity* is very important and constitutes what the system "knows." The pattern of connectivity is the connections between the various units of the system plus the weight (positive or negative) that is assigned to the connections between sets of units. Since units may receive input from various units and output to various units, each of which may have different weights, the pattern of connectivity among various units can be quite complex, especially if the weighting is multiplicative rather than additive.

The *rule of propagation* is a rule that takes the output vector, which represents the output values from the units, and combines that output value with the connectivity matrices (associated with the various units) to provide a net input for each type of input to each unit. Besides having a propagation rule, an *activation rule* is needed "whereby the net inputs of each type impinging on a particular unit are combined with one another and with the current state of the unit to produce a new state of activation" (p. 51).

A means is also needed to *modify the patterns of connectivity* between the various units as a function of experience by either developing new connections, losing connections, or modifying the strengths of associations between connections that already exist. And finally, any PDP model needs a clear *representation of the environment* in which it exists.

Parallel distributed processing models are neurally inspired models as opposed to computer-inspired models. They appear to offer a realistic model for how the brain processes information, given that neurons operate in terms of milliseconds, whereas computers operate in terms of nanoseconds. Mental processes that involved a hundred or so steps must operate in parallel if the resulting processes, such as perception, memory retrieval, speech processing, or sentence comprehension are to take no more than a second or so (which is usually the time that such processes involve).

A major difference between PDP approaches and serial approaches is that "almost all knowledge is *implicit* in the structure of the device that carries out the task rather than *explicit* in the states of the units themselves" (Rumelhart *et al.*, 1986a, p. 75). Hence, knowledge is a function of the "tuning" of the connections between units rather than "stored" as declarative knowledge within units.

Because of the essentially constructive nature of PDP models, they have robust ability to generalize automatically to new situations and they are also especially "tunable" to changing environments.

Baars's Global Workspace Theory of Consciousness

A theoretical model of consciousness that borrows from and expands the notion of parallel distributed processing is described by Baars (1983, 1985, 1987, 1988). In Baars's model, the nervous system is seen as a distributed collection of specialized parallel processors. These specialized processors cooperate and compete with each other for access to an integrative domain called a "global workspace." Whereas the global workspace appears to be closely associated with conscious functions, the specialized processors are thought to be largely unconscious.

For Baars, conscious and unconscious processes are vastly different.

Whereas unconscious processes are highly efficient in their own specialized tasks (characterized by low errors, high speed, and little mutual interference), conscious processes are computationally inefficient (characterized by high errors, low speed, and mutual interference). Whereas unconscious processes are relatively isolated, autonomous in reference to each other, and have limited range over time, conscious processes can relate conscious contents to each other rather easily, and hence have great range over different contents over time.

In his 1987 article, Baars reviews the evidence that the nervous system acts as an (unconscious) parallel distributed system and the reticular-thalamic system as the neural analogue to the (conscious) global workspace. Baars writes:

> (T)here is reliable evidence that most anatomical structures in the brain subserve very specific functions. Under these circumstances it is natural to view the brain as a parallel distributed system, and at least two well-known interpreters of brain function have done so. Arbib has for some years argued that motor systems should be viewed as collections of multiple specialized processors, operating independently of each other to a considerable degree (e.g., Arbib, 1980). And recently Mountcastle (1978) has interpreted the columnar organization of the cerebral cortex in terms of distributed "unit modules." (Baars, 1987, p. 217)

For Baars, the definition of a "processor" is recursive. A processor will often be part of a structured coalition of processors, or a processor may be functionally decomposable into many components or processors. "Thus, functionally separable processors can only be defined momentarily, within the context of a single task—in some other task or context, processors may be rearranged in some other way; perhaps in a different organization they are functionally inseparable from a superordinate processor" (1987, p. 219). Hence, different processors may be superprocessors or subprocessors, depending on the task at hand and the cerebral circuitry involved. Although such a definition complicates theoretical matters making the definition of processors somewhat circular, it does give tremendous flexibility to the system, a flexibility akin to that of the human psyche.

The global workspace "is really a publicity organ for the distributed system" (Baars, 1987, p. 215). It allows processors to gain access to the global workspace to posit a problem that may be solved by the other processors. The global workspace should be able to send (output) and receive (input) information. Concerning input, there should be competition of access between mutually incompatible contents. That this occurs psychologically is evidenced by the finding that conscious contents compete with all other incompatible conscious contents. In terms of output, information from the global workspace should be available to many different subsystems. Baars cites evidence from event-related potentials (Thatcher & John, 1977) and the orienting response (Sokolov, 1963) suggesting that this indeed is the case.

For Baars, the reticular-thalamic system behaves like a global workspace in a parallel distributed system. The reticular-thalamic system incorporates the classical brain stem reticular formation, the nonspecific nuclei of the thalamus, and the fibers that project, in diffuse fashion, upward from the thalamus to "activate" the cortex. The reticular-thalamic system is involved in wakefulness, the orienting response, the focus of attention, and the "most central integrative processes of the brain" (Baars, 1987, p. 224).

Baars concludes that "there is considerable neurophysiological evidence to suggest that the reticular-thalamic system is the major substrate of conscious experience, while the cortex and perhaps other parts of the brain may provide the content of conscious experience" (p. 226).

Differential Emotions Theory

No history of the cognitive revolution in psychology would be complete without a section devoted to affect. Hand in hand with the cognitive explosion in psychology has been a tremendous increase in the theorizing and research concerning emotion, mood, and affect. Emotions, feelings such as joy, interest, sadness, anger, and guilt, have ceased to be of interest to only the clinician, but have become the focus of interest of academic psychologists. Although several psychologists including Kagan (1972), Plutchik (1962, 1980), and Tomkins (1962, 1963) have done much to propel emotion and affect into the scientific spotlight, this section will focus primarily on Carroll Izard's (1977) differential emotions theory.

Izard's theory places emotion as centrally important in motivation, social communication, cognition, and action, and takes its name "from its emphasis on discrete emotions as distinct experiential/motivational processes" (1977, p. 43). His theory is based on five key assumptions:

(1) Ten fundamental emotions constitute the principal motivational system for human beings. (2) Each fundamental emotion has unique motivational and phenomenological properties. (3) Fundamental emotions such as joy, sadness, anger, and shame lead to different inner experiences and different behavioral consequences. (4) Emotions interact with each other—one emotion may activate, amplify, or attenuate another. (5) Emotional processes interact with and exert influence on homeostatic, drive, perceptual, cognitive, and motor processes. (1977, p. 43)

The ten fundamental emotions include: interest-excitement, enjoyment-joy, surprise-startle, distress-anguish, anger-rage, disgust-revulsion, contempt-scorn, fear-terror, shame/shyness-humiliation, and guilt-remorse. According to differential emotions theory, personality is a complex of six organizational subsystems including the homeostatic, drive, emotional, perceptual, cognitive, and motor systems. These six subsystems of personality generate four types of motivation: drives, emotions, affect-cognitive interactions, and affective-cognitive structures. Whereas drives result from tissue deficit or change, emotions are the experiential-motivational phenomena that have adaptive functions regardless of tissue needs. An affect-cognitive interaction is a motivational state resulting from the interaction between an affect or patterns of affect and cognitive processes; while affective-cognitive structures are "psychological organizations of affect and cognition—traitlike phenomena that result from repeated interactions between a particular affect or patterns of affect and a particular set or configuration of cognitions" (1977, p. 45).

Izard defines an emotion as "a complex process with neurophysiological, neuromuscular, and phenomenological aspects" (1977, p. 48). In addition to the emotion system, two other biological systems operate in conjunction with the emotional system, that is, the brain stem reticular system and the glandular-visceral system in an auxiliary fashion. Since emotions rarely function independently of other systems, various patterns of emotion are usually always present and interacting with other systems, such as the perceptual, cognitive, and motor systems. According to Izard, differential emotion theory postulates the continuous presence of emotion in consciousness; although emotional processes can operate relatively independent of cognition, cognition interacts with emotional processes almost all of the time. For Izard, effective personality functioning results from the balanced and integrated interaction of emotions, cognitions, and the motor system, and auxiliary and other life systems.

Consciousness, Emotion, and Cognition

Izard defines consciousness as "the total array of sensations, perceptions, cognitions, and affects that characterize the individual" (1977, p. 137). If consciousness is assumed to be distinct from its contents, the special states of consciousness may be characterized by changes in the structures and operations of consciousness. According to differential emotions theory, affect is so basic and pervasive in consciousness that the primary fundamental emotions constitute the basic structures of consciousness.

Given that emotion constitutes or characterizes ordinary states of consciousness, emotion is prior to or "precedes" the perception of the world. Hence perception is a "prediction" based on past experience and current affective patterns. Perception, for Izard, is influenced in endless ways by the great variety of affect combinations.

In addition to emotion, most operations of consciousness involve *representations*. The usual contents of consciousness result from "a unique type of representation by which one re-presents (duplicates, imitates) to one's self some other aspect of the world" (1977, p. 144). For Izard, however, unlike some other cognitive psychologists, it is the emotions that are the organizing forces in consciousness, not representations or schema. It is the emotions that organize sensory data and reorganize information in creative ways. Affects exert control by means of an intraindividual communication system composed of feedback loops and interactive systems. According to differential emotions theory, the organization of consciousness is as follows:

> Sensations from both interocepters and exterocepters provide the basis for consciousness. Consciousness at its most basic level is awareness of sensation. Emotion is the most fundamental organization of sensations that has significance or meaning (and that has specific experiential, motivational properties). The very basic sensory-cortical process that produces affect lays the ground work for perception, cognition, and all other operations of consciousness. Consciousness that consists of awareness of "pure sensation" or of sensations that is only loosely organized by the usual perceptual-cognitive processes is attained by adults only under unusual conditions. Ordinary states of consciousness are characterized by affect and, most importantly, in human beings, by emotion; and the emotions in consciousness influence all perception, cognition, and behavior. (Izard, 1977, p. 155)

Given the above definition of consciousness, ordinary states of consciousness are characterized by combinations of emotion, perception, and cognition in terms of affective-cognitive orientations that seem automatic due to "innate neural programs that interrelate affective and perceptual-cognitive processes and partly because much of the framework for interpreting the world as we sense it has resulted from strong and early-learned affective-cognitive structures" (1977, p. 155). Hence, most adults have difficulty in achieving altered states of consciousness because the operations and structures of consciousness are firmly entrenched.

Special or altered states of consciousness, according to Izard, only result if and when the individual can break the affective-cognitive bonds that couple affect and cognitive structures, since they "provide the principal structures of ordinary consciousness" (1977, p. 158). Special or altered states of awareness or consciousness are then the result of major shifts in the affective-perceptual-cognitive processes that characterize consciousness. For Izard, an altered state of consciousness results from a radical change of interest and a breakdown or collapse of strong, early-learned affective-cognitive processing patterns. Special states of consciousness may result from radical shifts in the perceptual-affective-cognitive apparatus due, for example, to psychoactive drugs, extraordinary strong drives, or intense sensory pleasure that combines excitement and sexual stimulation. Altered states of consciousness are then usually the result of a radical shift in interest and a breakdown of very stable and well-learned affective-cognitive processing patterns.

Concluding Remarks

Although Izard's differential emotions theory goes a long way toward integrating emotion and affect with cognition and consciousness, it should be noted that cognitive psychology has tended to ignore affect. In the words of Zajonc (1980):

> Contemporary cognitive psychology simply ignores affect. The words *affect, attitude, feeling,* and *sentiment* do not appear in the indexes of any of the major works on cognition (Anderson, 1976; Anderson & Bower, 1973; Bobrow & Collins, 1975; Crowder, 1976; Kintsch, 1974; Lachman, Lachman, & Butterfield, 1979; Norman & Rumelhart, 1975; Schank & Adelson, 1977; Tulving & Donaldson, 1972). Nor do these concepts appear in Neisser's (1967) original work that gave rise to the cognitive revolution in experimental psychology. (p. 152, Footnote 3)

Any comprehensive theory and approach to mapping subjective experience must assess affect, in addition to cognition, volition, perception, and attention. Izard's approach does that and in a way that places affect in a position of great importance in contrast to most cognitive approaches to consciousness.

Consciousness and the Unconscious

To complete this chapter, it is important to address the role of the unconscious in consciousness. An edited book by K. S. Bowers and D. Meichenbaum entitled *The Unconscious Reconsidered* (1984) goes a long way in trying to understand the role of the unconscious in the production and manifestation of consciousness as seen from the recent cognitive revolution. Although there is not enough space to do justice to all the chapters in that book, the chapters by Meichenbaum and Gilmore (1984) and Kihlstrom (1984) (and Kihlstrom's subsequent article in *Science*, 1987), will be reviewed to illustrate how these psychologists conceptualize the manner in which unconscious psychological processes influence and form the substratum for the manifestation of consciousness.

The chapter by Meichenbaum and Gilmore (1984) delineates consciousness in terms of cognitive events, cognitive processes, and cognitive structures. For Meichenbaum and Gilmore, cognitive events are the conscious identifiable thoughts and images that occur within an individual's stream of consciousness. Cognitive processes, on the other hand, are "those processes that shape mental representations, transforming them and constructing schemas of experience and action" (p. 275). Whereas cognitive events are conscious, cognitive processes often operate on an automatic or unconscious level.

Cognitive structures, in turn, are the enduring characteristics of a person's cognitive organization that are the "theoretical constructs offered to explain the perception, interpretation, transformation, organization, and recall of information" (p. 283). They are the schemas by which a person understands himself and the world, they are the systems which provide meaning to existence.

Particular supraordinate cognitive structures, called *core organizing principles*, are inferred cognitive structures that operate on and influence behavior without conscious knowledge of the individual. It is these unconscious cognitive structures that can lead to psychopathology, due to the fact that these cognitive structures determine how a person will experience and perceive cognitive events. Because an individual's cognitive structures seem the "executive processor" for thinking, feeling, and behavior, it is these unconscious systems that allow individuals to impute meaning to situations and operate on behavior in predetermined ways.

Kihlstrom (1984), after reviewing a multistore and a unistore model of memory, presents a revised model of memory. In this model, incoming stimuli are processed by the sensory-perceptual system (an unconscious system), which, in turn, is guided by the stored procedural knowledge system, also unconscious. The sensory-perceptual and the procedural knowledge systems interact with the declarative knowledge system and attentional processes to form the "full perceptual construction (or memory reconstruction) of the object or event" (p. 168) resulting in a conscious percept. This conscious percept is both data driven ("bottom-up") and conceptually driven ("top-down") and results from the influence of the attentional resources of the subject, unconscious procedural knowledge, and sensory-perceptual data in interaction with the storehouse of declarative knowledge.

Kihlstrom then goes on to indicate how amnesia, repression, and dissociative phenomena associated with hypnosis can be explained or integrated with this model. His approach suggests that consciousness is the end result of attentional processes in interaction with declarative and procedural knowledge systems and a perceptual-sensory store that permits dissociation via "the weakening, fracturing, or breaking of the associative links between semantic representations of percepts and memories, and episodic representations of the self in spatiotemporal context" (1984, p. 195). Consciousness, in Kihlstrom's model, is the end result of attentional processes and sensory input in interaction with various unconscious structures.

In his 1987 article in *Science,* "The Cognitive Unconscious," Kihlstrom expands on his 1984 book chapter. He hypothesizes a "tripartite division of the cognitive unconscious." The first division includes in the domain of procedural knowledge "a number of complex processes that are inaccessible to introspection in principle under any circumstances" (p. 1450) and are mental processes that can only be known indirectly by inference. They can be described as unconscious in the strict sense of the term and they are responsible for the "construction" of a person's ongoing thought, experience, and action. Whereas some unconscious procedural knowledge appears to be innate, other types become automatized through use and practice.

Research on subliminal perception and implicit memory (an inferred change in memory resulting from a change in task performance that is attributable to information acquired during a previous learning episode for which the subject has become amnestic) reveals what Kihlstrom called "preconscious declarative knowledge." These are percepts and memories that are activated to some degree by current or prior inputs and hence able to influence thought, action, and experience. These percepts and memories, however, have not acquired the required activation for representation in working memory, and hence, for conscious awareness.

In addition to unconscious procedural knowledge and preconscious declarative knowledge, research on hypnosis and related states also suggests a category of subconscious declarative knowledge. These are:

> mental representations, fully activated by perceptual inputs or acts of thought, above the threshold ordinarily required for representation in working memory, and available to introspection under some circumstances, (that) seem nevertheless inaccessible to phenomenal awareness. (Kihlstrom, 1987, p. 1451)

These are memories and experiences that appear dissociated from conscious awareness and are yet, in principle, able to be consciously experienced by the self or "I." In this case, it appears that complex, deliberate attentional processes are operating unconsciously.

For both Kihlstrom and Meichenbaum and Gilmore, it is the "cognitive unconscious" or the cognitive structures (which appear to define similar domains) that form the "backdrop" or unconsciousness from which consciousness derives. The proclivity to perceive and structure experience according to prior models is then the result of an individual's cognitive structures or memory stores that have become or remain unconscious. With these theorists, it is the *interaction* between these different systems that will determine the nature of resulting conscious experience.

CONCLUSIONS

That concludes a sampling of the cognitive revolution that has transformed psychological science. Whether defined in terms of schemas, processing units, or the procedural knowledge domain, all theorists define and infer the existence of various cognitive structures or subsystems that interact in various ways to "construct" that phenomenon we call consciousness. Consistent with a major premise of this book, it is these structures or subsystems of consciousness that need to be better understood, not only in terms of their nature and "substance," but also in terms of their interrelations and interactions with each other.

Quantifying the Structures and Patterns of Consciousness

An Empirical-Phenomenological Approach

INTRODUCTION

The last 30 years have seen tremendous growth in the theorizing on the nature of consciousness (Baars, 1987, 1988; Fischer, 1971, 1978; Hilgard, 1980; Mandler, 1985; Marsh, 1977; Silverman, 1968; Tart, 1975) and its various altered (Tart, 1969, 1972) or alternate (Zinberg, 1977) states as induced by meditation (Naranjo & Ornstein, 1972; Pekala, 1987), drugs (Harman et al., 1972), hypnosis (Weitzenhoffer, 1978), EEG biofeedback (Brown, 1974), and many other altered state induction procedures (White, 1972). Since consciousness, by definition, is "awareness, especially of something within oneself" (*Webster*, 1970, p. 177), it would seem that introspection or phenomenological assessment (Battista, 1978) might be a very useful means to map subjective experience.

Yet, despite a great deal of theorizing on the enumeration (Krippner, 1972; Ludwig, 1972; White, 1972), nature (Singer, 1977; Zinberg, 1977), and organization of states of consciousness (Fischer, 1978; Fishkin & Jones, 1978; Tart, 1977), with the exception of studies that have focused on a particular state of consciousness (Johnson, 1979; Osis et al.,

1973; Shapiro, 1980; Smith, 1978; Tart, 1971; Vogel et al., 1972, for example), there has been relatively little systematic and comprehensive research into the structures of consciousness and its various states through the observation of subjective experience. Although much theorizing exists on the nature of consciousness and its various states, there is less than adequate phenomenological research to evaluate the validity of that theorizing. There are probably several reasons why phenomenological methods have not been utilized as well as they might have in trying to understand consciousness.

THE LACK OF PHENOMENOLOGICAL RESEARCH

The Hope of Neurophysiological Approaches

One of the reasons for the lack of systematic and comprehensive phenomenological research on consciousness is related to the expectation that neurophysiological methods, especially electroencephalography, could be used to map the structures and organization of consciousness (Hilgard, 1969; Kamiya, 1968). But the use of such an approach has not led to great advances in our understanding of particular EEG rhythms with general states of awareness, such as sleeping, dreaming, and waking (Lindsley, 1960).

Moreover, evidence on the lack of a relationship between the occurrence of the "alpha experience" (Kamiya, 1968) and the strength or density of the EEG alpha activity "calls into question the entire enterprise of 'mapping consciousness' neurophysiologically" (Plotkin, 1979, p. 1145). This suggests that neurophysiological methods may not be able to comprehensively map subjective experience, an opinion that was also voiced by L. C. Johnson (1970) soon after the initial excitement over EEG biofeedback and the "alpha high" experience.

Distrust of Introspection

A second reason for the lack of systematic phenomenological research into states of consciousness concerns the difficulty involved in trying to devise a phenomenological methodology to adequately and unobtrusively map the structures of conscious experience. Ever since the turn-of-the-century structuralists, such as Wundt (1897) and Titchener (1898), were attacked for their obtrusive methods of introspection (Angell, 1907) and the uselessness of mapping the structures of subjective experience through introspection (Watson, 1913), psychologists have been hesitant to assess the nature of phenomenological experience from an introspective approach.

When Titchener attempted to investigate the structures of consciousness by retrospection upon a few seconds of subjective experience, such a method was ridiculed for "freezing" and hence destroying the most fundamental property of consciousness—its evanescent and fleeting quality (Angell, 1907). More recently, due to behaviorism's hegemony during the 20th century (Robinson, 1979) and the acceptance by psychologists of behaviorism's philosophical and methodological assumptions, the mind or consciousness has been seen to be of dubious epistemological status (Lieberman, 1979). As a result, introspection was seen as an inherently flawed tool for the investigation of consciousness.

MODERN INTROSPECTION

But just as introspection was superseded by behaviorism, so behaviorism began to be superseded by cognitive psychology. It was in the late 1950s and early 1960s that a shift from purely behavioral to more cognitive approaches in psychology began to make their appearance. Interest in such diverse areas as sensory deprivation, attention, sleeping and dreaming, and imagery prompted psychologists to turn their attention from purely overt behaviors to stimuli of a more covert, physiological, or cognitive nature (Holt, 1964).

Cognitive approaches to psychology became the heir to behaviorism's long-standing hegemony in experimental psychology (Baars, 1986). Such approaches attempted to retain the gains and methods of behaviorism, while adapting methodology and theory to embrace cognition and its component processes. As testimony to the burgeoning interest in cognition, the 1970s witnessed the birth of several new journals addressed specifically to cognition: *Cognition* (1971), *Memory and Cognition* (1973), *Cognitive Science* (1977), and *Cognitive Therapy and Research* (1977).

The emergence of cognitive psychology and the renewal of interest in consciousness (Hilgard, 1980) has brought the return of introspection as an acceptable psychological methodology. Since its inception, a leading cognitive-behavioral journal, *Cognitive Therapy and Research*, has continued to publish articles using introspection or *phenomenological assessment* (as contemporary introspection is now called) in the assessment of cognition (Hurlburt, 1980; Rogers & Craighead, 1977), affect (Harrell *et al.*, 1981; LaPointe & Harrell, 1978), and related processes (Kendall & Korgeski, 1979; Mahoney, 1977).

In 1979 introspection was defended in psychology's leading journal, the *American Psychologist*, by an article entitled "Behaviorism and the Mind: A (limited) Call for a Return to Introspection" (Lieberman, 1979). Introspection has been used to study daydreaming (Singer, 1978), modes of conscious experience (Klinger, 1978; Parks *et al.*, 1988), the biological rhythms of waking fantasy (Kripke & Sonnenshein, 1978), imagery (Wharton, 1988), and imagination (Singer, 1981). Since Singer (1978, 1981), Hurlburt (Reise & Hurlburt, 1988), and Klinger (1971) are reliably mapping the *stream* of consciousness and the nature of the day-dreaming experience without stopping and hence destroying the nature of that experience, this strongly suggests that similar methodological approaches may be used to systematically and unobtrusively map the *structures* of conscious experience. With neurophysiological approaches to mapping consciousness being called into question, a phenomenological or introspective approach may be the only means to adequately and comprehensively investigate the structures of conscious experience.

If a phenomenological methodology for assessing and mapping the structures of consciousness is found to be reliable and valid, then it can be used to determine the particular phenomenological parameters associated with a specific stimulus condition. Such parameters could then be used to quantify the phenomenological state associated with a particular stimulus condition. This would then provide a means by which states of consciousness (Tart, 1975; Zinberg, 1977) associated with various stimulus conditions or induction procedures used to produce altered states of consciousness (Tart, 1972) could be empirically compared to one another.

FROM CLASSICAL TO CONTEMPORARY INTROSPECTION

Reliability and Validity

It is of interest that classical introspection became obsolete due to its failure to demonstrate adequate reliability and validity. According to Boring (1953), classical introspection

> went out of style after Titchener's death (1927) because it had demonstrated no functional use . . . and also because it was unreliable. Laboratory atmosphere crept into the descriptions, and it was not possible to verify, from one laboratory to another, the introspective accounts of the consciousness of action, feelings, choice, and judgment. (p. 174)

Controversies over imageless thought and Titchener's stimulus-error (Boring, 1929/50) cast further doubt over the validity of classical introspection and it became, as Boring said, functionally useless.

As in the past, there has recently been much controversy over the reliability of introspective data. Nisbett and Wilson (1977) have indicated that with regard to accessing cognitive processes, introspective access "is not sufficient to produce generally correct or reliable reports" (p. 233). Smith and Miller (1978), on the other hand, suggest that the assessment of cognitive processes may not be as inaccessible as Nisbett and Wilson indicate.

Nisbett and Wilson may be partially correct when relating individuals' attributions or cognitions to their actions. But when asked to describe, not the reasons (the why), but the content (the what) of their subjective experience, people are much more accurate, as Ericsson and Simon (1980), Lieberman (1979), and Singer and Kolligian (1987) have shown. Lieberman's summary of the literature has indicated that although phenomenological assessment can sometimes be misleading or wrong, the classical and modern literature of introspective research has shown that such "data can be highly reliable and useful, helping not only to predict specific behavior, but to discover fundamental principles of learning and performance (e.g., Weber's law, and the role of imagery in verbal memory)" (1979, p. 332).

Along similar lines, Singer and Kolligian (1987) indicate that "these reports using questionnaires all converge in suggesting that people can generally provide reasonably valid and reliable indices of their own differential patterns of ongoing inner thought through relatively short questionnaires" (p. 542).

The question of the accuracy of phenomenological assessment also suggests that validity may be difficult to confirm. Although the research reviewed by Ericsson and Simon (1980), Klinger (1978), Lieberman (1979), and Singer (Singer & Kolligian, 1987) indicate that introspective data can be both valid and useful, behaviorists like Rachlin (1974) and Skinner (1974, 1989) have strongly questioned the value and validity of introspective reports and have gone so far as to proclaim them superfluous.

Polemics notwithstanding, the question of the validity of introspective data must be based on empirical research. As with other areas of psychological research, the validity of introspective or phenomenological data will finally reside "in ruling out artifacts, in replications, and ultimately, in the usefulness of data or theory for making possible other forms of prediction, and perhaps, control" (Klinger, 1978, p. 227). Because of the covert nature of subjective data, however, questions of validity will probably be harder to investigate than with overt behaviors. Hence, a critical, empirical assessment of the validity of phenomenological assessment is also necessary.

Retrospective Phenomenological Assessment

Since behaviorism defined its variables in terms of specific behaviors and stimulus settings, the reliability and validity of such variables could be more easily observed, assessed, and evaluated than could cognitions, affects, imagery, or awareness levels. This suggested to me that by combining the strengths of behaviorism's overt variables with introspection's covert events, phenomenological assessment might be made more reliable and valid. By evaluating phenomenological experience in reference to specific behaviors and stimulus conditions, I hoped to increase the reliability and validity of phenomenological assessment by tying that assessment to observable and repeatable stimulus conditions (Pekala & Wenger, 1983). (A stimulus condition is any stimulus environment in which the participant is involved, including the participant's own behavior, and any verbal instructions and experimental manipulations enacted upon the individual.)

Such a methodology would retrospectively assess subjective experience in reference to specific stimulus conditions and allow for the various structures of phenomenological experience (i.e., imagery, cognition, attention, affect) to be investigated and evaluated in reference to those conditions. As long as the assessment is based on accurate retrieval from memory, the research evidence indicates that such retrospective verbalization can be both reliable and valid (Ericsson & Simon, 1980). Such an assessment might also allow one to map the relationship between a stimulus condition and its corresponding phenomenological parameters.

By asking individuals to retrospectively assess their phenomenological experience during a given stimulus condition, such a method of retrospective phenomenological assessment might not only (1) yield an introspective methodology that is both reliable and valid, but (2) allow for the various structures of subjective experience to be systematically assessed, and (3) generate a methodology for assessing and quantifying states and altered (Tart, 1977) or alternate (Zinberg, 1977) states of consciousness.

OPERATIONALIZING AND QUANTIFYING THE STRUCTURES AND PROCESSES OF CONSCIOUSNESS

Chapters 2 and 3 suggested that consciousness can be thought to be composed of certain structures, processing units, or schemas and a means to regulate awareness of those structures, units, or schemas, probably through some type of attentional mechanisms. Since we must first agree as to what consciousness is before it can be assessed and measured, we will briefly review several of the approaches discussed in the prior chapters that attempted to determine the major domains of consciousness.

Husserl's Intentionality Doctrine

One of the ways to break down or define consciousness is in terms of the *noesis-noema doctrine* promulgated by Husserl (1913/72). Husserl, the father of philosophical phenomenology, defined consciousness as *intentional*. For Husserl, *noema* are the objects, the data of consciousness that result from consciousness being intentional, that is, "consciousness is consciousness *of* something." That something is the noema: "the noema, as distinct from the real object as well as from the act, turns out to be an unreal or ideal entity which belongs to the same sphere as meanings or significations" (Gurwitsch, 1967, p. 129). For Husserl, there are "noema corresponding to every act of memory, expectation, representation, imagination, thinking, judging, volition, and so on" (1913/72, p. 130). Whereas noema represent the objects of intentionality, the *processes* or acts of intentionality are the *noeses*. Thus, the acts of thinking, perceiving, hearing, and so forth are also noeses, the processes by which consciousness is consciousness of something. Consciousness, being intentional, involves the processes or noeses of apperceiving or apprehending the noema.

The Cognitive Psychologists

The cognitive revolution has brought *schemas* to the forefront of understanding consciousness. Schemas, the building blocks for representations, are the "stuff" out of which consciousness is constructed for most of the cognitive psychologists. For Mandler (1985), "we can be conscious only of experiences that are constructed out of activated schemas. We are not conscious of the process of activation or the constituents of the activated schemas" (p. 57). Schemas are the "contents" of consciousness.

For Mandler, attention is not coextensive with consciousness. Attention "is the process whereby a specific part of the space-time continuum is automatically made available for further processing" (1984, p. 62). Attention is the "window" through which activated schemas are brought into awareness and made the subject of conscious experience. Because of the limited capacity of attentional mechanisms, consciousness is also of limited capacity. It is attention and the "subsequent activation of selected cognitive representations (schemas)" (1984, p. 62) that results in a subset of activated schemas forming "the unified phenomenal conscious experience" (p. 62) of the individual, that is, his or her particular stream of consciousness at the moment.

For Baars (1987), consciousness is relational, content sensitive, internally consistent, serial, and of limited capacity. Whereas various distributed parallel processors (localized in the cortex and other parts of the brain) appear to generate the various contents of consciousness, Baars's global workspace in the form of the extended reticular-thalamic activating system (ERTAS) (Baars, 1988) appears to be the major substrate for conscious experience. It is the ERTAS that is involved in the orienting response, focal attention, alertness, and so forth; it is the gatekeeping function that "illuminates" the contents of various parallel distributed processors, by taking "input from specialized modules in the brain, and broadcasting this information globally to the nervous system as a whole" (1988, p. 227).

For Izard (1977) emotion forms the basic organization of sensation. The basic sensory-cortical processes that produce affective experience (the emotions) lay the groundwork for all other operations of consciousness. Ten primary affects—interest-excitement, enjoyment-joy, surprise-startle, distress-anguish, anger-rage, disgust-revulsion, contempt-scorn, fear- terror, shame-shyness-humiliation, and guilt-remorse—form the basis for affective experience. These combine with cognitive processes, drives, homeostatic mechanisms, and the perceptual and motor systems to form the personality.

Consciousness, then, is the total matrix of sensations, perceptions, cognitions, and affects that characterize the individual. Whereas ordinary states of consciousness are characterized by combinations of emotions, perceptions, and cognitions in affective-cognitive orientations that appear automatic due to innate neural programs and early-learned affective-cognitive structures, altered states of consciousness occur when the bonds coupling affects and cognitive structures are broken, due to psychoactive drugs, extraordinary strong drives, or radical shifts in the perceptual-affective-cognitive structures.

The Consciousness Psychologists

Whereas I have chosen Mandler, Baars, and Izard to serve as spokesmen for the cognitive psychologists who have tried to develop models for consciousness, I have chosen Silverman (1968), Fishkin and

Jones (1978), and Tart (1975, 1977) to represent the consciousness psychologists, those psychologists interested not so much in cognitive psychology per se, but rather in consciousness and states of consciousness.

All four of these theorists have chosen to place attention in a prominent position in their theorizing. Silverman argues that altered states of consciousness are a function of the way attention is deployed; alterations in attention, in turn, lead to alterations in consciousness. Silverman breaks down attention into three dimensions: attentional intensiveness, extensiveness (scanning), and selectiveness (field articulation).

Whereas attentional intensiveness refers to how absorbed or involved a person becomes in reference to internal and external stimuli, extensiveness refers to the degree of "sampling" of the elements of the stimulus field—whether that field is narrow or wide. Selectiveness of attention, on the other hand, "refers to responses which determine which elements in a stimulus field exert a dominant influence on the perceiver" (Silverman, 1968, p. 1203), that is, whether the subject responds to the discrete elements of the field or takes a more holistic or global perspective.

For Fishkin and Jones (1978), attention is a "movable window" between what is potentially available to consciousness and what actually "gets into" consciousness. The location of the attentional window partially determines what gets into consciousness. The size of the window determines the breadth of attention, the rate of window movement determines the rate of shifts in attention, while the pattern of window movement determines the temporal sequence of attentional shifts. The fluidity of the *potentially available to consciousness* (PAC) and its structure determines the amount of material to enter consciousness and the specifics of that material. Finally, the distribution and amount of available energy determines tradeoffs between the rates of attention shifts, the intensity of consciousness, and the rigidity of PAC contents.

For Tart (1969, 1975, 1977), *awareness-attention* constitutes the major "energy" source of consciousness. Awareness, for Tart, "refers to the basic knowledge that something is happening to perceiving or feeling or cognizing in its simplest form" (Tart, 1975, p. 27). *Structures*, or subsystems, for Tart can be hard- or soft-wired and are the mechanisms by which consciousness is experienced. Ten subsystems or structures are hypothesized to comprise a particular state of consciousness, in addition to awareness-attention. These include: exteroceptors, interoceptors, input processing, memory, sense of identity, evaluation and decision making, motor output, subconscious, emotion, and space-time. States of consciousness, for Tart, are a function of the *patterns* among the aforementioned structures of consciousness and awareness-attention.

Quantifying Consciousness

Given the aforementioned review, any phenomenological approach to consciousness should attempt to measure or quantify attention, since it is implicated by all the aforementioned consciousness and cognitive psychologists. Thus, any phenomenological approach to consciousness should attempt to somehow define and measure the different phenomenological aspects of attention, along the lines of Silverman or Fishkin and Jones. It appears that any phenomenological approach to consciousness should also attempt to map and quantify the major subsystems, structures, schemas, parallel distributed processors, or noetic "building blocks" of consciousness. Although this might be particularly difficult, a consensus as to what might be the major structures or schemas of consciousness, somewhat like the classification of Tart (1977), would probably represent a good beginning point in trying to understand consciousness.

Hence, both the major contents of consciousness, and the processes or means by which these contents are "illuminated," cognized, perceived, and so forth by consciousness, that is, the noema and the noeses (Husserl, 1913/72), would need to be addressed in any comprehensive phenomenological quantification of consciousness.

Besides quantifying consciousness, a phenomenological methodology would also need to be able to define and quantify states of consciousness.

OPERATIONALIZING AND QUANTIFYING A STATE OF CONSCIOUSNESS

According to Mandler (1985), a state of consciousness "is constructed out of the most general structures currently being activated by current concerns and environmental requirements" (p. 60). A state of consciousness is a *construction* out of specific cognitive, affective, perceptual, and other structures that are activated due to the constraints of the organism and that of the environment.

Tart (1975, 1977), who has probably spent more time theorizing how to understand various states of consciousness than any other theorist, also views states of consciousness as constructions. According to Tart (1975), states of consciousness are a function of various subsystems or structures of mind that combine in particular patterns to form a specific or discrete state of consciousness. A state of consciousness is a unique configuration or system of psychological structures or subsystems, a configuration that maintains its integrity or identity as a recognizable system in spite of variations in input from the environment and in spite of various (small) changes in subsystems. (1975, p. 62)

For Tart, it is the pattern or organization between these different elements that determine the particular state of consciousness experienced. Tart has defined two basic categories of states of consciousness: an altered state of consciousness and an identity state of consciousness. An altered state of consciousness is a state of consciousness in which there is a significantly different pattern of organization among structures in comparison to ordinary, waking consciousness and the phenomenological perception of being in a radically different state of awareness, that I have elsewhere defined as the *subjective sense* of (being in) an *altered state* (SSAS) (Pekala & Wenger, 1983).

An identity state of consciousness, on the other hand, is a state of consciousness that is distinguished from other identity states by a significantly different pattern structure among dimensions (in comparison to ordinary, waking consciousness or other states). There is not, however, the perception of being in an altered state of consciousness. Thus, identity states are nonaltered states of consciousness characterized by a significant pattern change among dimensions in reference to other identity or altered states, but no SSAS.

Whereas Tart defines states of consciousness as a function of pattern organization among subsystems, Singer (cited in Zinberg, 1977) has suggested that it is primarily intensity, and not pattern, parameters that determine a particular state of consciousness. The approaches of Mandler, Tart, and Singer suggest that a methodology capable of quantifying both pattern and intensity parameters of consciousness might yield a viable means of mapping states of consciousness. In summary, one can draw upon the theorizing of Mandler, Tart, and Singer to define a state of consciousness as "the particular intensity and pattern of associated phenomenological parameters that characterize one's subjective experience during a given time period" (Pekala & Wenger, 1983, pp. 252–253) that are a function of both environmental and organismic variables.

Since a state can be defined as "any well-defined condition or property that can be recognized if it occurs again" (Ashby, 1963, p. 17), to the extent that a phenomenological methodology can be used to determine if and when a particular state of consciousness occurs, then a methodology to define and map states of consciousness would be theoretically possible. If such a methodology is found to be both reliable and valid, one then has at one's disposal an empirical methodology capable of mapping the structures and patterns of consciousness in a very practical manner.

Retrospective Phenomenological Assessment

I have previously reported on a phenomenological methodology to do the above (Pekala, 1980, 1985a; Pekala & Kumar, 1984, 1986, 1987, 1988, 1989; Pekala & Levine, 1981, 1982; Pekala & Wenger, 1983). The methodology involves the retrospective completion of a paper-and-pencil self-report inventory in reference to an immediately preceding stimulus condition. The inventory is composed of items that assess various aspects of subjective experience (dimensions and subdimensions of consciousness) such as: imagery, attention, awareness, memory, positive and negative affect, internal dialogue, rationality, arousal, volitional control, and altered experience. These dimensions do not necessarily represent statistically independent dimensions, but rather dimensions of subjective experience found, through cluster and factor analysis (Hunter, 1977), to be relatively consistent and stable structures of consciousness in several different stimulus conditions.

In completing the questionnaire, subjects retrospectively rate their phenomenological experience during a given time period by marking on a five- or seven-point Likert scale how their subjective experience corresponds to the items of the inventory. (To date, the self-report instruments have used both five- and seven-point Likert scales. Although I tend to prefer the seven-point scale, lack of appropriate optical scanning computer sheets necessitated using the five-point scale for several studies.) As an example, subjects are asked to rate their experience of internal dialogue, that is, whether they were silently talking to themselves a great deal or were not talking to themselves at all. In this particular case, participants have to mark one of the five or seven points along the Likert scale that best corresponds to their subjective experience of internal dialogue. They evaluated that experience in reference to the two end points of "I was silently talking to myself a great deal" versus "I did not engage in any silent talking to myself."

The person's scores for those items making up a particular (sub)dimension of consciousness are then averaged to arrive at an intensity score for each of the various (sub)dimensions of consciousness (Hunter & Gerbing, 1979). These scores allow for intensity parameters of subjective experience to be assessed and quantified, as per the recommendations of Singer (cited in Zinberg, 1977). By giving the questionnaire to many individuals in a particular stimulus condition (or repeatedly to the same individual in the same stimulus condition) Pearson r correlation coefficients can be computed between the various (sub)dimensions of consciousness. One can then use the coefficients to construct a correlation matrix of the various (sub)dimensions. This matrix represents a quantification of the pattern or relationships between dimensions. It meets Tart's (1972, 1975, 1977) criteria for his pattern approach for defining states of consciousness.

By means of t-tests, analyses of variance, and multivariate analyses of variance, dimension intensity scores for the dimensions and sub-dimensions of consciousness associated with a variety of stimulus conditions can be statistically compared. By comparing correlation matrices associated with different stimulus conditions [using the Jennrich (1970) test to statistically compare corresponding correlation matrices], the pattern or organization among dimensions can be statistically evaluated and compared for significant differences.

Research on the above methodology of *retrospective phenomenological assessment* (RPA), since participants retrospectively assess their phenomenological experience associated with a given stimulus condition, found RPA to be both reliable and valid (Pekala & Kumar, 1984, 1987; Pekala & Levine, 1982; Pekala & Wenger, 1983; Pekala *et al.*, 1986). During several different stimulus conditions, such as sitting quietly with eyes open or closed, experiencing an erotic fantasy, reading mildly arousing erotica, relaxing to one's breathing after having experienced progressive relaxation, or experiencing a hypnotic induction, several groups of undergraduates were found to complete RPA self-report inventories in a reasonably consistent and reliable manner. In addition, the different stimulus conditions were characterized by expected differences in intensity and pattern parameters among the (sub)dimensions of consciousness, indicating that the (sub)dimensions of the inventories possessed construct and discriminant validity.

Stimulus-State Specificity

The results from the aforementioned studies indicated that the same stimulus conditions were found to be associated with nonsignificantly different intensity and pattern parameters while different stimulus conditions were generally found to be associated with significantly different intensity and/or pattern parameters (Pekala & Kumar, 1986; Pekala & Wenger, 1983). These results supported the principle of stimulus-state specificity (principle of specificity), which posits that

> across groups of randomly selected individuals, the same behaviors in the same stimulus settings (the same stimulus conditions) will be associated with the same intensities and patterns of phenomenological experience (the same

phenomenological state), while different stimulus conditions will be associated with different intensities and/or patterns of phenomenological experience. (Pekala & Wenger, 1983, p. 255)

Since this principle posits a correspondence between subjective events and overt behaviors across groups of individuals in particular stimulus settings, it permits the intensity and/or patterns of phenomenological experience associated with similar and dissimilar conditions to be compared with one another.

The use of RPA inventories, in conjunction with the principle of specificity, allows for states of consciousness associated with various stimulus conditions to be compared and statistically assessed. Besides allowing for the attentional, perceptual, imaginative, volitional, affective, and cognitive structures of subjective experience to be statistically evaluated, RPA can thus be used to

compare states of subjective experience associated with such procedures as hypnosis, meditation, EEG biofeedback, progressive relaxation, drug intoxification, etc., to determine the extent to which these induction procedures are associated with altered states such as an "alpha high" (Kamiya, 1968) or a "trance state" (Weitzenhoffer, 1978), that are significantly different from non-altered states of consciousness. (Pekala & Levine, 1981, p. 44)

PSYGRAMS, PIPS, HYPNOGRAPHS, AND ICONS

In addition to using these self-report questionnaires to quantify and map various intensities and patterns of phenomenological experience, several graphing devices have been developed to visually depict these intensity/pattern parameters. Whereas *psygrams*, or graphs of the psychophenomenological state of consciousness of a group of individuals, allow for the state of consciousness of a group of individuals to be depicted in terms of pattern (and intensity) parameters, *pips* (phenomenological intensity profiles) allow for the profile of the various (sub)dimension intensity scores of an individual or group of individuals to be depicted and compared. *Icons*, on the other hand, give a rather condensed visual representation of the (intensity) phenomenological state associated with a given individual, as opposed to pips (which present that data in more linear form). And finally, *hypnographs* are graphs of the hypnoidal (Pekala & Nagler, 1989) effects associated with various stimulus conditions.

FORMAT FOR THE NEXT SECTION

The following four chapters will describe the development, nature, and use of the self-report inventories with particular reference to the Phenomenology of Consciousness Inventory (PCI) (Pekala, 1982, 1991b), the most refined and current RPA instrument for mapping and quantifying states of consciousness, and the Dimensions of Attention Questionnaire (DAQ) (Pekala, 1985d, 1991a), the instrument for mapping subjective aspects of attention. Since the PCI and the DAQ are based on predecessor inventories, the predecessor inventories to the PCI and then the DAQ will first be described, with particular reference to reliability and validity.

II

The Instruments

Development, Reliability, and Validity of the Phenomenology of Consciousness Questionnaire

Since the Phenomenology of Consciousness Inventory (PCI) is similar to and contains many of the items found in predecessor instruments, the Phenomenology of Consciousness Questionnaire (PCQ) and the (Abbreviated) Dimensions of Consciousness Questionnaire (A)DCQ, the development of the PCQ and the (A)DCQ will be presented first. This chapter will focus on the PCQ while the next chapter will discuss the (A)DCQ.

CONSTRUCTION OF THE PHENOMENOLOGY OF CONSCIOUSNESS QUESTIONNAIRE

Based on Battista's (1978) eight elements of phenomenological experience, Tart's (1975, 1977) 11 subsystems of consciousness, Krippner's (1972) and Ludwig's (1972) altered states of consciousness, and Silverman's (1968) dimensions of attention, the following dimensions or content areas of consciousness were identified: self-awareness, body image, (altered) state of awareness, alertness, attention (intensity, extensitivity, and selectivity), volition, space-time, perception, positive affect, negative affect, imagery, internal dialogue, memory, rationality, meaning, and a miscellaneous category (Pekala, 1980; Pekala & Levine, 1981).

Items were constructed for each of these content areas. The form of these items was patterned after the Post-Session Questionnaire (PSQ) developed by Osis, Bokert, and Carlson (1973) to assess phenomenological experience during meditation. Each item consisted of extreme statements that anchored a seven-point Likert scale. The items were randomly ordered, yielding an initial questionnaire of 60 items. Several pilot studies were completed on this initial questionnaire, during which time items were added, deleted, and modified.

PILOT STUDIES

First and Second Pilot Studies

For the first pilot study 20 subjects experienced the baseline condition of sitting quietly with their eyes open for four minutes and then completed the questionnaire in reference to the four-minute period. They were also asked to write down their impressions of how appropriately the questionnaire assessed what they had experienced and any areas of experience they felt the questionnaire did not adequately assess. Based on their feedback, many of the items of the questionnaire were modified and ten additional items dealing more specifically with the other content areas were added to the original 60 items.

For the second pilot study, 15 subjects completed the expanded questionnaire after experiencing an identical baseline condition. Since the instructions for the first two pilot studies did not tell the subjects what to expect while they sat quietly, several of the subjects of the second pilot study indicated that if they knew what they would be involved in doing and had some practice at doing it, it would be easier for them to retrospectively rate their subjective experience.

For this purpose, an initial practice period was instituted before the baseline condition for the third pilot study and a means was devised that monitored the subjects' consistency at completing the questionnaire. Five items of the questionnaire (those dealing with awareness, attention, affect, internal dialogue, and imagery) were duplicated with synonyms substituted for a few of the words in each of the items. Thus, there were two sets of five items with nearly identical wording. Five of the previous 70 items that seemed rather ambiguous were eliminated and the set of duplicate items were included in their place.

Third Pilot Study

At the beginning of the third pilot study, 27 subjects were given a short explanation of the nature of introspection and what that might involve. After sitting quietly for one minute with their eyes closed, the subjects completed a ten-item practice questionnaire very similar to the longer inventory. Since this short questionnaire contained several items similar in content with several other items, these item-pairs were reviewed with the subjects, letting them know how consistent they were at introspection.

The subjects then experienced three criterion time periods, each of which was followed by completion of the 70-item inventory. There were two four-minute periods of sitting quietly with eyes open (EO condition) and one four-minute period during which subjects were instructed to be aware of their breathing. This last period was preceded by 15 minutes of progressive relaxation. (This condition was labeled the relaxation/meditation, or RM, condition.)

Pearson *r* correlations were computed between the five pairs of duplicate items, using the data from all three periods for all subjects. Pearson correlations for the five pairs were: .47, .62, .68, .83, and .87. A new pair of items was substituted for the pair with the lowest correlations since the content of these items was diffuse and vague and seemed to be the reason for their low reliability. (This substitution was made when the final form of the questionnaire was constructed.)

The subjects' responses to the items of the questionnaire for the third pilot study were then cluster analyzed, collapsing across all three criterion time periods. A multiple group oblique cluster analysis (Hunter & Gerbing, 1979) with communalities in the diagonals of the correlation matrix was employed using Hunter's PACKAGE program (Hunter & Cohen, 1971) to determine those items that had their highest loadings in the content areas for which they were written.

Items that loaded higher on a different cluster from which they were assigned were eliminated as were items that had very low loadings. Reclustering then occurred until the items making up the final clusters all had their highest cluster loading in that cluster. Based on this procedure, the final version of the questionnaire, which was named the Phenomenology of Consciousness Questionnaire (PCQ), consisted of 60 items, drawn from 15 different content areas.

The particular content areas (and the number of items in each) were: body image (5), time sense (3), state of awareness (3), attention (direction, 3; absorption, 3), volitional control (5), self-awareness (4), perception (3), positive affect (4), negative affect (3), imagery (4), internal dialogue (3), rationality (3), memory (2), meaning (3), and alertness (3). Six items made up a miscellaneous category. The results of these pilot studies indicated that this methodology seemed quite adequate to assess the structures of subjective experience.

Fourth Pilot Study

A fourth pilot study comparing the conditions of sitting quietly with eyes open, attention to one's breathing (that was preceded by relaxation), and reading erotica also indicated that the former was an easy task for subjects to do that seemed quite appropriate for assessing ordinary, waking consciousness.

DEVELOPMENT OF THE PHENOMENOLOGY OF CONSCIOUSNESS QUESTIONNAIRE

Format

Two hundred and forty-nine introductory psychology students, who were seen in groups ranging in size between 30 to 40 students, were used to further develop and refine the questionnaire (Pekala, 1980). There were 179 females and 70 males. At the beginning of the study the subjects were told about the general nature of the experiment and the fact that they would be involved in introspection. They were then asked to sit quietly with their eyes closed for one minute. They completed a short ten-item practice questionnaire in reference to the eyes-closed period to give them some initial practice in introspection.

The subjects were then instructed to sit quietly with their eyes open without reading, writing, or talking (eyes-open condition). They were told that after several minutes of doing this they would be asked to report on their experience just like they had done after the one-minute practice session. The experimenter left the room and returned four minutes later. Each subject completed the PCQ in reference to the previous time period. (Although there were other assessment conditions that subjects experienced, these other conditions will be presented later, after the analysis of the results concerning the eyes open condition are presented.)

Pearson *r* Correlations for the Duplicate Item-Pairs

Pearson *r* correlations were computed for the subjects' responses to the five pairs of duplicate items of the PCQ. Correlations ranged from

.47 for the item-pair dealing with state of awareness to .83 for the internal dialogue item-pair, and averaged .67 across all five pairs. [These item-pairs became the reliability index (RI) item-pairs for the Phenomenology of Consciousness Inventory.]

Confirmatory Cluster Analysis

Since the number and composition of clusters was specified in advance, an oblique multiple groups cluster analysis (Hunter & Gerbing, 1979) was used on the subjects' responses to the 60-item PCQ. With communalities in the diagonals of the correlation matrix, Hunter's PACKAGE program (Hunter & Cohen, 1971) was used. This initial analysis resulted in 10 of the 15 clusters having coefficient alphas of .60 or greater.

After this initial analysis, confirmatory cluster analysis (Hunter, 1977) was used, purifying the clusters of items that were heterogenous, so as to arrive at clusters composed of homogeneous items. This was done by checking for the extent to which items of a given cluster had the same meaning, by checking the degree to which the cluster loadings of the items within each cluster had the same general pattern, and by noting the extent to which items within each cluster paralleled, in terms of cluster loadings, the items outside that particular cluster.

Items failing to meet the above criteria were removed and the remaining items of the clusters were then reclustered with another multiple groups cluster analysis, checking to make sure that coefficient alpha increased for each of the reclustered clusters. Those clusters correlating highly were also combined to see if the resulting supracluster was internally consistent, that is, had an equal or higher coefficient alpha. This procedure resulted in several clusters being subclusters of more general and inclusive clusters. This was true of all the resulting supraclusters except one. The attention cluster had a coefficient alpha (.72) less than one of its subclusters, direction of attention (.76). Since this seemed due to the much lower alpha for the absorption subcluster (.58), both subclusters were still combined, especially since the correlation between subclusters was high ($r = .63$).

This process of confirmatory cluster analysis yielded ten major clusters or dimensions of consciousness that were composed of only 39 of the original 60 items of the PCQ. Of these ten clusters, four clusters were composed of two or more subclusters. (Coefficient alpha averaged .73 across all ten clusters.) These dimensions (and associated subdimensions) included: internal dialogue, awareness (self-awareness, state of awareness), visual imagery (amount, vividness), positive affect, volitional control, altered experience (meaning, perception, time sense, body image), attention (direction, absorption), negative affect, memory, and alertness. Of the 15 dimensions found in the third pilot study, only rationality failed to find empirical support as a cluster or subcluster of phenomenological experience.

Exploratory Factor Analysis

As a check on the above dimensions, an exploratory factor analysis was done on all 60 items of the PCQ. Although this type of analysis tends to blur the distinctions between clusters arrived at by the multiple groups cluster analytic approach, it "will usually find those dimensions which are completely outside the investigator's frame of reference" (Hunter & Gerbing, 1979, p. 35).

The analysis consisted of a principal components factor analysis that was followed by Varimax rotation. Orthogonal factors were extracted for factors with eigenvalues of greater than one. Nine factors were generated, accounting for 43% of the variance. As can be seen from Table 5.1, except for the collapsing of attention and memory, the clusters arrived at by this blind empirical analysis were exactly the same as the clusters arrived at by confirmatory cluster analysis.

Another exploratory factor analysis was also performed, but with only the 37 items of the final confirmatory cluster analysis. (The consistently lower coefficient alpha for the alertness dimension in both the cluster and factor analyses made its inclusion as a reliable major dimension of consciousness questionable. For this reason, it was not included in subsequent analyses.) Seven factors were generated that accounted for 46% of the variance. Almost invariably, the factors were composed of items that were grouped together according to the clusters or subclusters arrived at by confirmatory cluster analysis.

FORMAT FOR THE PCQ STUDY

Besides giving the PCQ in reference to the eyes-open (EO1) sitting quietly condition just reported, the PCQ was also given to the 249 subjects in reference to three other stimulus conditions: a second eyes-open sitting quietly condition (EO2), a reading erotica (RE) condition, and a relaxation/meditation (RM) condition. The RE condition consisted of a short passage of about 1000 words that took approximately four minutes to read. It consisted of a slightly modified excerpt from a short story entitled "The Veiled Woman," taken from *Delta of Venus* by A. Nin (1978) (Pekala, 1980).

Table 5.1. Exploratory Factor Analysis for the Eyes-Open Condition across All Items[a]

Item number	Content	Factor loading	Cluster loading
	Factor		
Altered experience (alpha = .80; variance = 7%)			
30	Religious, spiritual experience	.55	.51
55	Change in body perspective	.52	.48
67	Dizzy and disoriented	.51	.56
70	Strange and dreamlike state	.50	.67
68	Sacredness or deep meaning	.49	.53
56	Ineffability	.47	.47
66	Objects in the world change	.44	.43
39	Profound and enlightening ideas	.44	.43
61	Change in the perception of time	.43	.50
48	Change in the perception of space	.39	.48
15	Body expanded into the world	.39	.42
21	Extraordinary sensory changes	.37	.44
29	Separation between self and environment	.35	.38
73	Transcendence of opposites	.35	.38
33	Fantastic thoughts and images	.29	.29
74	Questionnaire easy to complete	.24	.25
Awareness (alpha = .80; variance = 7%)			
60	Self-awareness	.73	.71
49	Conscious and aware of self	.72	.77
52	Certain of unusual state of consciousness	.67	.76
57	Unusual state of consciousness	.60	.71
54	Aware of body sensations	.54	.54
17	Nonordinary state of awareness	.47	.48
40	Aware of ego and personality	.36	.34
53	Change in the passage of time	.34	.31
Imagery (alpha = .80; variance = 7%)			
23	Amount of imagery	.73	.77
63	Amount of imagery	.72	.81
46	Vividness of imagery	.70	.75
36	Distinctness of imagery	.67	.70
45	Imagery versus thought	.55	.56
34	Mind and extent of thoughts	−.42	.38
25	Attention to field of consciousness	.24	.25
Attention/memory (alpha = .76; variance = 5%)			
44	Focus of attention	.70	.65
43	Thoughts: logical or illogical	−.68	.58

(continued)

Table 5.1. (*Continued*)

Item number	Content	Factor loading	Cluster loading
	Factor		
51	Distraction/absorption	.50	.55
58	Involved/detached in experience	.46	.57
65	Attention's direction	.46	.42
27	Remembering experience	−.44	.52
19	Control over attention	−.36	.36
41	Memory	−.36	.47
26	Understanding experience	−.34	.46
Negative affect (alpha = .70; variance = 4%)			
38	Feelings of irritation	.69	.77
31	Anger	.62	.60
71	Pleasure/unpleasure	.58	.62
69	Shame and guilt	.54	.48
59	Peacefulness/excitement	.44	.38
Alertness (arousal) (alpha = .57; variance = 3%)			
32	Awareness intensity	.55	.73
37	Perceptual sensitivity/intensity	.53	.43
18	Direction of attention	.49	.44
29	Alertness/drowsiness	.43	.42
Positive affect (alpha = .75; variance = 4%)			
22	Sexual feelings	.82	.79
72	Sexual feelings	.81	.77
47	Feelings of love	.56	.68
62	Feelings of joy and bliss	.34	.46
35	Suggestibility	.34	.37
Volitional control (alpha = .56; variance = 3%)			
42	Control	.56	.73
28	Actively involved/letting go	.50	.61
50	Control of thoughts and images	.47	.66
16	Sense of time	−.41	.06
Internal dialogue (alpha = .91; variance = 4%)			
24	Silently talking to oneself	.89	.92
64	Silently talking to oneself	.89	.92

[a]From Pekala & Levine (1981). Reprinted with permission of the publisher. Copyright 1981, Baywood Publishing Co., Inc.

The RM condition consisted of standard progressive relaxation instructions to which a four-minute meditational interlude was added. The condition began with the experimenter explaining the technique of progressive relaxation and demonstrating how the different muscle groups of the body were involved in achieving relaxation. He then read the progressive relaxation instructions while the students tensed and then relaxed the different muscle groups of their body with their eyes closed. After this the experimenter paused for four minutes while the participants relaxed to their breathing.

Whereas the EO1 and RE conditions were experienced during one experimental session, the EO2 and RM conditions were experienced during a second experimental session held two weeks later at the same time and place.

RELIABILITY

It was predicted that phenomenological experience would be reliably assessed by the PCQ during the three stimulus conditions of EO2, RE, and RM using the dimensions of the PCQ found in the final cluster analysis of the PCQ during the first eyes-open condition (EO1). It was also predicted that the dimensions would be stable structures of subjective experience.

Item-Pair Reliability

To determine how consistent the subjects were at reporting their experience, Pearson r correlations were computed for the subjects' responses to the five pairs of duplicate items of the PCQ for all conditions. The average correlation across all five item-pairs for the two baseline conditions (EO1 and EO2) was .70, and across all conditions, .65. Only one of the five item-pairs had statements whose content was identical (internal dialogue), and here the correlations averaged .83 for the two baseline conditions and .76 across all four conditions.

In order to determine how accurate the subjects' responses were in reference to these five item-pairs, a difference score was computed for each subject for each condition. It represented the absolute difference between the intensity ratings of the items for each item pair. In interpreting this difference score, a zero score represents an exact correspondence between the subject's responses to the two items of each item-pair, while a difference score of six represents completely opposite responses to the two items of the pair (when using a seven-point Likert scale). (Random responding by the subjects would yield an average difference score of three.)

Fifty-two percent of all responses to these duplicate item-pairs across all four conditions were direct hits (a difference score of zero), and 81 percent of all responses were within a one-unit difference score. The average difference score across all five item-pairs for all subjects was .84.

Coefficient Alpha Results

Coefficient alphas for 11 dimensions and subdimensions were computed. Across all nine major dimensions of consciousness, coefficient alphas averaged .79 for the second baseline condition, .72 for the erotica condition, and .70 for the relaxation/meditation condition. (The first baseline condition had an average alpha of .76.) Averaged across all four conditions, alphas for the PCI dimensions ranged from a high of .86 for internal dialogue to a low of .56 for negative affect, and averaged .74 for

Table 5.2. Dimensions of Consciousness and Corresponding Alphas for Each of the Four Stimulus Conditions

	Condition[a]				
Dimension	First baseline	Second baseline	Erotica	Relaxation/ meditation	Average
Imagery	.84	.85	.86	.79	.84
Imagery amount	.78	.83	.80	.76	.79
Imagery vividness	.77	.84	.76	.73	.78
Attention	.72	.80	.64	.57	.68
Direction	.76	.81	.68	.56	.70
Absorption	.58	.69	.36	.43	.52
Positive affect	.77	.81	.80	.74	.78
Altered experience	.73	.80	.76	.72	.78
Altered meaning	.63	.68	.66	.73	.68
Altered perception	.54	.45	.37	.54	.48
Altered time	.53	.73	.61	.61	.62
Altered body image	.49	.66	.45	.64	.56
Awareness	.86	.86	.81	.75	.82
Self-awareness	.81	.81	.68	.56	.76
State of awareness	.79	.83	.80	.77	.80
Negative affect	.65	.62	.50	.46	.56
Memory	.61	.57	.64	.75	.64
Internal dialogue	.91	.90	.81	.80	.86
Volitional control	.74	.86	.67	.72	.75
Average (major dimensions)	.76	.79	.72	.70	.74

[a] n for all conditions equals 249.

the nine major dimensions. Concerning the subdimensions of consciousness, coefficient alphas for all the subdimensions averaged .67 across all four conditions. Table 5.2 lists these coefficients for each of the four stimulus conditions.

Cluster and Factor Analyses

In addition to the coefficient alpha results, in order to assess the stability of the various dimensions, the 37 items of the PCQ found in the first baseline condition that were of acceptable reliability were submitted to cluster and factor analyses for the other three stimulus conditions. An oblique multiple groups cluster analysis with communalities in the diagonals of the correlation matrix was performed on the subjects' responses to the PCQ for the second baseline and the two treatment conditions. The cluster loadings for each of the dimensions indicated the relative stability and consistency of these dimensions. More than 90% of the items making up the nine dimensions continued to load highest on their assigned dimension across all conditions.

A principal components factor analysis, followed by Varimax rotation, was also done for each of the four conditions using the items of the nine dimensions. The analysis found several of the dimensions, arrived at by cluster analysis, to be combined and several of the subdimensions making up a particular cluster analytic dimension to be split, especially for the treatment conditions. Nevertheless, most of the items composing the factors of these exploratory factor analyses clustered together in terms of the subdimensions and dimensions arrived at by cluster analysis (Pekala, 1980).

Seven factors, accounting for 50% of the variance, were found for the second baseline condition (seven factors accounted for 46% of the variance for the first baseline condition). Five factor accounted for 39% of the variance for the erotica condition, and six factors accounted for 40% of the variance for the relaxation/meditation condition.

TEST-RETEST RELIABILITY

Subjects enacted the same behavior, that is, sitting quietly with their eyes open, in the same stimulus condition on two different occasions. To determine the extent to which their subjective experiences were similar, dimensions intensity scores were computed for each subject for each (sub)dimension in each condition. This was done by averaging the subject's responses to the items that made up a particular (sub)dimension, as per the recommendations of Hunter and Gerbing (1979).

By comparing each subject's intensity score for each (sub)dimension across the two baseline conditions using the Pearson r correlation coefficient, one has a measure of the test-retest reliability for each dimension. Correlations ranged from .56 for altered experience to .34 for memory and negative affect and averaged .43. Pearson r's for all subdimensions averaged .40. See Table 5.3 (which also includes the Pearson r's when comparing the first baseline and the erotica conditions and the second baseline and the relaxation/meditation conditions).

VALIDITY: INTENSITY EFFECTS

It was predicted that the same stimulus conditions (the baseline conditions of eyes-closed sitting quietly experienced twice) would be

Table 5.3. Test–Retest Reliabilities for the Dimensions of Consciousness

| Dimension | Comparison[a] | | |
	First and second baselines	First baseline and erotica conditions	Second baseline and relaxation/ meditation conditions
Imagery	.41	.21	.02*
Imagery amount	.38	.21	.04*
Imagery vividness	.40	.23	.08*
Attention	.39	−.05*	.03*
Direction	.28	−.01*	.04*
Absorption	.39	.02*	.02*
Positive affect	.43	.27	.31
Altered experience	.56	.41	.38
Altered meaning	.58	.40	.41
Altered perception	.29	.30	.16
Altered time	.38	.24	.23
Altered body image	.44	.24	.23
Awareness	.44	.40	.19
Self-awareness	.43	.34	.13
State of awareness	.43	.35	.15
Negative affect	.34	.38	.32
Memory	.34	.18	.06*
Internal dialogue	.50	.26	.17
Volitional control	.44	.18	.17
Average (major dimensions)	.43	.26	.18

[a] All correlations are significant at the $p < .05$ level except from those marked with an asterisk (*).

associated with the same (nonsignificantly different) intensities and patterns of phenomenological experience, while different stimulus conditions would be associated with significantly different intensities and patterns of phenomenological experience. Specifically, it was predicted that the erotica condition would be associated with significantly greater absorbed attention, volitional control, positive affect, imagery amount and vividness, but decreased internal dialogue in comparison to the corresponding baseline condition (these predictions were based on the fourth pilot study reported earlier). On the other hand, the relaxation/meditation condition would be associated with significantly greater altered awareness and altered experiences, inward and absorbed attention, and imagery vividness, but lesser self-awareness, volitional control, positive affect, negative affect, imagery amount, and internal dialogue than the baseline condition (predictions were based on the third and fourth pilot studies).

Dimension Intensity Differences between the Baseline Conditions

To test for overall intensity differences for the dimensions of consciousness between the two baseline conditions, multivariate analyses were enacted with the nine major PCI dimensions as the dependent variable and Conditions (baseline 1 versus baseline 2) as the repeated-measures factor. Unexpectedly, significant differences were found [F (9,240) = 12.75, $p < .001$]. However, omega-square, the index reflecting the "amount of variability accounted for by the experimental treatment" (Keppel, 1973, p. 549), was only 2%, indicating small, but nevertheless significant, differences between the two baseline conditions.

Paired t-tests were then computed between the two baseline conditions for the nine dimensions of consciousness and their subdimensions. As Table 5.4 shows, the first baseline condition was associated with significantly greater alterations in subjective experience for the (sub)dimensions of awareness, imagery, positive affect, and altered experience.

Dimension Intensity Differences between Treatment and Baseline Conditions

Multivariate analyses found significant differences in intensities of subjective experience between the erotica and baseline (EO1) conditions [F (9,240) = 45.66, $p < .001$]. Paired t-tests were computed for the dimensions and subdimensions. As hypothesized, the erotica condition was associated with greater, and more vivid, imagery, more absorbed attention, more positive affect, and less internal dialogue than the baseline

Table 5.4. Dimension Intensity Comparisons between the Two Baseline Conditions[a]

	Condition				
	First baseline		Second baseline		
Dimension	Mean[b]	S.D.	Mean	S.D.	t value[c]
Imagery	3.47	1.57	3.08	1.70	3.51**
Imagery amount	3.30	1.75	2.98	1.90	2.49*
Imagery vividness	3.65	1.71	3.18	1.90	3.75***
Attention	3.74	1.28	3.65	1.08	0.88
Direction	3.63	1.61	3.60	1.67	0.34
Absorption	3.85	1.42	3.75	1.46	1.21
Positive affect	2.60	1.56	1.81	1.50	7.63***
Altered experience	1.91	1.00	1.47	0.44	7.13***
Altered meaning	1.46	1.32	1.22	1.33	3.17**
Altered perception	1.43	1.44	0.90	1.16	5.38***
Altered time sense	2.50	1.58	1.90	1.66	5.22***
Altered body image	2.45	1.41	1.98	1.37	4.72***
Awareness	2.20	1.29	1.60	1.33	4.89***
Self-awareness	1.97	1.55	1.71	1.52	2.51*
State of awareness	2.07	1.45	1.52	1.44	5.52***
Negative affect	0.99	1.24	0.89	1.17	1.22
Memory	4.67	1.15	4.65	1.05	0.25
Internal dialogue	3.87	1.95	3.62	2.12	1.94
Volitional control	3.71	1.39	3.75	1.60	−0.42

[a]From Pekala & Levine (1982). Reprinted with permission of the publisher. Copyright 1982, Baywood Publishing Co., Inc.
[b]Higher values denote increased amounts ranging from none or little (rating = 0) to much or complete (rating = 6).
[c]$df = 248$; * = $p < .05$; ** = $p < .01$; *** = $p < .001$.

condition. It was associated with less, instead of more, volitional control, however. Table 5.5 tabulates these comparisons.

Concerning the comparisons between the relaxation/meditation and the second baseline (EO2) conditions, multivariate analysis found a significant difference between conditions [F (9,240) = 137.1, $p < .001$]. Paired t-tests were computed comparing conditions for the (sub)dimensions of consciousness. As hypothesized, all comparisons between conditions were in the expected direction except for imagery vividness. Significant differences between conditions were also found for the other (sub)dimensions of consciousness besides those hypothesized, as Table 5.6 indicates.

Table 5.5. Dimension Intensity Comparisons between the First Baseline
and the Erotica Conditions[a]

| | Condition | | | | |
| | First baseline | | Erotica | | |
Dimension	Mean[b]	S.D.	Mean	S.D.	t value[c]
Imagery	3.47	1.57	4.59	1.27	−9.71**
Imagery amount	3.30	1.75	4.64	1.48	−10.41**
Imagery vividness	3.65	1.71	4.53	1.27	−7.36**
Attention	3.74	1.28	4.43	1.02	−6.54**
Direction	3.63	1.61	4.37	1.26	−5.69**
Absorption	3.85	1.42	4.49	1.17	−5.62**
Positive affect	2.60	1.56	3.27	1.49	−5.82**
Altered experience	1.91	1.00	1.96	1.20	−0.78
Altered meaning	1.46	1.32	1.52	1.29	−0.68
Altered perception	1.43	1.44	1.57	1.28	−1.36
Altered time sense	2.50	1.58	2.35	1.66	1.15
Altered body image	2.45	1.41	2.61	1.37	−1.48
Awareness	2.20	1.29	2.18	1.38	−1.68
Self-awareness	1.97	1.55	2.24	1.63	−2.32*
State of awareness	2.07	1.45	2.14	1.53	−0.76
Negative affect	0.99	1.24	0.92	1.08	0.85
Memory	4.67	1.15	4.67	1.07	−0.04
Internal dialogue	3.87	1.95	1.37	1.61	18.11**
Volitional control	3.71	1.39	3.24	1.35	4.29**

[a] From Pekala & Levine (1982). Reprinted with permission of the publisher. Copyright 1982, Baywood
Publishing Co., Inc.
[b] Higher values denote increased amounts ranging from none or little (rating = 0) to much or complete
(rating = 6).
[c] $df = 248$; * = $p < .05$; ** = $p < .001$.

Dimension Intensity Differences between Treatment Conditions

In order to determine if the two treatment conditions may have
been significantly different from baseline yet similar to each other, multivariate analyses and paired t-tests were computed, testing for significant
differences between conditions. Not only were the relaxation/medita-
tion and erotica conditions significantly different across all dimensions
[$F (9,240) = 174.6$, $p < .001$], but all individual comparisons were
significant.

Table 5.6. Dimension Intensity Comparisons between the Second Baseline and the Relaxation/Meditation Conditions[a]

	Condition				
	Second baseline		Relaxation/ meditation		
Dimension	Mean[b]	S.D.	Mean	S.D.	t value[c]
Imagery	3.08	1.70	2.03	1.49	7.41*
Imagery amount	2.98	1.90	2.28	1.83	4.23*
Imagery vividness	3.18	1.91	1.77	1.56	9.39*
Attention	3.65	1.38	5.40	0.86	−13.66*
Direction	3.58	1.67	5.12	1.07	−12.45*
Absorption	3.75	1.46	4.97	1.08	−10.83*
Positive affect	1.81	1.50	1.47	1.24	3.27*
Altered experience	1.47	1.07	3.10	1.08	−21.46*
Altered meaning	1.22	1.33	2.21	1.63	−9.69*
Altered perception	0.90	1.16	2.39	1.64	−12.67*
Altered time sense	1.90	1.66	4.07	1.59	−17.01*
Altered body image	1.98	1.37	4.16	1.58	−17.68*
Awareness	1.60	1.33	4.56	1.10	−30.15*
Self-awareness	1.71	1.52	4.09	1.65	−17.94*
State of awareness	1.52	1.44	4.88	1.11	−31.49*
Negative affect	0.89	1.17	0.41	0.75	6.34*
Memory	4.65	1.06	2.84	1.73	14.47*
Internal dialogue	3.62	2.11	1.70	1.65	12.38*
Volitional control	3.75	1.61	1.65	1.27	17.94*

[a] From Pekala & Levine (1982). Reprinted with permission of the publisher. Copyright 1982, Baywood Publishing Co., Inc.
[b] Higher values denote increased amounts ranging from none or little (rating = 0) to much or complete (rating = 6).
[c] $df = 248$; * = $p < .001$.

VALIDITY: PATTERN EFFECTS

Pattern Differences between the Baseline Conditions

It was predicted that the baseline conditions would be associated with the same patterns of subjective experience. Correlation matrices were constructed between the nine dimensions of consciousness for each of the two baseline conditions. A matrix expressing the differences between these two matrices were also computed. Of the 36 correlation differences, only four were significant at the .05 level. Thus, there appear to have been only minimal differences between the patterns of dimensions in the two baseline conditions.

To more precisely test for differences between the patterns of dimensions for the two conditions, the Jennrich (1970) test was used. The Jennrich test is a multivariate test that statistically assesses for significant differences in two independent correlation matrices. (When it is used with correlated groups, as it is here, it is a more conservative test of significant differences than with independent correlation matrices.) By using the Jennrich test, it is possible to determine whether two correlation matrices, and hence the patterns associated with the corresponding stimulus conditions, are significantly different from one another. The nine major PCI dimensions were used to construct correlation matrices for the four stimulus conditions. (Degrees of freedom, df, for all comparisons using nine dimensions was 36.) When comparing the two baseline conditions, the Jennrich test yielded a chi-square value of 31.59, which was not significant ($p > .05$).

Pattern Differences between the Treatment and Baseline Conditions

It was predicted that the treatment conditions would be associated with patterns of phenomenological experience significantly different from that of baseline. The correlation matrices representing the patterns among the nine dimensions of consciousness for the erotica and relaxation/meditation conditions were constructed. The differences matrix between the correlations of the erotica and the first baseline conditions yielded 14 out of 36 differences that were significant at the .05 level. The difference matrix between the correlations of the second baseline and the relaxation/meditation conditions had 21 out of 36 differences that were significant.

To more precisely test for pattern differences, the Jennrich test was utilized. The Jennrich test comparison between the first baseline and erotica conditions was significant [chi-square (36) = 106.64, $p < .001$], as was the comparison between the second baseline and the erotica conditions [chi-square (36) = 97.54, $p < .001$]. The comparison between the second baseline and the relaxation/meditation conditions was significant [chi-square (36) = 130.24, $p < .001$], as was the comparison between the first baseline and the relaxation-meditation conditions [chi-square (36) = 127.18, $p < .001$]. Concerning the correlation matrices of the erotica and relaxation/meditation conditions, the Jennrich test indicated that they too were significantly different from one another [chi-square (36) = 178.56, $p < .001$].

RELIABILITY, REACTIVITY, STABILITY, AND VALIDITY

Reliability

In spite of the difficulties involved in assessing internal experience (Kendall & Korgeski, 1979), any methodology attempting to map phenomenological experience should be adequately reliable. The coefficients obtained from the five duplicate item-pairs demonstrated that subjects can be reasonably consistent at reporting the nature of their subjective experience. The other measure of reliability used, the difference score, indicated that the subjects were moderately accurate at responding to items of similar or identical content in the same general way, even in differing types of conditions. An average coefficient alpha of .74 for the nine dimensions of consciousness supports the above.

These results strongly suggest that subjects can be consistent at rating the items of the PCQ in reference to their subjective experience, provided it follows upon the period to be assessed and that period is of relatively short duration.

Reactive Effects of Introspection

Subjects were sensitized to the fact that they would be involved in introspection into their stream of consciousness. Such self-observation may have altered the nature of their subjective experience more than if they had not been sensitized to it. The dimension intensity results for the first baseline condition did indicate mild alterations in awareness, imagery, affect, and altered experience. These results agree with the findings of Hunt and Chefurka (1976) who found that merely having subjects sit quietly for ten minutes while they observed their subjective experience led to greater anomalous subjective experiences to the extent that they were "sensitized" to that experience.

Although Hunt and Chefurka did not take their subjects through a second session to see if their results would replicate, the present study did. The second baseline condition found significantly less alterations in subjective experience than the first condition. This suggests that besides sensitization to subjective experience, the novelty of doing introspection in the first baseline condition may have led to alterations in consciousness that were reduced when that condition was repeated.

Test-Retest Reliability

A practice effect associated with the repetition of the same baseline condition may be partly responsible for the relatively low test-retest reliabilities found. But it should also be taken into account that "states" and not "traits" were being assessed. Since one's state of consciousness at a particular moment in time is much more liable to disruption or change than a trait, an average correlation of .43 for all nine dimensions may not be especially low.

These relatively low reliabilities are suggestive, however. They indicate that the intensities of phenomenological experience can vary to a moderate degree for individual subjects in this repeated stimulus condition. Yet if the intensities are averaged across a group of subjects, the subjective experiences associated with the baseline condition tends to be the same, or only mildly different, when it is repeated.

Stability of the Dimensions of Consciousness

Despite the rather large intensity variations for the dimensions in several different stimulus conditions, the nine major dimensions of consciousness continued to remain internally consistent or stable. This was shown by relatively stable coefficient alphas and cluster loadings across the various conditions for the cluster analyses. The results of the factor analyses also support this conclusion, since the factors obtained were composed of the various (sub)dimensions found through cluster analysis.

Tart (1975, 1977) has suggested that consciousness is composed of certain structures or subsystems that retain their basic function in spite of variations in the intensity and/or the quality of their activity. The stability of these dimensions in several differing conditions is supportive of Tart's theorizing on the stability of the structures or dimensions of consciousness.

Validity

Based on the instructional sets of the baseline and treatment conditions, predictions were made as to how the treatment conditions would differ from the baseline conditions for specific dimensions of consciousness. Almost all of the predictions were in the expected directions. These results indicate that the PCQ appeared to be validly assessing various aspects of phenomenological experience and are supportive of the construct and discriminant validity of the inventory.

STATES OF CONSCIOUSNESS

The unexpected intensity changes between the two baseline conditions were generally small, as shown by an average omega-square of

2%. The two baseline conditions were also much more similar to each other, in terms of intensities of phenomenological experience, than they were to the treatment conditions. This suggests that the intensities of phenomenological experience for the two baseline conditions were similar, although not identical, to each other.

In contrast, the patterns between the dimensions of these two stimulus conditions, as measured by the Jennrich test, remained the same (nonsignificantly different). This suggests that the patterns between the dimensions of consciousness may not necessarily change as the intensities of the dimensions do. This appears to offer tentative support for Tart's (1975) theorizing that it is primarily the patterns between subsystems, and not the intensities of the subsystems, that determine a particular state of consciousness.

An Altered State of Consciousness

Besides the predicted changes in intensity between the baseline and treatment conditions, there were also significant differences in the pattern of the dimensions between the baseline and erotica and the baseline and the relaxation/meditation conditions. Thus, the states of consciousness associated with the erotica and relaxation/meditation conditions were different in both pattern and intensity from those of baseline.

That dimension or subdimension that most significantly differentiated between the treatment and the baseline conditions, that is, evinced the greatest proportion of variance attributable to differences between conditions, was the state of awareness subdimension in the baseline-relaxation/meditation comparison. No significant differences were found between the first baseline and erotica conditions for this subdimension. The two baseline conditions, however, did have significant differences in intensity for this subdimension.

These results suggest that the relaxation/meditation condition, but not the erotica or baseline condition, can be characterized as being associated with an altered state of consciousness if the criteria hypothesized by Tart (1975) to differentiate altered states of consciousness from other states are used. These criteria include: (1) changes in pattern among the dimensions of consciousness and (2) the *subjective sense* of (being in) an *altered state*, herein abbreviated SSAS, radically different from one's ordinary or normal state of awareness.

The relaxation/meditation condition was associated with not only a significant pattern change, but a significant perceived alteration of consciousness as assessed by the state of awareness subdimension. On the other hand, the first baseline condition, in comparison to the second, was associated with a mild SSAS but no pattern difference.

An Identity State of Consciousness

While the relaxation/meditation condition was associated with experience that can be labeled an altered state of consciousness, the subjective experience of the erotica condition can be labeled an identity state of consciousness. An identity state is Tart's (1975) term for a specialized version of a nonaltered state of consciousness that has an overall pattern of functioning that distinguishes it from other identity states. It is composed of psychological structures that possess unique properties not present in other identity states, but it is not perceived as a radically different state of consciousness. Since the structure or pattern of phenomenological experience during the erotica condition was much different from the baseline state, but there was not a significant difference in SSAS, the experience associated with the erotica condition can be labeled an identity state of consciousness.

CONCLUSIONS

Although the validity of retrospective phenomenological assessment will ultimately reside "in the usefulness of the data or theory for making possible other forms of prediction and perhaps control" (Klinger, 1978, p. 227), the results suggest that this methodology can be a reliable and valid means for mapping various types of subjective experience. The next chapter will present reliability and validity data on a revision of the PCQ.

6

Development, Reliability, and Validity of the (Abbreviated) Dimensions of Consciousness Questionnaire

DEVELOPMENT OF THE DIMENSIONS OF CONSCIOUSNESS QUESTIONNAIRE

The Dimensions of Consciousness Questionnaire (DCQ) was developed by revising the 37-item Phenomenology of Consciousness Questionnaire (PCQ). For any dimensions or subdimensions of the PCQ containing less than four items, additional items, similar in content, were written so that each (sub)dimension consisted of four items. The dimensions of positive and negative affect were expanded from four and three items, respectively, to eight items each; this was done to include subclasses of affect associated with each dimension. Thus, positive affect had two items each dealing with joy, sexual excitement, love, and peace/calmness, while negative affect had two items each assessing anxiety, guilt, depression, and anger.

Two dimensions of consciousness that were assessed in previous research that did not reach criterion level reliability, that is, rationality and alertness, were again included with additional items written so that each of these dimensions was composed of four items. An additional dimension of four items dealing with arousal/relaxation was also included.

The revision of the PCQ became an inventory of 80 items composed of the same dimensions and subdimensions as the 37-item PCQ plus the dimensions of alertness, rationality, and arousal. Items for the DCQ were arranged in a randomized block design, so that no two items of similar content would be adjacent. The dipoles of each item were also oppositely arranged. Thus, the items of a particular dimension or subdimension had half of those items with the left dipole addressed to more normal subjective experience, while the other half of the items had the left dipole addressed to more altered subjective experience.

DEVELOPMENT OF THE ABBREVIATED DIMENSIONS OF CONSCIOUSNESS QUESTIONNAIRE

Besides the larger inventory of 80 items, a shorter questionnaire of 40 items was constructed. The abbreviated questionnaire had two items from each of the dimensions or subdimensions of consciousness, except for four items from the dimensions of volitional control and memory. (In the event certain major dimensions would cluster together, all resulting dimensions would be composed of four items, except for memory and control. Hence all four items from these dimensions were used. Only those two items correlating highest with each other for memory and control, however, were used to compute dimension intensity scores for these dimensions.)

Pairs of items composing a particular dimension or subdimension for the shortened questionnaire were chosen as follows: if the (sub)dimension of the 37-item PCQ consisted of only two items, those were the items used. If the (sub)dimension was composed of three or more items, those two items having the highest correlation with one another were chosen. For those items just written on which there were no statistical data available, items most similar in content were chosen. Rather than including all the items for the four pairs of positive and negative affect items, only those dealing with sex and anger were used.

Items for the Abbreviated Dimensions of Consciousness Questionnaire, or ADCQ, were also arranged in a randomized block design. Two forms of the ADCQ were constructed of exactly the same items, arranged into two different sequences. As with the PCQ, both the DCQ and the ADCQ had five pairs of duplicate items of similar or identical content interspersed throughout the questionnaire; this permitted assessment of intratest consistency for individual participants.

PROCEDURE AND HYPOTHESES

Approximately 300 subjects were used in the study with the (A)DCQ (Pekala & Wenger, 1983). They were seen in six groups averaging approximately 50 people per group. At the beginning of the study the general nature of the experiment was explained. After completing consent forms, the experimenter presented an instruction sheet that explained to the participants the nature of their task and also defined the major concepts of the questionnaire. Subjects were advised that since introspection into one's subjective experience is something that may be difficult, they were not to hurry, but were to take their time and thoughtfully complete the questionnaire when asked to do so.

After completing a one-minute practice session and a ten-item practice questionnaire (just like the DCQ) to give the subjects some practice at introspection, participants were told:

> For the next few minutes I'd like you to sit quietly and think about whatever you like. I'd like you not to read, write, talk, or close your eyes, however. I'll be sitting outside the room during this time and after several minutes, I'll be back in and ask you to write about your experience. Any questions?

After these instructions were repeated the experimenter left the room. She returned four minutes later and had the participants complete the DCQ in reference to the four-minute period of sitting quietly.

The experimenter then told the participants that they would be asked to experience several other conditions and would be required to write about them as they did before. Although all individuals first experienced the sitting quietly with eyes-open (EO) condition just described, each of the six groups of participants received a different sequence of second and third conditions, both of which were followed by completion of the ADCQ in reference to that condition. The six groups of participants and the sequence of conditions they experienced are listed in Table 6.1.

The instructions for the second and third EO conditions were the same as the instructions for the initial EO condition. The instructions for the sitting quietly eyes-closed (EC) condition were the same as for the EO condition, except the participants were told to close their eyes. As with the EO condition, instructions for all the other conditions were repeated once.

For the erotic fantasy (EF) condition, individuals were told to close their eyes and reexperience the most erotic sexual experience that they could remember. The experimenter left the room, returned four minutes later, and asked the research participants to complete the ADCQ in

Table 6.1. Sequence of Conditions Experienced by the Six Groups of Participants[a]

Group number	Number of subjects	Condition[b] 1	Condition[b] 2	Condition[b] 3
1	67	Eyes open	Eyes closed	Eyes open
2	55	Eyes open	Eyes open	Eyes closed
3	60	Eyes open	Eyes closed	Relaxation/ meditation
4	36	Eyes open	Eyes closed	Eyes closed
5	45	Eyes open	Eyes closed	Erotic fantasy
6	41	Eyes open	Eyes closed	Eyes closed
Questionnaire used		DCQ	(A)DCQ Form 1	(A)DCQ Form 0

[a] From Pekala & Wenger (1983). Reprinted with permission of the publisher.
[b] Conditions 1–3 are combined with sitting quietly.

reference to the time period specific to the fantasy. (Whereas the DCQ was completed in reference to the first condition, the ADCQ was completed in reference to the second and third conditions.) The relaxation/meditation (RM) condition was the same as the relaxation/meditation condition reported earlier with the PCQ.

Based on the aforementioned material, the following hypotheses were entertained:

1. The DCQ will be found to be more reliable than the 37-item PCQ.
2. The ADCQ will be found to be as reliable as the 37-item PCQ.
3. The ADCQ will be able to validly assess and discriminate variations in phenomenological experience across similar and dissimilar conditions. More specifically, the following were predicted:
   a. In comparing eyes open (EO) sitting quietly (baseline) and relaxation/meditation (RM) across the same group of participants, the same differences in dimension intensity and pattern results will be found as were found when these conditions were compared with the PCQ.
   b. In comparing an erotic fantasy (EF) with baseline (EO) across the same group of participants, similar differences in dimension intensity and pattern results will be found as was demonstrated when baseline was compared with reading erotica with the PCQ.
4. Across several different groups of participants, the same stimulus conditions will be associated with the same (nonsignificantly

different) intensities and patterns of phenomenological experience, while different stimulus conditions will be associated with intensities and/or patterns of phenomenological experience significantly different from one another (the principle of *stimulus-state specificity*).

RELIABILITY OF THE DIMENSIONS
OF CONSCIOUSNESS QUESTIONNAIRE

It was predicted that the DCQ would be more reliable then the 37-item PCQ. This prediction was assessed (1) in terms of the five pairs of reliability items of similar or identical content embedded in the DCQ, and also (2) in terms of coefficient alphas for each of the (sub)dimensions of consciousness.

Item-Pair Reliability

To determine the participant's intratest consistency, Pearson r correlations and difference scores were computed for each participant's responses to the five pairs of reliability items. Pearson r correlations for these five reliability pairs averaged .69 across all individuals during the EO condition and ranged from .46 for state of awareness to .85 for internal dialogue. Difference score values, representing the absolute difference between the two intensity ratings for the items of each item-pair averaged .89 across all five pairs for all participants with mean values ranging from .59 for internal dialogue to 1.29 for state of awareness.

Cluster and Factor Analyses

The reliability of the various (sub)dimensions of the questionnaire was also assessed by means of coefficient alphas. Before the coefficients were computed, however, the data from the participant's responses to the DCQ were cluster and factor analyzed to obtain unidimensional scales.

All of the items of the DCQ for all individuals were submitted to an oblique multiple groups cluster analysis with communalities in the diagonals of the correlation matrix (Hunter & Gerbing, 1979). After this initial cluster analysis, each cluster was tested for unidimensionality; that is, the extent to which the items "share a common core—the attribute which is to be measured" (Nunnally, 1967, p. 274). This was done by an analysis of the items of each cluster: (1) making sure the item of a given cluster had the same general meaning, (2) checking the degree to which the cluster loadings of the items within each cluster had the same general pattern, and (3) checking the extent to which items within each cluster paralleled in terms of cluster loadings, the items outside that particular cluster (Hunter, 1977).

Items not meeting these criteria were eliminated and the resulting items reanalyzed with another oblique multiple groups cluster analysis "until a set of unidimensional scales were obtained" (Hunter & Gerbing, 1979, p. 8). This process of confirmatory cluster analysis resulted in the elimination of six items (two from positive affect, and one each from negative affect, imagery amount, imagery vividness, and self-awareness).

To determine if there were any aspects of subjective experience not being appropriately mapped by the cluster analytic approach, the DCQ was also submitted to an exploratory factor analysis (Hunter & Gerbing, 1979). A principal components factor analysis, followed by Varimax rotation, was performed on all 80 items of the DCQ with factors extracted having eigenvalues of greater than 1.0. Fifty-one percent of the variance was accounted for by 13 factors. The obtained factors, almost invariably, were composed of items that clustered together in terms of the dimensions and subdimensions arrived at by cluster analysis, and no new factors appeared to be obtained that were not already being assessed by the questionnaire's (sub)dimensions.

Coefficient Alphas

Since the resulting 74-item DCQ was composed of unidimensional cluster analytic (sub)dimensions, coefficient alphas were computed for each dimension and subdimension. Table 6.2 tabulates the alphas for each of the (sub)dimensions while also listing the PCQ alphas obtained from earlier research. As can be seen from the table, all dimensions and subdimensions had coefficient alphas of .70 for above, for an average alpha across all eleven major dimensions (excluding alertness) of .81. (As with the results of the PCQ, the alertness dimension was dropped as a reliable dimension of consciousness due to its low reliability, alpha = .53.)

RELIABILITY OF THE ABBREVIATED DIMENSIONS OF CONSCIOUSNESS QUESTIONNAIRE

It was predicted that an abbreviated version of the DCQ would be as reliable as the 37-item PCQ. Pearson r correlations for the five pairs of duplicate items for Form 1 of the ADCQ (given to 304 participants dur-

Table 6.2. Dimensions of Consciousness and Corresponding Alphas
for the PCQ, the DCQ, and the ADCQ

	Questionnaire[a]				
Dimension	PCQ[b]	DCQ	DCQ (short form)	ADCQ (Form 0)	ADCQ (Form 1)
Imagery	.84	.89	.82	.90	.89
Imagery amount	.79	.85	.80	.91	.91
Imagery vividness	.78	.82	.71	.83	.86
Attention	.68	.85	.75	.79	.77
Direction	.70	.86	.79	.82	.81
Absorption	.52	.76	.60	.49	.56
Positive affect	.78	.85	.91	.91	.91
Altered experience	.78	.84	.74	.76	.72
Altered body image	.56	.76	.64	.53	.54
Altered perception	.48	.76	.59	.57	.57
Altered time	.62	.71	.69	.78	.71
Altered meaning	.56	.70	.61	.65	.59
Awareness	.82	.80	.77	.83	.79
Self-awareness	.80	.81	.73	.75	.76
State of awareness	.76	.73	.66	.85	.82
Negative affect	.56	.80	.65	.70	.71
Memory	.64	.79	.76	.78	.64
Internal dialogue	.86	.78	.92	.91	.90
Rationality	—	.78	.72	.88	.81
Volitional control	.75	.77	.68	.77	.78
Arousal	—	.77	.80	.68	.71
Average (major dimensions)	.74	.81	.78	.81	.78

[a] n for all questionnaires except for PCQ equals 304; n for the PCQ equals 249.
[b] Coefficients represent the average of four conditions: eyes open (experienced twice), relaxation/meditation, and reading erotica.

ing the EC condition) averaged .76. (All item-pairs of the ADCQ were
the same as the DCQ except for a different item for the item-pair of state
of awareness.) Pearson r correlations for Form 0 of the questionnaire
(given to six groups of individuals during one EO, one EF, one RM, and
three EC conditions) yielded an average value of .75. Values ranged from
.60 and .61 for the item-pair of state of awareness to .84 and .82 for the
item-pair of internal dialogue for both forms, respectively, of the questionnaire. Average difference score values were slightly lower than
those reported for the DCQ.

Coefficient alphas for the (sub)dimensions were computed and are
listed in Table 6.2, along with the alphas for the (sub)dimensions of the
DCQ composed of only those items the same as the ADCQ (shortened

DCQ). Alphas averaged .78 for the 11 major dimensions of the ADCQ, Form 1; .81 for the ADCQ, Form 0; and .78 for the shortened DCQ. (Since none of the items of the ADCQ that were the same as the DCQ items were dropped using confirmatory cluster analysis, the dimensions of the ADCQ were also judged to be of unidimensional content, which appears confirmed by the coefficient alpha results.)

VALIDITY

In order to determine the validity of the (sub)dimensions of the questionnaire at discriminating among similar and dissimilar stimulus conditions, the intensity ratings for each (sub)dimension were first quantified for each participant for each condition. This was done by averaging the participant's responses to all items that made up a particular (sub)dimension.

Intensity Comparisons

The dimension intensity values of the EO and RM conditions of group 3 were compared using paired t-tests to assess whether the same results would be found as was demonstrated when comparing these same conditions with the PCQ. Across all 19 subdimensions and dimensions found significantly different with the 37-item PCQ, the ADCQ obtained significant differences in 17 of these and all were in the same direction as found with the PCQ. Phenomenologically, the RM condition, in comparison to the EO condition, was associated with less imagery and less vivid imagery; more absorbed and inward attention; less positive affect; more altered experiences involving body image, perception, time sense, and unusual meanings; greater alterations in self-awareness and state of awareness; less negative affect; decreased memory, internal dialogue, rationality, and volitional control; and increased body relaxation.

The dimension intensity ratings for the EO and EF (erotic fantasy) conditions of group 5 were compared using paired t-tests to assess whether similar results would be found as were demonstrated when reading erotica and EO were compared with the PCQ. The present research replicated seven of ten previously significant comparisons, all in the same direction, while also yielding four other significant comparisons. Phenomenologically, the EF condition was associated with more imagery and more vivid imagery, more inward attention, more positive affect, greater altered meaning, less negative affect, better memory, and less talking to oneself than the EO condition.

Pattern Comparisons

To assess for pattern differences between the stimulus conditions, the Box (1950) test was used. It allows for the assessment of significant differences between the covariance matrices of the stimulus conditions as a function of chi-square or F (Timm, 1975) and was used before a computer program was developed (Pekala & Kumar, 1985) that allowed utilization of the Jennrich (1970) test. (The correlation matrices comparisons reported in Chapter 5 were also initially done with the Box test. These matrices were later recomputed with the Jennrich test. This was not able to be done with the above, since these correlation matrices have since been lost.)

The correlation matrices for the EO and RM conditions were composed of all the major dimensions of the DCQ except for imagery, attention, and awareness, whose corresponding subdimensions were used instead. Conversion of the correlation matrices to covariance matrices and comparison of the covariance matrices associated with the EO and RM conditions yielded an F (105, 42,800) value of 1.42 that was significant at $p < .001$. Utilizing the same procedure while comparing the EF and EO conditions yielded an F (105, 24,300) value of 1.28. This was significant at $p < .05$. (The Box test was devised for two independent groups. When it is used with correlated groups, it is a more conservative test for differences than when used with independent groups.)

STIMULUS-STATE SPECIFICITY

To determine if the same stimulus conditions are associated with the same intensities and patterns of phenomenological experience while differing conditions are associated with differing intensities and/or patterns of phenomenological experience (principle of stimulus-state specificity), intensity and pattern comparisons were performed on the data from the last four groups of participants (groups 3 through 6). Groups 1 and 2 were not used since their second and third conditions were counterbalanced for order.

Intensity Comparisons

One-way analyses of variance were performed for the last four groups of individuals for all dimensions and subdimensions of consciousness for the first, second, and third conditions, that is, the eyes-open (EO), eyes-closed (EC), and mixed (MX) conditions. (The MX conditions consisted of two EC, one EF, and one RM condition.) The data analyses were performed using all the individuals in each of the groups, and then with only 36 individuals per group. Random sampling to reduce each group to 36 participants was done in order to equate the number of individuals involved in the intensity comparisons with the number of individuals involved in the pattern comparisons. (The Box test was utilized with an equal number of individuals in each group.) Since there were negligible differences when comparing the analyses involving unequal groups with those involving equal groups, only the latter analyses will be reported.

Whether using the DCQ or the shortened DCQ to assess for intensity differences for the 21 (sub)dimensions across the four groups of individuals during the EO condition, only one comparison was found to be significant. When using the ADCQ to assess for intensity differences across the four groups during the EC condition, again only one comparison was found to be significant. Since alpha was set at .05, the significant comparisons were most likely due to chance.

Concerning the MX condition, across the four groups, 15 of the 21 comparisons were significant. The RM condition was the most different of the four conditions when using the Tukey-HSD procedure for post hoc comparisons, followed by the EF condition. Table 6.3 tabulates these comparisons.

Pattern Comparisons

To assess for pattern differences among the same and differing conditions, the Box test was employed. Neither of the Box test comparisons for the four groups of participants in the EO condition [F (315, 28,560) = 1.06, $p > .05$] nor the EC condition [F (315, 28,560) = 1.04, $p > .05$] reached statistical significance. However, the Box test comparison across the group of mixed conditions yielded a significant effect [F (315, 28,560) = 1.36, $p < .05$].

OTHER RESULTS

Since the first two groups of subjects experienced the EO and EC conditions in counterbalanced order, the EO and EC conditions can be compared for significant (sub)dimension intensity and pattern differences between conditions and also order.

The EC condition was associated with significantly more imagery,

Table 6.3. Dimension Intensity Comparisons across Four Stimulus Conditions[a]

Dimension	Condition mean[b,c]				F^d ratio
	Eyes closed	Eyes closed	Erotic fantasy	Relaxation/ meditation	
Imagery	3.42e	3.58e	4.12e	1.72f	20.68***
Imagery amount	3.31e	3.74e	4.13e	1.64f	17.90***
Imagery vividness	3.51e	3.42e	4.11e	1.81f	15.71***
Attention	3.65e	4.39f	4.16ef	4.32ef	2.78*
Direction	3.68e	4.44ef	4.49ef	4.72f	3.45*
Absorption	3.61	4.33	3.82	3.92	2.02
Positive affect	1.67e	1.93e	4.26f	0.63g	33.47***
Altered experience	1.77e	1.96ef	2.12ef	2.43f	2.77*
Altered body image	2.35	2.61	2.99	3.18	2.36
Altered perception	1.44	1.29	1.86	1.60	1.30
Altered time	1.96e	2.51ef	2.18e	3.43f	5.79***
Altered meaning	1.33	1.40	1.46	1.51	0.09
Awareness	2.31e	1.88e	2.22e	3.24f	7.04***
Self-awareness	2.34e	1.88e	2.25e	3.23f	4.93**
State of awareness	2.28e	1.89e	2.18e	3.25f	5.70***
Negative affect	1.35	1.46	1.16	0.89	1.30
Memory	1.71ef	1.56e	1.21e	2.36f	5.05***
Internal dialogue	2.64e	2.62e	3.53ef	4.06f	4.84**
Rationality	2.03	2.15	1.61	2.21	1.13
Volitional control	3.04e	2.86e	2.57e	4.11f	6.39***
Arousal	1.79ef	1.32e	2.35f	0.78g	11.70***

[a]From Pekala & Wenger (1983). Reprinted with permission of the publisher.
[b]Higher values denote increased amounts ranging from none or little (rating = 0) to much or complete (rating = 6).
[c]All conditions having a particular letter (e,f,g) after the mean are significantly different from conditions without that particular letter.
[d]$df = 3/140$; * = $p < .05$; ** = $p < .01$; *** = $p < .001$.

more inward and absorbed attention, and greater alterations in time sense, unusual meanings, and state of awareness than the EO condition (omega-square averaged, across all (sub)dimensions, was 6%). Significant effects for order were found for negative affect and absorbed attention, while significant interactions between conditions and order were found for negative affect, self-awareness, and absorbed attention. (Omega-square, however, averaged less than 1% across all (sub)dimensions.)

Use of the Box (1950) test to assess for pattern differences did not find a significant pattern effect for type of condition [F (105, 152,800) = 0.84, $p > .05$], nor for order [F (105, 152,800) = 0.83, $p > .05$].

SUMMARY AND DISCUSSION OF RESULTS

Reliability of the DCQ

The results for the five pairs of reliability items indicated that the participants were responding to the items in a reliable manner. This is consistent with the reliability results when using the PCQ (Pekala & Levine, 1982) and with the reviews of Ericsson and Simon (1980), Lieberman (1979), and Singer (Singer & Kolligian, 1987), who suggested that although introspective data are not totally reliable, they can be reasonably reliable and reliable enough to yield useful information.

Coefficient alpha, the other measure of reliability used, assessed not only the individual's accuracy at completing the questionnaire, but also the internal consistency or unidimensionality of the dimensions mapped by the DCQ. An average alpha of .81 for all major dimensions mapped by the DCQ compares favorably with an average alpha of .76 for the nine dimensions of the PCQ. With alphas ranging from .77 to .89 for the DCQ's major dimensions, it can be concluded that the dimensions appear to be composed of items of internal consistency, which presupposes that the participants were accurate at completing the inventory.

Reliability of the ADCQ

It was expected that the ADCQ would be as reliable as the 37-item PCQ. Average Pearson r's for the two forms of the ADCQ of .76 and .75, and average alphas for the two forms of the ADCQ across all major dimensions of .81 and .78 indicate that the abbreviated version is as reliable as the 37-item PCQ and almost as reliable as the longer DCQ itself.

Discriminant and Construct Validity of the (A)DCQ

The (sub)dimensions of the (A)DCQ possess discriminant validity to the extent that the dimensions can discriminate among stimulus conditions according to the various aspects of subjective experience expected to be different in differing stimulus conditions. The RM condition, in comparison to baseline (EO) (for group 3), was associated with greater alterations in body image, time, meaning, self-awareness, and state of awareness; more inward attention; and decreased arousal, volitional control, rationality, internal dialogue, memory, negative affect, positive affect, and imagery amount and vividness, all in the expected direction. These results replicate those obtained with the PCQ when these conditions were compared and indicate that the (A)DCQ (sub)dimensions possess not only discriminant validity, but also construct validity since the (sub)dimensions appeared to be validly assessing the constructs for which they were developed.

In addition to the above intensity comparisons, the RM condition, in comparison to the EO condition, was associated with a significant pattern change. Since the RM condition, vis-à-vis the EO condition, had both a significant pattern change and a significant SSAS (subjective sense of altered state as measured by the state of awareness subdimension), it fits Tart's (1975) criteria for an altered state of consciousness. This finding replicates results obtained with the PCQ when RM and EO were compared (Pekala & Levine, 1982).

The comparisons between the EF and EO conditions support the validity of the (A)DCQ. Although three comparisons found significant when comparing reading erotica with baseline were not replicated, all other comparisons were: increased and more vivid imagery, more inward attention, greater positive affect (sexual excitement), and decreased internal dialogue during EF than EO. (The nonreplicated results probably relate to the fact that an erotic fantasy was being assessed instead of reading erotica as in the earlier study.)

The EF condition, vis-à-vis EO, also had a significant pattern change but a nonsignificant SSAS. These results suggest it can be labeled an identity state of consciousness using Tart's (1975) criteria. This finding also replicates the results obtained with the PCQ when reading erotica and EO were compared.

Retrospective Phenomenological Assessment and Stimulus-State Specificity

The aforementioned results indicate that a retrospective self-report methodology, such as that employing the questionnaires previously described, is a reliable and valid means for assessing and quantifying subjective experience in reference to specific stimulus conditions through the intensity and pattern parameters obtained from the questionnaires' items.

In addition, the hypothesis of stimulus-state specificity (principle of specificity) was found to be valid for the stimulus conditions assessed. Four groups of individuals experienced nonsignificant dimension intensity differences in regard to all but 1 of 21 dimensions and subdimensions of consciousness when assessed during either eyes-open or eyes-closed sitting quietly. There were also no significant pattern differences, as measured by the Box test, across the groups of participants for either of the above conditions. When comparing stimulus conditions that were different, 15 out of 21 comparisons were significantly different, as were the pattern comparisons among conditions.

CONCLUSIONS

Self-report questionnaires like the PCQ, DCQ, and (A)DCQ permit the researcher to reliably map subjective experience according to specific dimensions and subdimensions of consciousness. The questionnaire's use in retrospective phenomenological assessment (RPA) allows for subjective experience to be validly assessed in reference to particular stimulus conditions. The association of a particular phenomenological state with a specific stimulus condition, labeled the principle of specificity, may lead to a greater understanding of the structures of subjective experience, since such experience is tied to observable and repeatable stimulus conditions.

Chapter 7 will describe the Phenomenology of Consciousness Inventory, the most recent and refined general RPA self-report instrument, and its development, reliability, and validity.

The Phenomenology of Consciousness Inventory

INTRODUCTION

The Phenomenology of Consciousness Inventory (PCI) (Pekala, 1982, 1991b)[1] is a retrospective self-report questionnaire completed in reference to a preceding stimulus condition. As with the Phenomenology of Consciousness Questionnaire (PCQ) and the (Abbreviated) Dimensions of Consciousness Questionnaire, (A)DCQ, the PCI permits subjective experience to be phenomenologically quantified in terms of pattern parameters, as Tart (1975) indicates, and intensity parameters, as Singer (cited in Zinberg, 1977), suggests, thus allowing for the phenomenological values associated with a given stimulus condition to be empirically assessed.

The questionnaire consists of 53 items, each item consisting of two statements separated by a seven-point Likert scale. The questionnaire has two forms composed of the same items but arranged into two different sequences of items. The 53 items assess 12 dimensions of consciousness. Five dimensions have two or more subdimensions associated with them. The dimensions (and associated subdimensions) are: altered ex-

---

[1]The researcher or clinician interested in using the Phenomenology of Consciousness Inventory (PCI) (Pekala, 1982, 1991b) can procure the inventory, manual scoring sheets, and supporting materials from the Mid-Atlantic Educational Institute, Inc., 309 North Franklin Street, West Chester, Pennsylvania 19380-2765.

perience (body image, time sense, unusual meanings, perception), positive affect (joy, sexual excitement, love), negative affect (fear, anger, sadness), attention (direction, absorption), imagery (amount, vividness), self-awareness, state of awareness, internal dialogue, rationality, volitional control, memory, and arousal (decreased relaxation). The PCI also contains five pairs of reliability items. They are items of similar or identical content that are used to measure *intra*individual reliability.

DEVELOPMENT OF THE PHENOMENOLOGY OF CONSCIOUSNESS INVENTORY

The PCI is a third-generation questionnaire developed from the (A)DCQ, which in turn was developed from the PCQ. The PCI represents a modification of the (A)DCQ, primarily by incorporating Plutchik's (1980) four primary emotions (anger, fear, sadness, and joy) under the major dimensions of positive and negative affect and adding these subdimensions to the (sub)dimensions already mapped by the (A)DCQ.

Developing the PCI from the Pre-PCI

The PCI was developed by revising the (A)DCQ (reported in Pekala *et al.*, 1986). To review, the (sub)dimensions of the (A)DCQ included: imagery (amount, vividness), attention (direction, absorption), altered experience (body image, perception, time sense, unusual meanings), awareness (state of awareness, self-awareness), positive affect, negative affect, memory, internal dialogue, rationality, volitional control, and arousal. Each of these (sub)dimensions had four items each except for positive and negative affect, which, respectively, had two items each dealing with joy, sexual excitement, love/tenderness, and calmness, and anxiety, guilt, sadness, and anger.

The predecessor to the PCI, the pre-PCI, was constructed by utilizing all four items for each of the (sub)dimensions of the DCQ, except for positive and negative affect. For positive affect, two items for each of the (sub)dimensions (except calmness) were retained and two additional items were written. For negative affect, the two anger and sadness items of the DCQ were retained and two additional items were written for each. Four additional items were then written for the subdimension of fear. The result was an 84-item inventory composed of 11 dimensions, 6 of which had a total of 16 subdimensions.

Reliability Index Items

Five of the items of the pre-PCI are very similar or identical in content to five other items. These reliability item-pairs (dealing with the (sub)dimensions of sexual excitement, altered state of awareness, imagery amount, direction of attention, and internal dialogue) are used to monitor how consistent the participants are at completing the questionnaire. Subjects answering each pair identically would demonstrate a reliability index (RI) score of zero for each item-pair. Subjects responding oppositely would generate a reliability index score of six (using a seven-point Likert scale) for each item-pair, while subjects responding randomly would generate an *average* reliability index score of three. Marginal reliability was defined as an average (across all five item-pairs) RI score of greater than 2.0. Should the researcher want to eliminate any subjects with questionable or marginal reliability, as, for example, in trying to increase a validity coefficient, the PCI reliability index score allows for this to be done.

Subjects and Method

The pre-PCI was given to three groups of 112 subjects (subjects were Michigan State University psychology students, $n = 40, 40, 32$) within a one-week period. Subjects were asked to sit quietly with their eyes open and think about whatever they liked. After four minutes they completed the 84-item inventory in reference to sitting quietly with their eyes open.

Reliability Analyses

Pearson r correlation coefficients were computed for the five pairs of duplicate (intratest reliability) items. Item-pairs averaged .74 across all subjects. The average reliability index (the absolute difference score between the two items of each item-pair), averaged across all five reliability pairs, was .85 and only two subjects had a reliability index score of greater than 2.0.

Coefficient alphas for each dimension and subdimension of the pre-PCI were then computed. Alphas ranged from a high of .93 for imagery to a low of .65 for volitional control and averaged .82 across all major dimensions (.84 across all dimensions and subdimensions combined). The data from these 112 subjects and the data from the 304 subjects who completed the DCQ in previous research was then used to develop the

PCI. (For the positive and negative affect (sub)dimensions which had no previous DCQ coefficient alpha results, only the pre-PCI data was used.)

Those two or three items of each subdimension or dimension (if it had no associated subdimensions) correlating highest with each other were chosen and coefficient alphas computed using the values obtained with the pre-PCI and the DCQ. (Sub)dimensions evincing a high (above .70) coefficient alpha with both the pre-PCI and the DCQ that was not appreciably raised by the addition of a third item were composed of only two items. If the addition of a third item appreciably raised the alpha (by approximately .05), it was added.

The Phenomenology of Consciousness Inventory

This process resulted in 11 (sub)dimensions being composed of only two items and nine (sub)dimensions being composed of three items. One subdimension, meaning, had to have all four items in order to evince an alpha of .70. Due to a low correlation between self-awareness and state of awareness ($r = .38$), these dimensions, which previously had been subdimensions of the major dimension of awareness with the PCQ and the (A)DCQ, became separate dimensions with the PCI. All other (sub)dimensions were the same as the pre-PCI.

The result was a 53-item questionnaire consisting of 12 major dimensions and 14 subdimensions. Items of the PCI were arranged in a randomized block design so that no two items of similar content would be adjacent. The dipoles of each item were also oppositely arranged. Thus, the items of a particular dimension or subdimension had half of those items with the left dipole addressed to more normal subjective experience, while the other half of the items had the left dipole addressed to more altered subjective experience. Table 7.1 lists representative items of the PCI. (Appendix A lists all of the items of the PCI, Form 1. The two forms contain identical items, although they are arranged in different sequences for each form. The (sub)dimensions of the PCI and item numbers for both forms are contained in Appendix C.)

To give the reader an idea about the general meaning for each dimension and subdimension, the following will briefly review the general content of each of the (sub)dimensions.

The positive affect dimension consists of three subdimensions. Whereas the joy subdimension assesses feelings of ecstacy and extreme happiness, the sexual excitement subdimension addresses the extent of "intense sexual feelings." The love subdimension asks about feelings of love and loving-kindness.

Table 7.1. Representative Items of the Phenomenology of Consciousness Inventory

Dimension (subdimension)	
Left dipole	Right dipole

Attention (absorption)

I was forever distracted and unable to concentrate on anything.	I was able to concentrate quite well and was not distracted.

Internal dialogue

I was silently talking to myself a great deal.	I did not engage in any silent talking to myself.

Positive affect (joy)

I felt ecstatic and joyful.	I felt no feelings of being ecstatic or joyful.

Self-awareness

I was not aware of being aware of myself at all; I had no self-awareness.	I was very aware of being aware of myself; my self-awareness was intense.

Altered state of awareness

My state of consciousness was not any different or unusual from what it ordinarily is.	I felt in an extremely different and unusual state of consciousness.

Rationality

Conceptually, my thinking was clear and distinct.	Conceptually, my thinking was confused and muddled.

Altered experience (meaning)

I had an experience of awe and reverence toward the world.	I had no experience of awe and reverence toward the world.

Imagery (amount)

I experienced no or very few images.	My experience was made up almost completely of images.

The negative affect dimension monitors anger, sadness, and fear. The anger subdimension assesses feelings of being "very anger and upset" or enraged, while the sadness subdimension monitors feeling very, very sad or unhappy. The fear subdimension asks about feeling "very frightened" or being scared or afraid.

The altered experience dimension is composed of four subdimensions: altered body image, altered time sense, altered perception, and altered or unusual meaning. Altered body image addresses the extent to which subjects feel their bodily feelings expand into the world around them. Altered time sense addresses the extent to which "the flow of time changed drastically" or whether it seemed to "speed up or slow down." Concerning perception, this subdimension assesses changes in the perception of the world in terms of color, form, size, shape, or perspective. The unusual meanings subdimension assesses the extent to which a person reports an experience that might be labeled religious, spiritual, or transcendental, or has feelings of awe, sacredness, or reverence.

The imagery dimension is composed of two subdimensions: amount of imagery and vividness of imagery. Whereas imagery amount assesses the amount of imagery, the vividness subdimension assesses the extent to which visual imagery is "vivid and three-dimensional" or "as clear and vivid as objects in the real world." Attention likewise is composed of two subdimensions: direction of attention and absorption. Whereas direction addresses whether attention is directed toward "internal subjective experience" or "toward the environment around me." Absorption assesses whether the person was absorbed in what they were experiencing versus being "continually distracted by extraneous impressions."

The self-awareness dimension of the PCI assesses the extent to which the person is "aware of being aware of myself," versus having "lost consciousness" of themselves or not being aware of being aware of oneself. The altered state of awareness dimension, on the other hand, assesses being in "an extraordinarily unusual and nonordinary state of awareness" versus one's state of consciousness being no different than usual.

Whereas internal dialogue is addressed to the extent to which someone was silently talking to himself a great deal, the rationality dimension addresses whether thinking is clear and distinct, or rational and easy to comprehend, versus thinking being "confused and muddled" or "nonrational and very hard to comprehend."

Volitional control assesses the extent to which one has "complete control over what one is paying attention to" or is "willfully controlling" experience versus becoming passive and receptive to experience or having "images and thoughts pop into my mind without my control."

Memory assesses the subjects' perceptions that they can remember just about everything that they experienced versus not being able to remember what they experienced. And finally, the arousal dimension is really a measure of the extent of muscular tension, that is, the extent to which the muscles of the body are "very tense and tight" versus not feeling "tension or tightness at all."

Reliability of the PCI

Coefficient alphas for the PCI during eyes open (EO) sitting quietly ranged from a high of .92 for sexual excitement to a low of .69 for time sense and averaged .82 for all major dimensions and .82 for all dimensions and subdimensions combined. Table 7.2 lists the alphas for the various (sub)dimensions during eyes open sitting quietly (the two other stimulus conditions listed in the table are reported later). Of the 112

Table 7.2. Coefficient Alphas for the Phenomenology of Consciousness Inventory across Several Different Stimulus Conditions

	Stimulus condition[a]		
Dimension	Eyes open	Eyes closed	Hypnotic induction
Positive affect	.88	.85	.82
Joy	.82	.74	.54
Sexual excitement	.92	.91	.80
Love	.88	.80	.66
Negative affect	.87	.82	.74
Anger	.81	.69	.57
Sadness	.82	.78	.61
Fear	.90	.75	.53
Altered experience	.82	.75	.81
Altered body image	.74	.52	.70
Altered time sense	.69	.66	.68
Altered perception	.80	.56	.68
Altered meaning	.70	.54	.67
Visual imagery	.91	.80	.78
Amount	.90	.79	.76
Vividness	.82	.75	.66
Attention	.80	.75	.77
Direction (inward)	.84	.71	.75
Absorption	.79	.68	.80
Self-awareness	.77	.65	.78
Altered state of awareness	.83	.78	.87
Internal dialogue	.86	.85	.83
Rationality	.80	.69	.84
Volitional control	.71	.65	.76
Memory	.80	.69	.85
Arousal	.79	.80	.74
Average (major dimensions)	.82	.76	.80
Average (subdimensions)	.82	.73	.67
n	110	233	210

[a]Excludes subjects with a reliability index of > 2.0.

original subjects, two subjects had an item-pair difference score (reliability index) of greater than two and hence were excluded due to marginal reliability. (Eliminating these subjects did not appreciably change the coefficient alphas.)

PCI Gender Effects

Differences in phenomenological experience between males ($n = 42$) and females ($n = 68$) were assessed for all (sub)dimensions of consciousness mapped by the PCI. At the .05 level of significance, females reported significantly more imagery, more vivid imagery, and more inward attention than males.

Stimulus-State Specificity

It was predicted that the PCI would demonstrate nonsignificant intensity and pattern differences between the three groups of subjects experiencing the same stimulus condition. A one-way analysis of variance was performed for all dimension and subdimension intensity scores, testing for significant differences among the three groups of subjects. Across all (sub)dimensions, no significant differences ($p < .05$) were found.

To assess for pattern differences, correlation matrices that were composed of the correlations of the 12 major PCI dimensions of consciousness with each other were constructed for each of the three groups. These correlation matrices were then statistically assessed with a computer program (Pekala & Kumar, 1985) that operationalizes the Jennrich (1970) test. The Jennrich test statistically compares two independent correlation matrices for significant differences between them. None of the matrices were found to be significantly different from the others, suggesting there was *not* a significant pattern difference between them. (For the Jennrich test to be effective, there should be approximately five to ten times as many subjects as dimensions. Less than a 5 or 10 to 1 ratio will make it less likely that the Jennrich test will find a significant effect, if it exists, due to inadequate power. Hence, the aforementioned data analysis is suspect, due to a low ratio of subjects to dimensions.)

Conclusions

Reliability

The Pearson r coefficients, difference scores, and coefficient alpha results strongly indicated acceptable reliabilities for the (sub)dimensions of the PCI. These reliabilities are also comparable to the reliabilities obtained from predecessor questionnaires similar to the PCI (Pekala & Levine, 1981, 1982; Pekala & Wenger, 1983).

Stimulus-State Specificity

The nonsignificant intensity and pattern comparisons between the groups of participants for the PCI support the principle of stimulus-state specificity concerning intensity and pattern comparisons for the same stimulus conditions. These findings replicate previous research (Pekala & Wenger, 1983) and suggest no significant PCI intensity and pattern differences for the three stimulus conditions (although the pattern comparisons are suspect due to a low subject-dimension ratio).

USING THE PCI TO ASSESS TWO DIFFERENT STIMULUS CONDITIONS

Although the PCI was able to generate acceptable reliabilities for the eyes open sitting quietly condition, additional research was needed to: (1) determine if these reliabilities would replicate, especially when assessing other types of stimulus conditions, and (2) determine the construct and discriminant validity of the PCI. For this purpose, another study was run.

Subjects and Procedure

Two hundred and seventeen West Chester University college students, seen in groups of 99 and 118 individuals per group, experienced two stimulus conditions: eyes closed (EC) sitting quietly and the hypnotic induction (HI) procedure of the Harvard Group Scale of Hypnotic Susceptibility (HGSHS) (Shor & Orne, 1962). After each condition, subjects retrospectively completed the PCI. (These results were reported in Pekala *et al.*, 1986.)

All subjects first experienced the EC condition during which they were told to sit quietly with their eyes closed for several minutes. (The instructions for the EC condition were the same as the EC instructions for the (A)DCQ research.) Immediately after the four-minute EC condition, the subjects completed the PCI, Form 1, in reference to that condition.

After the EC condition, the subjects experienced the HI procedure of the HGSHS. (The HGSHS induction procedure was shortened approximately ten minutes by eliminating redundant phraseology between the beginning of the induction procedure but before the giving of the various behavioral suggestions.) After the eye catalepsy instructions but before the posthypnotic and amnesia instructions of the HGSHS, the subjects experienced a four-minute time period during which they were told:

> Continue to experience the state you are in right now. For the next several minutes I'm going to stop talking and I want you to experience the state you are in right now.

After the end of the hypnotic induction procedure and after writing down a list of the suggestions they remembered, the participants completed the PCI, Form 2, in reference to the time "when I stopped talking and I asked you to continue to experience the state you are in." (The time period from the end of the four-minute period to starting to complete the PCI averaged approximately 10 minutes.) Subjects completed the 11 response items of the HGSHS after completing the PCI. Subjects' scores on the Harvard were subsequently computed by adding their amnesia score to their score on the 11 response items of the Harvard Scale.

Results

Reliability

Reliability Index Scores. Pearson r's for the five pair of reliability items for the PCI during EC ($r = .53$) and HI ($r = .53$) were considerably lower than that obtained during the EO condition reported earlier. While only 2% of the EO participants (from the previous study) were marginally reliable completing the PCI (had an RI difference score of greater than 2), 11.4% of the EC subjects and 13.2% of the HI subjects had a difference score (reliability index) of greater than 2. Due to the lower Pearson r's for the EC and HI conditions, it was decided to run all analyses: (1) using only subjects with a reliability index of less than or equal to 2, and also (2) using all subjects. The following paragraphs will cite analyses using subjects with a reliability index of 2 or less while reporting analyses with all subjects in parentheses.

Coefficient Alphas. Coefficient alphas were computed for the various (sub)dimensions of consciousness. Alphas for the EC condition ranged from .85 for internal dialogue and positive affect to .65 for volitional control and self-awareness and averaged .76 (.73 across all subjects). Alphas for the HI condition ranged from .87 for state of awareness to .74 for negative affect and arousal and averaged .80 (.76 across all subjects). Alphas for all subdimensions during EC averaged .73 and .67 during HI. Table 7.2 (mentioned earlier) lists the coefficient alpha results for the EC and HI conditions and also the EO condition, eliminating subjects having a reliability index of greater than 2. In order that the researcher may have some idea as to the effect of eliminating unreliable subjects, Table 7.3 lists the alphas for the eyes closed and hypnosis conditions, *with* and *without* inclusion of marginally reliable subjects.

Table 7.3. Coefficient Alphas for the Phenomenology of Consciousness Inventory with and without Marginally Reliable Subjects

	Stimulus condition			
	Eyes closed		Hypnosis	
Dimension	With[a]	Without[b]	With	Without
Positive affect	.83	.85	.79	.82
Joy	.69	.74	.48	.54
Sexual excitement	.84	.91	.74	.80
Love	.75	.80	.62	.66
Negative affect	.81	.82	.71	.74
Anger	.68	.69	.44	.57
Sadness	.77	.78	.57	.61
Fear	.70	.75	.47	.53
Altered experience	.74	.75	.80	.81
Altered body image	.48	.52	.68	.70
Altered time sense	.62	.66	.65	.68
Altered perception	.56	.56	.65	.68
Altered meaning	.51	.54	.65	.67
Visual imagery	.78	.80	.74	.78
Amount	.69	.79	.62	.76
Vividness	.74	.75	.61	.66
Attention	.73	.75	.73	.77
Direction (inward)	.68	.71	.69	.75
Absorption	.64	.68	.74	.80
Self-awareness	.66	.65	.75	.78
Altered state of awareness	.71	.78	.82	.87
Internal dialogue	.75	.85	.71	.83
Rationality	.66	.69	.81	.84
Volitional control	.60	.65	.72	.76
Memory	.66	.69	.84	.85
Arousal	.78	.80	.73	.74
Average (major dimensions)	.73	.76	.76	.80
Average (subdimensions)	.67	.73	.62	.67
n	263	233	242	210

[a]Includes subjects with a reliability index of > 2.0.
[b]Excludes subjects with a reliability index of > 2.0.

Validity

It was predicted that the groups of subjects experiencing the same stimulus conditions would experience nonsignificantly different intensity and pattern parameters while subjects experiencing different stimulus conditions would experience significantly different intensity and pattern parameters.

Comparison across the Same Stimulus Conditions. Two groups of subjects each experienced the EC and HI conditions. Multivariate analysis of variance (MANOVA) were performed separately for the 12 major PCI dimensions and the 14 minor PCI dimensions, attempting to determine if the two groups of subjects would report significant intensity differences for the PCI (sub)dimensions. No significant main effects for groups were found when comparing either the major or the minor PCI dimensions.

In addition to the aforementioned multivariate analyses, *t*-tests were also performed in an attempt to look at each PCI (sub)dimension individually. Comparing all dimension and subdimension intensity scores for the two groups experiencing the EC condition by independent *t*-tests yielded no significant differences at the .05 level of significance for any (sub)dimension. (The same results were obtained using all subjects.) Concerning the HI condition, nonsignificant (sub)dimension intensity scores were also obtained across all (sub)dimensions. (Only 1 of the 26 (sub)dimensions, love, was significant when doing the analyses with all subjects.)

The Jennrich test comparison for the two groups of subjects in the EC condition (using the 12 major dimensions of the PCI to form the correlation matrix) yielded a chi-square value that was not significant. The Jennrich test comparison of the two groups of subjects in the HI condition also yielded a chi-square value that was not significant. (Using all subjects, neither the Jennrich test comparison of the subjects in the EC condition nor the HI condition was significant.)

Comparisons across Different Stimulus Conditions. Repeated-measures multivariate analyses of variance and paired *t*-tests were used to compare (sub)dimension intensity differences across the same subjects during the EC and HI conditions. It was predicted that the same results would be found as were demonstrated when the EC and relaxation/meditation (RM) conditions of earlier research were compared (Pekala *et al.*, 1985). During this earlier research, the RM condition, in comparison to EC, was associated with greater alterations in self-awareness, state of awareness, time sense, and body image; increased relaxation (decreased arousal); and decreased internal dialogue, imagery amount and vividness, positive and negative affect, rationality, memory, and volitional control.

Results of the repeated-measures MANOVA revealed a significant main effect for conditions (eyes-closed versus hypnosis) for the 12 major

Table 7.4. Means and Standard Deviations for the Phenomenology of Consciousness Inventory during Three Stimulus Conditions[a]

| | Stimulus condition[b] | | | | | |
| | Eyes open[c] | | Eyes closed[d] | | Hypnosis[d] | |
Dimension	Mean[e]	S.D.	Mean	S.D.	Mean	S.D.
Positive affect	2.71	1.56	3.43	1.56	1.43	1.24
Joy	2.68	1.79	3.39	1.81	1.52	1.40
Sexual excitement	2.26	1.93	2.72	2.00	0.87	1.45
Love	3.20	1.89	4.18	1.80	1.90	1.68
Negative affect	1.24	1.24	1.05	1.17	0.68	0.92
Anger	1.22	1.41	1.19	1.48	0.59	1.13
Sadness	1.64	1.66	1.33	1.59	0.73	1.16
Fear	0.86	1.32	0.62	1.15	0.72	1.25
Altered experience	2.07	0.96	2.04	0.97	2.48	1.14
Altered body image	2.70	1.33	2.75	1.39	3.11	1.61
Altered time sense	2.61	1.47	2.66	1.61	3.40	1.63
Altered perception	1.40	1.40	1.36	1.29	2.09	1.55
Altered meaning	1.71	1.22	1.57	1.18	1.61	1.34
Visual imagery	3.78	1.57	4.50	1.39	2.21	1.53
Amount	3.67	1.78	4.65	1.55	2.14	1.76
Vividness	3.89	1.55	4.36	1.56	2.27	1.67
Attention	3.71	1.27	4.13	1.21	3.95	1.31
Direction (inward)	3.80	1.66	4.09	1.33	3.87	1.55
Absorption	3.58	1.56	4.18	1.51	4.08	1.58
Self-awareness	4.20	1.25	4.10	1.28	3.11	1.61
Altered state of awareness	2.17	1.63	2.08	1.44	3.80	1.76
Internal dialogue	4.10	1.79	3.00	2.19	2.00	1.93
Rationality	4.21	1.39	4.42	1.38	3.21	1.75
Volitional control	3.95	1.36	4.06	1.38	2.62	1.64
Memory	4.25	1.06	5.19	0.96	3.80	1.69
Arousal	1.81	1.61	1.67	1.62	1.30	1.52

[a]From Pekala et al. (1986). Reprinted with permission of the publisher.
[b]Excludes subjects with a reliability index of > 2.0.
[c]n = 110 (Michigan State students).
[d]n = 173 (West Chester students).
[e]Higher numbers denote increased intensities.

PCI dimensions [F (12,159) = 36.89, $p < .0001$] and also the minor dimensions [F (14,157) = 29.98, $p < .0001$]. Table 7.4 lists the means and standard deviations for the EC and HI conditions for the current study and also the eyes-open condition of the previous study. The hypnotic condition, vis-à-vis the EC condition, was associated with decreased positive affect and negative affect, decreased imagery, self-awareness, internal dialogue, rationality, volitional control, memory, and arousal. The HI condition was also associated with increased altered experiences involving body image, time sense, and perception; increased alteration in state of awareness; and less inward attention. (Using all subjects yielded identical results, except the comparison for attention direction was no longer significant.) These findings replicated almost all comparisons obtained in the earlier research comparing RM and EC.

The Jennrich test comparison between the EC and HI conditions using subjects having a reliability index of less than 2 for *both* conditions ($n = 173$) yielded a chi-square value of 196.2 ($df = 66$), $p < .001$, suggesting a significant pattern structure difference between the two conditions. (Since the Jennrich test was devised for independent groups, when it is used with correlated groups, it is a more conservative test for differences than when used with uncorrelated groups.) This replicated earlier research (Pekala *et al.*, 1985) when relaxation/meditation and eyes-closed sitting quietly were compared for pattern differences. (Using all subjects in computing the correlation matrices for the pattern comparisons also resulted in a significant chi-square value.)

Exploratory Factor Analyses

To determine if an exploratory factor analysis (Hunter, 1977) would generate factors similar to the PCI (sub)dimensions (as another way of checking on the stability of the PCI (sub)dimensions across different stimulus conditions), a principal components factor analysis, followed by Varimax rotation, was enacted on all of the PCI items for the EC and HI conditions (including subjects with an RI of greater than two).

Orthogonal factors were then extracted for factors with eigenvalues of greater than one. For the EC condition eight factors were obtained. These eight factors were composed of items, most of which (74%) continued to load highest on its assigned PCI dimension or subdimension. Thus, of the 21 subdimensions and dimensions mapped by the PCI (excluding those five dimensions composed of two or more subdimensions so as not duplicate subdimensions), 16 had *all* their items loading highest on the factors obtained by this exploratory factor analysis.

For the HI condition eight factors were also extracted. Eighty-three percent of the PCI items continued to load highest on the factor that contained *all* of a particular (sub)dimension's assigned items and 19 of 21 (sub)dimensions had *all* their items found in factors obtained by this exploratory factor analysis.

Gender Comparisons

In regard to gender differences, only 1 of the 26 (sub)dimensions comparisons was significant when individual ANOVAs were completed; during eyes closed women scored higher on love than men, and during hypnosis women scored higher than men on absorption. (The MANOVA comparison for the PCI major and the minor dimensions in regard to gender was not significant.)

Discussion and Conclusions

Reliability

The reliability results obtained with the PCI from West Chester University students (across all subjects) were less than those obtained with the PCI with Michigan State University students. These differences may partially relate to the fact that the time constraints of the second study were much tighter than the first study. Hence, subjects may have felt somewhat pressured and were not quite so accurate. In addition, the West Chester students were run in much larger groups (about 100) than the Michigan State students (who were run in groups of about 30 to 50). The larger groups may have felt a more diffused sense of responsibility, and hence were less reliable. In any event, these results suggest that approximately 10 to 15% of subjects appear to have been relatively unreliable at introspection.

These results agree with those of Lieberman (1979) who reviewed data indicating that introspection is not always highly reliable, and suggests that a percentage of subjects may not be able to introspect accurately. Although the reliability index provides an excellent means for screening these unreliable subjects, the intensity and pattern analyses performed with or without these unreliable subjects indicated minimal differences.

Stability of the PCI (Sub)dimensions

The various (sub)dimensions of the PCI are stable dimensions of consciousness to the extent that the items composing the various (sub)dimensions continue to intercorrelate highly with each other across various stimulus conditions.

The PCI coefficient alphas (which are based on the correlations among the items) support the stability of the various major dimensions, as alphas of .82, .76, and .80 across the EO, EC, and HI conditions, respectively, indicate. (The lower alphas for the subdimensions suggest that they are relatively less stable dimensions of consciousness for the stimulus conditions assessed. Average alphas of .82, .73, and .67, respectively, for these subdimensions across all three conditions nevertheless indicate adequate reliabilities, and hence, stabilities for these subdimensions.)

Although the above coefficient alpha results eliminated subjects with a reliability index of greater than 2, the exploratory factor analyses did not. These analyses found that 16 and 19 of the PCI (sub)dimensions for the EC and HI conditions, respectively, continued to have all their items clustered together in terms of the empirically derived factors. The coefficient alpha and factor analysis results thus support the relative stability of the PCI (sub)dimensions.

Tart (1977) has suggested that consciousness is composed of certain structures or subsystems that retain their basic function in spite of variations in the intensity and/or the quality of their activity. The stability of these (sub)dimensions in several differing conditions is supportive of Tart's theorizing on the stability of the structures or dimensions of consciousness.

Validity

A crucial aspect of the cited study concerned the replicability of the principle of stimulus-state specificity, especially across the same stimulus conditions. The results of the study supported this principle across the same and different stimulus conditions for intensity comparisons and also for pattern comparisons.

The fact that groups of subjects experience the same phenomenological intensity and pattern parameters during the same stimulus conditions and different phenomenological intensity and pattern parameters during different stimulus conditions suggests the potential usefulness of this methodology for mapping states of consciousness across groups of participants for various stimulus conditions and comparing them to one another. Since a given stimulus condition has a corresponding phenomenological state, as assessed across groups of subjects (same condition specificity), various altered state induction procedures can be compared to one another and to previously defined baseline/attention-placebo conditions to determine to what extent such induction procedures are indeed associated and/or produce alterations in phenomenological experience.

The findings that the intensity comparisons between EC and HI replicated the (sub)dimension intensity results when EC and RM (relaxation/meditation) were compared (Pekala *et al.*, 1985) suggests the similarity between HI and RM. It also supports the construct and discriminant validity of the PCI since the PCI was able to discriminate the EC and HI conditions on the (sub)dimensions of the questionnaire in the same direction as earlier research as hypothesized. The paucity of gender differences concerning intensity comparisons also suggests that gender does not moderate phenomenological experience to any great extent as assessed by the PCI.

Further evidence for the reliability and construct and discriminant validity of the PCI will be given in Section IV, Chapters 11 through 16.

Development, Reliability, and Validity of the Dimensions of Attention Questionnaire

RATIONALE FOR AN ATTENTION QUESTIONNAIRE

It was discussed in a previous chapter that almost all consciousness researchers and theorists (Fishkin & Jones, 1978; Silverman, 1968; Tart, 1975, 1977) and cognitive psychologists interested in consciousness (Baars, 1987; Mandler, 1984, 1985) have attention in a very prominent position in their theorizing. Hence, any *comprehensive*, empirical phenomenological approach to consciousness should have a means to map and assess various aspects of attention.

When the Phenomenology of Consciousness Inventory (PCI) and predecessor instruments were developed, they assessed two aspects of attention: absorption (how intensely involved in the object of attention the subject is) and direction of attention (directed inward toward one's subjective experience or outward toward the environment), which were subsumed under the major dimension of attention. There are other aspects of attention, however, that are not adequately assessed by these two PCI subdimensions. Silverman (1968) suggested that attention can be conceptualized as composed of three related factors, factors that were derived from factor analytic studies: attentional intensiveness, extensiveness (scanning), and selectiveness (field articulation).

Attentional intensiveness refers to a subject's sensitivity to stimuli and how absorbed or involved he becomes in those stimuli. Whereas an ordinary state of consciousness, according to Silverman, involves a mid-range sensitivity to stimuli, "unusual hypersensitivity appears to be a precondition for an altered state of consciousness experience" (1968, p. 1208). This dimension corresponds to the absorption dimension of the PCI. Extensiveness of attention refers to the degree of sampling of the elements in the stimulus field. Whereas a person in an ordinary waking state is in a balanced state of scanning the environment, in an altered state of consciousness there is usually restricted scanning of the environment (for the person is preoccupied with a very narrow circle of internal or external stimuli), in terms of Silverman's theorizing.

Silverman's third variable, the selectiveness of attention, "refers to responses which determine which elements in a stimulus field exert a dominant influence on the perceiver" (p. 1203). Thus, whether the subject responds to the discrete elements of the field or takes a more holistic or global perspective represent differences in selectivity of attention. For Silverman, a person in a normal, waking state of consciousness generally has attentional control that is active, analytical, and sequentializing, whereas a person in an altered state has a passive, global-relational set of attentional selectivity. This attentional variable appears somewhat like the volitional control variable of the PCI, which maps the extent to which a person is actively or passively involved in the environment or his subjective self.

DEVELOPMENT OF ITEMS FOR AN ATTENTION QUESTIONNAIRE

It was decided that a phenomenological attentional questionnaire would have to map aspects of attentional experience that might become differentially activated during altered states of consciousness such as hypnosis (Hilgard, 1977), meditation (Pekala, 1987), daydreaming (Singer, 1966), out-of-the-body experiences (OBEs) (Monroe, 1971), and mystical experiences (Deikman, 1972; Yogananda, 1974). Such a questionnaire should also map the domains suggested by Silverman, but, in addition, it should address other aspects of attentional experience, such as vigilance, one-pointedness (as might occur in concentrative meditation), and locus (within or out of the body) for an OBE.

Examination of the literature suggested 12 dimensions of attention that might become differentially activated by the techniques used to elicit altered states. These attentional dimensions were labeled: flexibility, equanimity, detachment, perspicacity (as sense of attentional spatiality), locus (within or out-of-the-body), direction (directed inward or outward toward the environment), one-pointedness, absorption, control, vigilance, density, and simultaneity. (The two attention dimensions of the PCI and that of control were included as three of the above dimensions, since it was felt that they mapped pertinent aspects of attentional experience.) Items were written that appeared to assess aspects of attentional experience associated with the aforementioned dimensions.

Item format was patterned after the PCI. Each attentional item consisted of left and right dipole statements separated by a five-point Likert scale that was later converted to a seven-point scale. (A five- instead of a seven-point scale was used because optical scanning of a seven-point scale was unavailable at that time.) Three items were written for each of the dimensions.

Examples of representative items include (in terms of left dipole versus right dipole): "I was extremely vigilant and continuously observant of everything in my attentional field" versus "I was not vigilant or continuously observant of everything in my attentional field" (vigilance); "My attentional field felt crowded with too many thoughts, feelings, sensations, etc." versus "My attentional field was completely empty of any thoughts, feelings, sensations, etc. at all" (density); "My attention was totally directed toward the environment around me" versus "My attention was totally directed toward my own internal, subjective experience" (direction); "I felt I was willfully and actively controlling what I was attending to" versus "I stopped actively controlling what I was attending to and became passive and receptive to my experience" (control); "My consciousness felt spatially expanded beyond my body so that I felt my awareness to be simultaneously everywhere" versus "My consciousness did not feel spatially expanded beyond my body; I did not feel my awareness to be simultaneously everywhere" (perspicacity); and "I was aware of many sensations, thoughts, feelings, etc. simultaneously" versus "I was aware of only one sensation, thought, feeling, etc. at a time" (simultaneity). Table 8.1 lists several dimensions with representative items.

Two forms of the attention questionnaire were constructed. Both forms had identical items, although each form had a different sequence of items arranged in a randomized block design. The questionnaire contained five pairs of items of identical content. These items were used to assess for intrasubject reliability.

Table 8.1. Representative Items of the Attentional Questionnaire

Dimension	
Left dipole	Right dipole

Density

My mind was in a state of "no thought"; I was not aware of a single thought, feeling, sensation, etc.	My mind was continually occupied; I was always aware of thoughts, feelings, sensations, etc.

One-pointedness

I was able to easily and completely focus my mind on a single impression or event for as long as I wanted.	I found it impossible to focus my mind on a single impression or event for any length of time at all.

Simultaneity

I was aware of many sensations, thoughts, feelings, etc., simultaneously.	I was aware of only one sensation, thought, feeling, etc., at a time.

Flexibility

My attention was not very flexible; I felt my mind kept dwelling on thoughts, feelings, and sensations that I could not get out of my mind.	I felt my attention was very flexible; I could easily focus my attention on any thought, feeling, or sensation that came to my attention.

Perspicacity

My consciousness felt spatially expanded beyond my body so that I felt my awareness to be simultaneously everywhere.	My consciousness did not feel spatially expanded beyond my body; I did not feel my awareness to be simultaneously everywhere.

Vigilance

I was constantly aware of and scanning my internal or external environment for any changes in that environment.	I did not scan or try to be constantly aware of my internal or external environment for any changes in that environment.

STUDY 1

Design

In order to compare the attentional inventory in reference to an ordinary state of consciousness and an altered state, a study (reported in Pekala & Kumar, 1988) was designed so that subjects would experience several stimulus conditions: sitting quietly with eyes open or closed and the induction procedure of the Harvard Scale of Hypnotic Susceptibility (Shor & Orne, 1962). Whereas the baseline conditions would allow for the assessment of attentional experiences associated with normal, waking consciousness (eyes open sitting quietly) and subjective experience more akin to daydreaming (eyes closed sitting quietly), the hypnotic condition would allow for assessment of attentional alterations associated with hypnosis. In addition, by dividing subjects into low-, medium-, and high-susceptible subjects, it was hoped that the differential effects of hypnosis across the reported attentional experiences of low-, medium-, and high-susceptible subjects (as a test of discriminant validity) could be examined.

A previous study by Kumar and Pekala (1988) found that high susceptibles reported increased absorption during hypnosis in reference to eyes closed sitting quietly, while low susceptibles were less absorbed or more distracted during hypnosis than during eyes closed sitting quietly. It was hypothesized that the attentional absorption dimension would replicate the results of Kumar and Pekala and that additional differences between low- and high-susceptible individuals would emerge with the other attentional dimensions.

Method

Subjects and Materials

The subject pool consisted of 434 undergraduates enrolled in introductory psychology classes at West Chester University. Subjects knew beforehand that the study involved hypnosis; participation was voluntary.

The Harvard Group Scale of Hypnotic Susceptibility, Form A (Shor & Orne, 1962), was used to assess hypnotic susceptibility. The previously discussed attentional questionnaire was used to assess attentional experience.

Procedure

Four hundred and thirty-four subjects were seen in five groups of 75, 78, 42, 129, and 110. After the general nature of the study was explained and consent forms completed, 4 of the 5 subject groups ($n = 324$) were told to close their eyes, sit quietly, and think about whatever they liked. At the end of three minutes, they were asked to open their eyes and complete the 36-item questionnaire, Form 1, in reference to the time they sat with their eyes closed. The fifth group of subjects sat with their eyes open (n = 110). They were told to think about whatever they liked and after three minutes were asked to complete the same 36-item inventory, Form 1, in reference to the eyes-open period. (The subjects for this study also completed the PCI prior to completing the attentional instrument. The attentional inventory was "piggy-backed" onto the PCI.)

Upon completion of the questionnaire, all subjects experienced the induction procedure of the Harvard Scale. To accommodate to the time constraints of the study, the Harvard Scale was shortened by eliminating redundant phraseology in the induction phase. After the eye catalepsy instructions but before the posthypnotic suggestions and amnesia instructions, the subjects experienced a three-minute period during which they were told "to continue to experience the state you are in right now. For the next several minutes I'm going to stop talking and I want you to continue to experience the state you are in right now."

These instructions were repeated and the experimenter was silent for three minutes. The rest of the induction instructions were then given. After the end of the induction procedure and after writing down a list of the hypnotic suggestions remembered (and after removal of the amnesia), the participants completed the attentional inventory, Form 2, in reference to the time "when I stopped talking and I asked you to continue to experience the state you were in." The subjects then completed the 11 response items of the Harvard Scale.

Results

Preliminary Analyses

Each subject's responses to the attention questionnaire were first assessed for intratest reliability by means of the five pairs of reliability items embedded in the questionnaire. The inventory utilized a five-point Likert scale separating the two dipoles of each item. (This five-point scale was later converted to a seven-point scale for the data analysis.) Since the reliability item-pairs were very similar or identical in content, subjects could rate each item of a given pair in exactly the same manner, in which case they would obtain a absolute difference score for that item-pair of zero. If they rated the two items of the item-pair exactly oppositely, they would obtain an absolute difference score of 6 (after conversion to the seven-point scale). Subjects completing the inventory at random would generate an absolute difference score of 3.0 on the average. Subjects having a marginal reliability index (an average absolute difference score of greater than 2.00 for the five item-pairs) were eliminated.

Eliminating unreliable subjects resulted in 285 individuals having an acceptable reliability index for the eyes-closed condition, 89 having an acceptable reliability index for the eyes-open condition, and 345 having an acceptable reliability index for the hypnotic induction condition. This represents 88%, 81%, and 86%, respectively, of the subject pool.

Reliability Analyses

Subject's responses to the three items composing each dimension were averaged to arrive at an attention intensity score for each subject for each condition.

To determine reliability, coefficient alphas were computed for each dimension using all three items for the eyes open, eyes closed, and hypnosis conditions. Eight of the 12 dimensions were found to have coefficient alphas of above .60 when averaging across the three stimulus conditions. For the four dimensions that were left, eliminating one item from one of the dimensions resulted in an acceptable alpha (.71) for that dimension (detachment). Alphas across all 12 dimensions averaged .65. Table 8.2 lists the reliability coefficients for the stimulus conditions. (Three dimensions, flexibility, equanimity, and vigilance, had alphas of .47, .47, and .45, respectively. Analyses were still performed using these

Table 8.2. Coefficient Alphas for the Attention Questionnaire across Several Different Stimulus Conditions

Dimension	Stimulus condition[a]			
	Eyes open	Eyes closed	Hypnotic induction	Average
Flexibility	.40	.59	.42	.47
Equanimity	.29	.56	.56	.47
Detachment	.63	.67	.83	.71
Perspicacity	.54	.73	.71	.66
Locus	.65	.76	.79	.73
Direction	.77	.80	.84	.80
One-pointedness	.73	.71	.65	.70
Absorption	.73	.81	.83	.79
Control	.71	.76	.87	.78
Vigilance	.33	.37	.64	.45
Density	.54	.53	.75	.61
Simultaneity	.57	.68	.69	.65
Average	.57	.66	.72	.65
n	89	285	345	

[a] Excludes subjects with a reliability index > 2.0.

dimensions but with the realization that these dimensions were much less reliable than the others.)

Validity

Predictive Validity. To determine how well the 12 attention dimensions might predict hypnotic susceptibility, a regression analysis was done with the subjects' Harvard Group Scale scores as the dependent variable and the intensity scores for the 12 attention dimensions as the independent variables.

For the hypnotic induction condition, 10 of the 12 attention dimensions were utilized in the regression equation (direction and density did not meet criterion) with a resulting multiple R of .61 ($p < .0001$). Table 8.3 lists the multiple R's, the simple r's, and the unstandardized regression coefficients (whether using all dimensions or only those significant at the .01 level). Dimensions having the highest Pearson r correlations with hypnotic susceptibility were: absorption ($r = .56$), control ($r = -.48$), vigilance ($r = -.35$), locus ($r < -.33$), and perspicacity ($r = .30$).

Table 8.3. Attention Dimension Predictors of Hypnotic Susceptibility (Assessed during Hypnosis) from Stepwise Multiple Regression[a]

Dimension	Multiple R	Multiple R^2	Change in R^2	B[b]	B[c]	r[d]
Absorption	.56	.317	.317	.74	.72	.56**
Locus	.585	.342	.024	.18	.17	.33**
Control	.596	.356	.013	−.20	−.20	−.48**
Perspicacity	.601	.361	.006	.24	.25	.30**
Vigilance	.609	.370	.009	−.23	−.23	−.35**
Simultaneity	.609	.371	.0009	−.09	−.07	−.21**
Flexibility	.610	.372	.0005	.06	.06	−.25**
Detachment	.6101	.3722	.0004	.04		−.02
Equanimity	.6102	.3724	.0001	.03		.01
One-pointedness	.6103	.3725	.0001	−.03		.11*
Constant				3.07	3.26	

Simple correlations of dimensions not meeting inclusion criteria:

Direction						.21**
Density					−.02	−.20**

[a]From Pekala & Kumar (1988). Reprinted with permission of the publisher. Copyright 1988, Baywood Publishing Co., Inc.
[b]Unstandardized coefficients using all dimensions.
[c]Unstandardized coefficients using only dimensions significant at alpha < .01.
[d]* = $p < .05$; ** = $p < .001$.

As can be seen from the table, absorption accounted for the greatest percentage of the variance in terms of predicting susceptibility.

A regression analysis was also performed using the 12 dimensions for the eyes-closed condition. This resulted in an R of .29 ($p < .01$) between these dimensions and the Harvard Group Scale scores. (An analysis for the eyes-open condition was not completed due to the comparatively small n for that condition, $n = 89$.)

Several of the attention questionnaire dimensions (absorption, direction of attention, and control) were the same as (sub)dimensions of the PCI (being composed of almost exactly the same items). Since the PCI was given concurrently with the attention questionnaire, the relationship between the PCI dimensions and the same dimensions of the attention questionnaire were assessed via Pearson r correlations. Correlations of .68, .78, and .73, respectively, were found for absorption, direction, and control, suggesting these dimensions were tapping similar constructs with the attention questionnaire as with the PCI.

Discriminant Validity: Attention Intensity Comparisons as a Function of Individual Differences. To determine the nature of attentional intensity differences between eyes open/closed and hypnosis as a function of low, medium, and high hypnotic susceptibility, subjects having a reliability index of 2 or less for *both* the eyes open/closed and the hypnotic induction conditions ($n = 291$) were divided into three approximately equal groups of low (0–4, $n = 92$, $M = 2.33$), medium (5–7, $n = 105$, $M = 5.99$), and high (8–12, $n = 94$, $M = 9.41$) susceptible subjects.

Multivariate analyses of variance were then performed utilizing conditions (eyes open/closed, hypnosis) as the repeated measures factor, groups (low, medium, and high susceptibility), and subject groups (subjects were run in five groups, four of whom experienced eyes closed sitting quietly first, and one group, eyes open sitting quietly first) as between-group factors and the attention dimension scores as the dependent variables.

No significant multivariate main effects or interactions were found involving subject groups, which suggested no contraindications for combining the eyes open and closed subject groups. Concerning the other statistical comparisons, results indicated significant main effects for conditions [$F(12, 277) = 33.77$, $p < .0001$], and groups [$F(24, 552) = 5.67$, $p < .0001$], and a significant interaction between conditions and groups [$F(24, 552) = 3.26$, $p < .0001$].

Due to the significant multivariate effects, separate groups (3) by conditions (2) repeated measures ANOVAs were then performed for each of the attentional dimensions. Table 8.4 lists the F-test comparisons

Table 8.4. *F*-Test Comparisons for the Main Effects and Interaction for the Attention Questionnaire

| | Main effects[a] | | Interaction[c] |
	Conditions[b]	Groups[c]	
Flexibility	39.49***	7.92***	4.34*
Equanimity	28.51***	1.83	3.37*
Detachment	88.88***	2.96	0.35
Perspicacity	10.94**	10.63***	3.29*
Locus	20.09***	11.06***	4.87**
Direction	14.00***	8.94***	2.74
One-pointedness	3.40	0.64	1.33
Absorption	4.57*	41.32***	20.08***
Control	76.25***	36.82***	8.11***
Vigilance	27.96***	9.86***	11.11***
Density	41.35***	0.21	6.53**
Simultaneity	78.79***	1.77	2.38

[a] * = $p < .05$; ** = $p < .01$; *** $p < .001$.
[b] $df = 1/288$.
[c] $df = 2/288$.

for the main effects and the interactions. For the conditions main effect, 11 of the 12 dimensions significantly differentiated hypnosis from eyes open/closed. Hypnosis, vis-à-vis eyes open/closed, was associated with decreased attentional flexibility, control, vigilance, density, simultaneity, and, surprisingly, decreased absorption. It was also associated with increased equanimity, detachment, and perspicacity; a feeling of being out of one's body; and an inward-directed attentional focus.

Concerning the groups main effects, 7 out of 12 comparisons were significant. Student-Neuman-Keuls post hoc comparisons indicated that high susceptibles, vis-à-vis low susceptibles, reported decreased attentional flexibility, control, and vigilance and increased attentional perspicacity and absorption. Highs also reported a more inward attentional focus and an attentional locus "out-of-the-body."

Concerning simple main effects, during eyes open/closed, medium- and high-susceptible subjects reported significantly less control than lows. During hypnosis, mediums and highs reported significantly decreased flexibility and density, and increased perspicacity than lows. Highs, vis-à-vis mediums and lows, reported significantly increased absorption, decreased vigilance, and control, and more of a feeling of being out of one's body.

In addition, 8 out of 12 possible interactions between conditions and

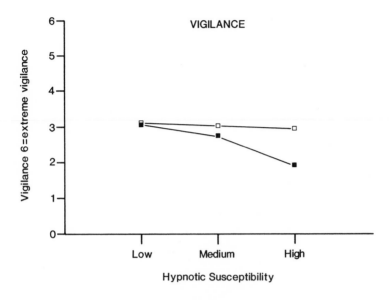

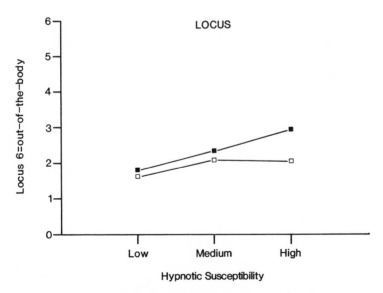

Figure 8.1. Intensity effects for two dimensions of attention as a function of conditions and hypnotic susceptibility (□, eyes open/closed; ■, hypnotic induction).

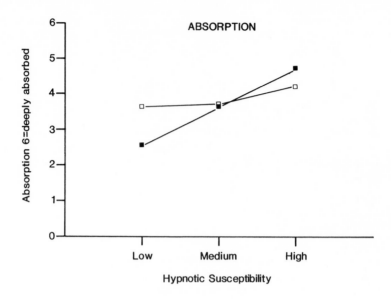

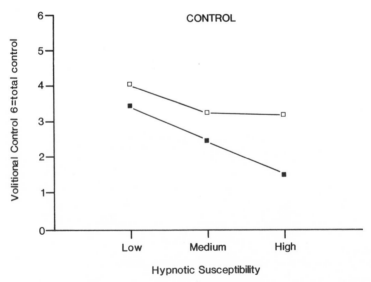

Figure 8.2. Intensity effects for two dimensions of attention as a function of conditions and hypnotic susceptibility (□, eyes open/closed; ■, hypnotic induction).

groups were significant, involving seven ordinal and one disordinal interactions. Figures 8.1 and 8.2 illustrate several of these interactions. For flexibility, equanimity, locus, control, vigilance, perspicacity, and density, hypnosis appeared to potentiate the reported differences between conditions for high as opposed to low (and medium, to a lesser extent) susceptible subjects. Whereas hypnosis was associated with increased absorption for high susceptibles, it was associated with decreased absorption, or increased distractibility, for lows.

Multivariate analyses of variance were also performed as a function of gender (male, female), groups (low, medium, high susceptibility), and conditions (eyes open/closed, hypnosis). Neither the main effect for gender nor the interactions with groups or conditions were significant.

Discussion

Reliability and Validity

Approximately 12 to 20% of the subjects were found to be less than adequately reliable at completing the attentional inventory (had a reliability index score of greater than 2.0). This is somewhat higher than that obtained with the PCI with these same subjects (Kumar & Pekala, 1989). The results may relate to the increased difficulty of being reliable with these items, due to the nature of their content and the fact that a more subtle differentiation is needed than when completing the PCI in reference to subjective experience. Thus, asking subjects to make subtle differentiations dealing with attention is probably more difficult to do than making such distinctions with consciousness in general. The fact that the Dimensions of Attention Questionnaire (DAQ) was piggy-backed on the PCI may also have had an effect if subjects became fatigued with completing the PCI and then began to complete the attentional items. In any event, it appears that attentional experience may be somewhat more difficult to assess than consciousness in general.

The coefficient alpha analyses suggest that 9 of the 12 dimensions of the attention questionnaire are reasonably reliable. The other three dimensions are not and research has been completed to increase reliability of those dimensions by writing additional items (Pekala & Forbes, 1990).

Regression analyses were able to generate a multiple R of .61 between the attention dimensions (during hypnosis) and subjects' resulting Harvard Group Scale scores, suggesting reasonable predictive validity. A multiple R of .61 is only somewhat less than the multiple R of .71 that was obtained when the PCI (sub)dimensions were used to predict hypnotic susceptibility (Pekala & Kumar, 1985) and suggests reasonably good predictive validity.

The finding that the three dimensions of the inventory that are the same as the PCI (and composed of almost identical items) gave Pearson *r* correlations of approximately .73 suggests that these dimensions are tapping the same subjective domains as that of the PCI (convergent validity). In addition, attentional experience appears to have been discriminated among low, medium, and high susceptibles suggesting evidence of discriminant validity.

Little differences in phenomenological attention were found for the dimensions between eyes open and closed. It is unknown as to whether this is due to the questionnaire's inability to make more subtle discriminations between these conditions or was due to a lack of significant differences in attentional experience between conditions. It would seem, however, that closing one's eyes should have some effect on attentional experience, at least as concerns direction of attention.

This lack of significant intensity differences between eyes open and closed suggests that the principle of specificity (specifically, different condition specificity) was not supported (although it was when comparing hypnosis against the eyes open/closed condition). The PCI, given to these same subjects, also failed to find significant intensity differences between eyes open and closed (Kumar & Pekala, 1989).

It appears, however, what when comparisons are made across the *same* subjects, as was done with the (Abbreviated) Dimensions of Consciousness Questionnaire [(A)DCQ] for the eyes open and closed conditions (Pekala & Wenger, 1983) instead of across *different* subjects, significant differences between the conditions were found. Such repeated-measures comparisons would reduce the error variance and thus be more likely to evince a significant effect, should it exist. Hence, whether the present results are evidence against the principle of different condition specificity for these two conditions, or is due to other reasons, must await future research.

Attentional Differences between Baseline and Hypnosis
as a Function of Individual Differences

The significant differences between conditions (baseline and hypnosis) for 11 of the 12 attention dimensions suggests that attentional experience is reported to be quite different between that occurring during hypnosis and eyes open/closed sitting quietly. In reference to these comparisons, not surprisingly, hypnosis was associated with decreased control, vigilance, and density (a decrease in thoughts, feelings, sensations, etc.); an increased feeling of detachment from the objects of attention; an increase in equanimous perception; a more inward attentional focus; the feeling that one's attention was located out of one's body; and a feeling of attentional expansion (perspicacity). Somewhat surprisingly, it was associated with decreased absorption and decreased flexibility. (The decreased absorption result may have been due to the increased distractibility of hypnosis vis-à-vis eyes open/closed for mainly the low susceptibles, which, nevertheless, had a significant effect when averaging across all subjects.)

Only one comparison, that of control, was significantly different between high susceptibles and low susceptibles during baseline (when analyzing the results separately for eyes open/closed and hypnosis). Yet there were many significant differences between lows and highs during hypnosis. That hypnosis appears to potentiate differences in attentional experience more for highs than lows during hypnosis than eyes open/closed is supported by the above results and also by the significant ordinal interactions for flexibility, equanimity, locus, control, vigilance, and density.

These findings agree with earlier research with the PCI (Kumar & Pekala, 1988) where hypnosis potentiated the phenomenological differences between hypnosis and baseline for high as opposed to low susceptibles and appear to highlight the importance of both trait, state, and situational variables (Hilgard, 1977) in regard to the reported attentional effects associated with hypnosis.

STUDY 2

Development of the Dimensions of Attention Questionnaire

Due to the low reliability of several of the attention dimensions reported in the first study, a second study was completed that used a revision of the earlier attentional instrument. The previous research found 4 of the 12 attention dimensions (detachment, flexibility, equanimity, and vigilance) with less than acceptable alphas.

For these dimensions, additional items were written so that each of these dimensions were composed of four items each (the other attention dimensions continued to be composed of only three items). An additional pair of reliability items were then written so that the DAQ had six pairs of reliability items.

The result was a 40-item inventory called the Dimensions of Attention Questionnaire (DAQ) (Pekala, 1985d, 1991a) that mapped 12 dimensions of attentional experience. Two forms of the DAQ were constructed. Both forms have the same items, although the sequence of items are differently arranged across the two forms. Attentional items were also arranged by randomized block design according to attentional dimension, so that no two attentional items from the same dimension would be adjacent. So that the reader will have some idea as to the nature of each of the DAQ dimensions, the next several paragraphs will describe the content of each of the attention dimensions. (The reader is referred to Appendix B for a list of each of the items as a function of attentional dimension.)

Attentional flexibility refers to the extent to which attention is "very flexible" and easily able to focus on thoughts, feelings, or sensations versus an inability to focus attention easily, that is, "I felt it very difficult to move and focus my attention." Attentional equanimity, on the other hand, refers to the ability to be "equally attentive to every thought, feeling, sensation, etc." versus not being equally attentive to the objects of attention.

Attentional detachment refers to being "very distant and detached" from feelings, thoughts, sensations rather than being "absorbed" in those thoughts, feelings, and sensations. Perspicacity refers to a spatial expansion of awareness. It was developed to help measure "mystical" aspects of attentional experience, such as Yogananda (1974) has reported experiencing. With perspicacious attentional experience, consciousness is reported to be spatially expanded, as if "consciousness felt like a sphere of awareness illuminating everything within it," versus the normal, nonaltered state when consciousness is not felt to be spatially expanded.

Attentional locus refers to whether consciousness is felt to be localized within or "out of" the body. Attentional direction refers to whether consciousness is directed toward the environment or toward one's own subjective, internal experience; and absorption, as with the PCI, refers to whether consciousness is "extremely distracted" or rather is "deeply absorbed."

One-pointedness was added to assess how focused attention can become, as with concentrative meditation. Attention can be "focused on a single subjective event to the exclusion of all other events" or attention can be focused on many different impressions. Attentional control is basically the same as volitional control with the PCI. One is able to either "let go" of attentional experience and become receptive to that experience or one can be actively involved in that experience.

Attentional vigilance refers to whether one is "extremely vigilant and continually observant of everything" in one's attentional field versus not being so vigilant and observant. Attentional density refers to the "amount" of thoughts, feelings, and sensations going through consciousness. One's attentional field can be "completely empty of any sensations, feelings, thoughts, etc." or one's attentional field can feel "crowded with too many sensations, etc." Finally, attentional simultaneity refers to whether attention is "aware of many sensations, thoughts, feelings, etc. simultaneously" or whether attention is only aware of one sensation, thought, and so on at a time.

After revision of the attention questionnaire into the DAQ, another study was completed that compared the attentional effects associated with three stress management conditions and a baseline comparison condition. (This study is reported in Pekala & Forbes, 1990.)

Design

This second study investigated the phenomenological effects of attention associated with four stimulus conditions: a baseline condition of eyes closed (of two-minute duration), a two-minute period following deep abdominal breathing, and two-minute periods embedded near the end of progressive relaxation instructions, and the induction procedure of the Harvard Group Scale of Hypnotic Susceptibility (Shor & Orne, 1962). The latter two conditions can be considered stress management techniques (American Society of Clinical Hypnosis, 1973; Berstein & Borkovec, 1973), while deep abdominal breathing is a short procedure that has also been associated with stress reduction (Fried, 1987).

The first study found significant main effects and a significant interaction between conditions (eyes closed/open, hypnosis) and susceptibility groups (low, medium, high) for various aspects of attentional experience. Hence, it was hypothesized that there would be significant attentional differences between stress management conditions (including baseline) for the present study, and that individuals of differing hypnotic susceptibility would report significantly different attentional experiences that might be further moderated by type of stimulus condition.

Method

Subjects and Materials

The subject pool consisted of 300 nursing students. The Harvard Group Scale of Hypnotic Susceptibility (Shor & Orne, 1962) was used to assess susceptibility. The previously defined DAQ (Pekala, 1985d) was used to map attentional experience.

Procedure

Three hundred subjects were seen in ten groups during two sessions spaced approximately one week apart. For the first session subjects sat quietly with their eyes closed for two minutes and then retrospectively completed the DAQ, Form 1, in reference to that time period. Subjects then experienced a slightly modified form of progressive relaxation (Bernstein & Borkovec, 1973) to which a two-minute sitting-quietly interlude was added near the end. Subjects then retrospectively completed the DAQ, Form 2, in reference to the two-minute period embedded in the progressive relaxation instructions immediately after the relaxation routine.

For the second session, subjects were taught deep abdominal breathing (Fried, 1987). Subjects did three rounds of deep abdominal breathing with their eyes closed and continued to sit quietly with their eyes closed for an additional two minutes. Afterward they completed the DAQ, Form 1, in reference to the two-minute period.

Subjects then experienced the induction procedure of the Harvard Scale (Shor & Orne, 1962). After the eye catalepsy instructions but before the posthypnotic suggestions and amnesia instructions, the subjects experienced a two-minute period during which they were told to continue to experience whatever they were experiencing at that time. After the end of the hypnosis procedure and after writing down a list of the hypnotic suggestions remembered (and after removal of the amnesia), the participants completed the DAQ, Form 2, in reference to the two minute time period.

Results

Preliminary Analyses

Dimensions of Attention Questionnaire inventories were available on 297 subjects for the baseline condition, 293 for progressive relaxation, 277 for deep abdominal breathing, and 280 for hypnosis. Completed data (without omissions or errors) on *all* inventories were available on 246 subjects, which represented 82% of the original subject pool. (No subjects were eliminated due to marginal unreliability, as was the case in the first study.)

Coefficient alphas across all 12 DAQ dimensions averaged .72, .75, .75, and .79, respectively, for the eyes-closed, progressive relaxation, breathing, and hypnosis conditions. Alphas for the individual dimensions, averaging across all four conditions, were: flexibility (.73), equanimity (.75), detachment (.78), perspicacity (.71), locus (.75), direction (.85), one-pointedness (.67), absorption (.82), control (.79), vigilance (.72), density (.76), and simultaneity (.73) (see Table 8.5).

Subjects were then divided into four (susceptibility) groups, based on their scores on the Harvard Scale: lows (scores of 0-4, $n = 68$, $M = 2.25$), low-mediums (5–6, $n = 51$, $M = 5.53$), high-mediums (7–8, $n = 70$, $M = 7.56$), and highs (9–12, $n = 57$, $M = 9.74$).

In order to compare conditions without confounding order effects, the baseline condition was compared against the breathing condition (the first set of conditions experienced each session) and the progressive relaxation condition was compared against the hypnosis condition (the second set of conditions). Multivariate analyses of variance were performed with (susceptibility) groups as the independent variable, conditions as the repeated-measures factor, and the DAQ dimension intensity scores as the dependent variables. Alphas was set at .01 for all MANOVA and ANOVA analyses to be conservative.

Progressive Relaxation versus Hypnosis

The multivariate analyses revealed a significant main effect for conditions and groups. The interaction between conditions and groups was

Table 8.5. Coefficient Alphas for the Dimensions of Attention Questionnaire across Several Different Stimulus Conditions

		Stimulus condition			
Dimension	Baseline	Progressive relaxation	Deep breathing	Hypnosis	Average
Flexibility	.74	.67	.75	.75	.73
Equanimity	.74	.72	.78	.75	.75
Detachment	.80	.77	.74	.79	.78
Perspicacity	.69	.65	.72	.78	.71
Locus	.67	.76	.74	.81	.75
Direction	.83	.83	.87	.86	.85
One-pointedness	.70	.64	.67	.65	.67
Absorption	.83	.78	.80	.86	.82
Control	.73	.80	.75	.88	.79
Vigilance	.60	.74	.75	.78	.72
Density	.64	.84	.73	.84	.76
Simultaneity	.71	.74	.70	.77	.73
Average	.72	.75	.75	.79	.76
n	297	293	277	280	

also significant. Due to the significant main effects and interaction, ANOVA analyses were performed for each of the 12 DAQ dimensions, with groups as the independent variable, conditions as the repeated-measures factor, and DAQ attentional intensity scores as the dependent variable.

Significant main effects were found for conditions for perspicacity, absorption, and control, with progressive relaxation being associated with increased perspicacity and absorption, but decreased control vis-à-vis hypnosis. Significant main effects for groups were found for perspicacity, locus, direction of attention, absorption, control, and vigilance. Repeated-measures post hoc comparisons were performed. To offset inflation of alpha levels for the six possible post hoc comparisons (per dimension), alpha was set at .002 using the Bonferroni (Kirk, 1968) adjustment procedure. The results revealed that high susceptibles (vis-à-vis low susceptibles) reported increased perspicacity, absorption, a more inward-focused attention, more of a feeling of being out of one's body, and decreased control and vigilance.

Significant interactions between conditions and groups were found for absorption, control, and vigilance. Whereas low susceptibles reported significantly increased absorption but significantly decreased control and vigilance during progressive relaxation than hypnosis, high susceptibles reported no significant differences between relaxation and hypnosis for either absorption, control or vigilance.

Deep Abdominal Breathing versus Baseline

The MANOVA analyses indicated significant main effects for conditions and groups when comparing baseline against deep abdominal breathing. The interaction between conditions and groups was not significant. Due to the significant main effects, ANOVAs were performed for each of the 12 DAQ dimensions with groups as the independent variable, conditions as the repeated measure, and DAQ intensity scores as the dependent variable.

Significant main effects were found for conditions for equanimity, detachment, perspicacity, locus, vigilance, and density. Breathing, vis-à-vis baseline, was associated with significantly increased attentional equanimity and detachment and significantly decreased attentional perspicacity, locus (more within the body), vigilance, and density.

Significant main effects ($p < .002$) were found for groups for locus, absorption, and control. Post hoc analyses (using the aforementioned Bonferroni correction procedure) revealed that high susceptibles reported significantly decreased control and an attentional locus that was more out-of-the-body than low susceptibles (the comparison for absorption approached significance, $p < .004$, with highs reporting being more absorbed than lows).

Factor Analyses

The DAQ results from each of the four stimulus conditions were also factor analyzed. The dependent variables consisted of the intensity scores for the 12 DAQ dimensions, and these variables were submitted to a principal components analysis followed by Varimax rotation (with an eigenvalue set at 1.0) for each of the three stress management conditions and also the baseline condition.

For each of the four Varimax solutions for the four conditions, there were four factors generated (see Table 8.6). For the baseline condition, detachment, direction, one-pointedness, and absorption were grouped together, as were perspicacity, locus, and control. The two other factors consisted of flexibility and equanimity; and vigilance, density, and simultaneity. For the progressive relaxation condition, the groupings were as follows: detachment; perspicacity, locus, one-pointedness, density, and simultaneity; flexibility and equanimity; and absorption, control, and vigilance.

For the deep abdominal breathing condition, the groupings were: detachment, direction, and absorption; perspicacity, locus, and control; flexibility and equanimity; and one-pointedness, vigilance, density, and simultaneity. The hypnosis condition factor solution led to the following breakdown: vigilance, density, and simultaneity; perspicacity, locus, absorption, and control; detachment, direction, and one-pointedness; and flexibility and equanimity.

Comparing across conditions indicates that flexibility and equanimity were found to be factored together in four of the four conditions. They appear to be somewhat similar to Silverman's (1968) selectivity factor, although this factor also loads highly on the extent to which sensations are sampled equally, suggesting that this dimension is probably an equanimity/selectivity factor. Concerning density and simultaneity, they were found to be factored together four of four times, and vigilance was grouped in this factor three of the four times. This factor appears to correspond to Silverman's extensivity factor.

Perspicacity and locus were found to be grouped together in the same factor four of four times, while control was grouped into this factor three of four times. It does not appear to fit into any of Silverman's three categories and is labeled a "diaphany" factor, since the items making up these dimensions suggest that attention has become passive and recep-

Table 8.6. Factor Analyses for the Dimensions of the Dimensions of Attention Questionnaire as a Function of Stimulus Condition

	Stimulus condition							
	Baseline		Progressive relaxation		Deep breathing		Hypnosis	
Dimension	Factor[a]	Loading	Factor	Loading	Factor	Loading	Factor	Loading
Flexibility	3	.74	3	.67	3	.75	4	.75
Equanimity	3	.76	3	.83	3	.83	4	.86
Detachment	1	−.83	1	−.78	1	−.88	3	−.80
Perspicacity	2	−.61	2	.63	2	−.68	2	.78
Locus	2	−.80	2	.74	2	−.87	2	.80
Direction	1	.79	4	.80	1	.73	3	.67
One-pointedness	1	.56	2	−.55	4	.62	3	.54
Absorption	1	.82	4	.82	1	.77	2	.60
Control	2	.72	4	−.63	2	.76	2	−.76
Vigilance	4	−.53	4	−.62	4	−.63	1	.71
Density	4	−.72	2	.81	4	−.65	1	.80
Simultaneity	4	−.75	2	.70	4	−.77	1	.82
Variance accounted for by the four factors:	65.3%		69.7%		68.7%		76.3%	

[a] Numbers in each column refer to the factor that the dimension loaded highest on, while the loading is the factor loading for that dimension for that factor. Dimensions having the same factor number per column thus denote the factor subsuming those dimensions for that stimulus condition.

tive, located more out-of-the-body, and more "tenuous," "transparent," and "spatialized."

The final factor, composed of the DAQ dimensions of detachment, direction, one-pointedness, and absorption, appears to fit Silverman's intensivity factor. Here, however, the clustering was not quite as definitive as with the other factors. Detachment factored into this factor three of the four times; direction, two of the four times; absorption, two of the four times; and one-pointedness only once.

Other Results

The second study also attempted to replicate the comparison between hypnosis and baseline, even though in the present study they occurred during different sessions (in the first study, the hypnosis followed the baseline condition during the same session). Significant MANOVA analyses were found for conditions, groups, and the interaction between conditions and groups. ANOVA analyses replicated almost all of the significant conditions and groups effects, and six of the eight interaction effects found significant in the first study (Pekala & Kumar, 1988).

Discussion

Reliability and Validity

The fact that subjects were not eliminated because of marginal reliability (only about 5% were marginally unreliable, that is, had a reliability index score of greater than 2.0) suggests that most all subjects were reasonably reliable at retrospection of attentional experience. The greater unreliability of the earlier study may relate to the tighter time constraints of that study, in addition to the larger group size.

The reliability results suggest that the dimensions of the DAQ are reasonably reliable. Considering the fact that the DAQ dimensions are composed of only three or four items, the coefficient alpha results appear quite good. The significant conditions and groups effects when comparing the hypnosis and baseline conditions replicates most of the results obtained during the first study and supports the discriminant validity of the DAQ.

The fact that the DAQ dimensions tended to factor together in terms of four general factors, that of attentional intensivity, extensivity, equanimity/selectivity, and diaphany, partially supports the theorizing and research of Silverman (1968), and also supports the construct validity of the DAQ.

Stress Management Results

The present study suggests that hypnosis and progressive relaxation are not equivalent stress management strategies as demonstrated in their associated attentional effects, although they may be more similar than different (9 of the 12 attentional dimensions were not found to be significantly different from one another). The analyses suggest that progressive relaxation differs from hypnosis concerning reported attentional effects associated with absorption, control, and perspicacity, although the differences across conditions are complicated by the significant interaction for two of these three (absorption and control). (There was also an additional significant interaction for vigilance.)

The interactions suggest that the reported attentional effects associated with hypnosis versus progressive relaxation are moderated by a person's hypnotic susceptibility such that low susceptibles report significantly greater alterations in attentional experience during progressive relaxation than hypnosis for absorption, control, and vigilance, but there are no such differences for high susceptibles. This suggests that progressive relaxation may be a "better" procedure to use with low susceptibles than hypnosis, at least if one wants to increase absorption and decrease vigilance and control. The significant main effects for groups also suggest that one's hypnotic susceptibility augments the reported attentional effects, but more so for hypnosis than the other strategies and baseline.

The data demonstrated attentional differences between eyes closed and deep abdominal breathing. The nature of these results suggests that deep abdominal breathing is reported to be associated with increased "calmness of mind," at least in reference to baseline, as demonstrated by increased detachment and equanimity and decreased vigilance and density (the "amount" of thoughts going through one's mind). Regardless of the psychophysiological effects of deep abdominal breathing (Fried, 1987), the data suggest important phenomenological effects associated with the practice of this technique, at least in comparison to a baseline condition.

In summary, the results of Study 2 not only support the reliability and validity of the DAQ[1] (Pekala, 1985d, 1991a), but they appear to have generated some interesting data concerning differences between progressive relaxation and hypnosis that may have important clinical implications.

---

[1]The researcher or clinician interested in using the Dimensions of Attention Questionnaire (DAQ) (Pekala, 1985d, 1991a) can procure the inventory, manual scoring sheets, and supporting materials from the Mid-Atlantic Educational Institute, Inc., 309 North Franklin Street, West Chester, Pennsylvania 19380-2765.

III

The Methodology

Graphing Devices for the Retrospective Phenomenological Assessment Instruments

Although a review of the methodology for using the Phenomenology of Consciousness Inventory (PCI) and other retrospective phenomenological assessment (RPA) instruments will not be given until the next chapter, this chapter will describe the several graphing devices that have been developed to diagram phenomenological experience. Once these devices have been described, it will be easier to review the methodological limitations of the PCI and similar instruments and their use with the graphing devices discussed below. (To simplify the following discussion, the different graphing devices will only be discussed in terms of the PCI. The Dimensions of Attention Questionnaire (DAQ) could just as easily been used to illustrate most of what will be discussed in terms of the PCI.)

PSYGRAMS

Introduction

The *psygram* is a dia*gram* of the *psy*chophenomenological state associated with a specific stimulus condition, hence the name psygram. It allows for the phenomenological pattern (and associated intensity) parameters of a given stimulus condition to be presented to the reader in pictograph form.

The psygram was developed primarily as an alternative to the correlation matrix for the illustration of pattern relationships among PCI dimensions. In attempting to determine the nature of the pattern structure from a 9- or 12-dimension correlation matrix, I was overwhelmed by the amount of data that I would need to integrate and compare if using a correlation matrix. This was especially difficult, given that the nature of a 12×12 correlation matrix (using the 12 major PCI dimensions) made it difficult to just match up one PCI dimension with that of another, let alone determine the nature of the correlations for more that several pairs of dimensions at once.

I felt this was due to the fact that a correlation matrix presents data that have to be digested sequentially, linearly, and digitally. If it were possible to present that same data in a visual-spatial manner, one could call on the simultaneous and holistic processing of the right, instead of the left, hemisphere (Ornstein, 1972) to cognize and understand the nature of the pattern relationships among dimensions. This device would hopefully allow the reader to more easily compare the nature of the associations between pairs of PCI dimensions than would be possible with the visual array of a correlation matrix.

I believe a psygram meets that need and does it extremely well. In the process of trying to publish papers in professional journals, some reviewers have complained that a psygram does not add anything new to the data contained in a correlation matrix, and hence they preferred the correlation matrix. I am convinced, however, that a psygram allows the reader to easily "see" the nature of the associations between pairs of PCI dimensions more easily than a correlation matrix because that information is presented visually instead of digitally. In the following section, you can decide for yourself which is the easier of the two modes of presentation to cognitively digest.

The Nature of a Psygram

A psygram consists of small circles, each representing a major dimension of consciousness, that are positioned on the circumference of a much larger circle. Intensity scores for each dimension are coded within the circles in terms of colors or black and white (using shading designations). For color-coding, a particular color corresponds to a particular intensity value from 0 to 6 (the (sub)dimension intensity ranges for a seven-point Likert scale); for black and white coding a variety of shading designations can be used. For the following example, intensity parameters have been coded in terms of rotated parallel lines.

To code for pattern relationships between dimensions, lines are drawn connecting the two circles. The lines between the different dimensions represent statistically significant correlations between the PCI dimensions that have been converted to coefficients of determination (simply the square of the Pearson *r* correlation coefficients). Hence, the lines represent the proportion of variance in common between the dimensions in question. Psygrams thus illustrate *not* the correlations between dimensions, but rather the *variance in common* between dimensions. It was decided to utilize coefficients of determination instead of correlations so that the reviewer could look at a psygram and tell from the drawing what percentage of variance two PCI dimensions have in common. It was felt that this was a better descriptor of the "pattern" relationships between dimensions than its associated correlation.

To make the exact magnitude of the coefficients of determination easy to determine, all lines connecting PCI dimensions have the exact coefficient, converted to a percentage, depicted next to its associated lines. (Coefficients based on negative correlations have a minus sign associated with them.) I have chosen to let each line represent approximately 5% of the variance in common. (If the researcher is without a color option, the lines representing negative correlations may be dashed and can be shown with a corresponding negative number.)

Thus, the more lines, the greater the variance in common and hence the higher the correlation between dimensions. To assure that only statistically significant correlations are represented, I have generally chosen to represent only those variances that denote a significant correlation between dimensions, with an alpha level of no greater than .05 (although I have also opted for an alpha value of .01 or .001 depending on the size of the sample and how conservative I want to be).

Figure 9.1 and Table 9.1 illustrate the relationship between a psygram and its corresponding correlation matrix. Table 9.1 depicts the correlation matrix for the 12 major dimensions of consciousness assessed by the PCI during the stimulus condition of eyes open sitting quietly. Figure 9.1 depicts the pattern of interrelationships among the 12 dimensions for the same stimulus condition in terms of various percentages corresponding to coefficients of determinations significant at the .01 level. Figure 9.1 also depicts the PCI mean intensity ratings for each dimension, coded in terms of rotated parallel lines within each circle.

As the reader can see, there is a strong association between altered state and altered experience, as there is between rationality and memory, memory and vivid imagery, and vivid imagery and inward absorbed

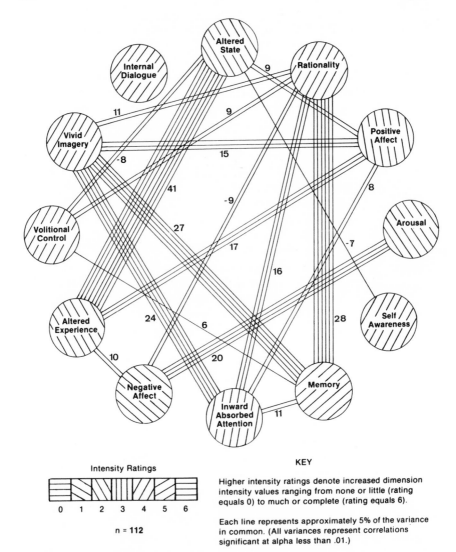

Figure 9.1. A PCI psygram: Eyes open sitting quietly. (From Pekala & Kumar, 1986. Reprinted with permission of the publisher.)

attention. The exact variance percentages are listed adjacent to their corresponding lines. Many other minor associations are also evident. A psygram thus provides an overall picture of the pattern of relationships in terms of connections or associations between pairs of dimensions for a specific stimulus condition. It can be conceptualized as a visual depiction of a phenomenologically based parallel distributed processing

Table 9.1. Intercorrelation Matrix of the 12 Dimensions of Consciousness Assessed by the PCI during Eyes Open[a,b]

	1	2	3	4	5	6	7	8	9	10	11	12
Self-awareness[c]	1.00	-.26**	.06	-.08	.15	.09	.07	-.08	.00	-.22*	-.03	-.10
State of awareness		1.00	-.03	.11	-.28**	-.07	.14	.30***	.12	.64***	-.02	.11
Internal dialogue			1.00	.04	-.02	-.21*	-.18	-.01	-.09	-.09	-.07	-.13
Rationality				1.00	.30***	.53***	-.23*	.00	-.30**	-.10	.40***	.33***
Volitional control					1.00	.25**	.17	-.14	-.05	-.10	.22*	.21*
Memory						1.00	-.18	.07	-.17	-.01	.33***	.52***
Arousal							1.00	.13	.45***	.22*	.04	.02
Positive affect								1.00	.01	.41***	.28**	.39***
Negative affect									1.00	.32***	.02	-.05
Altered experience										1.00	.08	.10
Vivid, visual imagery											1.00	.49***
Inward, absorbed attention												1.00

[a]From Pekala & Kumar (1986). Reprinted with permission of the publisher.
[b]$n = 112$.
[c]$* = p < .05$; $** = p < .01$; $*** = p < .001$.

(PDP) approach (McClelland & Rumelhart, 1988) to mapping the relationships among certain phenomenological processors or dimensions of consciousness.

So that the reader has some idea as to what psygrams are all about and how they can be useful, several psygrams of various stimulus conditions and subject types are presented.

States of Consciousness Associated with Specific Stimulus Conditions

Figures 9.2 through 9.4 (reported in Pekala, 1985a) represent psygrams of the states of consciousness associated with several stimulus conditions that were assessed by the Phenomenology of Consciousness Questionnaire (PCQ). (The PCQ has only nine major dimensions.) Figure 9.2 represents the state of consciousness associated with sitting quietly with eyes open. Waking consciousness, as assessed during this stimulus condition, is reported to be associated with little negative affect, mild alterations in awareness and experience, some positive affect, a moderate amount of vivid imagery and internal dialogue, moderate volitional control, an attentional state that is inwardly focused and relatively absorbed, and a relatively intact memory.

Figure 9.3 depicts the state of consciousness associated with reading erotic material (from Nin, 1978) of a mildly arousing nature. In relation to waking consciousness (Figure 9.2), there is a significant increase in imagery and positive affect, a loss of volitional control, and a slightly more inward and absorbed attentional focus. Internal talking to oneself is also significantly decreased in comparison to baseline. In terms of pattern relationships, Figure 9.3 is noticeably different (and statistically different as measured by the Jennrich test) from Figure 9.2. Although the relationship between imagery and attention and awareness and altered experience remain approximately the same as baseline, awareness and volitional control are now strongly coupled, while positive affect and altered experience and volitional control and altered experience have also become strongly coupled. Many more associations between various other dimensions are evident.

Concerning Figure 9.3, there is no perceived alteration in subjective experience (as assessed by the altered awareness dimension) in comparison to baseline. But since there is a significant pattern change, the phenomenological state associated with the reading erotica condition, in comparison to baseline, fits Tart's (1977) definition for an identity state of consciousness. (At a later point in this book I have found it more feasible to rename what Tart calls an identity state of consciousness as a discrete state of consciousness.)

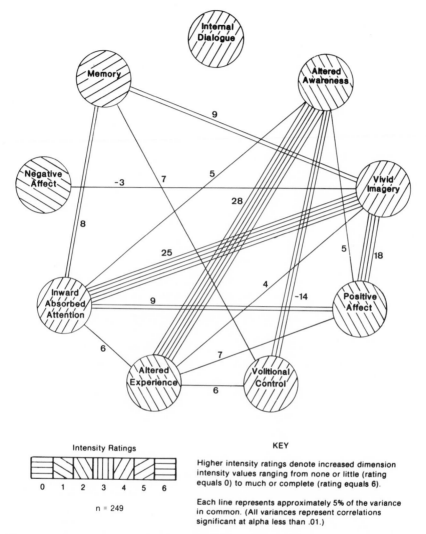

Figure 9.2. Psygram 1: Eyes open sitting quietly. (From Pekala, 1985a. Reprinted with permission of the publisher.)

Figure 9.4 depicts the state of consciousness associated with the stimulus condition of relaxing to one's breathing (after having experienced deep muscle relaxation). Attention has now become more absorbed and inwardly directed than in any of the other conditions. In comparison to baseline, there is a very significant loss of volitional control, greater alterations in awareness, memory, and altered experience,

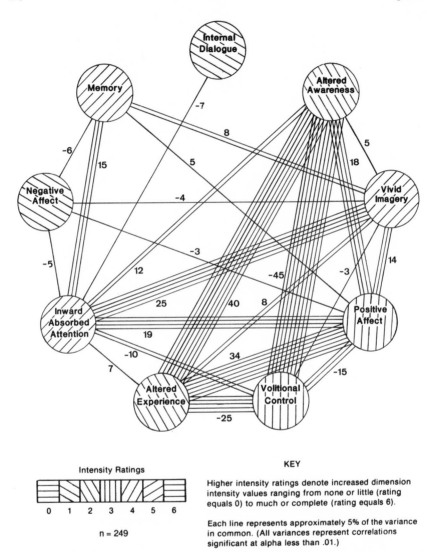

Figure 9.3. Psygram 2: Reading erotica. (From Pekala, 1985a. Reprinted with permission of the publisher.)

and significant decreases in the amount of internal dialogue and positive and negative affect. When comparing psygrams, there is also a significant pattern change among dimensions in comparison to the other conditions. Although awareness and volitional control are strongly coupled, the only other major connections concern memory and volitional control and awareness and altered experience.

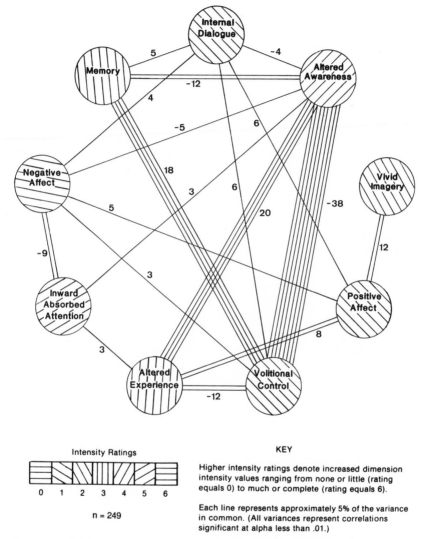

Figure 9.4. Psygram 3: Relaxation/meditation. (From Pekala, 1985a. Reprinted with permission of the publisher.)

Since the phenomenological state associated with the relaxation/meditation condition, in comparison to baseline, is associated with a significant pattern change and a significant perceived alteration in subjective experience (as assessed by the altered awareness dimension), it fits Tart's (1977) criteria for an altered state of consciousness. Retrospective phenomenological assessment thus permits the researcher to assess identity and altered states of consciousness associated with specific stimulus conditions, as defined by Tart, while psygrams allow for these phenomenological states to be visually depicted.

States of Consciousness Associated with Different Subject Types

Figures 9.5 and 9.6, respectively, depict the states of consciousness of low ($n = 60$) and high ($n = 60$) *absorption* individuals during eyes open sitting quietly. Absorption is a trait assessing "openness to absorbing and self-altering experiences" (Tellegen & Atkinson, 1974) that is mildly to moderately correlated with hypnotic susceptibility. Besides its correlation with hypnotic susceptibility, absorption has been found to be associated with differential responsivity to meditation (Greenfield, 1977), marijuana intoxification (Fabian & Fishkin, 1981), and electromyogram biofeedback (Qualls & Sheehan, 1981a,b).

Tellegen (1981) has hypothesized that the trait of absorption appears to tap eight content areas. These include: imaginative and oblivious involvement, affective responsiveness to engaging stimuli, responsiveness to high "inductive" stimuli, vivid reexperiencing of the past, expansion of awareness, powerful "inductive imagining," imaginal thinking, and cross-modal experiencing. Given the above, high-absorption individuals might differ phenomenologically from low-absorption-individuals; differences that may be evident in psygrams.

Figures 9.5 and 9.6 represent the assessment of eyes open sitting quietly with the Dimensions of Consciousness Questionnaire (DCQ), a precursor of the PCI. The DCQ was given to 304 undergraduates to complete immediately afterward in reference to eyes open sitting quietly. The states of consciousness of those 60 participants scoring lowest and highest on the absorption scale of Tellegen are represented by the psygrams (Pekala, 1985a).

A comparison of Figures 9.5 and 9.6 indicate that high-absorption subjects reported experiencing significantly more imagery and positive affect (sexual excitement), a greater loss in awareness, and increased alterations in subjective experience in comparison to lows (Pekala *et al.*, 1985). Especially noteworthy, however, are the pattern relationships among dimensions between highs and lows. (The patterns of association between highs and lows are significantly different as assessed by the Jennrich test.) For low-absorption subjects, rationality, volitional control, and awareness are all moderately coupled. A loss of control is associated with decreased rationality, both of which are associated with a loss of awareness. Besides an association between awareness and altered experience, the only other associations concern relationships be-

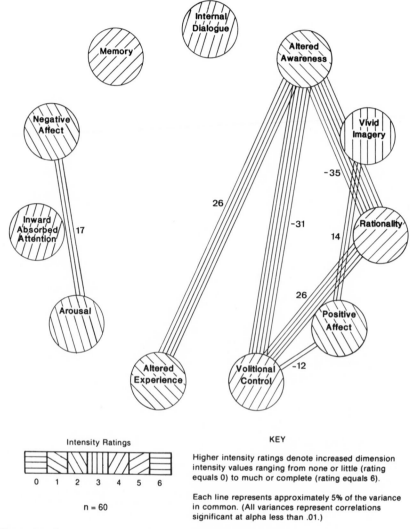

Intensity Ratings

0 1 2 3 4 5 6

n = 60

KEY

Higher intensity ratings denote increased dimension intensity values ranging from none or little (rating equals 0) to much or complete (rating equals 6).

Each line represents approximately 5% of the variance in common. (All variances represent correlations significant at alpha less than .01.)

Figure 9.5. Psygram 4: Low-absorption individuals: Eyes open sitting quietly. (From Pekala, 1985a. Reprinted with permission of the publisher.)

tween negative affect and arousal, vivid imagery and positive affect, and positive affect and volitional control

When comparing the low-absorption psygram with that of the high, most noticeable are the lack of relationships (for lows vis-à-vis highs) between imagery and attention, memory and rationality, and positive

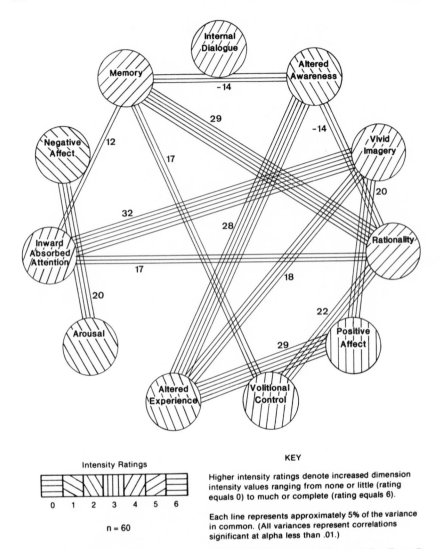

Figure 9.6. Psygram 5: High-absorption individuals: Eyes open sitting quietly. (From Pekala, 1985a. Reprinted with permission of the publisher.)

affect and altered experience. Also lacking are significant relationships between rationality and attention, volitional control and memory, and altered awareness and memory. The wealth of associations between many dimensions for highs but not lows suggests major differences in the reported patterning or processing of information for these two groups of individuals.

The psygram findings concerning attention appear consistent with the hypothesizing of Tellegen (1981) on the nature of absorption. Highs appear to couple inward and absorbed attention with imagery in a way not found with low-absorption individuals. The different pattern structure between highs and lows also suggests that highs are in a different state of consciousness, relative to lows, during ordinary waking consciousness. This may help explain why high-absorption individuals find it easier to be hypnotized or easier to enter other altered states of consciousness than lows.

Psygrams Assessed during Hypnosis

Probably one of the best ways to illustrate the possible usefulness of psygrams is to depict an altered state of consciousness and assess that state across groups of subjects thought to experience that state of consciousness differently. Figure 9.7 depicts the state of consciousness associated with a four-minute segment during the induction procedure of the Harvard Group Scale of Hypnotic Susceptibility (HGSHS) (Shor & Orne, 1962) assessed across individuals who subsequently scored low (HGSHS scores of 0–5) on that scale. (PCI intensity data are not depicted on the following psygrams.) During the four-minute period, subjects were told to just sit quietly and continue to experience the state they were in (Pekala & Kumar, 1985).

While Figure 9.7 depicts the "hypnotic state" across low-susceptible subjects, Figure 9.8 depicts the hypnotic state across high-susceptible subjects (HGSHS scores of 9–12). As the reader can easily see, whereas the various dimensions for low-susceptible subjects are highly correlated and hence strongly coupled to each other, very few dimensions are correlated with high-susceptible individuals. Hence, the dimensions of consciousness assessed by the PCI for high susceptibles are relatively independent of each other.

These results appear to support Hilgard's (1975) neodissociation theory of hypnosis. Hilgard's neodissociation theory of hypnosis postulates a hierarchy of control systems operating at any one time in a given individual and views hypnosis as modifying the hierarchical arrangement of these controls so that some become segregated (dissociated) from others (1975, p. 24).

The psygrams of Figures 9.7 and 9.8 (which are statistically different from one another using the Jennrich test) indicate that the subsystems or dimensions of consciousness for low susceptible subjects are highly associated during hypnosis, while that of highs are not. Thus, the structures or dimensions of consciousness of the highs, vis-à-vis lows, can be said to be independent (which statistically they are) of one another and

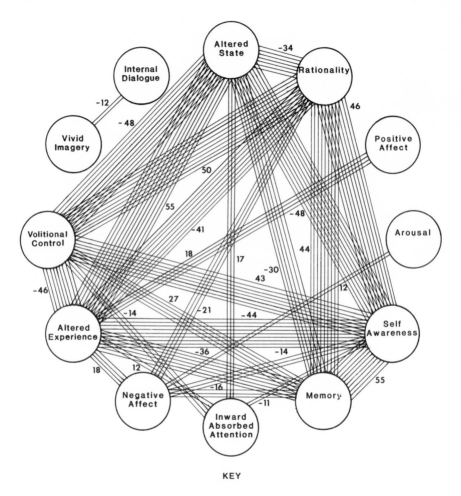

KEY

Each line represents approximately 5% of the variance in common.

(All variances represent correlations significant at alpha less than approximately .01.)

n=65

Figure 9.7. Low-susceptible individuals: Hypnotic induction. (From Pekala & Kumar, 1986. Reprinted with permission of the publisher.)

hence "disassociated" from one another. Whereas changes in rationality or volitional control consistently lead to changes in self-awareness or altered state (or vice versa) for lows, such changes are not necessarily found to occur for highs. Thus, lows appear to have a much more "rigid" structure or organizational pattern among most dimensions of consciousness during hypnosis while that of highs do not.

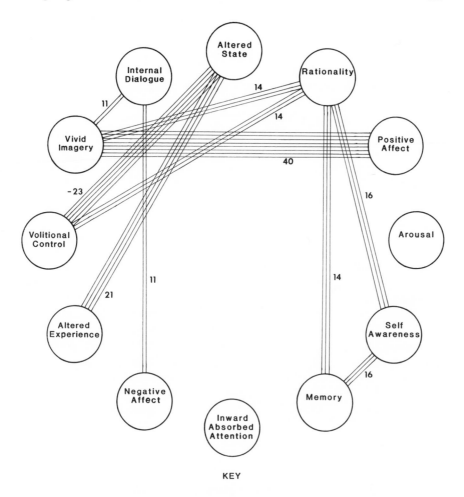

KEY

Each line represents approximately 5% of the variance in common.

(All variances represent correlations significant at alpha less than approximately .01.)

n=57

Figure 9.8. High-susceptible individuals: Hypnotic induction. (From Pekala & Kumar, 1986. Reprinted with permission of the publisher.)

Replication of such statistical independence between subsystems should help to shed greater light on Hilgard's neodissociation theory. These results suggest that the use of the PCI and psygrams appears to give a methodology whereby such theories about hypnosis and possibly other altered states can be statistically assessed and visually depicted.

Conclusions

Psygrams, graphs of the psychophenomenological state associated with various stimulus conditions (Pekala, 1985a), allow for baseline, identity, and altered states of consciousness (Tart, 1975, 1977) to be diagramed and visually presented. They hopefully will provide useful devices to diagram and understand states and altered states of consciousness and the various structures and patterns between structures comprising these states.

PIPS

Introduction

A *phenomenological intensity profile*, or *pip*, represents a graph of the (sub)dimension intensity variations across an individual or group of individuals. A pip permits the various (sub)dimensions of the PCI to be graphed to give a profile of an individual's or group's (sub)dimension intensity scores for the PCI (or the DAQ) for a given stimulus condition.

Quite simply, a pip has various dimensions or subdimension of the PCI along the horizontal axis and percentile scores or raw scores along the vertical axis. Pips provide a means to visually inspect the (sub)dimension intensity variations evident for a given individual or group of individuals, while also allowing for various individuals or groups of individuals to be compared with one another in different states of consciousness.

Format

I have chosen to construct PCI pips in two forms, A and B, and two modes, unscaled and scaled. The Form A pip depicts the 12 major dimensions mapped by the PCI, while Form B pips depict the 14 minor dimensions or subdimensions mapped by the PCI. In addition, a scaled pip depicts a given (sub)dimension intensity score in terms of percentiles, while an unscaled pip depicts the profile in terms of raw scores. Figure 9.9 illustrates a Form A scaled pip, depicting the 12 major PCI dimensions along the x-axis and the percentile scores of a PCI administration along the y-axis.

Percentile scores for the scaled pips were used instead of z or t scores, due to the possible nonnormality for various intensity distributions in various stimulus conditions. Scaled pips may be especially important to use when one wants to compare or graph the (sub)dimension

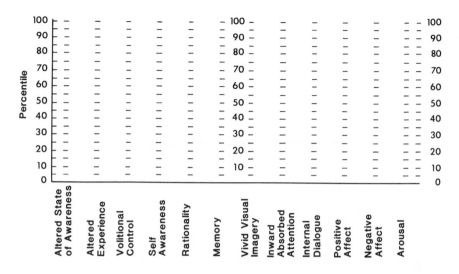

Higher scores denote percentile ranks of subjects having increased dimension intensity values ranging from none or little (score of 0) to much or complete (score of 100).

Figure 9.9. Phenomenological intensity profile using the PCI.

intensity scores of an individual or group of individuals in a particular altered state induction procedure, such as hypnosis. Obviously, scaled pips can only be used in reference to stimulus conditions or altered state induction procedures that have already been mapped and quantified by the PCI (or other self-report RPA instruments). Data on the stimulus conditions of eyes open (EO) sitting quietly, eyes closed (EC) sitting quietly, and a hypnotic induction (HI), as measured by the Harvard Group Scale (Shor & Orne, 1962), are currently available for the PCI. (Raw score conversion tables for Forms A and B of the PCI and also the DAQ are listed in Appendix E.)

Illustrating the Use of Pips

To illustrate the potential usefulness of pips, Figure 9.10 depicts the scaled pip of subjects during hypnosis who scored 0, 4, 8, and 12 on the Harvard Group Scale (assessed in reference to a four-minute period during the induction period; Pekala & Kumar, 1984). As can be seen from the graph, nonsusceptible hypnotic subjects (a Harvard scale score of 0) scored in the bottom 10th percentile concerning alterations in state

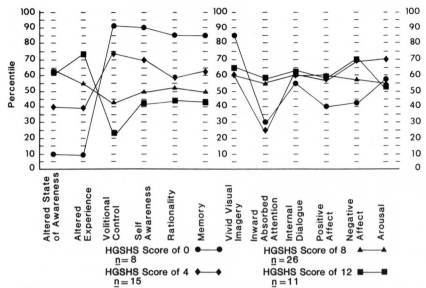

Higher scores denote percentile ranks of subjects having increased dimension intensity
values ranging from none or little (score of 0) to much or complete (score of 100).

Figure 9.10. Phenomenological intensity percentile scores for subjects during hypnosis
having HGSHS scores of 0, 4, 8, and 12. (From Pekala & Kumar, 1984. Reprinted with
permission of the publisher.)

of awareness and altered experiences, yet they scored in the 80th to 90th
percentiles concerning relatively intact memory, volitional control, self-
awareness, and rationality. Interestingly, they had the most vivid, visual
imagery of the four groups, scored in the 30th percentile concerning
inward, absorbed attention (indicating relatively distractible, outward-
directed attention), and experienced the least positive and negative
affect.

In contrast, highly susceptible subjects (a Harvard score of 12) were
in the 60th to 70th percentiles concerning alterations in awareness and
experience, had the least volitional control, and the least self-awareness,
rationality, and memory of all four groups. In terms of the profiles, it
appears that the low susceptibles were the most dissimilar of the four
groups.

Pip Interpretation

Although the pip was patterned after the Minnesota Multiphasic
Personality Inventory (MMPI) (Hathaway & McKinley, 1948), it cannot

be used in predicting, say, hypnotic susceptibility as the MMPI can in predicting psychopathology. By looking at an MMPI profile, a clinician can make judgments about an individual's personality functioning and attempt to make diagnostic predictions about that particular individual. Although a pip can be used to determine how much imagery, volitional control, or positive or negative affect a person reports during a given stimulus condition, such as hypnosis, visual perusal of a pip cannot be used to predict hypnotic susceptibility such as membership in low-, medium-, or high-susceptibility groups as measured by the Harvard Group Scale. This seems to be due to the fact that there is tremendous variation in the phenomenological correlates of being hypnotized as measured by the Harvard Group Scale.

In contrast to Figure 9.10, Figures 9.11 through 9.13 depict pips of individual subjects scoring 0, 6, or 12, respectively, on the Harvard Scale. Six subjects each are depicted for a given HGSHS score and they were randomly chosen from eight subjects having a HGSHS scores of 0, 15 subjects scoring 6 on the HGSHS, and 11 subjects scoring 12 on the HGSHS (total subject pool was 190). As the reader can see, although the

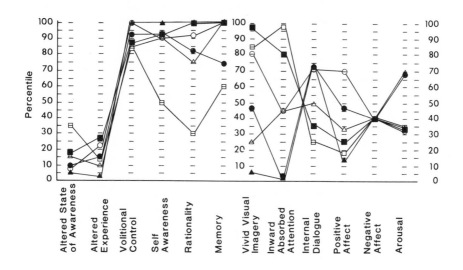

Higher scores denote percentile ranks of subjects having increased dimension intensity values ranging from none or little (score of 0) to much or complete (score of 100).

Figure 9.11. Phenomenological intensity percentile scores for six subjects during hypnosis having a HGSHS score of 0.

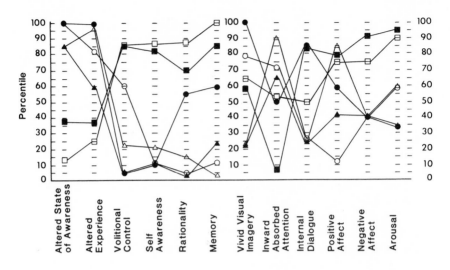

Higher scores denote percentile ranks of subjects having increased dimension intensity values ranging from none or little (score of 0) to much or complete (score of 100).

Figure 9.12. Phenomenological intensity percentile scores for six subjects during hypnosis having a HGSHS score of 6.

low-susceptible subjects appear to have pips that follow a general profile pattern, that of medium- and high- susceptible subjects do not.

As a check on this, several people were given pips of 8 low-, 8 medium-, and 11 high-susceptible subjects and asked to sort the pips according to profiles depicting the average of all subjects having HGSHS scores of 0, 6, and 12. There was no requirement that there should be a given number of profiles per group. The hit ratio (number of profiles successfully sorted) was 74%, 29%, and 59%, respectively, for low-, medium-, and high-susceptible subjects.

There are probably several reasons for the inability of pip visual analysis to predict hypnotic susceptibility. Whereas the MMPI is based on questionnaire items that largely assess various "trait" aspects of personality and psychopathology, the PCI is based on various highly fleeting and variable phenomenological "state" aspects of subjective experience. Given the variable nature of the stream of consciousness, such variability would be expected to reduce the relationship between susceptibility, assessed by the Harvard Scale, and the contents of consciousness during a single four-minute stimulus condition. This is supported

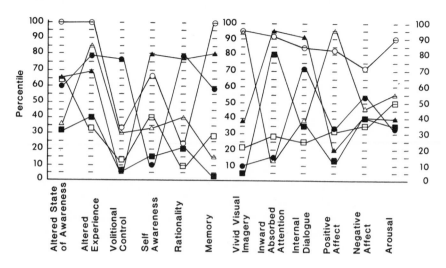

Higher scores denote percentile ranks of subjects having increased dimension intensity values ranging from none or little (score of 0) to much or complete (score of 100).

Figure 9.13. Phenomenological intensity percentile scores for six subjects during hypnosis having a HGSHS score of 12.

by the finding that the average test-retest reliability of the Phenomenology of Consciousness Questionnaire (PCQ), a precursor to the PCI, averaged only .43 across all dimensions of the PCQ, when completed in reference to two eyes-open sitting quietly conditions spaced a week apart (Pekala & Levine, 1982). Such moderate state-state correlations suggest that trait-state correlations between the Harvard Scale and the PCI may not be as high as trait-trait correlations between the MMPI and diagnostic categories. (This does not mean, however, that a linear combination of PCI (sub)dimensions intensity scores, such as would be obtained with a regression equation, may not be able to predict hypnotic susceptibility; see Chapter 14.)

It may also be the case that individuals who obtain a given score on the Harvard do not necessarily have exactly the same phenomenological experiences. As an example, a Harvard Scale score of 1 can be the result of the subjects passing one particular item out of a possible 12, while a Harvard Scale score of 6 can be the result of hundreds of different permutations of the 12 possible items. Since passing a given item may be associated with specific phenomenological experiences (for that item) that may be different from passing other items (Sheehan & McConkey, 1982), there may not be one specific phenomenological pattern that corresponds to a particular number of Harvard Scale items passed.

In addition, hypnosis may not generate one uniform state. There may be several "hypnotic" states, based not only on the instructions given to the subject, but the subject's own personality (Pekala, 1989). (See the next section of this chapter for additional data on this issue.) Hence, individual pips of high hypnotically susceptible individuals may be different because the subjects are using different modes of information processing during hypnosis (Sheehan & McConkey, 1982).

In conclusion, although the pip may not be a reliable means for visually predicting susceptibility on an individual basis, it can be a useful device for examining the various phenomenological parameters associated with various stimulus conditions, such as hypnosis, that a single individual or group of individuals have experienced.

ICONS

Introduction

An icon is another graphing device that allows the intensity scores of the PCI to be visually displayed. An icon is a device for displaying multivariate data (Cleveland, 1985; Everitt, 1978). Given a data pool that contains measurements on n cases involving p variables, an icon can be plotted (one for each case) with p different features for each icon. Although icons are not designed to communicate absolute numerical information, they are intended for recognizing clusters of similar objects and sorting or organizing objects that differ in many respects.

Although some theorists ridicule the use of icons, the cognitive science research has definitively shown that people can accurately categorize or sort multivariate data based on the appropriate visual cues (Garner, 1974; Spoehr & Lehmkuhle, 1982). An icon can be helpful in sorting individuals, or for visually cluster-analyzing response sets, in a way that would be quite difficult to do with, say, pips. Since the PCI is a multivariate instrument generating scores on 12 major and 14 minor dimensions of consciousness, the use of icons to display PCI (sub)dimension intensity effects across individual subjects or groups of subjects may be quite useful.

Whereas a pip has the various (sub)dimensions of the PCI on the x-axis and the intensity score for those dimensions on the y-axis to form a two-dimensional line graph, an icon is another means of displaying the same data in a two-dimensional format. The format I have adopted for icons uses the 12 major PCI dimensions. The various PCI intensities are then displayed on the face of an imaginary clock with each dimension corresponding to one of the 12 numbers on the clock; the distance from the origin corresponds to the various PCI dimensions' intensity scores.

Hence, whereas a pip (using the 12 PCI dimensions) of 12 subjects or 12 individual pips would be difficult to assess if one wanted to attempt to sort out different "types" or clusters of response sets, 12 individual icons, spaced adjacently, would allow the reader to more easily notice differences among individuals so that those individuals can be more easily differentiated than would be possible with pips.

Illustrating the Use of Icons

Design, Subject Pool, and Nature of Analysis

In order to demonstrate the usefulness of icons, this section will illustrate several icons associated with subjects of varying hypnotic susceptibility. (This section is partially based on Pekala, 1989, in press.) The subject pool consisted of the subjects from two studies (Pekala & Kumar, 1984, 1987). The 572 subjects experienced eyes closed sitting quietly for several minutes as a baseline condition. This was followed by the induction procedure of the HGSHS (Shor & Orne, 1962) to which was added a short sitting quietly period between the eye catalepsy item and the amnesia instructions of the Harvard Scale.

After the hypnosis, subjects retrospectively completed the PCI in reference to this sitting quietly period. Their hypnotic susceptibility was also determined based on their response to the Harvard Scale. After removal of marginally reliable subjects, subjects were divided into low- (Harvard Group Scale scores of 0–4, $n = 156$, $M = 2.40$), medium- (5–8, $n = 247$, $M = 6.53$), and high- (9–12, $n = 129$, $M = 10.21$) susceptible subjects. The subject pool was also divided into very-low- (0–1, $n = 47$, $M = 0.62$), and very-high- (11–12, $n = 49$, $M = 11.45$) susceptible individuals.

A three-tiered cluster analysis, employing K-means cluster analysis (Hartigan, 1975), was subsequently performed on the data using the K-means SYSTAT (Wilkinson, 1988b) data analysis program employing the 12 major PCI dimensions as the independent variables and subjects as the dependent variable. This clustering procedure is an iterative clustering procedure that assigns cases to a specified number of non-overlapping clusters. The "average" linkage method (Sokal & Michener, 1958) was chosen which "averages all distances between pairs of objects in different clusters to decide how far apart they are" (Wilkinson, 1988b,

p. 380). Clustering occurred on an $n + 1$ basis until fragmentation occurred, that is, cluster analysis occurred grouping subjects into 2, 3, 4, and so on mutually exclusive groups until one of the groups contained only one or a very few cases.

Cluster Analysis of Very-Low- and Very-High-Susceptible Groups

Separate cluster analyses were performed for the very-low- and very-high-susceptible groups until fragmentation occurred. This analysis yielded two cluster groups for the very-low individuals and two cluster groups for the very-highs. For the very-lows, the first cluster group was labeled "classic" very-lows, since their subjective experience, as reported by the 12 major dimensions of the PCI, appeared consistent with what refractory (Hilgard, 1965) subjects would report concerning their subjective experiences. The second group of very-lows were labeled "pseudo" very-lows since they reported experiences somewhat like what medium- or high-susceptible individuals would report during hypnosis. Whereas the former group reported subjective experience characterized by little alteration in altered state and experience, and almost complete control, self-awareness, memory, and rationality, the latter group reported moderate alterations in volitional control, self-awareness, rationality, and memory.

The cluster analysis of the very-highs yielded one group of subjects, who were labeled "classic" very-highs, since their phenomenological experiences were consistent with what somnambulists (Hilgard, 1965) would subjectively report during hypnosis. The second group of very-highs were labeled "fantasy" very-highs, since their experience was characterized by a predominance of imagery, positive affect, and rationality. Whereas the classic very-highs reported alterations in awareness and experience, losses of control, self-awareness, rationality, and memory, and little vivid imagery, the fantasy group reported a great deal of vivid imagery and moderate positive affect.

Figure 9.14 illustrates these four groups in terms of their associated icons (using the "star" icon command from SYGRAPH; Wilkinson, 1988a). As the reader can see, all four icons are quite different from one another.

Cluster Analysis of Low-, Medium-, and High-Susceptible Groups

Given the above cluster analysis, it was speculated if similar results would obtain with lows and highs, those subjects who scored 0–4 and 9–12 on the Harvard Scale, as was obtained with the very-lows and the very-highs.

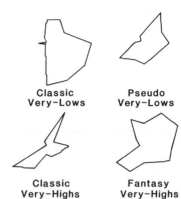

Classic
Very-Lows

Pseudo
Very-Lows

Figure 9.14. Icons for the four very-low/very-high susceptibility groups.

Classic
Very-Highs

Fantasy
Very-Highs

Hence, separate cluster analyses were performed for the low-, medium-, and high-susceptible groups using the same type of analysis as was completed with the very-lows and the very-highs. This analysis yielded three groups for the lows, two groups for the highs, and two groups for the mediums. Figure 9.15 illustrates their associated icons.

In comparing Figure 9.15 with Figure 9.14, the reader can seen that two of the three low cluster groups are very similar, if not identical, to the two very-low groups, and hence were labeled "classic" lows and "pseudo" lows, since their reported phenomenology was quite similar to that of the two very-low groups. A third cluster group of lows, labeled "dialoging" lows, was found that appeared quite similar to the "classic" lows, except that this group reported a great deal of internal dialogue.

A comparison of the icons for the highs with the very-highs also yielded two very similar groupings. The "classic" and "fantasy" highs reported phenomenological experiences very similar to the two very-high groups, as visually illustrated by the icons.

The similarity between the lows and highs and the very-lows and the very-highs, by inference, suggests that subjects who score 9–12 on the Harvard appear to report phenomenological experiences that cluster together almost identically to that of subjects who scored 11 and 12 on the Harvard. Similarly, individuals who scored 0–4 on the Harvard appear very similar phenomenologically to individuals who scored 0 and 1, except for a subgroup of individuals who report significant internal dialogue.

Cluster Analysis across All Subjects

Although there appear to be relatively distinct clusters of low and high, and very-low and very-high individuals, the question can be asked

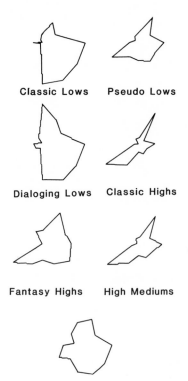

Classic Lows   Pseudo Lows

Dialoging Lows   Classic Highs

Fantasy Highs   High Mediums

Low Mediums

Figure 9.15. Icons for the low/medium/high susceptibility groups.

if these clusters would continue to hold up when cluster analyzing across all subjects, instead of just specific subsets of individuals.

For this purpose, a third cluster analysis was performed across all subjects (scores of 0–12). (Because of memory limitations in SYSTAT, a random sample of approximately one half of all subjects were used in this analysis.) The cluster analysis yielded four cluster groups, and Figure 9.16 illustrates these groups.

In comparing Figure 9.16 with Figures 9.14 and 9.15, the reader can see that two of the four icons of Figure 9.16 are very similar to two of the icons of Figure 9.14 and two of the icons of Figure 9.15, that is, the "classic" very-low and very-high and the "classic" low and high groups. Although this is partly due to the inclusion of the same subjects across the three sets of analyses, data analyses done with the lows and highs, while excluding the very-lows and very-highs (to achieve nonoverlapping subject groups), generated very similar results as the very-low and very-high groups (Pekala, in press).

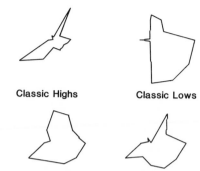

Classic Highs   Classic Lows

Figure 9.16. Icons for the four suscep-
tibility groups clustered across all subjects.   Dialoging Mediums   Nondialoging Mediums

A visual analysis of these three sets of icons suggests that there appear to be two distinct types of hypnotically susceptible individuals, in terms of reported PCI phenomenology, that occur whether looking across all subjects or only low- and high-susceptible subjects.

Conclusions

Icon visual analysis of PCI phenomenology as a function of suscep-tibility groups demonstrates how this approach can be useful in looking at the multivariate data generated by the PCI's 12 major dimensions across groups of individuals or individual subjects. The icon presents the PCI intensity data in a way that more easily allows for different types or clusters of subjects or individual subjects to be distinguished from one another than appears possible with pips. Icons may be especially useful when PCI (sub)dimension intensity values need to be compared across many different subjects.

HYPNOGRAPHS

Introduction

A *hypnograph* is a device to illustrate the "hypnoidal" state (Pekala & Nagler, 1989) that an individual experiences. A hypnoidal state is one (defined by a regression equation using the PCI) that is associated with the endorsement of PCI (sub)dimension intensity effects consistent with what high hypnotically susceptible individuals would endorse in refer-ence to a short (eyes closed) sitting quietly interval during the induction procedure of the Harvard Group Scale (Shor & Orne, 1962).

The PCI has been able to generate a validity coefficient of .65 (Pekala & Kumar, 1987) and .63 (Forbes & Pekala, 1991) between the actual Harvard Group Scale scores of a group of subjects and their predicted Harvard Group Scale (pHGS) scores (based on a regression equation using the regression coefficients obtained from another group of subjects).

The regression equation is composed of the unstandardized regression coefficients of ten of the PCI (sub)dimensions. It generates a pHGS score (based on a regression analysis reported in Pekala & Kumar, 1989, and listed in Table 14.3, page 317) that can theoretically range from $-.71$ to 11.77, although it usually ranges between 1 and 9 ($M = 5.97 \pm 1.82$). A score of 7 or above is indicative of being in a "hypnoidal" state (Pekala & Nagler, 1989), since high-susceptible individuals (individuals who scored 9 or above on the Harvard Scale) during hypnosis obtained averaged pHGS scores of 7 or above; such average scores were not obtained by highs during a baseline condition of sitting quietly with eyes closed or individuals during hypnosis or eyes closed who scored 8 or less on the Harvard Scale.

Whereas simple 1–10 depth scales give a subjective estimate of simple hypnotic "depth," the PCI pHGS score gives an intensity measure of the phenomenological experience associated with what subjects of varying hypnotic susceptibility would report during hypnosis. Being a linear combination of ten (sub)dimensions of the PCI, it may be a more stable measure of hypnotic "state" than linear depth scales, since it is sensitive to intensity variations along ten dimensions of subjective experience associated with being hypnotized.

A hypnograph allows the pHGS score associated with a particular stimulus condition to be graphed and compared to other stimulus conditions. Quite simply, a hypnograph is a bar graph that has the various stimulus conditions that an individual experiences along the x-axis, and the pHGS scores on the y-axis. A hypnograph thus illustrates the hypnoidal effects associated with various stimulus conditions and gives a measure of the extent to which the phenomenology of that state is consistent with what low or high hypnotically susceptible individuals would report during a sitting quietly period embedded in the Harvard Scale.

Illustrating a Hypnograph

Figure 9.17 illustrates the hypnograph of an individual whom we shall call Leo who was referred to a biofeedback clinic for headaches and flashbacks. He experienced frontal tension headaches radiating tem-

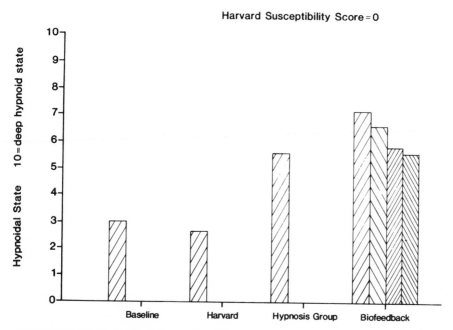

Figure 9.17. Hypnograph of the predicted Harvard Scale scores of Leo (▨, session 1; ▨, session 2; ▨, session 3; ▨, session 4).

porally approximately three times a week and also carried a post-traumatic stress disorder (PTSD) diagnosis. Leo obtained a Harvard Scale score of 0. Figure 9.17 illustrates his hypnoidal scores for baseline (eyes closed sitting quietly: pHGS score = 3.0), the Harvard Scale (score = 2.6), an eyes closed sitting quietly period (score = 5.6) during a hypnotherapy group (where he was taught self-hypnosis and given suggestions to deal with his headaches), and biofeedback training using analog and digital audio biofeedback (average score = 6.3).

As the reader can see, Leo was in a nonhypnoidal state during baseline and also during the Harvard Scale. Interestingly, he obtained a hypnoidal score of 5.6 during the hypnosis group, and somewhat higher hypnoidal scores during analog and digital EMG biofeedback training. This single case does not mean to imply that many low hypnotically susceptible individuals can experience greater hypnoidal effects during biofeedback than hypnosis or report greater hypnoidal effects during a clinical hypnosis trial than a more experimental hypnosis assessment session. However, the data do suggest that this individual experienced greater hypnoidal effects during both clinical trials than baseline or the

Harvard assessment. It illustrates how a hypnograph can be used to compare hypnoidal effects associated with different stimulus conditions across an individual.

Conclusions

Hypnographs provide a way to visually illustrate the hypnoidal effects associated with various stimulus conditions or altered state induction procedures across individual subjects or groups of subjects. They provide a way to visually compare such effects in a way that is easy to comprehend. Hypnographs, along with pips, icons, and psygrams, can provide the graphic means to illustrate the psychophenomenological data obtained from instruments like the PCI, the DAQ, and hopefully, other yet-to-be-developed RPA instruments.

RPA GRAPHING DEVICES CONSTRUCTION

Psygram Construction

Intensity Parameters

A psygram for the PCI is constructed using the format shown in Figure 9.1. The format consists of 12 small circles on the circumference of a much larger circle. (Although I have only constructed psygrams for the PCI major dimensions, they could also be constructed for the PCI minor dimensions or the DAQ dimensions.) Each of the 12 small circles corresponds to one of the 12 major dimensions of the PCI. The intensity values for each of the dimensions can be coded in black and white or color. If they are coded in black and white, I have found this easiest to do by coding the intensity values, which run from 0 through 6 (when using a seven-point Likert scale), in terms of rotated parallel lines, one integer corresponding to 30 degrees rotation clockwise, starting with zero at the negative x-axis.

Since I usually code intensity values with 0 to mean none or little, through 6, to signify "much or complete," the reader can usually tell at a glance which dimensions are activated and which are not. Differences in intensity values between dimensions may still be hard to recognize, however, and this is where color-coding intensity parameters can be so much more effective (if they can be done so commercially). If the psygram intensity values are coded in black and white, the exact intensity rating can still be listed inside the circle under the name of the particular dimension to clarify the intensity rating.

Pattern Parameters

The pattern relationships between dimension are depicted by means of lines connecting the various dimensions. Each line represents the proportion of variance in common between two dimensions and is simply the square of the correlation of the two dimensions.

Depicting only statistically significant correlations allows for only those relationships to be depicted that are not the result of chance. I have usually chosen a significance level of .01 so that the resulting variances would be more likely to be replicated across different groups of subjects. I also found that if I used the .05 level of significance when the number of subjects per group was very large (approximately 200 or more), there were so many lines on the psygrams due to more significant correlations and hence coefficients of determination that the resulting psygram became too complex and confusing to cognitively digest.

I have used the convention of having black lines represent percentages of coefficients of determination associated with positive correlations between dimensions and red to represent negative correlations (if the color option is available). When using only black and white, I have recently begun to depict coefficients of determination associated with negative correlations with a dashed (---) line and coefficients of determination associated with positive correlations with a straight (——) line. I have also used a single line to represent approximately 5% of the variance in common and multiple lines to represent multiples of 5%. Whether in color or black and white, I also label each line as to its exact percentage of variance in common, labeling negative variance percentages (correlations) with a negative number.

The lines representing the variance percentages in common are simply drawn approximately 1/32 of an inch apart from each other on the psygram format. The lines between each of the two circles then represent the variance percentages in common between the two PCI dimensions represented by those circles.

The use of this procedure allows for the pattern relationships between dimensions to be easily recognized and, in conjunction with the intensity codings, allows for the psychophenomenological state associated with a given stimulus condition to be put in diagram form. This psygram approach to mapping consciousness is especially appropriate when comparing states of consciousness associated with different stimulus conditions and/or subject types and allows the reader to easily see pattern differences across conditions and also intensity variations, especially if the intensity values are color-coded.

Pip Construction

Pips are phenomenological intensity profiles. They illustrate the intensity variations associated with the PCI major or minor dimensions in graph form and allow the researcher to visually assess for differences in intensity variations across the PCI dimensions.

Phenomenological intensity profiles are constructed relatively easily by using a graphics program such as Lotus 1-2-3. Whereas the x-axis represents the different major or minor dimensions of the PCI, the y-axis represents the intensity ratings. While unscaled pips use PCI or DAQ intensity ratings from 0 to 6 (when using a seven-point Likert scale) and hence are based on raw scores, scaled pips convert the raw scale to a scaled score before it is diagramed. If scaled scores are to be used (and norms are available), the researcher goes to the appropriate stimulus condition conversion table (see Appendix E for PCI and DAQ scaled scores for several conditions) to convert raw scores into scaled scores.

Icon Construction

An icon represents the 12 PCI major dimensions on the face of an imaginary clock. The 12 PCI dimensions correspond to the 12 hours on the clock, while the distance from the center of the clock is the PCI intensity rating for that dimension. Icons allow the PCI intensity ratings to be depicted more "compactly" than would be possible with a pip. Hence, if the researcher wants to compare intensity variations associated with 6 or 12 subjects and wants to check for overall differences between them, an icon would be a better displaying device than a pip. Where 12 separate pips or 12 sets of lines (corresponding to 12 subjects) on a single graph would be very hard to cognitively digest, 12 icons depicted adjacently is much easier to visually compare and evaluate.

Icons are constructed using the SYGRAPH (Wilkinson, 1988a) program. SYGRAPH and SYSTAT (Wilkinson, 1988b) are acronyms for the data analysis and graphics programs developed by Wilkinson. They provide the researcher with a very flexible data analysis and graphics system. "Star" icons are used and the experimenter needs merely to type in the values for the different PCI dimensions and the program will construct the icons.

To produce icons identical to those illustrated in this chapter, after typing the ICON command in SYSTAT, the following PCI major dimension intensity scores are typed in the following order: altered state of awareness, altered experience, volitional control, self-awareness, rationality, memory, imagery, attention, internal dialogue, positive affect, negative affect, and arousal.

Hypnograph Construction

Hypnographs allow for the "hypnoidal effects" (Pekala & Nagler, 1989) associated with a given stimulus condition to be visually displayed. Hypnoidal effects are the subjective effects associated with what subjects of varying susceptibility would report during hypnosis (in reference to a sitting quietly period embedded in the hypnosis) when using a standardized induction scale like the Harvard (Shor & Orne, 1962). Scores tend to range from 1 to 9. Scores under 3 are typical of what low-susceptible subjects (scores on the Harvard Scale of 0–4) would report on the Harvard while scores above 7 are illustrative of a "hypnoidal state" (Pekala & Nagler, 1989), since this is what high susceptibles (Harvard scores of 10–12) would report, on the average.

Hypnographs can be constructed using a variety of graphic programs. I generally use LOTUS 1-2-3 and use the y-axis for the hypnoidal state values from 0 to 10 and the x-axis for the different stimulus conditions that are to be graphed. A bar graph is then constructed for the different stimulus conditions experienced by the subject.

CONCLUSION

This concludes the chapter on the RPA graphing devices. The next chapter will review the administration and methodological and statistical limits for using the PCI and related instruments.

Using Retrospective Phenomenological Assessment Instruments

Theory and Praxis

ADMINISTRATION OF THE SELF-REPORT INSTRUMENTS

The Phenomenology of Consciousness Inventory (PCI), the Dimensions of Attention Questionnaire (DAQ), or another self-report instrument is administered by giving it to subjects to complete in reference to a preceding stimulus condition. Thus, if subjects sit quietly for four minutes, the questionnaire is completed after the four-minute period in reference to that time period. The PCI has been used in reference to time periods from two to four minutes, while the DAQ has been used in reference to time periods of two to three minutes. Asking subjects to complete the PCI or the DAQ in reference to longer time periods has not been investigated, although several researchers have given the PCI in reference to time periods as long as several hours (that research, to my knowledge, has not yet been published).

Previous to experiencing any stimulus condition for the first time, subjects should also be briefed as to the general nature of the task before them. Thus, if subjects are going to experience a baseline condition, such as eyes open sitting quietly for the first time (and would be subsequently completing the PCI), they may be told something like the following:

> I am interested in learning about your stream of consciousness, your subjective experience of yourself and the world around you. I will be asking you to engage in a short activity and then will ask you to write about your experience. I will ask about the sensations, perceptions, emotions, thoughts, images, and awareness levels that you experienced during the short time interval. In order for you to have some idea of what you will be asked about, I want you to read the set of instructions that will tell you what you will be asked to do.

These instructions (listed in the front of the PCI and the DAQ) acquaint the subjects with the upcoming task and sensitize them to the fact that they will be engaged in retrospective introspection, something which they do not usually do. Hence, subjects should read the instruction sheet that precedes the questionnaire itself before completing a self-report inventory for the first time.

The instructions explain how to complete the questionnaire and define several of the key concepts of the instrument. If subjects are going to use the questionnaire for the first time, the researcher may want the subjects to read the instructions before experiencing the first stimulus condition (the time period that subjects will afterward complete the PCI or the DAQ in reference to), although I have also had subjects read it afterward (but before completing the PCI or the DAQ) without any major ill effects.

Subjects then complete each item, putting their responses on the questionnaire itself or on an optical scanning sheet if the items are to be optically scored. In either case, subjects choose the rating for each item that best corresponds to their subjective experience during the time in question. Subjects do this for each of the items trying to be as accurate as they can without spending too much time on any one item.

After the subjects have experienced a given stimulus condition and are about to complete the self-report inventory for the first time, I usually tell them something like the following:

> Since introspection into your subjective experience is not something you normally do, it may be difficult. Please take your time and try to be as accurate as possible.

SCORING

Manual Scoring

The PCI and the DAQ can be scored manually or by computer after using optical scanning to convert scoring sheets to computer files. For manual scoring, subjects put their responses on the questionnaire itself, circling the number that best corresponds to their subjective experience. Scores are then transferred to the scoring sheets to manually compute intensity and reliability index scores.

Computerized Scoring

The PCI and the DAQ can also be computer scored. This is done by having the subjects put their responses on a computer data sheet which is subsequently optically scanned and converted to a computer file. The experimenter then uses a program to compute (sub)dimension intensity scores and reliability scores for each administration of the PCI or DAQ.

Intensity Scoring

SYSTAT (Wilkinson, 1988b) programs for converting the PCI, Forms 1 and 2, and the DAQ, Forms 1 and 2, from computer data to (sub)dimension intensity scores (and reliability data) are given in Appendix F. These programs give the reader an idea of various ways to approach the data transformations and are taken from the data contained in Appendixes C and D, respectively, which lists the items of the various (sub)dimensions of the PCI and the DAQ, including which items have to be reversed and the reliability item-pairs.

Pattern Scoring

A computer program (Pekala & Kumar, 1985), written in APL (Gilman & Rose, 1974), for testing correlation matrices for significant differences using the Jennrich (1970) test is available and listed in Appendix G. The APL program allows for two independent correlation matrices of n dimensions each to be statistically compared. APL was chosen, as opposed to FORTRAN or BASIC, since the APL program could be written in about 25 steps, which is much less than would be needed if FORTRAN or BASIC was used.

Once the program is keyed into the computer, the researcher needs only to type in the sample sizes for the two correlation matrices being compared, that is, the "M" and "N" of the program. The matrices, "X" and "Z," corresponding to sample sizes "M" and "N," respectively, are then keyed in, with only the lower left corner of the correlation matrix being input and with zeros in all other positions of the matrix (see Appendix G).

The program will then generate a chi-square value whose degrees of freedom is $p(p - 1)/2$, where p is the number of the dimensions of the matrix. The program illustrated in Appendix G employs sample sizes of 60 and 100, while the algorithm "X JENN Z" prompts the computer to issue the appropriate chi-square value. The program of Appendix G (p. 394) is written for a 3 × 3 correlation matrix. For a 12-dimension matrix, one simply changes steps 3, 5, 7, and 25 by substituting "12" for each of the "3s" used in the illustrated program. (Threes were used, instead of "12s," in the listed program so that the reader could easily test the program once it was typed in. The experimenter can then test the program using the smaller matrices, before changing the numbers to run a larger matrix problem.)

RATIONALE FOR THE USE OF RETROSPECTIVE PHENOMENOLOGICAL ASSESSMENT

As the review of Chapter 1 indicated, classical introspection went out of style after Titchener's death in 1927 because it demonstrated no functional use and because it was unreliable. Behaviorism then "took over" because it was quite easy to establish adequate reliability and proved itself to be quite functional and valuable.

Behaviorism defined its variables in terms of specific behaviors and stimulus settings. Thus, the reliability and validity of such variables could be more easily observed, assessed, and evaluated than could cognitions, affects, images, or awareness levels. This suggested to me that by combining the strengths of behaviorism's overt variables with introspection's covert events, phenomenological assessment might be made more reliable and valid. By evaluating phenomenological experience in reference to specific behaviors and stimulus settings, I hoped to increase the reliability and validity of phenomenological assessment by tying it to observable and repeatable stimulus conditions. (A stimulus condition is any stimulus environment in which the participant is involved, including the participant's own behavior, and any experimental manipulations enacted upon the individual. Experimental manipulations include verbal instructional sets and behavioral, physiological, biochemical, and related variables.)

The rationale for such a strategy has its roots in Angell's 1907 attack on structuralism. Angell attacked the structuralist's "state of consciousness" concept when he noticed that the elements of the state of consciousness that an individual reported were "dependent upon the particular exigencies and conditions which called them forth" (1907, p. 67). Hence, it was impossible to get an individual in one laboratory to agree with an individual in another laboratory. As a result, classical introspectionism failed.

This failure, I believe, was due in large measure to the fact that the "unit of measurement" was the individual observer. Given the vast individual differences across people, different people in different stimulus environments will report vastly different phenomena. However, randomly selecting a *group* of individuals and having them experience the same stimulus environments should greatly reduce the variance associated with individual differences and thus elucidate the phenomenological effects, across a group of individuals, associated with a given stimulus condition.

This is exactly what is done in retrospective phenomenological assessment (RPA). Subjective experience is assessed in reference to specific stimulus conditions and instructional sets, and the various structures of phenomenological experience such as imagery, cognition, affect, and so on are evaluated, quantified, and statistically assessed across groups of individuals. Following Angell (1907), since subjective experience is a function of the stimulus setting in which the individual is immersed, having a group of individuals retrospect in reference to a specific stimulus condition should make the subjective phenomena experienced a function of that condition, and hence give the subjective events assessed an overt referent. In addition, averaging across a group of individuals will reduce the variance associated with individual differences and thus allow for quantification of the *average* phenomenological intensity and pattern values associated with a given condition. The end result should be a more reliable and valid introspective methodology than that used in classical introspection.

As in the past, there has been controversy over the reliability of introspective data. Nisbett and Wilson (1977) have indicated that with regard to accessing cognitive processes, introspective access is "not sufficient to produce generally correct or reliable reports" (p. 233). Smith and Miller (1978), on the other hand, suggest that the assessment of cognitive processing may not be as inaccessible as Nisbett and Wilson indicate.

Nisbett and Wilson may be partially correct when relating individual's attributions or cognitions to their actions. But when asked to describe, not the reasons (the why) but the content (the what) of their subjective experience, people are much more accurate, as Ericsson and Simon (1980) and Lieberman (1979) have indicated. Lieberman's summary of the literature has indicated that although phenomenological assessment can sometimes be misleading or wrong, the classical and modern literature of introspective research has shown that such "data can be highly reliable and useful, helping not only to predict specific behavior, but to discover fundamental principles of learning and performance (e.g., Weber's law, and the role of imagery in verbal memory)" (p.

332). Hence, a review of the data suggests that a retrospective self-report methodology can be reliable, although that reliability must not be assumed but rather empirically demonstrated.

The question of the accuracy of phenomenological assessment also suggests that validity may be difficult to confirm. Although the research reviewed by Ericsson and Simon (1980), Klinger (1978), Lieberman (1979), and Singer and Kolligian (1987) indicates that introspective data can be both valid and useful, Rachlin (1974) and Skinner (1974) have strongly questioned the value and validity of introspective reports and have gone so far as to proclaim them superfluous.

Polemics notwithstanding, the question of the validity of introspective data must be based on empirical research. As with other areas of psychological research, the validity of introspective or phenomenological data will finally reside "in ruling out artifacts, in replications, and ultimately, in the usefulness of data or theory for making possible other forms of prediction and perhaps, control" (Klinger, 1978, p. 227). Because of the covert nature of subjective data, however, questions of validity will probably be harder to investigate than will overt behaviors. Hence, a critical, empirical assessment of the validity of phenomenological assessment is also necessary.

RATIONALE FOR THE PRINCIPLE
OF STIMULUS-STATE SPECIFICITY

Although adequate reliability and validity assures the potential usefulness of RPA, the fact that phenomenological experience is a highly fleeting and variable one suggests the *possibility* that the same stimulus conditions may nevertheless be associated with different intensities and patterns of phenomenological experience across groups of individuals. Such phenomenological variability across the same stimulus conditions, should it occur, would make it impossible to compare various stimulus conditions since there would be no consistent and repeatable baseline state associated with a particular stimulus condition.

Thus, if groups of subjects experience the same stimulus environments with the same instructional and experimental sets and yet report significantly different amounts of imagery, attentional focus, positive affect, and so on, it becomes difficult, if not impossible, to compare the phenomenological states associated with different stimulus conditions across groups of subjects if the same stimulus conditions are associated with different phenomenological experiences.

It is here that I coined the term of *stimulus-state specificity* (principle of specificity) (Pekala & Wenger, 1983) to denote the relationship between a particular stimulus condition and its corresponding phenomenological state. Concretely defined, this principle states that across groups of randomly selected individuals, the same behaviors enacted in the same stimulus settings (the same stimulus conditions) will be associated with the same intensities and patterns of phenomenological experience (the same phenomenological state), while differing stimulus conditions will be associated with different intensity and/or pattern parameters.

The purpose of specificity is just that: a principle that *presupposes* that a given stimulus condition will be associated with the same phenomenological parameters when assessed across groups of randomly chosen individuals. It needs further empirical validation. Although the research to date supports the principle of specificity for the same conditions (same-condition specificity), it is somewhat less robust for different conditions (different-condition specificity) (Kumar & Pekala, 1988; Pekala & Kumar, 1986; Pekala *et al.*, 1986). Hence, more research yet needs to be done.

The use of RPA, in conjunction with the principle of specificity, gives the researcher a methodology for assessing and evaluating phenomenological experience and allows for different and varying conditions to be compared with one another. Given that this is a relatively new methodology, more research needs to be done to determine if the reliability and validity of specificity holds up across various individuals and stimulus settings. The research to date has established that both RPA and same-condition specificity are valid, provided certain methodological and statistical limitations are followed. One of the purposes of this chapter will be to delineate the theoretical rationale, the methodology, and the statistical limits for when RPA and specificity appear valid and when that validity has not been empirically assessed. Although future research will undoubtedly change and modify what is written here, the following paragraphs will hopefully provide the basis for further research and hypothesis testing.

MAPPING STATES OF CONSCIOUSNESS
ACROSS GROUPS OF INDIVIDUALS

Tart (1975, 1977) has indicated that the study of states of consciousness must first be done on an individual basis. Only when the states of consciousness of individuals have been investigated will researchers be able to map states of consciousness across groups of subjects. Thus, Tart (1975) writes:

> I cannot emphasize too strongly that the mapping of experience and the use of the concepts of d-SoCs *must first be done on an individual basis. Only* then, *if* regions of great similarity are found to exist across individuals, can common names that apply across individuals be legitimately coined. (p. 144)

Yet the approach advocated in this book is basically a nomothetic as opposed to an idiographic approach. Hence, the (sub)dimension intensity and pattern parameters obtained by RPA are usually procured across groups of individuals. Such an approach was chosen mainly for two reasons.

Classical introspection was basically an idiographic approach, with single individuals introspecting and describing their subjective experiences. Based on introspection of individual subjects (including the researcher himself), the researcher then arrived at inferences concerning the structures of subjective experience. Yet classical introspection was found to be not only unreliable, but also useless, to quote Watson (1913). This was partially due to the tremendous individual differences in subjective experience across groups of individuals. If a given person thinks in terms of images, while another in terms of verbal thoughts, it will be extremely difficult for the above individuals to agree on the nature of their subjective experience.

Figures 10.1 and 10.2 are a contemporary illustration of this. These figures illustrate the frequency of subjects having different percentages of various aspects of subjective experience during four stimulus conditions: two conditions of eyes open sitting quietly, one condition of reading erotica, and one condition of relaxation/meditation (Pekala, 1980). As the reader can easily see, there is tremendous variation across individuals as to the amount of various aspects of subjective experience.

Given this great variability across individuals and the fact that one person may have high imagery vividness, low internal dialogue, and much positive affect, while another may have low imagery vividness, high internal dialogue, and much positive affect while just sitting quietly with their eyes open, mapping consciousness across single individuals may yield extremely conflicting results due to the tremendous variability of the human psyche. Thus, it seemed more appropriate to map aspects of subjective experience across groups of individuals, where individual differences would be "averaged out."

A second reason for mapping consciousness across groups of individuals concerns the need to quantify pattern structures. Although the phenomenological intensity profile (pip) and the icon are ways to depict

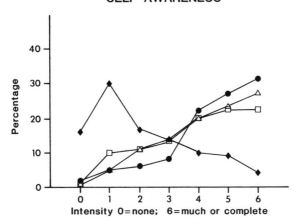

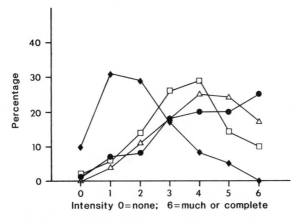

Figure 10.1. Percentage of subjects having a given phenomenological intensity score for the PCQ dimensions as a function of conditions. (△, First baseline; ●, second baseline; □, erotica; ◆, relaxation/meditation.)

intensity effects, there is no way to statistically determine the *degree* of relationships between different dimensions via pips or icons, although these devices do indicate the relationships between different intensities associated with the (sub)dimensions mapped by the PCI or the DAQ. On the other hand, pattern effects can be assessed by mapping subjective experience across groups of individuals and using the Pearson *r*

ALTERED EXPERIENCE

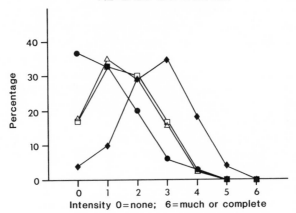

ALTERED STATE OF AWARENESS

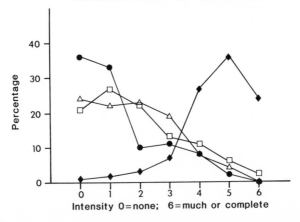

Figure 10.2. Percentage of subjects having a given phenomenological intensity score for the PCQ dimensions as a function of conditions. (△, First baseline; ●, second baseline; □, erotica; ◆, relaxation/meditation.)

correlation coefficient to compute the degree of association between different dimensions of consciousness. The Jennrich (1970) test can then be used to evaluate for pattern effects across different stimulus conditions and/or different subject types by statistically assessing correlation matrices.

The (sub)dimension intensity and pattern results obtained with this approach represent the state of consciousness associated with a stimulus condition that is the *average* intensity and pattern parameters obtained for the group of individuals assessed. It is granted that probably no individual will have exactly the same intensity values obtained for a group of subjects. In addition, it is also recognized that an individual's or group of individuals' intensity ratings for the various (sub)dimensions represent that person's or group's *perceived average* for the contents of consciousness experienced during a given time period. Although there may be problems associated with such perceived average values for each individual and across individuals, the benefits obtained from this approach appear to outweigh the deficits, as the following subsections of will indicate.

RETROSPECTIVE PHENOMENOLOGICAL ASSESSMENT

Administration of the RPA Inventory

The PCI is administered by giving it to subjects to complete in reference to an immediately preceding stimulus condition. Thus, if subjects sit quietly for four minutes, the questionnaire is completed after the four-minute period in reference to that time period. The PCI has been used in reference to time periods from two to four minutes. Asking subjects to complete the PCI in reference to longer time periods has not been investigated, although several researchers have given the PCI in reference to time periods as long as several hours (this research, to my knowledge, has not yet been published).

Time Period Length

In a review of verbal reports on subjective processes, Ericsson and Simon (1980) indicated that as long as such assessment is *remembered* rather than *inferred*, such retrospective verbalization can be both reliable and valid. My research with self-report questionnaires in RPA have been used with stimulus conditions having time intervals of approximately two to four minutes. Although RPA instruments have usually been completed immediately after the stimulus conditions under study, several studies (Pekala & Kumar, 1984, 1987; Pekala & Forbes, 1988; Pekala *et al.*, 1986) had an intervening time period of approximately ten minutes between the stimulus condition and subsequent completion of the PCI. The data obtained from these conditions (both immediately following the stimulus condition and after the short delay) have yielded results consistent with expected findings, which suggest that this approach for mapping subjective experience is valid for the time periods assessed.

The completion of the inventory in reference to time periods less than two and greater than four minutes has not been empirically assessed by myself. Based on my experience with this method, I would be comfortable with time periods from 20 seconds to 20 minutes, but time intervals outside these limits may be problematic.

Very short time periods may disrupt or "freeze" one's stream of consciousness. This argument was a major one that the functionalists used against the structuralists at the turn of the century when introspection was quite common. The functionalists' thesis was that an assessment period of several seconds as used by the structuralists (and also used in some contemporary thought sampling; Hurlburt, 1980; Klinger, 1978) was so short that it eliminated the most essential aspect of consciousness, its process and evanescent nature (Angell, 1907).

A time period of several minutes, on the other hand, should not so easily disrupt the flow or stream of consciousness and hence not so easily affect or change the phenomena during the act of measuring it. By sampling a several-minute time period, RPA will also tend to eliminate, through memory loss, transient and random events, thus making it easier for any "state" properties of consciousness to become evident and thus allow for such properties of consciousness to be more easily investigated.

Although time periods of up to 20 minutes would probably be valid, periods of 20 to 30 minutes or more may be problematic. Longer time periods may involve various changes in subjective experience; hence subjects will more likely need to "average" or infer their subjective experience over this time period. Thus, what subjects report may be more what they infer rather than what they remember and thus be less of a valid representation of their experience (Ericsson & Simon, 1980). In addition, asking subjects to complete the questionnaire in reference to a long period of time may result in the completion of the questionnaire in reference to the last several and first several minutes of the stimulus condition, due to recency and primacy effects, respectively. Hence, until more research is done in this area, the experimenter should probably assess relatively short time intervals. If longer time periods are assessed, the researcher should: (1) document evidence of the validity of this approach, or (2) indicate that what the subject is completing the PCI in reference to may be not only what he or she remembers, but also what he or she *infers*. Although such inferences concerning what subjects experience are interesting in their own right, the researcher should be aware that such inferences may not accurately reflect what the subjects actually experienced.

Elapsed Time between the Stimulus Condition
and Completion of the Inventory

Although the PCI was originally completed right after the experiencing of a given stimulus interval, it's use with hypnosis (Pekala & Kumar, 1984, 1987) necessitated an intervening time period of approximately ten minutes from the stimulus interval in question and subsequent completion of the PCI. (Between the experiencing of a three- or four-minute time period and completion of the PCI, subjects had to be brought out of hypnosis and complete the amnesia assessment; hence the delay.) Such a delay appeared to have no significant effect on reliability (how consistent subjects were at completing the inventory) and negligible effects on validity. However, no formal studies have been reported to assess the effects of intervening time intervals.

In my private practice, often I will see a patient in my office, do a hypnotic induction/assessment, and give the patient the PCI to complete when he or she gets home. In that case, the intervening time period between the hypnotic induction and completion of the PCI can be several hours or more. Although I have no formal data analysis of this procedure concerning validity, its use with my private clients *appears* to be valid and has also been found to be reliable. (I have completed two studies that assessed time delays of up to several days, but those data have yet to be analyzed.)

By completing the PCI or other RPA instruments in reference to time periods that have to be remembered days, weeks, or months ago, the subject will probably be relying more on inference than memory. Although such inferences concerning what subjects experience are interesting in their own right, the researcher should be aware that such inferences may not accurately reflect what the subjects really experience, but are probably a function of both memory and inference.

In the past I have been contacted by researchers who have had subjects complete the PCI in reference to a time period of an hour or more for an experience that may have occurred many years ago, that is, a drug experience of MMDA (3-methoxy-4,5-methylenedioxyamphetamine) before it was made illegal. Although the data collected via this approach are surely quite interesting, the researcher should be aware of the influences of inference and other variables on what such subjects relate in this type of retrospection (Bradburn et al., 1987).

Use of a Practice Questionnaire and Completion
of the Inventory for the First Time

Earlier research (Pekala, 1980) had subjects complete a short practice questionnaire of ten items that was very similar to the longer questionnaire (PCQ) before engaging in introspection for longer periods. Subjects usually completed it in reference to a one-minute period with eyes open or closed or in reference to the time period while they were traveling to the experiment. Three of the items of this practice questionnaire were very similar to three other items. After the subjects completed the questionnaire, the experimenter would review it with them, calling their attention to the three item-pairs. By having them compare their responses to the item-pairs, subjects could determine how consistent they were at completing the inventory. Subjects who completed the items by giving opposite or near opposite responses were told that they would have to be more consistent when completing the next questionnaire, while subjects that were reliable were told to keep up the good work (see Pekala, 1980).

Unpublished research (Pekala, unpublished study) examined the need of a practice session. Subjects were given a self-report inventory to complete in reference to eyes open, some of whom had the practice inventory preceding the longer inventory and some of whom did not. An average difference in Pearson rs of only .02 for the five pairs of reliability items, that is, .74 versus .72 (between subjects that had the practice session and those that did not, respectively), indicates that the practice session is not a necessity. Hence, I have dropped the use of the practice session in current research and clinical practice. And of course, after the subjects have completed the PCI for the first time, reading the instructions is also not a necessity.

Over the last several years, I have also been giving the PCI to psychiatric patients to complete in reference to various stress management conditions. With these patients I sometimes do not go over the instructions, although I will go over the first couple items of the questionnaire with the patients so that they understand what is expected of them. When I do this, there does not appear to be much of a difference in reliability, and the patients have been found to be as reliable as West Chester University students (who, however, were not as ego-involved in completing the inventory as the patients). Hence, either going over the instructions or reading the first several items of the inventory and making sure subjects or patients understand what is expected of them appear sufficient for most people. [With both the above populations, I find about 10 to 15% are marginally unreliable at completing a given administration of the PCI, i.e., obtain a reliability index score of greater than 2.0 (3.0 would be random responding).]

In unpublished research with the PCI I have also instructed subjects not to go back over the items of the inventory once they have scored a given item. This was done so they could not check their answers with previously completed items, in an attempt to determine to what extent subjects may be changing their responses as they complete the instrument to comply with the instructions of trying to be as accurate or consistent as possible. As with the comparison of subjects who used the practice questionnaire versus those who did not, although there was a slight drop in reliability, it was negligible.

Demand Characteristics, Response Bias, "Holding Back," and Expectancy

Since phenomenological assessment may be highly influenced by demand characteristics, the validity of RPA should also be demonstrated when such characteristics are controlled for or found to be of minimal influence. Two studies (Pekala et al., 1985; Pekala & Kumar, 1988) found expected results with RPA instruments that do not appear to have been due to demand characteristics (Orne, 1962). Thus, subjects of low, medium, and high absorption ability (a trait moderately correlated with hypnotic susceptibility) during the stimulus conditions of eyes open and eyes closed sitting quietly experienced significant alterations in the subjective experience of awareness, imagery, positive affect, altered experiences, and attention. Since the experimenter (who was blind to the experimental hypotheses) had no knowledge of who were of low, medium, or high absorption ability, demand characteristics appear to have been minimal and were probably not responsible for the results obtained (Pekala et al., 1985).

A follow-up study (Kumar & Pekala, 1989) comparing low, medium, and high hypnotically susceptible subjects (as assessed by the Harvard Group Scale) also obtained significant differences during the stimulus conditions of eyes closed sitting quietly and the hypnotic induction for the PCI (sub)dimensions of positive affect, altered experiences, state of awareness, self-awareness, and volitional control. The results during the eyes-closed condition likewise could not be attributable to demand characteristics since lows, mediums, and highs all participated in mixed groups with no experimenter knowledge as to who were of low, medium, or high susceptibility during eyes closed (which preceded the assessment of hypnotizability). These findings support the discriminant validity of the PCI; a validity not reducible to acquiescence to demand characteristics.

Response bias (Jones & Spanos, 1982), the extent to which subjects may skew their responses due to individual differences in perception, cognition, and/or personality, is an important issue concerning the reporting of phenomenological experience. The extent to which, during hypnotic induction assessment conditions, lows respond in counterde-mand fashion while highs respond in such a way to maintain a "good subject" role is a question to which little research has been addressed. Future psychophenomenological research will need to address this and also the extent to which responses may be skewed due to "holding back" (Sharf & Zamansky, 1963). Sequence effects leading to holding back phenomena, the extent to which subjects underreport certain sub-jective events because they know they will be hypnotized, or experience an altered state induction procedure later, have also not be assessed to any great extent.

A study (Nulton & Pekala, 1991) has recently been completed that assessed for order effects when hypnosis (as induced by the Harvard Scale) was counterbalanced with progressive relaxation. The results sug-gested an order effect for certain PCI (sub)dimensions. This research suggested that the order of conditions can have an effect on the nature of reported phenomenological experience, at least as assessed by the PCI. These types of influences will need to be considered when order or sequence may have important or unpredictable effects on the results.

Research has also been completed comparing the effects of expec-tancy on reported phenomenological experience (Pekala et al., 1991). Subjects first completed the PCI in reference to a time period where they imagined what it would be like to be hypnotized. They sat quietly for several minutes while they thought what they would experience subjec-tively had they been hypnotized. They subsequently completed the PCI in reference to what they *expected* they would have felt when being hypnotized. There were significant differences between what subjects expected they would experience during hypnosis and what they subsequently actually did experience (as assessed by the PCI (sub)di-mensions).

In addition, the data analysis indicated that the PCI was able to predict about 40% of the total variance (in reference to subjects' suscep-tibility as measured by the Harvard Scale); expectancy accounted for about one-fourth of that variance. This data suggest that how subjects expect they will feel about being hypnotized will have an impact on how they actually respond.

Since subjective experience is probably heavily influenced by the context of that experience (Baars, 1988), and especially the instructional set associated with a given stimulus condition, future research with the PCI and related instruments will need to comprehensively assess the role of response bias, demand characteristics, expectancy, holding back, and associated order effects.

Validity

The results of the above-cited studies and the other previously reported data on the PCI and related questionnaires (Kumar & Pekala, 1988; Pekala & Levine, 1982; Pekala & Wenger, 1983; Pekala *et al.*, 1989) suggest that the possible lack of data due to memory loss (by employing RPA) does not appear to significantly affect the validity of the obtained results. Thus, according to Ericsson and Simon (1980):

> Incompleteness of reports may make some information unavailable, but it does not invalidate the information that is presented. In an often cited remark, Duncker (1945) observed that "a protocol is relatively reliable only for what it positively contains, but not for that which it omits." (p. 11)

Hence, the validity of the self-report is not a function of what is lost through forgetting, but rather what is positively contained in the protocol. The PCI, the DAQ, and predecessor questionnaires have been able to validly discriminate dissimilar stimulus conditions in regard to both intensity and pattern parameters. Thus, the use of RPA appears, at this point, to be at least *adequately* valid for discriminating such stimulus conditions as eyes open/closed, hypnosis, relaxation/meditation, reading erotica, experiencing an erotic fantasy, or deep abdominal breathing from each other (these are the conditions so far assessed by my research).

Nevertheless, since RPA, by definition, is retrospective, memory loss will occur. Retrospective phenomenological assessment thus precludes a completely accurate assessment of the criterion time period. For this reason, RPA needs to be assessed and validated against concurrent verbalization (reporting on subjective events as they occur) to determine to what extent memory loss affects RPA.

Although the PCI and the DAQ, as a whole, have been found to be valid, the question of the validity of each and every (sub)dimension must await additional research. The reporting of increased imagery and positive affect during the erotica conditions with the Phenomenology of Consciousness Questionnaire (PCQ) and the (Abbreviated) Dimensions of Consciousness Questionnaire ((A)DCQ); the increased alterations in state of awareness and altered experiences; and decreased self-awareness, rationality, volitional control, and memory during relaxation/meditation and hypnosis with the (A)DCQ and the PCI (Kumar & Pekala, 1988; Pekala & Levine, 1982; Pekala *et al.*, 1986) supports the discriminant validity of these dimensions. The same holds for many of the DAQ dimensions (Pekala & Forbes, 1990; Pekala & Kumar, 1988). Although the validity of the dimensions of arousal and internal dialogue of the PCI and most of the DAQ dimensions were also supported, more research employing stimulus conditions differentially activating these dimensions is needed.

Reliability

Although a method must be considered reliable before it can be considered valid (reliability is a necessary condition for validity), validity was dealt with first since invalidity of a method negates its usefulness, no matter how reliable it is.

Until the research with West Chester University (WCU) students, RPA reliability had been very good, that is, only 2% of the PCI subjects [Michigan State University (MSU) students] had a reliability index of greater than 2 and the Pearson r and coefficient alpha results with the PCI, the PCQ, and the (A)DCQ were also quite good. The lower reliability results with the WCU students may have been due to several factors.

Whereas the MSU subjects were run in small groups, that is, 30 to 60 subjects per group, the WCU students were run in much larger groups. The increase in group size may have diffused responsibility for accurately completing the questionnaires and hence lowered the reliability. The time constraints of the WCU studies were also much tighter and hence the less time to complete the inventories may have decreased reliability. It is also possible the WCU students were less reliable because of some unexplained reason, possibly relating to differences between MSU and WCU students, although this seems less likely.

The West Chester data (Kumar & Pekala, 1988, 1989) and its 10–15% marginal unreliability is contrasted, however, with data obtained from 300 nursing students at Thomas Jefferson University. Here, across the stimulus conditions of eyes closed, hypnosis, deep abdominal breathing, and progressive relaxation, reliability index scores for the PCI were found to be only 4–5% unreliable (Pekala *et al.*, 1989). The nature of how data were collected for the Jefferson students was more similar, however, to how data were collected with the Penn State students than with the West Chester students. Hence, there was more time and the groups were smaller with the Jefferson and Penn State students than with the West Chester students. Marginal reliability may thus be at least partially a function of large group size (i.e., above 100 students per group) and rather tight time constraints.

To control for possible unreliability, the reliability index was instituted. It is simply the average absolute difference score of the five pairs of similar or identical items embedded within the questionnaire for the PCI and the six pairs of reliability items for the DAQ. Since an average reliability index score of 0 denotes perfect agreement with all item-pairs, while a reliability index score of 6.0 denotes completely opposite responses to the items of each item-pair (when using a seven-point Likert scale), random responding would generate an average reliability index score of 3.0. For this reason, it was decided to use a reliability index score of 2.0 as the upper limit for adequate (marginally reliable) reliability.

Although the decision of a cut-off score of 2.0 or less is somewhat arbitrary, exclusion of subjects with a reliability index score of greater than 2 with the WCU students raised average Pearson rs for the five reliability item-pairs from .57 to .65. A value of .65 is relatively comparable to that obtained with the MSU students during eyes open sitting quietly with the PCI and exactly the same as the average Pearson r results obtained with the PCQ across the four stimulus conditions of eyes open sitting quietly (experienced twice), reading erotica, and relaxation/meditation (Pekala & Levine, 1982).

The use of the reliability index with the WCU subjects (deletion of subjects with an reliability index of greater than 2.0) resulted in modest increases in coefficient alphas for the various (sub)dimensions. Yet it did not affect the dimension and pattern comparisons between similar or different stimulus conditions to even a mild extent. Hence, statistical comparison with or without marginally reliable subjects had small, statistically negligible effects when doing ANOVA analyses (Kumar & Pekala, 1988). The fact that there was not much difference between using or not using subjects with a reliability index of greater than 2.0 for intensity and pattern comparisons may partially relate to the large n's assessed, and smaller samples may have generated more differences. Nevertheless, these results are encouraging and suggest that provided the sample sizes are large, that is, approximately 100 subjects per group, 13% of the subjects having a reliability index score of greater than 2.0 seems to have little effect on intensity and pattern comparisons with the PCI. To give the researcher an idea of the range and distribution of these reliability scores, Table 10.1 lists the reliability index cumulative probabilities for the eyes-closed and hypnotic induction stimulus conditions when using the West Chester subject pool with 10 to 15% marginal reliability for the PCI.

Limitations

Given the small number of items per dimension, approximately 4.5, the PCI will probably not be able to make very fine phenomenological

Table 10.1. Reliability Index Frequency and Cumulative Percentage
for Subjects during Eyes Closed and a Hypnotic Induction

Reliability index score	Eyes closed[a]		Hypnotic induction[b]	
	Frequency	Cumulative percentage	Frequency	Cumulative percentage
0.0	1	0	8	3
0.2	12	5	14	9
0.4	27	15	21	18
0.6	34	28	22	27
0.8	25	38	36	42
1.0	32	50	26	52
1.2	37	64	31	65
1.4	17	70	19	73
1.6	16	76	19	81
1.8	16	83	10	85
2.0	16	89	4	87
2.2	8	92	9	90
2.4	6	94	8	94
2.6	1	94	7	97
2.8	2	95	3	98
3.0	6	97	3	99
3.2	2	98		
3.4				
3.6	2	99	1	100
3.8	1	99		
4.0				
4.2	1	100		
4.4	1	100		
4.6			1	100

[a]$n = 263$.
[b]$n = 242$.

discriminations. It has, however, made (sub)dimension intensity distinctions between the conditions of eyes open and eyes closed sitting
quietly (Pekala & Wenger, 1983), where the only difference between
conditions was the single behavioral event of eye closure and the data
being compared was a within-subjects comparison. Other, more recent,
research (Kumar & Pekala, 1989), however, found no significant differences for the PCI major or minor dimensions when eyes open and
eyes closed were compared (this was, however, a between-subjects
comparison).

Due to the fact that the PCI is composed of a relatively small number of dimensions and subdimensions, distinctions between various as-

pects of attention (intensity, extensivity, or selectivity; Silverman, 1968), imagery (visual, kinesthetic, or auditory), or memory (short-term, intermediate, or long-term), besides those already made with the PCI, cannot be made without expanding the questionnaire. The fact that the PCI was successful in making phenomenological distinctions between differing stimulus conditions suggests that other questionnaires, similar in format, could be constructed and used in RPA to make finer phenomenological distinctions for these aspects of consciousness. [This is why the DAQ (Pekala, 1985d, 1991a), to measure various aspects of attention, was constructed. The same limitations would apply to this inventory as the PCI.] Besides the limited number of items, the PCI's ability to make fine phenomenological distinctions will also depend on how many subjects are assessed and how reliably the subjects are completing the inventory.

STIMULUS-STATE SPECIFICITY

The use of RPA is based on the principle of stimulus-state specificity (principle of specificity) as far as comparisons among groups of subjects are concerned. This principle states that across groups of randomly selected subjects, the same stimulus conditions are associated with the same intensities and patterns of phenomenological experience (same condition specificity), while different stimulus conditions are associated with different intensity and/or pattern parameters (different condition specificity) (Pekala & Wenger, 1983).

Use of the principle of specificity allows for parallelisms to be drawn between stimulus conditions and phenomenological events and thus posits a means in which variations in phenomenological experience can be assessed by varying the stimulus environment. The research to date has supported the principle of specificity for the same stimulus conditions for intensity comparisons and for pattern comparisons for the PCI, provided the subject-to-dimension ratio is at least five to one (Kumar & Pekala, 1988, 1989; Pekala & Kumar, 1986, 1989; Pekala et al., 1986). The research to date has also supported different condition specificity for the most part, although two studies (Kumar & Pekala, 1989; Pekala & Kumar, 1988) found no intensity differences between eyes closed and eyes open with the PCI and DAQ, respectively, even though another study using a predecessor to the PCI did (Pekala et al., 1985). (As mentioned, this difference may relate to the fact that the former studies used a between-subjects comparison, while the latter study employed a within-subjects comparison.)

Same- and Different-Condition Specificity

Since the external validity of same-condition specificity is currently weak (there have not been any published data on populations other than college students, and only a handful of stimulus conditions have been investigated), I would recommend that this principle be empirically validated for same-condition specificity each time intensity and pattern comparisons are done when working with groups of individuals. If pattern comparisons are to be made, however, this is contingent on being able to run large numbers of subjects per group.

Same-condition specificity indicates that several groups of subjects who have experienced a given stimulus condition report nonsignificantly different intensity and pattern parameters for that stimulus condition. If the two groups experiencing an eyes-open condition or a relaxation/meditation condition are found to report significantly different intensity values or pattern structures for a given stimulus condition, inferences concerning comparisons between the eyes-open and relaxation/meditation conditions would be problematic since there is not a consistent baseline with which to compare them; that is, a given stimulus condition is not necessarily associated with a specific phenomenological state.

By empirically demonstrating same-condition specificity across groups of subjects experiencing the same stimulus condition, one is then justified in attributing intensity differences or pattern structure differences between different stimulus conditions to the nature of these conditions and not to perturbations within a given stimulus condition. Thus, by empirically establishing same-condition specificity with the population of interest, one is then justified in assessing for different-condition specificity between two or more different stimulus conditions.

The use of RPA in conjunction with the principle of specificity should be quite helpful in understanding and mapping subjective experience in reference to human behavior since specificity posits a correspondence between subjective experience and associated stimulus condition.

Benefits

One of the problems with classical and modern introspection has been the difficulty of establishing adequate reliability and validity. It is of interest that, according to Boring (1953), classical introspection

> went out of style after Titchener's death (1927) because it had demonstrated on functional use . . . and also because it was unreliable. Laboratory atmo-

sphere crept into the descriptions, and it was not possible to verify, from one laboratory to another, the introspective accounts of the consciousness of action, feelings, choice, and judgment. (p. 174)

A correspondence between subjective events and overt behaviors (in a particular stimulus setting) would not only help to increase the reliability of introspection, but would also help to increase the validity of introspection as well. Subjective experience could then be differentially and systematically investigated by varying the behaviors, neuropsychophysiological variables, and environmental and instructional stimuli of different stimulus conditions, which in turn would permit the various structures of phenomenological experience such as attention, imagery, and cognition to be evaluated and systematically and comprehensively compared.

This methodology can thus be used to not only map and quantify the various structures of consciousness, but it can be used to:

compare states of subjective experience associated with such procedures as hypnosis, meditation, EEG biofeedback, progressive relaxation, drug intoxification, etc. to determine the extent to which these induction procedures are associated with altered states such as an "alpha high" (Kamiya, 1968) or a "trance state" (Weitzenhoffer, 1978) that are significantly different from non-altered states of consciousness. (Pekala & Levine, 1981, p. 44)

Limitations

The principle of same-condition specificity only holds across groups of randomly selected individuals. It does not apply to individual assessments. Relatively low test-retest reliabilities from earlier research with the PCQ (Pekala & Levine, 1982) indicated that individuals have moderate variation in subjective experience (the second time) when the same stimulus condition is experienced twice. Although this finding was probably also due to habituation to some extent, the relatively low reliabilities were probably due to the fact that there is intraindividual variation in phenomenological experience. (Strictly speaking, the same stimulus condition being experienced twice by the same subjects is not "the same" stimulus condition the second time, since history and practice have influenced how subjects respond during the second administration. Hence, (sub)dimension intensity differences between a stimulus condition that is experienced twice does not appear to be a violation of same-condition specificity.)

Although there appear to be no *consistent* gender differences for the (sub)dimensions across various stimulus conditions (Pekala *et al.*, 1985, 1986), individuals who differ from one another in terms of certain personality characteristics may have significantly different intensities and patterns of phenomenological experience. Thus, individuals who scored low, medium, or high on absorption, a trait moderately correlated with hypnotic susceptibility, were found to differ significantly in regard to the intensities and/or patterns of phenomenological experience reported during eyes-open and eyes-closed sitting quietly (Pekala *et al.*, 1985) and eyes-closed sitting quietly and a hypnotic induction (Kumar & Pekala, 1988, 1989; Pekala *et al.*, 1986).

Methodologically, the principle of specificity may only hold when the (sub)dimensions of consciousness are assessed *molarly*, in the rather general, nonmeticulous manner of the items of the PCQ, the (A)DCQ, the PCI, or the DAQ. The items of the questionnaire ask the subject to make judgments regarding *nontrivial* aspects of subjective experience without meticulous "hair-splitting." Very specific judgments, as were done by the classical introspectionists, may not only make it harder to attain adequate reliability, but it may also lead to significant differences in the (sub)dimension intensity values across groups of individuals experiencing identical stimulus conditions. Hence, as with any other area of research, the methods of observation and evaluation will ultimately determine the nature of the data obtained.

ASSESSING STATES OF CONSCIOUSNESS WITH RPA

The concept of state of consciousness has had a less than respectable history. Back in 1907 Angell attacked the "more extreme and ingenuous conceptions of structural psychology" as the result of "an unchastened indulgence in what we may call the 'state of consciousness' doctrine" (p. 64), a doctrine that yielded introspective data "dependent upon the particular exigencies and conditions which call them forth" (p. 67). Angell believed that when analyzing for the elements of a particular state of consciousness, what the observer noticed was a function of the stimulus setting and condition that called them forth.

Angell's distrust of the concept of state of consciousness has been echoed by Hilgard (1980). Hilgard has noted how "discussions are not entirely clear about the concept of state of consciousness" (p. 21), not to mention the "problems in defining and characterizing altered or alternate states" (p. 22). Even Tart (1972, 1975, 1977) has indicated his dismay at the lack of precision in defining and operationalizing exactly what a state or altered state of consciousness is. Tart suggests that this lack of precision has led to a great deal of confusion, so that many people now use "the term, state of consciousness, to simply mean whatever is on their mind" (1977, p. 110)

Part of the problem involves one of definition. States of consciousness have been defined as being different from other states of consciousness (Krippner, 1972; Ludwig, 1972). Yet the ways in which such states are different from one another have not been systematically addressed. It has also been suggested that neurophysiology could help define and map the nature and structure of consciousness (Hilgard, 1969; Kamiya, 1968). Evidence, however, on the lack of a relationship between the occurrence of the "alpha experience" (Kamiya, 1968) and the strength or density of the EEG alpha activity "calls into question the entire enterprise of 'mapping consciousness' neurophysiologically" (Plotkin, 1979, p. 1145).

These results suggest that neurophysiological approaches may be inappropriate, by themselves, for assessing the subtleties of conscious experience. On the other hand, retrospective phenomenological assessment may be more appropriate. Angell (1907) has indicated that the elements of a state of consciousness are a function of the nature of the stimulus condition being assessed. The elements of a state of consciousness, however, are the various aspects of subjective experience an individual is experiencing (Boring, 1953). It then follows that the various aspects of subjective experience, that is, the (sub)dimensions of consciousness or attention, are at least partially a function of the stimulus condition being assessed. Comparing variations in subjective experience across stimulus conditions activating different aspects of that experience would thus allow for the various dimensions or structures of phenomenological experience to be systematically assessed.

A state can be defined as "any well defined condition or property that can be recognized if it occurs again" (Ashby, 1963, p. 17). Using this definition and the suggestions of Singer (cited in Zinberg, 1977), Tart (1975), Anderson (1983), and the PDP researchers (McClelland & Rumelhart, 1988), a state of consciousness can be defined as the particular intensity and pattern of associated phenomenological parameters that characterize one's subjective conscious experience during a given time period. Since retrospective phenomenological assessment using the PCI allows for subjective experience to be quantified in terms of intensity and pattern parameters, the PCI can be used to quantify states of consciousness.

Tart's Definitions

Tart (1975) has suggested that consciousness is composed of certain structures or subsystems that retain their basic function in spite of variations in the intensity and/or the quality of their activity. Tart also suggests that it is primarily patterns between subsystems and not the intensities or levels of activation of the subsystems themselves that determine a particular state of consciousness.

Tart has defined two types of states of consciousness: *altered states of consciousness* and *identity states of consciousness*. An altered state of consciousness, for Tart, is a state in which there are (1) changes in pattern among the dimensions or subsystems of consciousness, and (2) the subjective sense of (being in) an altered state (SSAS) radically different from one's ordinary or normal state of awareness. An identity state, on the other hand, is a specialized version of a nonaltered state of consciousness that has an overall pattern that distinguishes it from other identity states. It is composed of psychological structures that possess unique properties not present in other identity states, but it is not perceived as a radically different state of consciousness.

The use of the PCI in RPA permits operationalization of Tart's definitions. The altered state of awareness dimension allows one to quantify SSAS, while the correlation matrix among dimensions and the use of the Jennrich (1970) test allows for the quantification and statistical assessment of pattern structures.

Redefining Identity, Discrete, and Altered States of Consciousness

The use of the PCI, however, permits even greater differentiation than that contained in Tart's definitions. Obviously, altered or identity states will depend on how you define them and how one can operationalize these definitions. The PCI permits definition and quantification of states of consciousness in terms of both intensity and pattern parameters. Although Tart has suggested that it is primarily pattern structures that define a particular state of consciousness, as mentioned, Singer (cited in Zinberg, 1977) suggests that it is primarily intensity parameters that define states of consciousness. Since it is unknown at this time if and to what extent changes in intensities of certain phenomenological structures can lead to changes in pattern, or vice versa, until more research is done between *levels of activation* or the intensities of the subsystems of consciousness and the *patterns of connectivity* between subsystems, *both* should be used in defining states of consciousness.

Given the possibility of quantification of states of consciousness in terms of both intensity and pattern parameters, several combinations then become possible. These combinations include:

1. Nonsignificantly different intensity values and nonsignificantly different pattern values (between states of consciousness associated with two stimulus conditions).

2. Nonsignificantly different intensity values and significantly different pattern values.
3. Significantly different intensity values and nonsignificantly different pattern values.
4. Significantly different intensity values and significantly different pattern values.

Concerning (3) and (4) above, it can also be the case that:

5. There can be a nonsignificantly different SSAS value between conditions, or
6. There can be a significantly different SSAS value between conditions.

Thus, six possibilities become apparent and Tart's definitions cover only two of them. For this reason, some of the above states have been redefined so as to logically follow from the intensity and pattern parameters mapped by the PCI. Only those states will be discussed that have been found to empirically exist.

Identity States or I-States

Research has found that the same stimulus conditions are associated with the same (nonsignificantly different) intensities and patterns of phenomenological experience, that is, the basis for the principle of stimulus-state specificity (for the same conditions). Thus, these stimulus conditions have identical (nonsignificantly different) phenomenological states associated with them. States having such nonsignificantly different intensity and pattern parameters are herein called *identity states*, since the phenomenological intensity and pattern parameters are identical.

Notice that identity states (abbreviated I-states) is used here to mean a much different type of state than what Tart (1975, 1977) means by identity states. Whereas Tart's identity states have different pattern parameters, I am using the term to mean that such states have *identical* (nonsignificantly different) pattern and intensity parameters. And, of course, identity states are such states only in reference to other identity states.

Early research with the PCQ (Pekala & Levine, 1982) found that the same stimulus condition, when experienced twice by the same group of subjects, was associated with significantly different intensity values for several of the dimensions of consciousness and yet a nonsignificantly different pattern structure. Since the pattern structure was identical (nonsignificantly different) but the intensity values were different, these are herein defined as *identity-differing* (identical pattern, differing (sub)dimension intensities) or *I-D states*. They have the same pattern structure and yet the intensity values for certain (sub)dimensions can vary.

A comparison between eyes-open and eyes-closed stimulus conditions, counterbalanced for order (Pekala & Wenger, 1983), also found significant dimension intensity differences for several (sub)dimensions but no significant pattern differences. The eyes open and closed conditions would thus be I-D states in reference to one another. I-D states may be thought of as identity states involving greater depth or greater intensity; the greater depth or intensity concerning those particular (sub)dimensions significantly different between conditions. More research is needed exploring the ways in which I-D states are different from one another and the extent to which one may involve greater depth or intensity than another. (Notice that this definition highlights pattern effects as having the greater impact, at least in terms of definition, for defining an identity state of consciousness. This is partly due, however, to my bias, like Tart, in presupposing pattern effects as being more important than intensity effects.)

Discrete States or D-States

Research (Pekala & Levine, 1982; Pekala & Wenger, 1983) has found states such as reading erotica (RE) or experiencing an erotic fantasy (EF) that had significantly different (sub)dimension intensity values from baseline, a significantly different pattern structure from baseline, and yet were not perceived as altered states of consciousness, that is, there was not a significant SSAS from baseline. Thus, both intensity and pattern parameters were significantly different from baseline and yet neither state was perceived as an altered state of consciousness. Such states are herein labeled *discrete states* or D-states.

This term is used in the sense that Tart uses the term *discrete state of consciousness*: "a unique, dynamic pattern or configuration of psychological structures, an active system of psychological subsystems" (1975, p. 5). A discrete state of consciousness is any state of consciousness that in reference to any other state of consciousness, has a significantly different pattern structure and (sub)dimension intensity values. Since no D-states have been discovered that have a significantly different pattern structure and yet nonsignificantly different (sub)dimension intensity values, until proven otherwise D-states have both pattern and intensity parameters that are different from other D-states, although, like Tart, I regard the pattern structure as the more significant variable of the two.

Altered States or A-States

Research has also found states with significant intensity and pattern differences vis-à-vis baseline and also a significant SSAS. These states are herein labeled *altered states* or A-states. They are identical to what Tart has called an altered state of consciousness. An A-state is a D-state that also has a significant SSAS in comparison to another reference state of consciousness. Thus, although all A-states are D-states, not all D-states are A-states.

Mention should also be made that a particular A-state, such as relaxation/meditation, in reference to another A-state, like hypnosis (both altered states in reference to eyes open), can also be an A-state in reference to another A-state. As an example, both relaxation/ meditation (RM) and a hypnotic induction (HI) can be altered states in reference to eyes open and closed, and yet RM can be an altered state in reference to HI if it has a different pattern structure and a significantly greater SSAS than HI. To distinguish one altered state from another, I will use the term *discrete, altered state of consciousness*, or discrete A-state, to highlight the fact that one altered state can be altered from baseline, as can another altered state, and yet both can be quite different from one another. An important point to keep in mind is the *relativity* involved in these definitions and the fact that a given I-, D-, or A-state can be such a state only in reference to another state.

Thus, the universe of empirically assessed states to date include I-, D-, and A-states, or identity, discrete, and altered states of consciousness, respectively. Like Tart, this division is based more on pattern than intensity parameters. It is also a heuristic classification and not absolute. Depending on new data, it can be modified to accommodate that data. Future research should be able to determine the usefulness of the above classification.

A NOTE ON METHODOLOGY AS TO "FUNDAMENTAL STRUCTURES" OF CONSCIOUSNESS

The PCI (sub)dimensions were based on predecessor questionnaire (sub)dimensions, which, in turn, were based on a thorough perusal of the literature, identification of various dimensions or structures of consciousness, feedback from subjects regarding the appropriateness of the items composing those (sub)dimensions, and the refinement of the items making up those (sub)dimensions through cluster and exploratory factor analysis (Pekala & Levine, 1981, 1982; Pekala & Wenger, 1983).

Although this procedure was done so as to try to generate as comprehensive a mapping of consciousness as possible, no claim is made that the (sub)dimensions of the PCI are the fundamental nor the only dimensions of consciousness (the same concerns the dimensions mapped by the DAQ). Thus, the PCI is not a questionnaire that purports to map consciousness in terms of "fundamental" structures à la Wundt (1897) or Titchener (1898). Rather its goals are much more modest. It is a heuristic instrument for mapping states of consciousness given: (1) the empirically derived stability of the a priori defined and empirically corroborated structures of consciousness, and (2) their relatively reliable and valid assessment.

Obviously, if more items on alertness, a dimension of the PCQ and the (A)DCQ that did not reach criterion level reliability, were written (and/or written better), it may have developed into a reliable dimension of consciousness. But the research did not support it as a reliable dimension and hence it was dropped.

The lack of universal inclusiveness of the PCI, I feel, does not invalidate its usefulness and the same argument given for the reliability and validity of a four-minute assessment period, despite memory loss, is equally apropos here. Obviously, definitions have to be made and limits set as to what to include or omit in this type of inventory and it is granted that it (the PCI and other instruments like it) is a limited phenomenological instrument. But so are all psychological tests and assessment instruments.

Yet despite its limitations, it does allow one to differentiate and quantify various states of consciousness and do so in a way never done before. Thus, it is a useful instrument and an instrument that the researcher can use to help quantify and map consciousness, provided he is aware of the presuppositions underlying the use of the instrument and the limits to which it can be used.

The approach used to develop the PCI and predecessor instruments was cluster analysis. This approach was used so that concepts like attention, imagery, and awareness could be kept qualitatively and quantitatively separate and not combined into unnameable factors that factor analysis might yield. The fact that exploratory factor analyses with the PCQ, the (A)DCQ, and the PCI across various stimulus conditions blurred distinctions between clusters arrived at by confirmatory cluster analysis, yet did not yield any new clusters (Pekala & Levine, 1981, 1982; Pekala & Wenger, 1983; Pekala et al., 1986), supports the efficacy of the cluster analytic approach to mapping subjective experience, a conclusion consistent with the theorizing and research of Hunter (1977).

The empirical finding that various structures, such as imagery and attention, or rationality and memory, are differentially correlated depending on the stimulus conditions assessed (Pekala, 1985a) supports the judgment of using this approach to map the structures of consciousness instead of factor analysis (which generated different factor analytic solutions depending on the stimulus condition assessed). The finding that the various (sub)dimensions of consciousness remain relatively stable structures of subjective experience across different stimulus conditions (as assessed by the coefficient alpha results), also supports the usefulness of this approach in mapping these structures of consciousness and is consistent with the theorizing of Tart (1975) on the stability of these dimensions or subsystems.

This approach may be contrasted with the approach of Huba, Aneshensel, and Singer (1981), who used factor analysis to arrive at the "fundamental" structures of daydreaming. Obviously, if the basic research question is "What are the fundamental dimensions of consciousness?" then the factor analytic approach is probably the most efficacious means to arrive at that decision. However, if the researcher wants to map states of consciousness phenomenologically using the structures of consciousness accepted by common parlance, that is, imagery, attention, memory, and so forth, then cluster analysis is probably the technique to use since factor analysis will combine items and different phenomenological structures making the resulting factors difficult to name (Hunter & Gerbing, 1979). An a priori cluster analytic approach allows such structures to be kept distinct.

THE JENNRICH AND THE BOX TESTS

The Jennrich Test

To assess pattern effects between two independent groups of subjects, the Jennrich (1970) test is the statistical procedure to use. It allows two independent correlation matrices to be compared for significant differences in pattern between them. The Jennrich test, however, is a large-sample multivariate statistical procedure.

Nunnally (1967) suggests a good rule of thumb for determining how many subjects should be used to obtain useful data from factor analysis and other multivariate techniques. He indicates that "there should be at least ten times as many subjects as items" and "five subjects per item should be considered the minimum that can be tolerated" (p. 260). If the 12 major dimensions of the PCI are used in the pattern analysis, then according to Nunnally, a minimum permissible number of subjects per group should be about 60.

Use of the Jennrich test with various sample sizes over the last several years suggests, however, that 60 subjects per group may not give the researcher adequate power to reject the null hypothesis should a significant difference really exist. Hence, when at all possible, the researcher should attempt to use approximately ten times as many subjects as there are dimensions to be used in the pattern analysis.

A second problem associated with the Jennrich procedure is that until recently there has been no readily available statistical program to assess for significant pattern differences between correlation matrices using the Jennrich test. For this purpose a computer program using the computer language of APL (Gilman & Rose, 1974) has been developed to test for significant differences between correlation matrices that uses the Jennrich test (Pekala & Kumar, 1985). (It is listed in Appendix G.) If the computer APL software is unavailable, then the researcher cannot use the Jennrich formula, unless of course he can convert Jennrich's formula (given in his 1970 article) into a computer programming language such as FORTRAN.

The Box Test

If a program for using Jennrich's formula is unavailable, I recommend using the Box (1950) test to assess for pattern differences, especially if the only other choice is not to do the pattern analysis. The problem with this procedure involves the variances in the diagonals of the covariance matrices and the possibility that these variances, across different stimulus conditions, may be significantly different from one another. Should several of the variances (associated with several of the PCI dimensions) be significantly different, these significantly different variances could lead to a Box test comparison indicating significantly different determinants and hence pattern structures between conditions. Such differences in pattern structure could then have nothing to do with the correlations between dimensions but rather be a function of significantly different variances (in the diagonals of the correlation matrix) for several of the PCI dimensions. Thus, the Box test comparisons are problematic (as the reader shall see, so too are the Jennrich comparisons to some extent).

A partial solution to this dilemma is possible. If significant Box test results are found, one can test, using a Bartlett-Box F or similar statistic, for significant differences in variance between the stimulus conditions for the 12 PCI dimensions used to create the covariance matrices. If several of the variances are significantly different, then the significant Box test results may be the result of these significant variances and not the correlations. If little or no significant differences are found, then the researcher can be reasonably certain that the significant differences between covariance matrices are due to the correlations and not the variances.

Using the Jennrich and Box Tests

Mention should be made that both the Jennrich and the Box tests were devised for independent groups. When they are used with correlated groups, they are a more conservative test for significant differences than when used with independent groups. Although Steiger (1980) has developed a computer program using FORTRAN for testing for significant differences between two correlated groups, I have not been able to utilize it for the large matrix sizes, that is, 12 × 12, needed in the PCI pattern analyses. Unless the researcher is able to operationalize Steiger's program for correlated groups, I recommend using the Jennrich test while indicating its conservativeness.[1]

PSYGRAMS AND PATTERN COMPARISONS

Pattern Comparisons Based on the Twelve Major PCI Dimensions

The pattern comparisons are based on the 12 major PCI dimensions and not all 26 (sub)dimensions. This was done for two major reasons. A psygram of more than 12 circles becomes unnecessarily cluttered and the resulting pattern relationships are very hard to cognitively digest if more than 12 dimensions are diagramed. Since the psygram is a major vehicle for interpreting pattern relationships, I felt that the Jennrich test (and the Box test, if it has to be used), which adds statistical validity to the psygrams, should parallel the psygrams.

In addition, since the Jennrich test is a multivariate statistic, which requires approximately five to ten times as many subjects as dimensions, 26 (sub)dimensions would require a subject pool of approximately 260 subjects instead of a minimum of 120 subjects if 12 dimensions are used. Even using the bare minimum of five subjects per dimension would require approximately 130 subjects when using the 26 (sub)dimensions of the PCI.

---

[1] I would be interested in any statistical/computational approach to assess for significant pattern structure differences between dependent matrices that is not too difficult to compute with a program such as APL (Gilman & Rose, 1974).

Depicting Only Statistically Significant Variance Percentages

The convention of depicting only statistically significant variance percentages (based on correlations usually significant at the .01 level) was done so as to: (1) be statistically conservative, and (2) allow for the psygrams to be easily interpreted by not cluttering up the graph with needless nonsignificant lines. (I have also used limits of .05 and .001 if the number of subjects per condition was rather small or very large; see Pekala & Kumar, 1989.) Yet the Jennrich pattern test is based on the correlations of *all* 12 major dimensions with each other and thus includes those nonsignificant variances not depicted in the psygram. Hence, the researcher needs to be aware of what a psygram actually depicts and what has been statistically assessed of a given stimulus condition's phenomenological state through the Jennrich test.

Psygrams Based on 60 to 120 Subjects

The Jennrich test with the 12 PCI dimensions is valid with n's from upward of 120 subjects or more. When used with 60 to 120 subjects (five to ten times the number of subjects vis-à-vis dimensions), analyses completed by the author indicate that analyses that would have been significant had 120 subjects been used may not be significant if only 60 to 90 subjects were used. Hence, the Jennrich test appears especially conservative with small sample sizes, and the researcher may not have the power to yield a significant effect if less than 120 subjects are used.

Although it is relatively easy to get 120 subjects to experience a given stimulus condition if one has access to a large university population, it is more difficult (even with a university population) to get 120 low absorption or 120 low hypnotizable subjects, especially if one needs to run 600 to 800 subjects to generate the 120 low absorption subjects needed. Hence, the researcher may find himself, as I have done, trying to analyze pattern structures with less than 120 subjects per group. For one study (Pekala & Kumar, 1989) I have used an n as small as 40. (This is not a problem, however, if an n of 40 yields a significant pattern effect.)

When doing so it is important for the researcher to realize that: (1) the Jennrich test may miss a significant effect that may have been significant if larger sample sizes were used, and (2) psygrams based on 60 subjects or less may yield results that are harder to replicate, due to the fact that the correlations between dimensions can still vary a lot (a larger confidence interval for the "true correlation") in comparison to larger sample sizes.

Obviously, the researcher must work with the subjects he has available. Nevertheless, he must also be willing to recognize the limitations imposed on the data by the methods he uses to gather and statistically assess that data.

Group Size Limits When Using the Pattern Comparisons and Psygrams

The researcher should also be aware that when very different group sizes are being compared and psygrams constructed for these groups, the lower limit for the diagraming of variances based on significant correlations (adhering to the .01 significance level) will be different for different group sizes. Thus, for a group size of 60 subjects, a lower variance percentage limit of approximately 11% is generated when using the .01 significance level. Yet a group size of 120 subjects will generate a lower limit percentage of approximately 5.5% when using the .01 level. Thus, if two psygrams are being visually compared, one with 60 subjects per group and one with 120 subjects per group, the former will illustrate variance percentages of 11% or more, whereas the latter will illustrate percentages of 5.5% or more, if a .01 alpha level is adapted.

Hence, if the psygrams on which the pattern analyses are based are to be comparable, the researcher should try to compare pattern structures using groups of approximately equal size.

THE JENNRICH TEST AND PCI DIMENSION VARIABILITY: CORRECTING FOR VARIANCE DIFFERENCES

Significantly greater variability for a PCI dimension in one stimulus condition may lead to higher correlations for that condition than another stimulus condition which has significantly less variability. As a result, a significant Jennrich comparison may not be due to significant correlational differences in conditions among dimensions but rather be a function of higher correlations that are due to greater variability for particular PCI dimensions for one stimulus condition vis-à-vis another. In this case, the significant differences would then be an artifact due to greater dimension variability and *not* due to higher correlations among the dimensions of that condition.

As an example, if the variances of several PCI dimensions during hypnosis were significantly greater than an eyes-closed condition, significantly higher correlations for the hypnosis condition might be due to the greater variability of the various PCI dimension scores and not necessarily to "true" higher correlations. Hence, when using the Jennrich test, checking to make sure that higher correlations (if found) are not a function of greater variance is important.

My own research has indicated that most variance analyses will yield only one or two major PCI dimensions having significantly greater variances in one condition than another, but not necessarily in the direction that would inflate the correlation coefficients. Hence, although PCI dimension variability is not a major one, it is something that should be assessed if a significant Jennrich test is found that appears to be due to one stimulus condition having correlations much higher than another. If several significant variance differences are found between conditions, such that the higher correlations in one condition may be due to the greater variability for these dimensions, then the researcher should do supplemental Jennrich comparisons.

These supplemental analyses can be done in two ways. Correlation matrices can be constructed, but by eliminating the dimensions found to have significantly greater variability. Thus, if four PCI dimensions had greater variability in the direction that would inflate the correlation, the Jennrich test can be performed, but without the dimensions that may be inflationary, checking to see if a significant effect still exists. Thus, let us assume that the dimensions of attention, imagery, and positive and negative affect were found to be of significantly greater variability for an eyes-closed condition, that is being compared against a hypnosis condition. The researcher can construct matrices for each of these two conditions, but without these four dimensions, and compare for pattern comparisons using only 8 instead of 12 PCI dimensions.

The problem with this approach, however, is that if these dimensions were the ones that were responsible for the significant Jennrich differences in spite of the greater variability, deletion of these dimensions would allow the researcher to conclude that the matrices are not different when in fact they might be. Hence, probably a better procedure is to determine if the increased variability for the PCI dimensions may have led to significant pattern differences without deleting the problematic PCI dimensions. This involves using a procedure that corrects for a restriction of range of the correlations (Guilford & Fruchter, 1978).

For this correction procedure, those "inflated" correlations among PCI dimensions for each of the dimensions being compared are corrected. This involves getting an *estimated reduced correlation* for the PCI dimensions with the unrestricted range (the condition or group having the significantly increased variability) from the ones with the restricted range (the condition or group having the significantly decreased variability). This is done for all the correlations among PCI dimensions for the groups or conditions having significantly greater variability for which the variance analyses found significant differences in the inflationary direction.

Let us say, for example, that the dimensions of state of awareness, negative affect, and attention all had significantly greater variability for lows than highs for the hypnosis condition, while highs had greater variability for imagery. Let us further assume that for all four dimensions, the significantly greater variability was associated with the higher correlations. Thus, the correlations for state of awareness, negative affect, and attention for lows and imagery for highs with each of the other PCI dimensions of the matrices of lows and highs, respectively, would be correspondingly reduced for the subject group with the significantly greater variability. This would be done by estimating the correlation that would result if the group having the significantly greater variability had the same variance or variability as the group having the significantly lesser variability. These correlations would then be substituted in the matrix that had the inflated correlations.

Thus, for each of the dimensions of interest the standard deviation of the group or condition having the significantly lesser variability would be substituted in an equation (see below) similar to that of Guilford and Fruchter (1978, pp. 325–327) to generate correlations (for this PCI dimension with each other PCI dimension of the matrix) having the same variability as the correlation having the lesser variability. These correlations would then be substituted in the elements of the intercorrelation matrices for all PCI dimensions having significantly greater variability. For the PCI imagery dimension, for highs (using our example) this would involve correcting the correlation of imagery with each of the other PCI dimensions of the matrix of highs for the hypnosis condition, substituting the standard deviation of the lows in the modified equation of Guilford and Fruchter below.

As an example let:

r_c = the desired correlation corrected using the standard deviation of the group with the reduced variance.

r_u = the actual (unrestricted) correlation.

S_c = the standard deviation of the group that needs to be corrected, because its standard deviation is significantly higher than that of the other group.

S_u = the standard deviation of the group having a standard deviation significantly lower than that of the other group.

Then:

$$r_c = \frac{r_u(S_c/S_u)}{[1 - r_u^2 + r_u^2(S_c^2/S_u^2)]^{1/2}}$$

The corrected (reduced) correlations are then substituted in the correlation matrix, substituting a corrected correlation for each correlation of the dimension (with each other dimension of the matrix) that has the significantly greater variability. If imagery for high hypnotically susceptibles had a significantly greater variability than imagery for low hypnotically susceptibles, then in the correlation matrix for high susceptibles all of the imagery correlations with the other dimensions of the matrix (altered experience, attention, rationality, volitional control, etc.) would be reduced, using the formula above. The Jennrich test is then repeated and if a significant difference between matrices is still found, then differences between the matrices cannot be attributed to the significantly greater variability of the aforementioned dimension(s).

CONCLUSIONS

This chapter concludes the methodological and statistical limits for using RPA instruments in assessing and quantifying phenomenological intensity and pattern data. The following section will illustrate just what the previously defined methodology has been able to do in attempting to understand and predict human behavior and experience.

IV

Applications

11

The Trait of Absorption and Subjective Experience

INTRODUCTION

Previous research with predecessor instruments to the Phenomenology of Consciousness Inventory (PCI), that is, the Phenomenology of Consciousness Questionnaire (PCQ) and the (Abbreviated) Dimensions of Consciousness Questionnaire ((A)DCQ), assessed state manifestations of the trait of absorption. Absorption, "the openness to absorbing and self-altering experiences" (Tellegen & Atkinson, 1974), is a personality trait moderately correlated ($r = .38$) with hypnotic susceptibility. Absorption seems to describe an individual's proclivity toward complete attentional involvement in one's perceptual, imaginative, and ideational faculties (Fabian & Fishkin, 1981; O'Grady, 1980). Although subsequent studies (Finke & MacDonald, 1978; Spanos & McPeake, 1975; Yanchar & Johnson, 1981) have confirmed the correlation between hypnotic susceptibility and absorption, more recent studies (De Groot et al., 1988) have suggested that the correlation may be an artifact and due to expectancy and related variables. Despite the above controversy, absorption has been found to be associated with differential responsivity to meditation (Greenfield, 1977), EMG biofeedback (Qualls & Sheehan, 1981a,b), and marijuana intoxification (Fabian & Fishkin, 1981).

Unlike many behavioral-type questionnaires that have not been successful at assessing personality characteristics associated with altered-state induction procedures such as hypnosis (Hilgard, 1965), the items of the absorption questionnaire assess phenomenological experiences; experiences concerned with such subjective processes as attention, imagery, cognition, awareness, perception, and so forth. The significant differences found for hypnosis and the other conditions as a function of absorption may relate to the absorption questionnaire's ability to assess trait aspects associated with "state" changes in phenomenological experiences, which the previously enumerated altered-state induction procedures can be thought to induce (Singer, 1977; Tart, 1977; Zinberg, 1977).

Zuckerman, Persky, and Link (1967) have suggested the importance of distinguishing between trait and state aspects of subjective experience as they relate to altered state induction procedures such as hypnosis. Given this trait-state interface, using a phenomenological state instrument to investigate the parameters of various subjective experiences as these relate to the trait of absorption may help to determine why some individuals can more easily enter altered states of consciousness. Self-report questionnaires, capable of mapping and quantifying states of consciousness in terms of pattern changes, as Tart (1975, 1977) recommends, and intensity changes, as Singer (cited in Zinberg, 1977) suggests, may be able to assess and map alterations in phenomenological experience as a function of absorption.

Several studies were undertaken to investigate the relationship between absorption and phenomenological experience. Self-report questionnaires, developed by the author (reported in Pekala & Levine, 1981, 1982; Pekala & Wenger, 1983) were used to quantify phenomenological experience. Whereas study 1 attempted to correlate absorption with the (sub)dimensions of consciousness mapped by the PCQ (defined earlier in the book), studies 2 and 3 attempted to replicate the results and further refine them.

STUDY 1

This study assessed the relationship between absorption and the (sub)dimensions of consciousness monitored during the stimulus conditions of eyes open sitting quietly (experienced twice), reading erotica, and relaxation/meditation. Eyes open sitting quietly was chosen as a condition similar to normal waking consciousness; relaxation/meditation was chosen as a hypnoticlike condition that is associated with an altered state of consciousness; and reading erotica was used to assess an absorbed but nonaltered state of awareness. A second personality trait not related to hypnotic susceptibility, introversion-extraversion

(Eysenck, 1952), was also included to determine if this trait (as assessed by items of a more behavioral nature) would be found to correlate with the (sub)dimensions of the state questionnaire.

It was predicted that absorption would positively correlate with greater alterations in state of awareness and self-awareness; increased inward and absorbed attention; decreased volitional control; and increased alterations in subjective experience dealing with time, perception, body image, and meaning. These predictions follow from the nature of absorption as defined by Tellegen (1981) and the (sub)dimensions of consciousness that the questionnaires are capable of mapping.

Method

Subjects and Materials

The subjects were 249 introductory psychology students (179 females and 70 males) who participated in return for credits toward their final grade. Only the absorption and introversion-extraversion subscales of Tellegen's Differential Personality Questionnaire (DPQ) (now the Multidimensional Personality Questionnaire) (Tellegen, 1977) were used. The absorption scale was used to tap "openness to absorbing and self-altering experiences" (Tellegen & Atkinson, 1974), whereas the three scales of social closeness, social potency, and impulsiveness were used to assess the trait of introversion-extraversion. The absorption scale has a coefficient alpha of .89, whereas the introversion-extraversion scales have alphas of .87, .88, and .86. The PCQ was used to map subjective experience.

Procedure

Subjects participated in groups of about 35 individuals each. After the general nature of the study was explained, subjects experienced two four-minute stimulus conditions, that is, sitting quietly with eyes open, and the reading of mildly arousing erotica. Immediately following each condition, the subjects completed the PCQ in reference to that condition. At the end of the first session the participants completed the DPQ.

The subjects returned a week later at the same time and place and experienced two more conditions. These included a second eyes-open sitting quietly condition and a relaxation/meditation condition that consisted of standard progressive relaxation instructions to which was added a four-minute meditational interlude. During the meditational interlude, the subjects relaxed to their breathing. Immediately after each condition the participants completed the PCQ in reference to that condition (this was done in reference to the meditational interlude for the relaxation condition).

Results

Significant correlations ($p < .05$) were found between absorption and the following (sub)dimensions during the following stimulus conditions: awareness and state of awareness ($r = .17$) during the two eyes open conditions and the relaxation/meditation condition; altered experience and altered meaning, perception, time sense, and body image ($r = .18$) during the first eyes-open condition and the relaxation/meditation condition; imagery and imagery amount ($r = .19$) during the two eyes-open conditions; attention ($r = .14$) during the first eyes-open condition and the relaxation/meditation condition; and imagery vividness ($r = .16$) and direction of attention ($r = .14$) during the first eyes-open condition.

When correlating the trait of introversion-extraversion (summing across social closeness, social potency, and impulsivity) with the various (sub)dimensions, only altered meaning was positively correlated with extraversion for two of the four stimulus conditions.

Discussion

Except for the significant correlation between the subdimension of meaning and extraversion, the results indicated that introversion- extraversion does not appear to moderate phenomenological experience as assessed by the PCQ. On the other hand, significant, but low, correlations between absorption and several of the (sub)dimensions suggest that the ability to become involved in absorbing and self-altering experiences is mildly associated with significant alterations in attention, awareness, imagery, and the subjective altered experience of time, perception, body image, and meaning.

STUDY 2

To replicate the significant results, a second study was conducted. Six groups of subjects experienced eyes open and eyes closed sitting quietly. Whereas eyes open was used as a measure of normal waking consciousness, eyes closed was chosen to assess a waking conscious state where daydreaming and imagery might be more prominent (Singer & Pope, 1981). (Although the six groups of subjects experienced a third stimulus condition—either eyes open, eyes closed, relaxation/meditation, or an erotic fantasy—these results are not further addressed here.)

In addition, the study also compared differences in phenomenological state across low, medium, and high absorption individuals. It was predicted that during eyes open and eyes closed, high absorption individuals, in comparison to lows, would experience greater alterations in the intensities of subjective experience associated with the (sub)dimensions of consciousness correlating with absorption. It was also predicted that the state of consciousness of high absorption subjects, as assessed by the state questionnaire's pattern parameters, would be significantly different from that of low absorption individuals during both eyes open and eyes closed.

Method

Subjects and Materials

Subjects consisted of 304 introductory psychology students (217 females and 87 males) who participated in return for credits toward their final grade. Tellegen's absorption scale was again used to assess absorption. The (A)DCQ was used to map subjective experience. It has been described earlier in the book.

Procedure

Participants were seen in six groups of about 50 people each. After the general nature of the study was explained, the subjects completed the absorption questionnaire. They then experienced two four-minute stimulus conditions; the eyes-open and eyes-closed conditions mentioned earlier. Immediately at the end of each condition, the participants completed the ADCQ in reference to that condition. (Although the ADCQ was completed in reference to the eyes closed condition, a longer version of the ADCQ, the DCQ was completed in reference to the eyes-open condition. Only those items of the DCQ which were the same as the ADCQ, however, were used in the data analysis.)

Results

The subjects' scores for the trait of absorption were correlated with the subjects' intensity ratings for the (sub)dimensions of consciousness mapped by the ADCQ during the eyes-open and eyes-closed conditions. As can be seen in Table 11.1, significant correlations were found

Table 11.1. Correlation of Absorption with the
Dimensions of Consciousness[a]

	Condition[b,c]	
Dimension	Eyes open	Eyes closed
Internal dialogue	.11	.07
Awareness	.16**	.20***
Self-awareness	.16**	.15**
State of awareness	.12*	.19***
Imagery	.17**	.26***
Imagery amount	.21***	.28***
Imagery vividness	.10	.19***
Positive affect	.21***	.26***
Volitional control	.10	.08
Altered experience	.28***	.24***
Altered meaning	.23***	.22***
Altered perception	.17**	.14*
Altered time	.20***	.14*
Altered body image	.16**	.18**
Attention	.13*	.16**
Direction	.12*	.11
Absorption	.10	.18***
Negative affect	−.02	−.02
Memory	−.04	−.09
Rationality	.10	.06
Arousal	−.05	−.09

[a]From Pekala et al. (1985). Reprinted with permission of the publisher.
[b]$n = 304$.
[c]$* = p < .05$; $** = p < .01$; $*** p < .001$.

for most of the (sub)dimensions and all of the significant results of study 1 were replicated.

Intensity Differences among Low, Medium, and High Absorption Subjects

To further evaluate phenomenological experience as a function of absorption, three groups of 60 subjects each were selected for further analysis. Group 1 consisted of those 60 subjects scoring lowest on the absorption questionnaire ($M = 14.5$), group 3 consisted of those 60 individuals scoring highest on absorption ($M = 29.9$), whereas group 2 were those 60 subjects having absorption scores midway between those of groups 1 and 3 (M = 22.5). A one-way analysis of variance (ANOVA) was performed for the eyes-open and eyes-closed conditions for the subjects' intensity ratings for the (sub)dimensions, testing for significant differences among the three groups.

For the eyes-open condition, significant differences ($p < .05$) were found for the dimensions and associated subdimensions of internal dialogue, awareness, imagery, positive affect, and altered experience. Post hoc comparisons revealed that high absorption individuals (in comparison to lows) experienced significantly more imagery; greater positive affect; and greater alterations in self-awareness, meaning, perception, time sense, and body image. Moderate absorption individuals (in comparison to lows) reported significantly more imagery; greater alterations in meaning, time sense, and body image; and increased internal dialogue.

For the eyes-closed condition, significant differences between groups were found for awareness, imagery, positive affect, altered experience, and attention. High absorption individuals experienced greater alterations in state of awareness; more imagery and more vivid imagery; greater positive affect; increased absorption; and greater alterations in meaning and body image in comparison to lows. Moderate absorption subjects (in comparison to lows) also experienced greater alterations in state of awareness; increased imagery and more vivid imagery; more positive affect; increased absorption; and greater alterations in body image.

Pattern Differences among Low, Medium, and High Absorption Subjects

To assess for pattern differences, correlation matrices that were composed of the correlations of the 11 major dimensions of consciousness with each other were constructed for each condition. These correlations were then compared using the Jennrich (1970) test.

Comparison of the correlation matrices associated with low and high absorption subjects for the eyes-open condition yielded a chi-square value of 80.70, which was significant at the .05 level (df = 55). Comparison of the correlation matrices between lows and mediums was also significant (chi-square = 81.32), while that between mediums and highs was not.

Comparison of the correlation matrices associated with low and high absorption subjects for the eyes-closed condition was not significant (chi-square = 68.63, df = 55, $p > .05$). The comparisons between lows and mediums and mediums and highs were also not significant.

Discussion

Trait-State Correlations

The correlations between absorption and many of the (sub)dimensions of consciousness attest to the construct validity of the questionnaires. The fact that the correlations are relatively low may relate to the fact that absorption was correlated with various fleeting and highly variable phenomenological experiences, that is, the contents of one's stream of consciousness. Thus, the myriad of subjective events that can pass through one's stream of consciousness (Singer, 1977) may decrease the probability of more stable, or trait, phenomenological contents becoming evident during the relatively short time period assessed.

States of Consciousness as a Function of Absorption

Tart (1977) has argued that it is primarily pattern parameters that define a state of consciousness. Whereas altered states are distinguished from other states by (1) changes in the pattern among the structures or dimensions of consciousness and (2) the perception of being in a radically different state of consciousness, an identity state has an overall pattern that makes it different from other states of consciousness, but there is not perceived alteration in state of consciousness.

Using Tart's criteria, both high and medium absorption subjects during the eyes-open condition were found to be in a different identity state of consciousness relative to lows (a discrete state of consciousness, using the criteria defined in Chapter 10). Both groups of individuals experienced a significantly different organization among the dimensions of consciousness, yet neither group reported a significant alteration in state of awareness (as assessed by the PCI awareness dimension).

With eye closure, most of the significant intensity differences found between groups during eyes open were replicated. However, no significant pattern differences were now evident between groups. Hence, using Tart's definitions, it cannot be said that highs were in an altered state of consciousness in reference to lows during eyes closed, for although there was a significant perceived alteration in consciousness, there was not a significant pattern difference.

Conclusions

The trait of absorption will help to determine who will be susceptible to a hypnotic induction (Yanchar & Johnson, 1981). It will also determine who will report experiencing greater alterations in subjective experience during ordinary, waking consciousness. Yet eye closure will lead to reported intensity alterations in imagery, awareness, attention, and subjective experience that are further augmented with the experience of a hypnoticlike induction procedure (relaxation/meditation) (Pekala *et al.*, 1983). This leads to speculation that various hypnotic or altered-state induction procedures may accentuate already significant differences in the reported intensities of phenomenological experience across individuals of different absorption and possibly hypnotic ability.

STUDY 3

In an attempt to replicate the aforementioned results with the PCI, a third study was conducted (reported in Kumar & Pekala, 1988).

Method

Subjects, Materials, and Procedure

Subjects were 217 students from introductory psychology classes. The PCI (Pekala, 1982) was used to map subjective experience, while the Harvard Group Scale of Hypnotic Susceptibility (Shor & Orne, 1962) was used to measure hypnotic susceptibility.

Participants were seen in two groups. After the general nature of the study was explained, subjects sat quietly with their eyes closed for two minutes and were asked to think about whatever they liked. Afterward they completed the PCI in reference to their subjective experience. Subjects were then given the Harvard Group Scale, shortened approximately ten minutes to accommodate to the time constraints of the study. After the eye catalepsy instructions but before the posthypnotic suggestion and amnesia, subjects experienced a four-minute period during which they were told to continue to experience the state they were in. After coming out of the hypnosis and after writing down a list of the suggestions remembered, subjects completed the PCI in reference to the four-minute sitting quietly period.

Results

Preliminary Analyses

All subjects who had a reliability index of 2 or under were divided into three groups of low ($M = 15.6$, $n = 57$), medium ($M = 21.8$, $n = 57$), and high ($M = 28.4$, $n = 53$) absorption subjects.

Intensity Comparisons

A multivariate analysis of variance (MANOVA) was then performed using conditions (eyes closed, hypnosis) as a repeated-measures factor, and absorption groups (low, medium, high) as a between-groups factor. The dependent variables were the intensity scores of the 12 major PCI dimensions and the 14 minor dimensions. High correlations between the minor dimensions and their corresponding major dimensions warranted separate MANOVAs for the PCI major and minor dimensions. Alpha was set at .05.

For the 12 PCI major dimensions, the results indicated significant main effects for conditions ($F = 33.55$, $df = 12,159$, $p < .0001$) and absorption groups ($F = 2.62$, $df = 24,316$, $p < .001$). The conditions by absorption groups comparison approached significance ($F = 1.54$, $df = 24,316$, $p < .06$). For the PCI minor dimensions, there were significant main effects for conditions ($F = 28.28$, $df = 14,157$, $p < .0001$) and absorption groups ($F = 2.42$, $df = 28,312$, $p < .001$). The conditions by absorption groups comparison approached significance ($F = 1.50$, $df = 28,312$, $p < .06$).

As the multivariate analyses yielded significant results, separate conditions (2: eyes closed, hypnosis) by absorption groups (3: low, medium, high) analyses of variance (ANOVAs) were performed for each of the PCI major and minor dimensions.

Significant main effects for absorption groups were found for altered experience (body image, perception, meaning), altered state of awareness, and volitional control. Post hoc analyses revealed that high absorption subjects (vis-à-vis lows) reported significantly more altered experiences involving body image, perception, and meaning; greater alteration in state of awareness; more love; increased absorption; and decreased volitional control and self-awareness. Medium subjects, relative to lows, reported significantly greater alterations in perception and state of awareness and decreased volitional control. (The significant effects comparing hypnosis versus eyes closed will be reported in Chapter 12.)

A one-way analysis of variance was then performed *separately* for the eyes-closed and hypnotic induction conditions for the subjects' intensity ratings for the PCI (sub)dimensions of consciousness, testing for significant differences among the three absorption groups (Kumar & Pekala, 1988). For the eyes-closed condition, significant differences ($p < .05$) were found for the dimensions and associated subdimensions of positive affect, altered experience, and altered state of awareness. Post hoc comparisons using the Student-Neuman-Keuls procedure revealed high absorption subjects (in comparison to lows) experienced significantly more feelings of love; significantly more altered experiences involving time sense, body image, perception, and unusual meanings; and a significantly greater altered state of awareness (subjective sense of altered state, SSAS). Table 11.2 tabulates these comparisons.

For the hypnotic induction condition, significant differences between the three groups were found for altered experiences, visual imagery, attention, self-awareness, altered state of awareness, and volitional

Table 11.2. Dimension Intensity Comparisons across Low, Medium, and High Absorption Individuals during Eyes Closed

	Group mean[a,b]			
Dimension	Low	Medium	High	F ratio[c]
Positive affect	3.27!	3.18!	3.83	3.43*
Joy	3.22	3.15	3.69	1.66
Sexual excitement	2.59	2.57	3.20	2.15
Love	4.02!	3.83!	4.61	3.41*
Negative affect	1.25	0.93	1.06	1.26
Anger	1.50	1.02	1.12	1.86
Sadness	1.48	1.20	1.40	0.56
Fear	0.78	0.56	0.65	0.57
Altered experience	1.70!	1.90!	2.58	16.92***
Altered body image	2.40!	2.50!	3.34	9.68***
Altered time sense	2.34!	2.62!	3.06	3.26*
Altered perception	1.02!	1.26!	1.84	7.31***
Altered meaning	1.20!	1.39!	2.19	14.69***
Visual imagery	4.40	4.45	4.71	0.91
Amount	4.49	4.57	4.63	0.33
Vividness	4.28	4.25	4.68	1.51
Attention	4.13	4.02	4.20	0.40
Direction (inward)	4.17	4.02	4.09	0.20
Absorption	4.08	4.01	4.37	1.03
Self-awareness	4.27	4.19	3.75	2.84
Altered state of				
awareness	1.74!	2.06!	2.61	5.86**
Internal dialogue	2.73	3.17	3.13	0.79
Rationality	4.22	4.32	4.51	0.67
Volitional control	4.33	3.89	3.82	2.27
Memory	5.07	5.05	5.28	0.95
Arousal	1.90	1.61	1.60	0.68

[a]Higher values denote increased amounts ranging from none or little (rating = 0) to much or complete (rating = 6).
[b]Groups having an exclamation mark(s) (!) are significantly different from groups not having that exclamation mark(s) as determined by the Student–Newman–Keuls post hoc procedure.
[c]$df = 2/187$; $*p < .05$; $**p < .01$; $***p < .001$.

control. Post hoc comparisons revealed that during the hypnotic induction, highs relative to lows experienced greater alterations in body image, perception, and unusual meanings; greater absorption; decreased self-awareness; increased SSAS; and decreased volitional control. Moderate absorption subjects, relative to lows, reported greater altered perception, increased absorption, decreased self-awareness, increased SSAS, and decreased volitional control. Table 11.3 tabulates these comparisons.

Table 11.3. Dimension Intensity Comparisons across Low, Medium, and High Absorption Individuals during Hypnosis

Dimension	Group mean[a,b]			F ratio[c]
	Low	Medium	High	
Positive affect	1.34	1.48	1.57	0.51
Joy	1.43	1.57	1.70	0.53
Sexual excitement	0.75	1.10	0.83	1.04
Love	1.82	1.77	2.18	1.03
Negative affect	0.62	0.69	0.85	0.92
Anger	0.62	0.59	0.70	0.13
Sadness	0.60	0.82	0.93	1.14
Fear	0.63	0.68	0.94	1.00
Altered experience	2.16!	2.38!	3.04	11.10***
Altered body image	2.27!	3.10!	3.73	6.33**
Altered time sense	3.30	3.37	3.67	0.80
Altered perception	1.54	2.08!	2.73!!	9.92***
Altered meaning	1.37!	1.34!	2.29	10.72***
Visual imagery	1.96	2.50	2.29	2.03
Amount	1.76!	2.59	2.24!	3.60*
Vividness	2.16	2.41	2.34	0.40
Attention	3.53	4.13!	4.24!	5.62**
Direction (inward)	3.50	4.05	4.07	2.78
Absorption	3.56	4.27!	4.50!	5.96**
Self-awareness	3.44	3.07!	2.60!	4.16*
Altered state of awareness	3.33	3.94!	4.30!	4.95**
Internal dialogue	1.67	2.10	2.30	1.65
Rationality	3.53	3.18	2.83	2.47
Volitional control	3.07	2.56!	2.16!	4.89**
Memory	3.99	3.81	3.53	1.12
Arousal	1.46	1.38	1.09	1.00

[a]Higher values denote increased amounts ranging from none or little (rating = 0) to much or complete (rating = 6).
[b]Groups having an exclamation mark(s) (!) are significantly different from groups not having that exclamation mark(s) as determined by the Student–Newman–Keuls post hoc procedure.
[c]$df = 2/187$; *$p < .05$; **$p < .01$; ***$p < .001$.

Pattern Comparisons

Pattern comparisons between the three groups of subjects were also computed. Correlation matrices that were composed of the correlations of the 12 major dimensions of the PCI were constructed for the three groups of subjects for the eyes-closed and hypnotic induction conditions. Comparison of the correlation matrices (via the Jennrich test) associated with the low and high absorption subjects during the eyes-closed condition yielded a chi-square value of 89.33, which was significant ($p <$ .05). Comparison of the correlation matrices of low and medium and medium and high absorption subjects during the eyes-closed condition was not significant. Pattern comparisons between lows and highs, lows and mediums, and medium and high absorption subjects during hypnosis were not found to be significant.

Conclusions

These results replicated many of the intensity results obtained earlier between low and high absorption subjects as assessed by the (A)DCQ. (The fact that all comparisons with the (A)DCQ were not replicated with the PCI may relate to the larger n used with the (A)DCQ study. Whereas the (A)DCQ study used the 60 lowest, middle, and highest absorption subjects from a pool of 304 individuals, the PCI study used the lowest, middle, and highest 60 subjects from a pool of approximately 170 subjects.) The PCI intensity results suggest that low, vis-à-vis high, absorption subjects report alterations in subjective experience that are further intensified when these subjects are hypnotized.

If one uses Tart's (1975, 1977) criteria (or the criteria set forth in Chapter 10) to define an altered state of consciousness vis-à-vis a non-altered state as distinguished by changes in pattern among the structures of consciousness and the subjective sense of (being in) an altered state of consciousness, then high absorption individuals were in an altered state of consciousness vis-à-vis low absorption individuals during the eyes-closed sitting quietly condition. Highs had a significantly different phenomenological pattern structure from that of lows and they also perceived their state of consciousness as assessed by the altered state of awareness dimension to be significantly different from lows. No significant pattern differences were found, however, when comparing lows and highs during hypnosis. This is surprising, considering that hypnosis would be presumed to intensify differences between lows and highs, as it did with the intensity comparisons.

Notice also that the pattern results for the eyes-closed condition is different (and reversed) from the results of study 2. In that study pattern effects were not found to be significantly different between low and high absorption subjects during eyes closed, although they were during eyes open. This difference between studies suggests that the pattern comparison results, at least concerning the trait of absorption, appear to be less robust than the intensity comparisons. (The inability to replicate the pattern comparisons may relate to the fact that the Jennrich comparisons used approximately 60 instead of the recommended 120 subjects per group.)

12

Using the PCI to Investigate Trait-State Aspects of Hypnosis and Several Stress Management Conditions

STUDY 1

Rationale

Given the relationship between hypnotic susceptibility and absorption (r = .38) (Tellegen & Atkinson, 1974), it was hypothesized that the results found with low, medium, and high absorption subjects (reported in Chapter 11) would also be found with low, medium, and high hypnotically susceptible subjects. By using the Phenomenology of Consciousness Inventory (PCI) to investigate the phenomenological parameters of hypnosis across low, medium, and high susceptible subjects, this might help to provide evidence concerning the trait-state controversy in hypnosis. This controversy concerns the extent to which "hypnotic responsiveness is more a matter of the characteristics of the subject than of the state produced by the hypnotic induction" (Hilgard, 1975, p. 20).

If the results indicate that high susceptible subjects report phenomenological alterations in subjective experience prior to a hypnotic induction (i.e., in reference to a baseline eyes-open or eyes-closed stimulus condition), this would support the importance of trait or individual differences measures in determining the extent to which such differences are involved in the resulting hypnotic state. On the other hand, increased phenomenological alterations during a hypnotic induction, as opposed to a baseline stimulus condition such as eyes closed sitting quietly, would implicate the importance of an induction in augmenting susceptibility.

There is rather definitive evidence that (1) there are pronounced individual differences as regards hypnotic susceptibility across subjects, and that (2) a hypnotic induction does lead to increased alterations in subjective experience consistent with increased hypnotic responsiveness, at least for many subjects (Brown & Fromm, 1986; Hilgard, 1965, 1977). The present research was done to determine if the above results would be found when assessing the phenomenological correlates of a hypnotic induction procedure and a baseline comparison condition of eyes closed sitting quietly across low, medium, and high susceptible subjects.

Predictions

Thus, the present study (reported in Kumar & Pekala, 1988) was undertaken to determine which phenomenological variables may be involved in trait and state aspects of hypnotizability and to what extent such variables are differentially implicated across low, medium, and high susceptible subjects. Given the absorption results reported in Chapter 11 and Hilgard's (1965, 1977) review of the importance of both state and trait aspects of hypnotizability, the following predictions were made:

1. Low, medium, and high hypnotizable subjects will report significant (sub)dimension intensity differences for awareness, imagery, positive affect, altered experience, and attention during both the eyes-closed and hypnosis conditions. These predictions follow from previous results when assessing low, medium, and high absorption subjects during eyes open and eyes closed sitting quietly and the correlation between absorption and hypnotic susceptibility.

2. Due to the experimental research (Hilgard, 1965) that a hypnotic induction leads to greater alterations in phenomenological experience during hypnosis vis-à-vis a baseline comparison condition, the hypnotic induction will evince greater alterations in phe-

nomenological experience than will the eyes-closed condition. This result will be found for low, medium, and high susceptible subjects.

3. Following experimental and clinical research (Brown & Fromm, 1986; Hilgard, 1965, 1977) that the hypnotic induction affects high susceptible subjects more than low susceptible subjects, high susceptible individuals will report a significantly greater degree of alteration in phenomenological experience when comparing the hypnotic induction against eyes closed than will low susceptible subjects.

Research Design

Students ($n = 263$; 88 men, 175 women) from several sections of introductory courses in psychology participated. Completed data were available on 217 students (72 men, 145 women). The participants knew in advance that the study involved hypnosis. The Harvard Group Scale of Hypnotic Susceptibility, Form A (Shor & Orne, 1962) was used to measure hypnotic susceptibility. The PCI was used to map phenomenological experience.

Participants were run in two groups. After the general nature of the study was explained, subjects were asked to sit quietly with their eyes closed and think about whatever they liked. At the end of four minutes, they opened their eyes and completed the PCI, Form 1, in reference to the time they sat with their eyes closed.

Upon completion of the PCI, subjects experienced the induction procedure of the Harvard Scale, which was shortened approximately ten minutes to accommodate to the time constraints of the study. After the eye catalepsy instructions but before the posthypnotic suggestion and amnesia, the subjects experienced a four-minute time period during which time they were told to "continue to experience the state you are in right now. For the next several minutes I'm going to stop talking and I want you to continue to experience the state you are in right now."

After repeating these instructions, the experimenter was silent for four minutes. The rest of the Harvard Scale instructions were then given. After the end of the induction procedure and after writing down a list of the hypnotic suggestions subjects remembered (and after removal of amnesia), the participants completed the PCI, Form 2, in reference to the time "when I stopped talking and I asked you to continue to experience the state you were in." Subjects then completed the 11 response items of the Harvard Scale.

Nature of the Results

Preliminary Analyses

Subjects' responses to the PCI were first assessed for intraindividual reliability. This was done by computing average absolute difference scores for each subject for the five pairs of reliability items (pairs of items of very similar or identical content) embedded in the questionnaire for the eyes-closed and hypnotic induction conditions. An average absolute difference score (reliability index; RI) of 0 indicates perfect reliability. Subjects with marginal RIs of 2 or higher were eliminated from the analysis. This resulted in 195 subjects having an acceptable RI for the eyes-closed condition, 190 subjects for the hypnotic induction condition, and 173 subjects with acceptable RIs for both conditions.

Three groups of subjects were then formed, based on the distribution of scores on the Harvard scale: low (0–5; $M = 3.25$), medium (6–8; $M = 7.16$), and high (9–12; $M = 10.27$).

Hypnotic Susceptibility Comparisons

MANOVAs were performed on the intensity scores for the major PCI dimensions and the subdimensions utilizing conditions (eyes closed, hypnosis) as the repeated-measures factor and susceptibility groups (low, medium, high susceptibility) as the between-subjects factor. (High correlations between the minor dimensions and their corresponding major dimensions warranted separate MANOVAs for the major and minor dimensions.) Alpha was set at .01.

For the 12 major PCI dimensions, the results indicated significant main effects for conditions [$F(12, 154) = 36.89$, $p < .0001$], and susceptibility groups [$F(24, 316) = 5.26$, $p < .001$]; and a significant interaction for conditions by susceptibility groups [$F(24, 316) = 3.21$, $p < .001$]. For the 14 minor dimensions, the results demonstrated significant main effects for conditions [$F(14, 157) = 29.98$, $p < .0001$], and susceptibility groups [$F(28, 312) = 3.21$, $p < .001$]; and a significant interaction between conditions and susceptibility groups [$F(28, 312) = 3.06$, $p < .001$].

Due to the significant MANOVAs, separate conditions (repeated factor) by susceptibility groups (2 x 3) ANOVAs were then performed for each of the PCI (sub)dimensions (see Table 12.1). For the conditions main effect, the hypnotic condition was associated with significantly less positive affect (joy, sexual excitement, love); negative affect (anger, sadness); visual imagery (amount, vividness); self-awareness, internal dialogue, rationality, volitional control, and memory; and significantly

Table 12.1. *F*-Test Comparisons for the Phenomenology of Consciousness Inventory as a Function of Conditions and Susceptibility Groups

Dimension	Main effects[a]		Interaction
	Conditions	Groups	
Positive affect	202.27***	6.01**	1.01
Joy	138.05***	5.95**	0.37
Sexual excitement	115.45***	1.90	1.49
Love	166.94***	5.34**	0.64
Negative affect	13.45***	0.79	0.66
Anger	21.32***	0.30	0.47
Sadness	21.09***	0.58	0.93
Fear	0.81	1.39	0.60
Altered experience	26.90***	32.39***	6.03**
Altered body image	6.25*	26.81***	1.73
Altered time sense	31.78***	12.89***	2.00
Altered perception	41.62***	10.48***	7.86**
Altered meaning	0.22	14.02***	3.98*
Imagery	254.14***	0.46	6.42**
Amount	232.74***	0.42	1.79
Vividness	174.20***	1.38	11.19***
Attention	2.08	11.00***	5.88**
Direction (inward)	2.58	6.55**	2.52
Absorption	0.30	10.85***	5.77**
Self-awareness	69.74***	19.55***	14.24***
Altered state of awareness	155.62***	26.20***	10.01***
Internal dialogue	32.46***	1.49	0.69
Rationality	60.48***	8.61***	12.95***
Volitional control	102.99***	33.98***	11.72***
Memory	105.92***	9.21***	17.17***
Arousal	6.46*	4.41*	1.92

[a]$* = p < .05$; $** = p < .01$; $*** = p < .001$.

more altered experience (time sense, perception) and altered state of awareness than the eyes-closed condition.

Significant main effects for susceptibility groups were found for positive affect (joy, love), altered experience (body image, time sense, perception, meaning), attention (direction, absorption), self-awareness, altered state of awareness, rationality, volitional control, and memory.

When assessing for simple main effects, post hoc comparisons for the eyes-closed condition revealed that high susceptibles, relative to low susceptibles, reported significantly greater alterations in body image, time sense, meaning, and altered state of awareness. Medium susceptibles, compared to low susceptibles, reported significantly increased alterations in body image and state of awareness.

Post hoc comparisons for the hypnotic induction condition revealed that high susceptibles, vis-à-vis low susceptibles, reported significantly increased absorbed attention, greater altered experience (body image, time sense, perception, meaning), and increased alterations in state of awareness. High susceptibles also reported significantly less imagery vividness, self-awareness, rationality, volitional control, and memory. Medium susceptible subjects, vis-à-vis low susceptibles, reported significantly more altered experience (body image, time sense, perception, meaning), absorbed attention, and altered state of awareness; and significantly less imagery vividness, self-awareness, rationality, volitional control, and memory. High susceptibles, relative to mediums, reported significantly more altered experience (perception, meaning) and absorption, and significantly less rationality, volitional control, and memory.

Concerning the significant interactions (alpha = .01), graphs of the means indicated significant ordinal interactions between conditions and susceptibility groups for altered experience (perception), imagery vividness, self-awareness, altered state of awareness, rationality, volitional control, and memory. For all of the PCI (sub)dimensions, the hypnotic induction condition (compared to eyes closed) was associated with a significantly *greater* increase in altered experience (perception) and altered state of awareness, and a significantly greater decrease in imagery (vividness), rationality, self-awareness, volitional control, and memory for the high (and medium) susceptible groups relative to the low susceptible group. A significant disordinal interaction was found for absorption. Whereas high susceptible subjects reported a more absorbed attentional focus during hypnosis, low susceptible subjects reported being less absorbed (or more distracted) during the induction than eyes closed. Figures 12.1 and 12.2 illustrate several of the significant interactions.

Table 12.2 lists the correlation coefficients among the major PCI dimensions, absorption, and hypnotic susceptibility. The upper right matrix lists the correlations during hypnosis and the lower left matrix does the same during eyes closed. Notice that the correlations are very different between conditions.

Discussion and Interpretation

The three predictions were supported by the results. As predicted, significant differences across low, medium, and high susceptibles were found for many PCI (sub)dimensions. The hypnotic condition (vis-à-vis eyes closed) was also associated with significant changes across most of

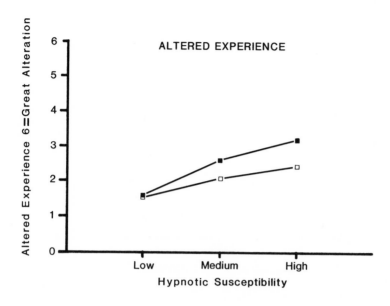

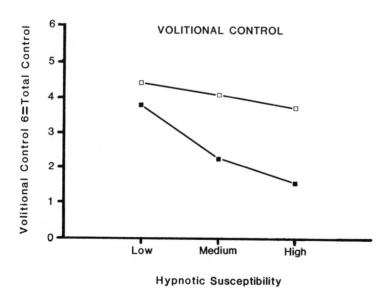

Figure 12.1. Significant PCI dimension interactions as a function of conditions and suscep-tibility group. (□, Eyes closed; ■, hypnotic induction.)

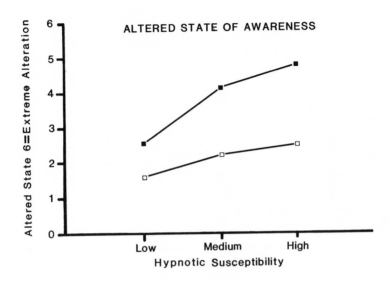

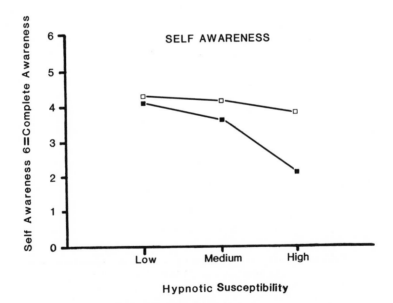

Figure 12.2. Significant PCI dimension interactions as a function of conditions and susceptibility group. (□, Eyes closed; ■, hypnotic induction.)

Table 12.2. Intercorrelation Matrices for Absorption, Hypnotic Susceptibility, and the 12 Major PCI Dimensions during Hypnosis[a] and Eyes Closed[b]

	1	2	3	4	5	6	7	8	9	10	11	12	13	14
Absorption[c]	.	.27f	-.25f	.26f	.07	-.22e	-.24e	-.16a	-.11	.10	.06	.34f	.10	.29f
Susceptibility	.27f	.	-.55f	.60f	-.15a	-.41f	-.65f	-.41f	-.28f	.19a	.03	.56f	-.12	.44f
Self-awareness	-.08	-.14	.	-.71f	.29f	.65f	.67f	.65f	.28f	-.11	-.06	-.61f	.15	-.38f
State of awareness	.20e	.21e	-.50f	.	-.25e	-.57f	-.75f	-.45f	-.29f	.07	.02	.70f	-.14	.47f
Internal dialogue	.10	-.08	.17a	.00	.	.24e	.25f	.20e	.07	.07	.13	-.10	.16a	-.11
Rationality	.10	-.05	.12	.06	-.03	.	.65f	.61f	.17a	-.09	-.16a	-.59f	.28f	-.25f
Volitional control	-.08	-.18a	.36f	-.13	.09	.40f	.	.47f	.34f	-.04	.00	-.67f	.15a	-.48f
Memory	.13	.13	.04	-.01	-.10	.59f	.33f	.	.15	-.04	-.10	-.46f	.18a	-.21e
Arousal	-.11	-.13	.13	-.11	.17a	-.28f	-.12	-.31f	.	-.05	.31f	-.25e	.13	-.38f
Positive affect	.24e	.26f	-.05	.15	-.15a	.26e	.10	.34f	-.34f	.	.22e	.27f	.36f	.11
Negative affect	-.01	.08	-.05	.02	.18a	-.24e	-.21e	-.12	.38f	-.14	.	.17a	.17a	-.12
Altered experience	.41f	.32f	-.29f	.59f	-.07	.16a	.02	.14	-.23e	.36f	-.08	.	-.01	.37f
Vivid, visual imagery	.15	.19a	-.09	.16a	-.18a	.47f	.15	.44f	-.28f	.41f	-.09	.29f	.	.04
Inward, absorbed attention	.05	.18a	-.22e	.17a	-.15a	.48f	.21e	.43f	-.33f	.25e	-.11	.22e	.34f	.

From Kumar & Pekala (1988). Reprinted with permission of the publisher.

[a]Intercorrelations for the hypnotic induction condition are listed in the upper right of the matrix.

[b]Intercorrelations for the eyes closed condition are listed in the lower left of the matrix.

[c]n = 173.

[a]p < .05.

[e]p < .01.

[f]p < .001.

the PCI (sub)dimensions for the susceptible groups (as it was for the absorption groups for many PCI (sub)dimensions). In addition, the significant ordinal interactions for the susceptible groups suggests that hypnosis potentiated the differences between these two conditions for the high (and medium) relative to the low susceptible group.

The results support both a trait and state interpretation of hypnotic susceptibility, at least in terms of subjects' self-reported phenomenological effects. The "trance controversy" in hypnosis (Hilgard, 1975; Shor, 1959, 1962) concerns the extent to which trait, situational, and state variables account for more of the variance of hypnotic responses. Whereas trait theorists assert that more of the variance is due to trait variables, situational theorists (Sarbin & Coe, 1972) suggest that the situational context is of primary importance, and state theorists suggest the "enhancement of hypnotic-like behavior as a consequence of induction procedures" (Hilgard, 1975, p. 21). These positions are not necessarily mutually exclusive.

Tellegen (1979) has argued for the need to consider *interacting* variables on resulting hypnotic responsiveness. The results of the reported study highlight the importance of an interaction between trait and state/situational variables. The importance of a subject's hypnotic ability (trait) was found to be evident in the nonhypnotic context of eyes closed sitting quietly. Phenomenological differences were further augmented during hypnosis, presumably the result of "state" effects associated with the hypnotic induction, although *situational* cues and the contextual environment probably also had a major effect on the resulting self-reports.

STUDY 2

Rationale

The previously cited research found that high susceptible subjects, relative to low susceptible subjects, reported significantly greater alterations in subjective experience for various dimensions of phenomenological experience, and that hypnosis, vis-à-vis eyes closed, was also associated with further alterations in subjective experience.

The Kumar and Pekala study highlighted the importance of the interaction between a subject's hypnotic ability (trait), the contextual environment or situation of the subject, that is, eyes closed versus an hypnotic induction, and the resulting phenomenological *state* reported by the subject. The present study (reported in Kumar and Pekala, 1989) was designed to replicate the previous findings with a different group of subjects. It was predicted that:

1. During hypnosis and a baseline condition (eyes open/closed), high susceptible subjects will report the phenomenological effects previously reported, relative to low susceptible subjects.
2. The hypnotic induction (vis-à-vis eyes open/closed) will be associated with increased relaxation (decreased arousal); greater alterations in state of awareness and experiences involving body image, time sense, perception, and unusual meanings; and decreased volitional control, self-awareness, internal dialogue, positive and negative affect, rationality, and memory.
3. Since a hypnotic induction appears to have a more significant effect on high than low susceptibles (Brown & Fromm, 1986; Hilgard, 1977; Kumar & Pekala, 1988; Orne, 1959; Shor, 1979), phenomenological intensity differences (hypnosis compared to eyes open/closed) will be significantly greater for high than low (and medium) susceptible subjects.

Research Design

The subject pool for this study consisted of 434 undergraduates enrolled in introductory psychology classes at West Chester University. Subjects knew beforehand that the study involved hypnosis; participation was voluntary. Whereas, the Harvard Group Scale of Hypnotic Susceptibility, Form A (Shor & Orne, 1962) was used to assess susceptibility, the PCI was used to map phenomenological experience.

The 434 subjects were seen in five groups of 75, 78, 42, 129, and 110. After the general nature of the experiment was explained, four of the five subject groups ($n = 324$) were told to close their eyes, sit quietly, and think about whatever they liked. At the end of three minutes, they were asked to open their eyes and complete the PCI, Form 1, in reference to the time they sat with their eyes closed. The fifth group of subjects sat with their eyes open ($n = 110$). They were told to think about whatever they liked and afterward completed the PCI in reference to the eyes open period. Upon completion of the questionnaire, all subjects experienced the induction procedure of the Harvard Scale. To accommodate to the time constraints of the study, the Harvard Scale was shortened by eliminating redundant phraseology in the induction phase.

After the eye catalepsy instructions but before the posthypnotic suggestions and amnesia instructions, the subjects experienced a three-minute period during which they were told to "continue to experience the state you are in right now. For the next several minutes I'm going to stop talking and I want you to continue to experience the state you are in right now." These instructions were repeated and the experimenter was silent for three minutes. The rest of the instructions were then given. After the end of the induction procedure and after writing down a list of the hypnotic suggestions remembered (and after removal of the amnesia), the participants completed the PCI, Form 2, in reference to the time "when I stopped talking and I asked you to continue to experience the state you were in." The subjects then completed the 11 response items of the Harvard Scale.

Nature of the Results

Preliminary Analyses

Although the initial subject pool consisted of 434 subjects, completed data (completion of all paper-and-pencil tests without errors or omissions) were available on 375 subjects (237 females and 138 males). This represented 86% of all subjects tested.

Each subject's responses to the PCI were assessed for intratest reliability by means of the five pairs of reliability items embedded in the questionnaire. Subjects having a marginal reliability index (an average absolute difference score of greater than 2.0 for the five item-pairs) were eliminated.

Eliminating unreliable subjects resulted in 251 individuals having an acceptable reliability index (RI) for the eyes-closed condition, 84 having an acceptable RI for the eyes-open condition, 342 having an acceptable RI for the hypnotic induction condition, and 310 subjects having an acceptable RI for *both* the eyes open/closed and the hypnotic conditions. This represented 90%, 88%, 91%, and 83%, respectively, of the subject pool (after elimination of subjects with incomplete data).

Reliability Analyses

To determine internal consistency reliability for this administration of the PCI, coefficient alphas were computed for each (sub)dimension of the PCI. Table 12.3 lists the reliability coefficients for the three stimulus conditions. For the 12 major dimensions reliabilities ranged from .57 for volitional control to .91 for internal dialogue during eyes open, and 89% of all alphas were .70 or above. These results are quite similar to those reported earlier (Pekala *et al.*, 1986) where the same three stimulus conditions were assessed. (A table of the coefficient alphas for the three conditions for that earlier research was presented in Table 7.2, page 133.)

Table 12.3. Coefficient Alphas for the Phenomenology of Consciousness Inventory across Several Different Stimulus Conditions

Dimension	Stimulus condition[a]			Average
	Eyes open	Eyes closed	Hypnotic induction	
Positive affect	.83	.86	.87	.85
Joy	.73	.70	.69	.71
Sexual excitement	.92	.93	.90	.92
Love	.75	.78	.79	.77
Negative affect	.80	.82	.84	.82
Anger	.71	.74	.68	.71
Sadness	.82	.79	.83	.73
Fear	.63	.79	.83	.75
Altered experience	.75	.78	.88	.80
Altered body image	.60	.67	.74	.67
Altered time sense	.73	.77	.82	.77
Altered perception	.49	.65	.83	.66
Altered meaning	.63	.60	.76	.66
Visual imagery	.85	.90	.77	.84
Amount	.82	.85	.84	.84
Vividness	.77	.82	.56	.72
Attention	.72	.73	.75	.73
Direction (inward)	.65	.69	.78	.71
Absorption	.66	.73	.72	.70
Self-awareness	.61	.76	.83	.73
Altered state of awareness	.85	.80	.92	.86
Internal dialogue	.91	.89	.89	.90
Rationality	.58	.75	.87	.73
Volitional control	.57	.71	.75	.68
Memory	.72	.79	.84	.78
Arousal	.82	.84	.60	.75
Average (major dimensions)	.75	.80	.82	.79
Average (subdimensions)	.71	.75	.77	.74

[a]Excludes subjects with a reliability index of > 2.0.

(Sub)Dimension Intensity Comparisons as a Function of Individual Differences

To determine the nature of phenomenological intensity differences between eyes open/closed and hypnosis as a function of low, medium,

and high hypnotic susceptibility, subjects having a reliability index of
two or less for *both* the eyes open/closed and the hypnotic induction
conditions were divided into three approximately equal groups of low
(0–4, $n = 100$, $M = 2.41$), medium (5–7, $n = 110$, $M = 6.00$), and high (8–
12, $n = 100$, $M = 9.37$) susceptible subjects.

Subjects' responses to the items that composed each (sub)dimen-
sion were averaged to arrive at an intensity score for each subject for
each condition for all 26 (sub)dimensions. Multivariate analyses of variance were then performed for the PCI major and also the PCI minor
dimensions utilizing conditions (eyes open/closed, hypnosis) as the
repeated-measures factor, and susceptibility groups (low, medium, and
high susceptibility) and subject groups (subjects were run in five
groups) as the between-groups factors. The PCI (sub)dimension intensity scores served as the dependent variable.

Although a significant main effect was found for subject groups for
the PCI major dimensions ($F = 1.45$, $df = 48/1122$, $p < .03$), individual
ANOVA analyses indicated that none of the 12 comparisons were significant at the .05 level. Interactions between subject groups, groups, and
conditions were not significant. A significant main effect for the PCI
minor dimensions was not found for subject groups, and all interactions
were nonsignificant except for the subject groups by conditions interaction ($F = 1.50$, $df = 56/1122$, $p < .02$). Individual ANOVAs indicated that
only 1 of the 14 interaction comparisons (unusual meanings) was significant at the .05 level. The results suggested that there were little significant intensity differences between the five groups across the PCI
(sub)dimensions, and hence gave no contraindications for combining
the eyes-open and eyes-closed subject groups.

MANOVAs for the PCI major dimensions indicated significant main
effects for conditions [$F(12, 294) = 50.04$, $p < .0001$], and susceptibility
groups [$F(24, 586) = 7.44$, $p < .0001$], and a significant interaction between conditions and susceptibility groups [$F(24, 586) = 4.24$, $p <
.0001$]. Multivariate analysis of the PCI minor dimensions also yielded
significant main effects for conditions [$F(14, 294) = 34.97$, $p < .0001$],
and susceptibility groups [$F(28, 586) = 5.20$, $p < .0001$], and a significant
interaction between conditions and susceptibility groups [$F(28, 586) =
1.87$, $p < .006$].

Due to the significant multivariate effects, separate susceptibility
groups (3) by conditions (2) between × within ANOVAs were then performed for the PCI (sub)dimensions. Table 12.4 lists the F-test comparisons for the main effects and the interactions for all (sub)dimensions
(alpha was set at .01). For the conditions main effect, 20 out of 26 PCI
(sub)dimensions significantly differentiated hypnosis from eyes open/

Table 12.4. *F*-Test Comparisons for the Phenomenology of Consciousness Inventory as a Function of Conditions and Susceptibility Groups: Study 2

| | Main effects[a] | | |
Dimension	Conditions[b]	Groups[c]	Interaction[c]
Positive affect	292.78***	2.86	0.14
Joy	143.17***	5.15**	0.53
Sexual excitement	219.75***	1.26	0.59
Love	282.52***	2.87	0.11
Negative affect	36.30***	5.36**	1.60
Anger	23.74***	7.00**	1.85
Sadness	58.92***	2.45	1.89
Fear	3.91*	3.12*	0.71
Altered experience	43.21***	43.59***	13.75***
Altered body image	6.46***	28.51***	6.79**
Altered time sense	49.17***	30.96***	7.75**
Altered perception	50.91***	19.59***	7.33**
Altered meaning	1.10	20.40***	4.28*
Imagery	174.50***	0.28	2.84
Amount	196.71***	2.40	1.66
Vividness	103.12***	0.82	4.01*
Attention	1.06	10.72***	3.05*
Direction (inward)	1.95	2.82	0.93
Absorption	0.00	17.92***	4.07*
Self-awareness	83.94***	31.75***	26.30***
Altered state of awareness	222.63***	54.52***	11.33***
Internal dialogue	84.64***	2.89	6.03**
Rationality	82.47***	15.52***	11.58***
Volitional control	221.47***	39.86***	21.00***
Memory	146.25***	11.89***	25.70***
Arousal	5.05*	3.80*	3.49*

[a]$* = p < .05; ** = p < .01; *** = p < .001.$
[b]$df = 1/293.$
[c]$df = 2/293.$

closed. Hypnosis vis-à-vis eyes open/closed was associated with significantly decreased positive (joy, love, sexual excitement) and negative (anger, sadness) affect; imagery amount and vividness; and self-awareness, internal dialogue, rationality, volitional control, and memory. It was also associated with an increased altered state of awareness and increased altered experiences involving body image, time sense, perception, and meaning.

Concerning the susceptibility groups main effect, 15 out of 26 comparisons were significant. Student-Neuman-Keuls post hoc comparisons collapsing across hypnosis and eyes open/closed (alpha = .01) indicated that high susceptibles, vis-à-vis low susceptibles, reported significantly increased joy; increased altered experiences involving body image, time sense, perception, and meaning; a more altered state of awareness; a more internally oriented, absorbed attentional focus; and decreased self-awareness, rationality, volitional control, and memory.

Analyses were also performed separately for the eyes open/closed and the hypnosis conditions assessing for simple main effects. During eyes open/closed, high susceptibles, vis-à-vis low susceptibles, reported significantly more altered experiences involving body image, time sense, perception, and meaning; increased absorption and altered state of awareness; and decreased rationality and volitional control. Mediums, vis-à-vis lows, reported more altered experiences involving body image, time sense, perception, and meaning; an increased altered state of awareness; and decreased rationality and volitional control. Highs, vis-à-vis mediums, reported increased absorption and decreased rationality.

During hypnosis, high susceptibles, relative to low susceptibles, reported increased altered experiences involving body image, time sense, perception, and meaning; increased absorption and a more altered state of awareness; and decreased internal dialogue, rationality, volitional control, memory, self-awareness, and arousal. Medium susceptibles, relative to lows, reported increased altered experiences involving body image, time sense, perception, and meaning; an increased altered state of awareness; and decreased rationality, volitional control, memory, and self-awareness. Highs, relative to mediums, reported increased altered experiences involving body image, time sense, perception, and meaning; increased absorption and a more altered state of awareness; and decreased self-awareness, internal dialogue, volitional control, and memory. Table 12.5 tabulates the group means for the various PCI (sub)dimensions during hypnosis.

In addition, 10 out of 26 possible interactions between conditions and susceptibility groups were significant ($p < .01$). For altered experience (in general), altered body image, altered perception, altered time sense, self-awareness, altered state of awareness, internal dialogue, rationality, volitional control, and memory, hypnosis appeared to potentiate the reported differences between conditions for high as opposed to low (and medium, to a lesser extent) susceptible subjects. As with the earlier study, low susceptibles reported being *more* distracted during hypnosis than the eyes-closed sitting quietly comparison period. Figures 12.3 and 12.4 illustrate several of these interactions.

Table 12.5. Dimension Intensity Comparisons across Low, Medium, and High Susceptible Individuals during Hypnosis

Dimension	Group mean[a,b]			F ratio[c]
	Low	Medium	High	
Positive affect	1.12	1.65!	1.61!	3.50*
Joy	1.18	1.79!	1.75!	3.89*
Sexual excitement	0.71	1.04	0.98	0.95
Love	1.50	2.13	2.11	2.93
Negative affect	0.79	0.66	0.70	0.35
Anger	0.79	0.65	0.43	1.47
Sadness	0.86	0.66	0.82	0.51
Fear	0.73	0.67	0.83	0.26
Altered experience	1.81!	2.64!!	3.15!!!	30.74***
Altered body image	2.33	3.41!	3.81!	16.99***
Altered time sense	2.73	3.57!	4.07!	11.87***
Altered perception	1.43!	2.14!!	2.80!!!	14.13***
Altered meaning	1.01!	1.73!!	2.22!!!	14.63***
Visual imagery	2.53	2.27	1.95	2.11
Amount	2.19	2.31	2.14	0.16
Vividness	2.86	2.24!	1.76!	7.09**
Attention	3.30!	4.08!!	4.61!!!	18.59***
Direction (inward)	3.30	4.00!	4.40!	8.78***
Absorption	3.30!	4.21!!	4.91!!!	18.99***
Self-awareness	3.96!	3.00!!	2.07!!!	27.39***
Altered state of awareness	2.68	4.22!	4.75!	32.44***
Internal dialogue	2.28	2.08	1.68	1.49
Rationality	4.04!	3.10!!	2.34!!!	17.48***
Volitional control	3.81!	2.32!!	1.57!!!	45.79***
Memory	4.54!	3.78!!	2.94!!!	16.23***
Arousal	1.68	1.43	0.77!	6.35*

[a] Higher values denote increased amounts ranging from none or little (rating = 0) to much or complete (rating = 6).
[b] Groups having an exclamation mark(s) (!) are significantly different from groups not having that exclamation mark(s) as determined by the Student–Newman–Keuls post hoc procedure.
[c] $df = 2/187$; *$p < .05$; **$p < .01$; ***$p < .001$.

Multivariate analyses of variance were also performed as a function of gender (male, female), susceptibility groups (low, medium, high susceptibility), and conditions (eyes open/closed, hypnosis). Neither the main effect for gender nor the interactions with groups or conditions were found to be significant.

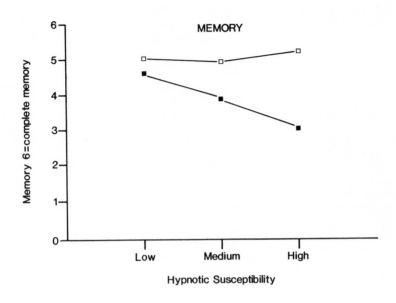

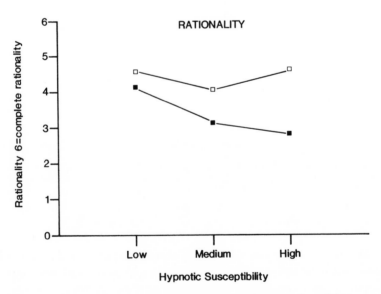

Figure 12.3. Significant PCI dimension interactions as a function of conditions and susceptibility group. (□, Eyes open/closed; ■, hypnotic induction.)

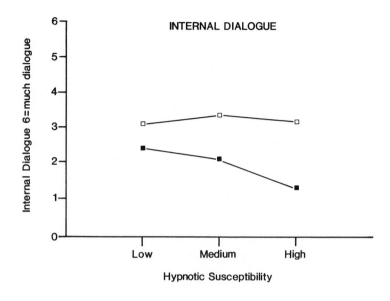

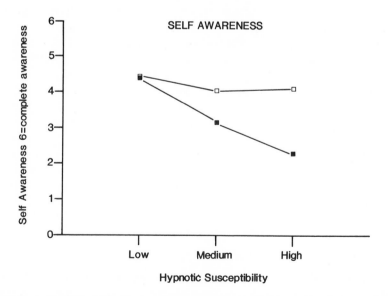

Figure 12.4. Significant PCI dimension interactions as a function of conditions and susceptibility group. (□, Eyes open/closed; ■, hypnotic induction.)

Discussion and Interpretation

Replication

All the hypotheses were supported by the results. There were significant PCI (sub)dimension intensity differences between hypnosis and eyes open/closed. In addition, there were also significant differences between low, medium, and high susceptibles, not only during hypnosis but also the baseline condition. Significant ordinal interactions for several (sub)dimensions were found as they were for earlier research.

The many PCI (sub)dimensions that were found to be significantly different for lows and highs during the baseline condition of eyes open/closed, without a hypnotic induction, highlight the importance of trait variables in accounting for hypnotic susceptibility. The fact that some subjects can experience and report hypnotic effects without an induction (Barber & Calverly, 1966) may be related to the aforementioned PCI intensity differences during eyes open/closed. If highs are reporting decreased volitional control, increased absorption, and a greater alteration in awareness during normal waking consciousness, that is, eyes open or closed, it may not be surprising that they can also report hypnotic effects without an induction.

The increased differences between low, medium, and high susceptible subjects during the induction, in comparison to baseline, and the significant ordinal interactions for many dimensions also highlight the importance of not only situational cues associated with experiencing an hypnotic induction, but also the state effects associated with experiencing that induction. It appears that the induction not only significantly changed the PCI intensity ratings for most subjects, but potentiated the differences between baseline and hypnosis for highs in comparison to lows.

Tellegen (1979) highlighted the importance of *interacting* variables on resulting hypnotic susceptibility. The present research supports that theorizing in that trait, situational, and state variables are involved in the resulting reported phenomenological effects.

Summary and Concluding Remarks

The present study replicates previous research (Kumar & Pekala, 1988) and highlights the importance of one's hypnotic ability in reporting, and possibly in experiencing, a variety of phenomenological contents of consciousness not only during hypnosis, but also during normal waking consciousness. The importance of a hypnotic induction (a "state" variable) and the situational cues associated with that induction was also supported by the present research. An interaction of trait, state, and situational variables can not only potentiate certain reported phenomenological effects (notably absorption) for a given subject type (such as high susceptibles), but it can also obviate the same phenomenological effects for other subject types (e.g., lows).

As the present study did not control for "holding back" (Sharf & Zamansky, 1963) and response bias (Jones & Spanos, 1982), further research will be needed to examine the significance of nonspecific variables relative to the trait, state, and situational effects in accounting for the variance of hypnotic responses.

STUDY 3

Introduction

This study (reported in Pekala et al., 1989) investigated the phenomenological effects associated with four stimulus conditions: baseline, deep abdominal breathing (DAB), progressive relaxation, and the induction procedure of the Harvard Group Scale. The latter two strategies can be considered stress management techniques (American Society of Clinical Hypnosis, 1973; Bernstein & Borkovec, 1973), while the former, DAB, is a short procedure that also has been associated with stress reduction (Fried, 1987). A baseline condition of eyes closed sitting quietly was chosen as a comparison procedure.

The present study represents an expansion of the earlier studies (Kumar & Pekala, 1988, 1989) by assessing for phenomenological differences between hypnosis and progressive relaxation, and DAB and a baseline condition, while also monitoring hypnotic susceptibility. It was hypothesized that subjects would be reliable at completing the PCI. It was also hypothesized that there would be significant phenomenological differences between the stimulus conditions. Individuals of differing hypnotic susceptibility would report phenomenological differences among themselves, with high susceptibles reporting greater "hypnotic" effects, that is, decreased volitional control, rationality, and self-awareness and increased altered state of awareness and altered experiences, than low susceptibles. Such differences might be further influenced by the type of stress management condition experienced. In addition, it was hypothesized that the phenomenological comparisons between hypnosis and eyes closed would replicate that of previous research (Kumar & Pekala, 1988, 1989).

Method

Subjects, Materials, and Procedure

The subject pool consisted of 300 nursing students. Subjects knew that the study involved hypnosis. Participation was voluntary. The Harvard Group Scale of Hypnotic Susceptibility was used to assess susceptibility. The PCI was used to map phenomenological experience.

The 300 subjects were seen in ten groups during two sessions spaced approximately one week apart. For the first session subjects sat quietly with their eyes closed for two minutes. During the two minutes they were told to "think about whatever you like." After the two minutes, subjects retrospectively completed the PCI, Form 1, in reference to that time period.

Subjects then experienced a slightly modified form of progressive relaxation (Bernstein & Borkovec, 1973) to which a two-minute sitting quietly interlude was added near the end. For the progressive relaxation, the experimenter first demonstrated the different muscle groups that would be tensed and relaxed and subjects could briefly tense and relax the muscles. Subjects subsequently sat with their eyes closed while the experimenter did the progressive relaxation routine. Before coming out of the procedure, subjects sat quietly for two minutes. For this two-minute interval subjects were told to go on relaxing more and more deeply on their own. After the end of the progressive relaxation instructions, subjects completed the PCI, Form 2, in reference to the two-minute period.

For the second session, subjects were taught deep abdominal breathing (Fried, 1987). For this strategy, the experimenter first demonstrated DAB, and all subjects stood up and practiced doing three rounds of DAB on their own. They then sat down and did three rounds of DAB on their own with their eyes closed and continued sitting quietly for two additional minutes. Subjects were told by the experimenter to sit quietly with their eyes closed for several minutes and experience what it feels like to sit quietly like this. Afterward they completed the PCI, Form 1, in reference to the two-minute period. Subjects then experienced the induction procedure of the Harvard Scale (shortened by eliminating redundant phraseology prior to the hand-lowering suggestion). After the eye catalepsy instructions but before the posthypnotic suggestions and amnesia instructions, the subjects experienced a two-minute period during which they were told to continue to experience whatever they were experiencing. The experimenter was silent for two minutes during this time; the rest of the instructions were given. At the completion of the hypnosis procedure and after writing down a list of the hypnotic suggestions remembered (and after removal of the amnesia), the participants completed the PCI, Form 2, in reference to the time when the experimenter stopped talking and asked the subjects to continue to experience whatever they were experiencing during that time. The subjects then completed the 11 response items of the Harvard Scale.

Results

Preliminary Analyses

PCI inventories were available on 297 subjects for the baseline condition, 293 for progressive relaxation, 277 for DAB, and 280 for the hypnosis condition. Completed data, however (without omissions or errors), across *all* inventories were available on 246 subjects, which represented 82% of the original subject pool. (The loss of 18% of the subject pool was due primarily to incomplete inventories or inventories without identification numbers, which made it impossible to obtain completed PCIs across all four conditions.) Coefficient alphas across all 12 major PCI dimensions *for all subjects* averaged .81, .81, .82, and .83, respectively, for the eyes-closed, progressive relaxation, breathing, and hypnosis conditions, and averaged .77, .72, .76, and .76 for the minor PCI dimensions (see Table 12.6).

Subjects were then divided into four (susceptibility) groups, based on their scores on the Harvard Scale: low (0–4, $n = 68$, $M = 2.24$), low-medium (5–6, $n = 51$, $M = 5.53$), high-medium (7–8, $n = 70$, $M = 7.56$), and high 9–12, $n = 57$, $M = 9.74$). PCI intensity scores were then computed for each dimension and subdimension by averaging those items that comprised each (sub)dimension.

In order to compare conditions without confounding order effects, the progressive relaxation condition was compared against the hypnosis condition and the baseline condition was compared against the DAB condition. Multivariate analyses of variance were performed with (susceptibility) groups as the independent variable, conditions as the repeated-measures factor, and the PCI (sub)dimension intensity scores as the dependent variables. Due to the correlation between the major and minor PCI dimensions, analyses were performed separately for the major and minor PCI dimensions. Alpha was set at .01 for all MANOVA and ANOVA analyses.

Table 12.6. Coefficient Alphas for the Phenomenology of Consciousness Inventory across Several Stress Management Conditions

	Stress management condition[a]				
Dimension	Baseline	Progressive relaxation	DAB	Hypnosis	Average
Positive affect	.86	.84	.84	.87	.85
Joy	.84	.75	.75	.72	.77
Sexual excitement	.90	.80	.86	.85	.85
Love	.79	.76	.76	.78	.77
Negative affect	.82	.74	.83	.77	.79
Anger	.66	.61	.59	.61	.62
Sadness	.79	.62	.79	.64	.71
Fear	.69	.62	.69	.73	.68
Altered experience	.84	.86	.88	.90	.87
Altered body image	.73	.76	.77	.79	.76
Altered time sense	.70	.78	.84	.86	.80
Altered perception	.61	.72	.70	.81	.71
Altered meaning	.77	.74	.74	.78	.76
Visual imagery	.90	.82	.84	.84	.85
Amount	.84	.75	.85	.80	.81
Vividness	.83	.74	.74	.73	.76
Attention	.82	.75	.83	.80	.80
Direction (inward)	.81	.76	.86	.82	.82
Absorption	.75	.69	.74	.80	.75
Self-awareness	.71	.82	.67	.85	.76
Altered state of awareness	.81	.89	.87	.90	.87
Internal dialogue	.86	.86	.87	.80	.85
Rationality	.72	.85	.79	.85	.80
Volitional control	.66	.72	.76	.79	.73
Memory	.82	.85	.86	.89	.86
Arousal	.86	.72	.84	.73	.79
Average (major dimensions)	.81	.81	.82	.83	.82
Average (subdimensions)	.77	.72	.76	.76	.76
n	297	293	277	280	

[a]Includes all subjects (those with a reliability index of > 2.0 have been included).

Discriminant Validity

Progressive Relaxation versus Hypnosis. There were significant main effects for conditions [$F = 9.81$, $df = 12/231$, $p < .0001$] and groups [$F = 4.07$, $df = 36/689$, $p < .001$]; the interaction between conditions and groups approached significance [$F = 1.58$, $df = 361/689$, $p < .018$].

Repeated-measures (groups × conditions) ANOVAs were subsequently performed for each of the 12 major PCI dimensions, with PCI intensity scores as the dependent variable and conditions as the repeated measure. Significant main effects for conditions found that progressive relaxation, vis-à-vis hypnosis, was associated with increased positive affect; inward-absorbed attention, rationality, memory, and self-awareness; and a decreased altered state of awareness.

Significant main effects for groups were found for positive affect, altered experience, inward-absorbed attention, self-awareness, state of awareness, rationality, volitional control, memory, and arousal. Repeated-measures post hoc comparisons [using the LMGLH program of SYSTAT (Wilkinson, 1988b), which takes into account unequal ns] were performed. To offset inflation of alpha levels for the six sets of post hoc comparisons (per (sub)dimension), alpha was set at .002, using the Bonferroni (Kirk, 1968) correction procedure. The results indicated that high susceptible individuals, vis-à-vis lows, reported increased positive affect, altered experiences, and altered state of awareness, and decreased self-awareness, rationality, volitional control, memory, and arousal.

High susceptible individuals, vis-à-vis low-medium individuals, reported increased altered experience and altered state of awareness. High-medium susceptible individuals, vis-à-vis low susceptibles, reported increased positive affect, altered experience, inward-absorbed attention, and altered state of awareness, and decreased self-awareness, rationality, volitional control, memory, and arousal. Low-medium, vis-à-vis low susceptibles, reported increased inward-absorbed attention and altered state of awareness, and decreased self-awareness, volitional control, and memory.

Due to the near-significant interaction between groups and conditions, interaction effects between groups and conditions were also examined for each PCI dimension. Significant interactions (at the .001 level) were found for altered experience, self-awareness, altered state of awareness, and volitional control. Low susceptibles found progressive relaxation to be associated with significantly greater alterations in experience and state of awareness and significantly decreased volitional control than hypnosis. In contrast, except for self-awareness, high susceptibles found hypnosis and progressive relaxation to be relatively equivalent strategies.

For the PCI minor dimensions there were significant main effects for conditions [$F = 4.55$, $df = 14/229$, $p < .001$] and groups [$F = 3.33$, $df = 42/683$, $p < .001$]. The interaction between conditions and groups was not significant [$F = 1.31$, $df = 42/683$, $p < .093$]. The MANOVA analyses were followed by ANOVA analyses. Significant differences between conditions were found with progressive relaxation associated with more joy, love, and altered body image, and increased inward and absorbed attention than hypnosis.

Significant main effects analyses for groups followed by post hoc comparisons (using the same statistical limits as defined above) revealed that high, vis-à-vis low, susceptibles reported more love, increased absorption, and increased alterations in body image, time sense, perception, and unusual meanings. Highs, vis-à-vis, low-mediums, reported increased absorption and increased alterations in body image, time sense, perception, and unusual meanings. High-mediums, vis-à-vis lows reported more love, joy, and a more absorbed attentional focus, and increased alterations in body image, time sense, perception, and meaning.

Deep Abdominal Breathing versus Baseline. For the PCI major dimensions MANOVAs revealed significant main effects for conditions [F = 16.60, df = 12/231, p < .0001] and groups [F = 2.05, df = 36/689, p < .001]. The interaction between conditions and groups was not significant [F = 1.39, df = 36/689, p < .068].

ANOVA comparisons for conditions revealed that the interval immediately following the breathing condition, vis-à-vis baseline, was associated with significantly less imagery and less vivid imagery, less positive affect and altered experiences, and a less intact memory.

ANOVA comparisons for groups revealed significant differences for altered experience and state of awareness with post hoc comparisons revealing that high and high-medium susceptibles reported greater altered experiences and a more altered state of awareness than lows. Highs, vis-à-vis low-mediums, also reported a more altered state of awareness.

MANOVA analyses for the PCI minor dimensions found significant main effects for conditions [F = 12.91, df = 14/229, p < .0001] and groups [F = 2.25, df = 42/683, p < .001]. The interaction between conditions and groups was not significant [F = 1.39, df = 42/683, p < .056]. ANOVA comparisons between conditions revealed the baseline condition, vis-à-vis breathing, was associated with significantly more joy, sexual excitement, love, imagery amount, and imagery vividness, and greater alterations in body image, time sense, perception, and unusual meanings. ANOVA groups analyses and subsequent post hoc comparisons indicated that high susceptibles reported significantly greater alterations in body image, time sense, perception, and unusual meanings than did low susceptibles.

Hypnosis Compared against the Baseline Condition. Because previous research compared hypnosis against baseline (Kumar & Pekala, 1988,

1989), the present study also assessed for differences between these conditions, although the hypnosis condition in the present study was experienced a week later and after DAB. (The earlier studies had hypnosis immediately following the baseline condition.)

For the PCI major dimensions there was a main effect for conditions [$F = 35.32$, $df = 12/231$, $p < .0001$] and groups [$F = 3.90$, $df = 36/689$, $p < .001$], and a significant interaction between conditions and groups [$F = 2.98$, $df = 36/689$, $p < .001$].

ANOVA comparisons for conditions revealed that hypnosis, vis-à-vis baseline, was associated with significantly less positive affect, imagery, self-awareness, internal dialogue, rationality, volitional control, memory, and arousal. It was also associated with significantly more altered experiences and an altered state of awareness.

ANOVA comparisons for groups revealed significant differences for altered experience, self-awareness, state of awareness, rationality, volitional control, and memory. High susceptibles reported greater alterations in altered experience and state of awareness, and decreased self-awareness, rationality, volitional control, and memory than low susceptibles. ANOVA comparisons for the conditions by groups interaction revealed significant interactions for altered experience, attention, self-awareness, state of awareness, internal dialogue, rationality, volitional control, memory, and arousal. The aforementioned comparisons replicated most of the results obtained previously (Kumar & Pekala, 1988, 1989).

For the PCI minor dimensions there was a significant main effect for conditions [$F = 22.49$, $df = 14/229$, $p < .0001$], and groups [$F = 3.34$, $df = 42/683$, $p < .001$], and a significant interaction between conditions and groups [$F = 2.58$, $df = 42/683$, $p < .001$].

ANOVA comparisons for conditions revealed that hypnosis, relative to baseline, was associated with decreased joy, sexual excitement, love, sadness, imagery amount and vividness, and a greater alteration in body image, time sense, perception, and meaning. ANOVA comparisons for groups revealed that high susceptibles, vis-à-vis low susceptibles, reported significantly more joy and love, and greater alterations in body image, time sense, perception, and meaning. There were significant interactions for altered body image, time sense, and perception, imagery vividness, and absorption. (These results replicated most of the comparisons obtained previously.)

Discussion

The coefficient alpha reliability results suggest that subjects were reliable at completing the PCI for the different stress management conditions assessed and baseline. Since only 4%, averaging across all four conditions, were marginally reliable, they were not excluded from the analysis. The fact that these subjects were *more* reliable than subjects from two previous studies (Kumar & Pekala, 1988, 1989) is intriguing. This may relate to several reasons. The nursing students were more task oriented than the West Chester students from the two earlier studies, based on their behavior during the studies. The nursing students also had somewhat more time (15 extra minutes) and hence time constraints were not as tight. In addition, the nursing students were run in smaller groups than the subjects of the earlier studies and, of course, the two subject pools were different—one was from West Chester University and the other from Thomas Jefferson University.

The significant differences between hypnosis and progressive relaxation and DAB and baseline suggest that the PCI (sub)dimensions are able to discriminant subjective differences between these stimulus conditions and support the discriminant validity of the PCI for these conditions. Significant differences between low, low-medium, high-medium, and high susceptibles found in earlier studies (Kumar & Pekala, 1988, 1989) also support the discriminant validity of the PCI in assessing for subjective effects as a function of individual differences.

CONCLUDING REMARKS

The significant main effects for low, medium, and high hypnotically susceptible individuals support the many studies suggesting differential responsivity to hypnosis as a function of hypnotic susceptibility (Brown & Fromm, 1986). It appears that such effects occur in conditions not labeled hypnotic, including progressive relaxation and even sitting quietly with one's eyes open or closed.

The interaction effects evident from the several studies suggest that an induction procedure, be it hypnosis or even progressive relaxation, appears to facilitate alterations in subjects' subjective experiences. Since context effects (Council & Kirsch, 1989) and expectancy (Kirsch, 1985) were not assessed, it is not known how important such variables are, in terms of necessary and sufficient conditions, for producing the subjective phenomena associated with hypnosis. But when subjects expect to be hypnotized, the data suggest that such hypnotic procedures will potentiate alterations in subjective experience, but more so for medium and high susceptibles than lows.

Finally, the data also suggest that increased absorption, a trait commonly associated with being hypnotized (Brown & Fromm, 1986; Hilgard, 1965, 1977), is not necessarily an occurrence across all types of subjects. The fact that low susceptibles reported becoming less absorbed (or *more* distracted) during hypnosis than a baseline comparison condition suggests that being increasingly absorbed during hypnosis is not necessarily characteristic of all subjects. As with most areas of psychological inquiry, the result appears to be an interaction of trait and situational variables.

The Differential Organization of the Structures of Consciousness during Hypnosis

The previous chapter demonstrated the interaction of trait and situational/state variables in the reported phenomenology of hypnotic susceptibility. The data concerned phenomenological intensity effects, that is, those intensity effects thought important by Singer (cited in Zinberg, 1977) in determining an altered state of consciousness. The question can be asked as to what happens to the *pattern* effects among dimensions of consciousness during hypnosis vis-à-vis a baseline condition as a function of hypnotic susceptibility. This was the issue that Tart (1975, 1977) suggested would be paramount in determining a particular state of consciousness, and what the parallel distributed processing (PDP) researchers (McClelland & Rumelhart, 1988) assert are of primary importance in understanding how the brain processes information.

STUDY 1

Introduction

Hence, the following section presents a methodology to determine the changes in the pattern of phenomenological subsystems of consciousness in response to hypnosis (reported in Pekala & Kumar, 1986). Its purpose was two-fold: (1) to present a methodology that makes possible the study of the interrelationships among phenomenological subsystems of consciousness as reported by a self-report phenomenological state instrument such as the Phenomenology of Consciousness Inventory (PCI), and (2) to use that methodology to investigate the organization of the structures of consciousness during hypnosis and a baseline condition for low, medium, and high susceptible subjects.

It was hoped that a study of the interrelationships among various phenomenological subsystems of consciousness would allow for an evaluation of the possible differential phenomenological effects of hypnosis vis-à-vis a baseline condition. Furthermore, by examining for the differential pattern of interrelationships across low, medium, and high susceptible subjects, it was also hoped that a broader picture of the phenomenological effects of hypnosis as a function of individual differences would be obtained.

Investigating the Organization of the Structures of Consciousness during Hypnosis

Hypnosis has been hypothesized to differentially affect various phenomenological subsystems of consciousness, (e.g., imagery, memory, volition, or rationality). Although the relationship between hypnosis and individual phenomenological subsystems such as volition (Bowers, 1981), absorption (Tellegen & Atkinson, 1974; Yanchar & Johnson, 1981), visual imagery (Spanos & McPeake, 1975), and alterations in state of consciousness (Hilgard, 1969, 1975) have been studied, investigations aimed at comparing how these and other phenomenological subsystems relate to each other inside and outside of hypnosis has, to my knowledge, not been addressed.

Pekala, Wenger, and Levine (1985), using a precursor to the PCI, the Dimensions of Consciousness Questionnaire (DCQ), found not only DCQ (sub)dimension intensity differences, but also pattern differences (using the major dimensions of the DCQ in correlation matrices) between low and high absorption (Tellegen, 1981) subjects. As absorption is a trait correlated with hypnotic susceptibility (Tellegen & Atkinson, 1974; Yanchar & Johnson, 1981), it is reasonable to expect that the results obtained with absorption would extend to susceptibility, particularly since hypnosis has been shown to result in greater alterations in phenomenological experience for high vis-à-vis low susceptible subjects (Hilgard, 1965; Kumar & Pekala, 1988; Orne, 1977; Shor, 1979).

In addition, if hypnosis results in a reorganization of the subsystems of consciousness (Hilgard, 1977), there might also be significant pattern differences between a hypnotic condition and a baseline condition, like eyes closed sitting quietly, for low, medium, and high susceptible subjects.

To test the previous theorizing, two hypotheses were entertained:

1. High susceptible subjects will report a significantly different pattern of relationships among phenomenological subsystems (as assessed by the PCI) than low susceptible subjects for the hypnotic induction condition and possibly the baseline condition of eyes closed sitting quietly.

2. Hypnosis, vis-à-vis this baseline condition, will result in a significantly different pattern of relationships among the phenomenological subsystems of consciousness for high, medium, and possibly low susceptible subjects.

Comparing States of Consciousness

The present methodology also allows for states of consciousness, as defined by Tart (1975), to be statistically assessed and visually compared. According to Tart (1975), an *altered state of consciousness*, in reference to another state of consciousness, can be defined in terms of: (1) a significant pattern difference among various subsystems of consciousness and (2) the degree to which a given state of consciousness, vis-à-vis another state, is perceived as associated with a perceived alteration in subjective experience or the *subjective sense of altered state* (SSAS) (Pekala & Kumar, 1986).

A psygram allows for the state of consciousness associated with a particular stimulus condition to be visually graphed in terms of the pattern structures, while the state of awareness (altered state) dimension quantifies the perceived alteration in subjective experience.

Given the above, high susceptible subjects, during hypnosis, might then be characterized as being in an altered state of consciousness relative to lows if there is a significant pattern difference and a significant SSAS. Similarly, high, medium, and possibly low susceptible subjects during hypnosis might be in an altered state in reference to a baseline state, such as eyes closed, if significant pattern and SSAS effects are found between hypnosis and eyes closed for each of these three subject groups.

While hypotheses 1 and 2 addressed pattern effects, hypotheses 3 and 4 addressed the SSAS effects:

3. High susceptibles, compared to lows, will report a greater altera-

tion in the state of awareness dimension of the PCI for hypnosis and possibly the baseline condition.

4. Hypnosis, vis-à-vis the baseline condition, will result in a significantly greater alteration in the state of awareness dimension for high, medium, and possibly low susceptible subjects.

Research Design

The same subject pool, materials, and procedures, cited in Chapter 12 concerning the first hypnosis study on the trait-state/situational effects associated with hypnotic susceptibility, were used. Subjects sat quietly for several minutes with their eyes closed and they also experienced the hypnotic induction procedure of the Harvard Scale (Shor & Orne, 1962). After each condition they retrospectively completed the PCI.

Results

Harvard Group Scale Preliminary Analyses

Three groups were formed by dividing subjects into those scoring in the lowest (0–5, $M = 3.25$), middle (6–8, $M = 7.16$), and highest third (9–12, $M = 10.27$) of the Harvard Scale.

Pattern Comparisons as a Function of Hypnotic Susceptibility

Dimension intensity scores were computed for each subject for each condition by averaging those items that composed each PCI major dimension. Intercorrelation matrices of the 12 major PCI dimensions were then computed for the eyes-closed and the hypnotic induction conditions for low, medium, and high susceptible subject groups. The correlation matrices were subsequently compared with an APL computer program (Pekala & Kumar, 1985) of Jennrich's (1970) chi-square test, which makes it possible to determine if the correlation matrices, and hence the patterns among the dimensions of consciousness for the various groups, are significantly different from one another.

Comparison of the correlation matrices associated with low ($n = 66$) and high ($n = 59$) susceptibles for the eyes-closed condition yielded a chi-square value of 82.82, $p < .10$ (degrees of freedom for all analyses using Jennrich's test were 66). Whereas correlations for lows ranged from $-.43$ to .62 with 21 out of 66 correlations significant at $p < .01$, correlations for highs ranged from $-.48$ to .63 and 15 correlations were significant at $p < .01$.

Comparison of the correlation matrices for the eyes-closed condition between mediums (n = 70) and lows (chi-square = 74.72, $p < .25$), and mediums and highs (chi-square = 66.40, $p < .50$) were not significant. Medium susceptible subjects had correlations ranging from $-.65$ to .65, of which 20 were significant at $p < .01$.

A chi-square value of 108.25, which was significant ($p < .005$), was found for the comparison of the correlation matrices associated with lows (n = 65) and highs (n = 57) for the hypnotic induction condition. Whereas correlations for lows had a range of $-.69$ to .74, with 29 out of 66 significant at $p < .01$, correlations for highs had a range of $-.48$ to .63 with only 11 significant at $p < .01$. Although the comparison between the correlation matrices associated with mediums (n = 68) and lows was significant (chi-square = 87.35, $p < .05$), that comparing mediums and highs was not (chi-square = 75.84, $p < .25$). Mediums had 21 correlations significant at $p < .01$, ranging from $-.67$ to .62.

Pattern Comparisons between Eyes Closed and the Induction

To assess for pattern differences between eyes closed and the induction as a function of low, medium, or high susceptibility, intercorrelation matrices for the 12 PCI dimensions were constructed for the eyes-closed and induction conditions across low (n = 58), medium (n = 63), and high (n = 52) susceptible subjects. (Only those subjects who had a reliability index of 2 or less during *both* the eyes-closed and induction conditions were used so that the pattern comparisons would be done across groups composed of the same subjects.) Comparisons for low (chi-square = 117.58, $p < .001$) and medium (chi-square = 93.40, $p < .025$) groups were significant, while that for highs (chi-square = 82.39, $p < .10$) approached significance. (Because the Jennrich test was devised for independent groups, when it is used with correlated groups, it is a more conservative test than when used with uncorrelated groups.)

Variance Comparisons

To determine if significant variance differences among low, medium, and high susceptible groups were responsible for the significant chi-square values for the Jennrich tests, the Bartlett-Box F test was utilized to assess for homogeneity of variance for low, medium, and high susceptible subjects during the eyes-closed and hypnosis conditions. (Significantly greater PCI variability among low susceptible subjects, vis-à-vis high susceptibles, could account for higher correlations among the PCI dimensions for the low susceptibles relative to the highs.) For the eyes-closed condition, two of the 12 PCI dimensions had significantly different variances, that is, negative affect ($F = 3.69$, $p <$ .05) and memory ($F = 5.60$, $p < .01$). Only for memory, however, were the variances for lows significantly greater than that of highs. For the hypnosis condition, only for the dimension of altered state of awareness were there significantly different variances among groups ($F = 5.33$, $p <$ .01), with lows having significantly greater variability than highs.

Psygram Analyses

To determine the nature of the differences in the pattern of relationships for the aforementioned groups, psygrams were constructed for each group for each condition. (The average intensity scores for each dimension have been omitted from the following psygrams so as not to complicate the graphs. To save space, psygrams for the medium susceptible subjects are also omitted.)

Figure 13.1 depicts the psygram of low susceptible subjects during eyes closed sitting quietly. Figure 13.1 is contrasted with Figure 13.2, a psygram of low susceptibles during the hypnotic induction. (As mentioned, these patterns are significantly different from one another as assessed by statistical comparison of the correlation matrices.) Notice how the associations (variance percentages) among dimensions have become much more intense and frequent for the induction condition compared to the eyes-closed condition.

Figure 13.3 depicts the psygram of high susceptibles during eyes closed, while Figure 13.4 depicts the psygram of highs during hypnosis. In contrast to the previous psygrams, the hypnotic induction for highs is associated with less frequent and less intense variance percentages than eyes closed (the Jennrich comparison between these correlation matrices approached significance), an effect opposite to that seen with low susceptible subjects.

In addition, although the psygrams of lows (Figure 13.1) and highs (Figure 13.3) during eyes closed appear similar, the psygrams for lows (Figure 13.2) and highs (Figure 13.4) during hypnosis are vastly (and significantly) different.

Altered State Intensity Comparisons

A one-way analysis of variance (low, medium, and high susceptible subjects) revealed a significant main effect for the altered state of awareness dimension of the PCI for the eyes-closed condition [$F = 4.07$, $df = 2/192$, $p < .02$] and the hypnotic induction condition [$F = 37.44$, $df = 2/187$, $p < .0001$]. Mediums and highs for both conditions reported a

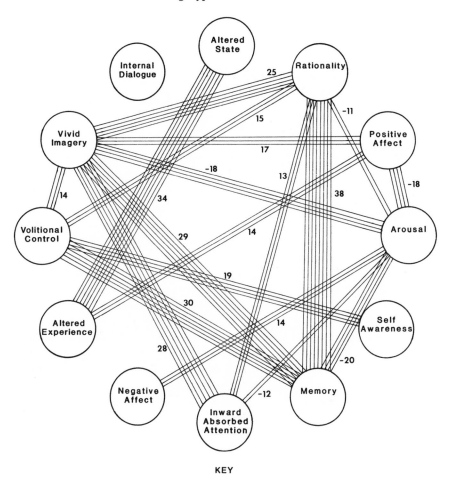

KEY

Each line represents approximately 5% of the variance in common.
(All variances represent correlations significant at alpha less than approximately .01.)

n = 66

Figure 13.1. Low-susceptible individuals: Eyes closed sitting quietly. (From Pekala &
Kumar, 1986. Reprinted with permission of the publisher.)

significantly greater alteration in awareness than lows (Student-
Newman-Keuls post hoc comparison).

Paired t tests revealed that lows [$t = 3.30$, $df = 57$, $p < .01$], mediums [$t = 8.68$, $df = 63$, $p < .001$], and highs [$t = 10.72$, $df = 52$, $p < .0001$]
all reported a greater alteration in state of awareness for the hypnotic
induction condition vis-à-vis the eyes-closed condition.

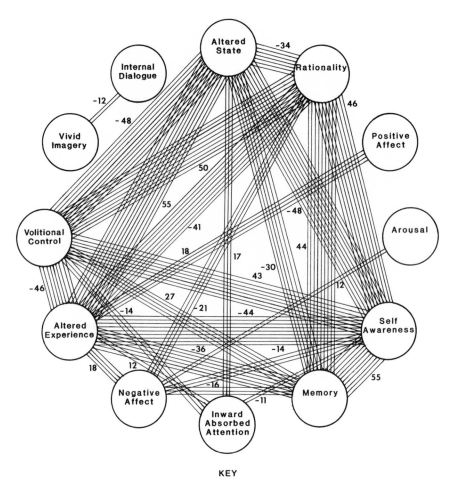

KEY

Each line represents approximately 5% of the variance in common.

(All variances represent correlations significant at alpha less than approximately .01.)

n = 65

Figure 13.2. Low-susceptible individuals: Hypnotic induction (HGSHS). (From Pekala & Kumar, 1986. Reprinted with permission of the publisher.)

Discussion and Interpretation

Pattern and Intensity Comparison Results

Hypotheses 1 and 2 were generally supported. High susceptible subjects were found to report a significantly different organizational

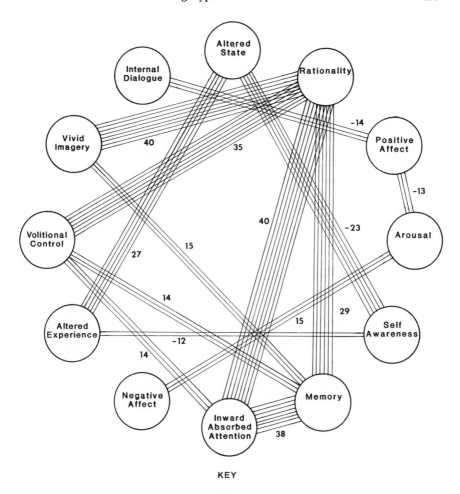

KEY

Each line represents approximately 5% of the variance in common.

(All variances represent correlations significant at alpha less than approximately .01.)

n = 59

Figure 13.3. High-susceptible individuals: Eyes closed sitting quietly. (From Pekala & Kumar, 1986. Reprinted with permission of the publisher.)

structure from that of lows for the hypnotic induction condition. (This was not the case for the eyes-closed baseline condition, however.) Diagraming the pattern results via the psygrams supported this, as the very different psygrams for these two groups for the hypnotic induction condition indicates. The data also support the conclusion of significantly

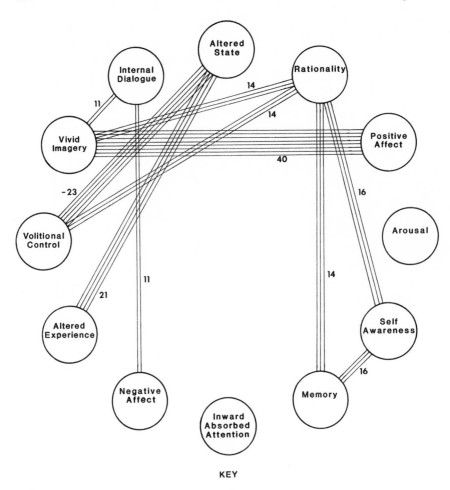

KEY

Each line represents approximately 5% of the variance in common.

(All variances represent correlations significant at alpha less than approximately .01.)

n = 57

Figure 13.4. High-susceptible individuals: Hypnotic induction (HGSHS). (From Pekala & Kumar, 1986. Reprinted with permission of the publisher.)

different patterns of relationship among PCI dimensions between hypnosis and eyes closed sitting quietly for low and medium susceptible subjects.

Hypotheses 3 and 4 were also supported. Not only did highs and mediums report a significantly greater alteration in state of awareness than lows for the hypnotic induction and baseline condition, but highs, mediums, and lows also reported that the hypnotic induction was associated with a greater alteration in state of awareness than the eyes-closed condition.

States of Consciousness as a Function of Susceptibility

According to Tart (1975), an altered state of consciousness can be defined, in reference to other states, by means of a significant pattern difference and a significant SSAS (subjective sense of altered state). High susceptible subjects were found to report a significantly different pattern among PCI dimensions, relative to lows, during the hypnotic induction condition. Highs also reported experiencing a significantly greater SSAS, vis-à-vis lows, during the induction. Thus, using Tart's definitions, high susceptible subjects can be said to have been in an altered state of consciousness relative to lows during the hypnotic induction. In contrast, this cannot be said to be the case during the eyes-closed condition, since the Jennrich comparison only approached significance.

Discrete Altered States of Consciousness

Comparison of the patterns among PCI dimensions for hypnosis and eyes closed across low, medium, and high susceptible subjects indicated that the induction condition, relative to eyes closed, was perceived as an altered state of consciousness for low and medium susceptible subjects. This was because low and medium groups, when comparing the induction to the baseline condition, were found to report a significantly different structure and a significantly greater alteration in state of awareness. Highs also reported a significantly greater SSAS relative to baseline, but only a near-significant difference in structure. This suggests that the hypnotic induction may have had less of an effect on subsystem pattern structure for high than medium and low susceptible subjects. As mentioned, however, the Jennrich comparison, used for independent groups, is a more conservative test of differences when used with correlated groups. Thus, this comparison may also have been significant if a test for correlated correlation matrices were used.

Although all three subject groups reported the induction condition to be associated with a greater alteration in state of awareness (SSAS) from the eyes-closed condition, visual depiction of the structures via psygrams indicated that the altered state of consciousness during hypnosis reported by high susceptibles was quite different from that reported by lows. Tart (1975) has coined the term, *discrete altered state of consciousness*, to denote the fact that a given altered state may be differ-ent from another altered state, and yet both may be altered from a reference state of consciousness. Such states are discrete since each are composed of a *unique* pattern or organization of structures. Thus, the altered state of consciousness associated with hypnosis (vis-à-vis eyes closed) reported by low susceptible subjects was different from that reported by medium (or high) susceptible subjects.

Differential Pattern Effects as a Function of Susceptibility

The psygram data suggest that low susceptible subjects responded to the hypnotic induction in a much different manner than high suscep-tibles. The plethora of associations for lows during hypnosis suggests that alterations in many of the subsystems of consciousness mapped by the PCI (altered state, rationality, self-awareness, memory, altered expe-rience, and volitional control) led to rather consistent alterations in asso-ciately coupled subsystems.

With the exception of a strong association between positive affect and imagery, there was a lack of associations between subsystems for highs during hypnosis (which cannot be attributable to differences in the distribution of scores for highs vis-à-vis lows due to the lack of signifi-cant variance differences). This result suggests that when the experi-menter told the subjects to "just continue to experience the state you are in"; whereas lows had subsystems that became even more tightly associ-ated, highs appeared to report a trend ($p < .10$) to "uncouple" sub-systems of consciousness (in reference to the previous baseline state).

There appears to be interesting parallels between the hypnotic be-havior of high susceptibles during hypnosis and the phenomenological pattern effects demonstrated with the psygram data for high suscepti-bles. A high susceptible during hypnosis is able to completely dissociate pain in, let us say, the hand from the rest of the body as if the hand were completely separated from it. Somewhat similarly, thoughts or feelings of a traumatic memory can become functionally divorced from the mem-ory, or the whole memory itself separated from other memories, leading to amnestic experiences or even multiple personality (Kluft, 1984) for high susceptibles that is not possible for lows.

The psygram of high susceptibles during hypnosis was constructed from the self-reports of subjects who were told to just sit quietly and continue to experience the state they were in. The instructions allowed for a very open stimulus set to be enacted. The fact that low susceptibles had various phenomenological dimensions of consciousness highly coupled with one another while highs had little comparative coupling suggests a significant pattern structure difference for highs, vis-à-vis lows, during hypnosis. Such a difference appears to be congruent with the hypnotic experiences and behaviors of highs mentioned above. Hypnosis is associated with phenomenological subsystems of consciousness for high susceptibles that become "loosely coupled," which may then be subsequently enabled by the hypnotist (or the subject via self-hypnosis) to be "manipulated" without affecting other phenomenological subsystems due to the lack of associations between subsystems. That such hypnotic phenomena are unable to be experienced by low susceptibles is supported by the psygram results for lows during hypnosis. Here, subsystems of consciousness became even more tightly coupled.

Pattern comparisons among the psygrams concerning specific dimensions also uncovered certain patterning effects that may be specific to a given subject group. Whereas low susceptibles have rationality strongly coupled with memory during eyes closed ($r = .62$), highs have rationality most strongly coupled with vivid, visual imagery and inward, absorbed attention ($r = .63$). [This may be why "trance logic" (Orne, 1971) is more likely to occur for high than low susceptible subjects.] In addition, whereas memory was statistically independent from attention for lows during eyes closed, memory was strongly coupled with inward, absorbed attention for highs ($r = .62$). This suggests that highs during eyes closed may be processing information (and possibly storing it) in a much different manner from that of lows.

Summary and Concluding Remarks

The data from this study support the feasibility of using this methodology for mapping and diagraming states and altered states of consciousness associated with hypnosis. The use of the Jennrich test and psygrams to visually illustrate the relationships among PCI dimensions allow for the *pattern* of relationships among subsystems of consciousness to be quantified and statistically assessed. The use of the altered state of awareness dimension allows for SSAS effects to be quantified. This approach thus allows for states of consciousness, as defined by Tart (1975, 1977), associated with various stimulus conditions and altered state induction procedures to be quantified and statistically assessed in a way never before possible.

Self-report phenomenological state instruments like the PCI and a means to diagram that data using psygrams or similar devices may thus provide a means to access the "state of consciousness" associated with hypnosis and possibly other altered-state induction procedures. In addition, by assessing such altered-state induction procedures across groups of subjects differing in various traits such as hypnotic susceptibility, one may then determine how individual differences measures may affect reported phenomenological experiences.

STUDY 2

Introduction

A second study attempted to replicate the results from the afore-mentioned study with a new subject group. (This second study, reported in Pekala and Kumar, 1989, will be briefly reviewed.) The subject pool consisted of 231 introductory psychology students who experienced the identical two stimulus conditions reported earlier, that is, eyes closed sitting quietly and the induction procedure of the Harvard Group Scale. After each stimulus condition, subjects completed the PCI in reference to their subjective experience of a three-minute period for the eyes-closed period and an equivalent period embedded in the Harvard Scale.

Subjects were divided into low (0–5), medium (6–8), and high (9–12) susceptibility groups based on their Harvard Scale scores, and intercorrelation matrices were constructed for each group for each condition, using the 12 major PCI dimensions. Matrices were subsequently compared by the Jennrich test. For the eyes-closed condition, significant differences were found between lows and highs and lows and mediums. For the hypnosis condition, significant differences were found between lows and high, lows and mediums, and mediums and highs. These results replicated all the significant results obtained in the first study, plus additional significant results that were not found significant in the first study (Pekala & Kumar, 1986).

Using the Jennrich test to compare the eyes-closed against the hypnosis condition yielded significant results for the low and medium susceptible groups, but not that of highs. These results also replicate that obtained earlier. Hence, the results of an additional study replicate and support the *replicability* of this approach for assessing pattern structures across stimulus conditions and subject groups.

Data Analysis with the Combined Subject Pool

Both the cited study and the prior one used approximately 60 to 80 subjects per group for the Jennrich comparisons. Although this is the minimum limit needed (12 PCI dimensions times 5 subjects per dimension, for approximately 60 subjects per group), analyses should be performed with approximately 120 subjects per group (Nunnally, 1967) to allow for a more definitive determination of the pattern effects between stimulus conditions as a function of susceptibility groups.

Since the two studies were practically identical, the subject pools were combined and the data reanalyzed, attempting to get more subjects per susceptibility group. In order to keep group size somewhat similar across susceptibility groups, subjects were divided into low (0–4, $n = 111$, $M = 2.40$), low-medium (5–6, $n = 88$, $M = 5.49$), high-medium (7–8, $n = 99$, $M = 7.50$), and high (9 -12, $n = 106$, $M = 10.18$) susceptible subjects.

Correlation matrices were constructed for the four groups for the two conditions, and the Jennrich test was used to assess for pattern differences. Although none of the comparisons among the four susceptibility groups for the eyes-closed condition were significant, all the comparisons among the four groups for the hypnosis condition were significant, except for that between highs and high-mediums. Comparing the four susceptibility groups as a function of eyes closed versus hypnosis indicated that for lows, low-mediums, high-mediums, and highs, hypnosis was associated with a significant pattern difference vis-à-vis eyes closed.

Additional pattern analyses looking at the very-low (those subjects who scored 0–1 on the Harvard Scale) and the very-high (11–12) susceptibles supported the previous analyses. These analyses indicated that the associations among PCI dimensions for the very-lows were even greater, while the associations for very-highs were very loosely coupled (except for strong associations between vivid imagery and rationality, and imagery and positive affect).

The data from the combined studies indicated that "hypnosis has differential effects upon the reported organization of the phenomenological structures of consciousness across low and high susceptible subjects" (Pekala & Kumar, 1986, p. 537). The results, assessed across the very-low and very-high susceptible groups, further supported phenomenological pattern differences. Thus, very-lows reported an increased association among PCI dimensions as the very-lows moved from eyes closed to hypnosis, while very-highs reported a reorganization of subsystems from that reported during eyes closed:

> In terms of Hilgard's (1977) neodissociation theory, hypnosis appears to increase the association among subsystems of consciousness for very-lows, possibly making it more difficult for subsystems of consciousness for very-lows to be manipulated without affecting other associatively-coupled sub-

systems. In contrast, hypnosis appears to: maintain a lower level of association among subsystems of consciousness for very-highs (than very-lows);
and decrease that level of association for particular subsystems of consciousness, while more strongly coupling imagery to rationality and positive affect.
(Pekala & Kumar, 1989, p. 18)

ASSESSING THE JENNRICH PATTERN ANALYSES BY A SOPHISTICATED FACTOR ANALYTIC APPROACH

Introduction

The approach of comparing correlation matrices by the Jennrich
(1970) test and descriptively comparing correlation matrices associated
with differing stimulus conditions and subject groups is a relatively
novel approach recently developed (Pekala, 1985a,c) to try to map and
diagram states and altered states of consciousness. The novelty of this
approach, however, makes it somewhat controversial, and the question
can be asked if the results obtained by this approach would replicate
using a more traditional, multivariate approach. For this purpose, the
following paragraphs will report briefly on a study (Pekala & Bieber,
1990), where the combined Jennrich and psygram analyses discussed in
the previous section were reanalyzed by a sophisticated factor analytic
approach.

The data from the combined subject pool mentioned earlier were
reanalyzed by a multigroup factor analytic approach involving a statistical procedure developed by Bieber (1986) to determine structural similarity and dissimilarity across factor analytic solutions derived for several groups. In traditional factor analysis, solutions are generated for each
of the different groups that are factored analyzed and then a determination of factorial similarity is made on the basis of visual comparison. The
visual comparison approach, however, is highly subjective.

In the multigroup factor analysis approach advocated by Bieber
(1986), factors are generated on the basis of their group structure. If a
factor is found to exist within the structure of each group examined, it
would be labeled a "universal" factor. If a factor is found that uniquely
exists within a single group, it is identified as "unique" and is group
specific.

Given this multigroup approach, groups may be determined to be
factorially totally similar, that is, all factors within one group are present
in the other. Or they may be determined to be partially similar (or
dissimilar)—some of the factors in one group are present in the other, or
they may be totally dissimilar where none of the factors present in one
group are present in the other groups. Whereas the Jennrich test would

reject the hypothesis of similarity in either of the latter two instances above, using the Bieber approach the nature of the differences can be statistically determined to be either partially or totally dissimilar.

Hence, analyses were completed to determine: (1) the structural nature of the factor solutions associated with the phenomenological experience of low, low-medium, high-medium, and high susceptible individuals during eyes closed and hypnosis; (2) if the nature of these solutions suggest pattern similarity or dissimilarity; (3) if the factor solutions obtained during hypnosis are "pattern equivalent" to those obtained during eyes closed; and (4) whether the approaches advocated by Bieber (1986) and Pekala (1985a) lead to the same or similar solutions.

Design and Analysis

Using the Bieber approach, the statistical design resembles a large multivariate analysis of variance with eight cells: a two by four design employing two conditions (eyes closed and hypnosis) and four susceptibility groups (low, low-medium, high-medium, and high) with 12 variables (the 12 major PCI dimensions).

In order to facilitate the analyses at the cell level, the subjects within each cell were randomly divided into two groups and each group was factor analyzed separately. Hence, 16 initial factor analyses were performed using generalized least-squares estimation (Joreskog & Goldberger, 1972) with a maximum of four factors retained in each. These 16 factors were then subjected to a multigroup factor analysis.

Two invariant or universal factors were obtained for the eyes-closed condition across all four susceptibility groups. One factor was found to be composed of altered experience, altered state of awareness, (negative) self-awareness, (negative) volitional control, and (negative) rationality. The second factor was composed of rationality, imagery, memory, inward, absorbed attention, and volitional control. The first factor was labeled an awareness/altered state factor, while the second was labeled a cognition/memory factor. No unique factors were found specific to any of the four susceptibility groups, and this is consistent with the Jennrich analyses from the two pooled studies reported earlier, where none of the four susceptibility groups were found to be significantly different from one another for the eyes-closed condition.

For the hypnosis condition, two universal factors were found to be common to all four groups. Whereas the first factor was exactly the same as the awareness/altered state factor found for the eyes-closed condition, the second factor consisted of positive affect, negative affect, imagery, and altered experience. It was labeled an affect/imagery factor.

In addition, two unique factors were generated, one for the low susceptibiles and one for the high susceptible individuals for the hypnosis condition. For the low susceptibles, the unique factor to emerge consisted of (negative) absorbed, inward attention (or increased distractibility), increased arousal (decreased relaxation), and (negative) positive affect. This factor was labeled a distractibility/negative affect factor. For the high susceptibles, the factor to emerge consisted of rationality, (negative) arousal, imagery, memory, and altered state. This unique factor was labeled a rationality/imagery factor.

To review, the Jennrich analyses for the four susceptibility groups for hypnosis revealed significant pattern differences between low and high susceptibles, lows and low-mediums, lows and high-mediums, and low-mediums and highs. The hierarchical factor analyses for the hypnosis condition appears congruent with this analysis. Although there were two universal factors common to all four groups, a unique factor was found for low susceptibles and a different unique factor was found for high susceptibles.

> Thus, the phenomenological pattern structures of low and high susceptibles were not only unique to themselves, but different from each other and also from low-mediums and high-mediums for the hypnosis condition. Superimposed on this pattern solution difference, however, is a pattern similarity concerning awareness/altered state and affect/imagery. (Pekala & Bieber, 1990, p. 316)

In addition, the aforementioned Jennrich analyses found that the eyes-closed and the hypnosis conditions were significantly different from one another for low, low-medium, high-medium, and high susceptible individuals. The hierarchical factor analysis found one factor in common among eyes closed and hypnosis, with a factor specific to the four susceptibility groups during eyes closed, another specific to the four groups for hypnosis, and one factor each unique to the low and high susceptible groups during hypnosis.

Conclusions

Thus, all of the hierarchical factor analyses (Bieber, 1986) supported the Jennrich analyses (Pekala & Kumar, 1989) mentioned earlier and demonstrate the use of the Jennrich analyses and associated psygrams as a legitimate means for assessing pattern structure among susceptibility groups and stimulus conditions. Whereas the Jennrich analyses and associated psygrams assess for significant differences between groups and/or stimulus conditions and descriptively illustrate those differences, the hierarchical analyses attempt to not only assess for group differences, but to factorially determine the specific nature of these differences.

The results suggest the complementarity of Bieber's (1986) and Pekala's (1985a,c) approaches for analyzing pattern structure differences across differing subject pools and stimulus conditions and illustrate that the approach presented in this book is consistent with more traditional factor analytic approaches for understanding multivariate data.

14

Predicting Hypnotic Susceptibility with the PCI

INTRODUCTION

One of the most useful aspects of self-report instruments may concern their ability to predict aspects of human behavior and experience. In a review of the clinical use of hypnosis, Wadden and Anderton (1982) indicated that many studies that use hypnosis frequently omit the assessment of hypnotic susceptibility. Reasons for omission usually include fear of poor response to test suggestions (which may then affect the client's response to treatment), the belief that susceptibility is not important in treatment outcome, or the obtrusiveness of administration and time of administration, when using a scale like the Harvard Group Scale of Hypnotic Susceptibility (Shor & Orne, 1962) or the Stanford Hypnotic Susceptibility Scale (Weitzenhoffer & Hilgard, 1962). And yet without adequate assessment of that susceptibility, it becomes uncertain to what extent the hypnotic intervention enacted is causally related to the therapeutic results obtained.

Standard assessment instruments may also not be used because the clinician is more interested in the cognitive and affective effects of the hypnotic intervention and not with the behavioral manifestations usually assessed by standard instruments. Consistent with this are the remarks by Orne (1977) that standard assessment instruments measure the hypnotic process only to the extent that the behavioral assessment validly reflects alterations in an individual's subjective experience. Similarly, Shor (1979) has advocated the use of phenomenological variables in understanding hypnosis. The aforementioned remarks of Orne and Shor, coupled with the fact that clinicians tend to avoid assessing susceptibility with the standard assessment instruments, suggests that self-report instruments like the Phenomenology of Consciousness Inventory (PCI) may be an appropriate means to measure susceptibility in a quicker and less obtrusive fashion than more traditional scales.

Another means to assess susceptibility consists of the use of hypnotic "depth" inventories, such as the Field Inventory (Field, 1965). It was developed to measure hypnotic depth and consisted of 38 true-false items derived empirically from a pool of 300 items found to correlate with hypnotic susceptibility. The Field Inventory, consisting of six factors derived from factor analysis, obtained an r of .51 between the Stanford scale and the items of the inventory (Field & Palmer, 1969), suggesting the possible usefulness of such an approach in assessing susceptibility. Whereas the Field Inventory is composed of only six dimensions, the PCI is composed of 12 major and 14 minor dimensions and hence may be a more effective instrument in measuring hypnotic depth than the Field Inventory.

STUDY 1

The previous chapters of this book have documented the usefulness of the PCI in discriminating phenomenological experiences among low, medium, and high absorption and susceptible individuals (Kumar & Pekala, 1988, 1989). Hence it was decided to determine if it might be an appropriate instrument for predicting hypnotic susceptibility. It was hoped that the PCI would be able to predict hypnotic susceptibility, as assessed by the Harvard Group Scale, in terms of the (sub)dimensions of the inventory and do so in a way so as to be statistically meaningful and clinically useful. It was also hoped that the results would hold up under cross-validation.

Research Design

The subjects and data obtained from the previously cited first hypnosis study (Chapter 12) were used to determine how well hypnotic susceptibility, as measured by the Harvard Group Scale (Shor & Orne, 1962), could be predicted from the PCI (sub)dimension intensity scores (this study is based on the published report by Pekala & Kumar, 1984). For that study two groups (n = 131 and 132) of subjects experienced a short sitting quietly eyes-closed period and subsequently completed the PCI in reference to it. They then experienced the induction procedure of the Harvard Group Scale and subsequently completed the PCI retrospectively in reference to a several-minute sitting quietly period embedded near the end of the Harvard Scale.

Stepwise multiple regression and discriminant analyses were performed on the data (after eliminating unreliable subjects using a reliability index score of 2.0 as a cutoff) using the subject's Harvard Group Scale score as the dependent variable and the PCI (sub)dimensions as the independent variables. This was done for both the hypnosis and eyes-closed conditions.

Nature of the Results

Regression Analyses

The Eyes-Closed Condition. Concerning the eyes-closed condition, Table 14.1 lists the results of the multiple regression analysis across all 26 (sub)dimensions. Twenty-one percent of the variance was accounted for using these (sub)dimensions. (Using only statistically significant (sub)dimensions resulted in an R^2 of .14.)

For cross-validation subjects were randomly divided into two groups and the subjects of the first group were used to generate regression coefficients to predict the hypnotic susceptibility of the second group of participants (using all 26 (sub)dimensions). Whereas a stepwise multiple regression of the subjects' PCI (sub)dimensions during eyes closed ($n = 106$) resulted in an R of .50 (R^2 of .25), cross-validation on group 2 ($n = 89$) (using the unstandardized regression coefficients from the first group of subjects) resulted in an r of .15, which was not significant.

The Hypnosis Condition. Table 14.2 illustrates the results of the multiple regression analysis across all 26 (sub)dimensions during the sitting quietly period embedded in the Harvard Scale. The analysis generated an R of .71 for an R^2 of .51.

Subjects were again randomly divided into two groups. The subjects of the first group of participants during hypnosis were used to generate regression coefficients to predict hypnotic susceptibility for the second group. A stepwise multiple regression of the subjects' responses during hypnosis ($n = 104$) across all 26 (sub)dimensions resulted in an R of .76 (an R^2 of .57), which cross-validated on group 2 ($n = 86$) yielded an r of .59 for an r^2 of .35.

Two other stepwise multiple regressions were also performed.

Table 14.1. PCI (Sub)Dimension Predictors of Hypnotic Susceptibility (Assessed during Eyes Closed) from Stepwise Multiple Regression[a]

Dimension	Multiple R	Multiple R^2	Change in R^2	Simple r[b]
Altered body image	.302	.091	.091	.30***
Positive affect	.333	.111	.020	.24***
Volitional control	.362	.131	.020	−.12
Attention direction	.387	.150	.019	.17*
Sadness	.408	.166	.016	.09
Joy	.423	.179	.013	.24***
Memory	.430	.185	.006	.17*
Altered time sense	.438	.192	.007	.20**
Self-awareness	.447	.200	.008	−.07
Sexual excitement	.450	.203	.003	.14
Altered state	.453	.205	.002	.29**
Imagery vividness	.455	.207	.002	.21**
Absorption	.457	.209	.002	.15*
Altered perception	.459	.210	.001	.10
Altered meaning	.460	.212	.002	.22*
Fear	.461	.212	.0004	.06
Arousal	.461	.213	.0005	−.12
Rationality	.461	.213	.0002	.08
Internal dialogue	.462	.213	.0001	.07
Negative affect	.462	.213	.0001	.08

Simple correlations of (sub)dimensions not meeting inclusion criteria:

Love	.22**
Anger	.04
Altered experience	.29***
Imagery	.20**
Imagery amount	.14
Attention	.19

[a]From Pekala & Kumar (1984). Reprinted with permission of the publisher.
[b]* = $p < .05$; ** = $p < .01$; *** = $p < .001$.

Using only the (sub)dimensions of the PCI significant at the .05 level of significance generated an R of .70 for an R^2 of .49 across all subjects. (Table 14.2 lists the unstandardized regression coefficients for this analysis.) These significant (sub)dimensions were then used in a stepwise multiple regression of only group 1 subjects during hypnosis and used to predict susceptibility for group 2 subjects. This resulted in an R of .73 (an R^2 of .54), which cross-validated on group 2 subjects yielded an r of .62 for an r^2 of .39.

Table 14.2. PCI (Sub)Dimension Predictors of Hypnotic Susceptibility (Assessed during Hypnosis) from Stepwise Multiple Regression[a]

Dimension	Multiple R	Multiple R^2	Change in R^2	B^b	B^c	r^d
Volitional control	.633	.400	.400	−.84	−.83	−.63***
Attention	.653	.427	.026	.57	.58	.43***
Love	.669	.448	.021	.14	.11	.17*
Altered state	.678	.461	.013	.20	.19	.56***
Imagery amount	.685	.470	.009	−.09		.01
Altered meaning	.691	.478	.007	.24	.23	.37***
Anger	.695	.484	.007	−.36		−.12
Memory	.700	.489	.005	−.17	−.18	−.38***
Rationality	.704	.496	.008	.28	.30	−.39***
Positive affect	.706	.499	.002	.30	.28	.18*
Altered body image	.708	.501	.002	−.19	−.16	.41***
Self-awareness	.710	.504	.003	−.16	−.14	−.51***
Negative affect	.711	.506	.002	.28		−.02
Altered perception	.712	.507	.001	.11	.12	.36***
Visual imagery	.713	.508	.002	−.21		−.12
Attention direction	.714	.509	.001	−.17	−.19	.30***
Sadness	.714	.509	.0001	−.04		.01
Joy	.714	.510	.00004	.02	−.03	.21**
Constant				6.79	6.60	

Simple correlations of (sub)dimensions not meeting inclusion criteria:

Sexual excitement		.08
Fear		.06
Altered time sense	.02	.37***
Imagery vividness	−.23	−.24***
Absorption		.44***
Internal dialogue		−.13
Arousal		−.26***
Altered experience		.52***

[a]From Pekala & Kumar (1984). Reprinted with permission of the publisher.
[b]Unstandardized coefficients using all dimensions.
[c]Unstandardized coefficients using only dimensions significant at alpha < .05.
[d]* = $p < .05$; ** = $p < .01$; *** = $p < .001$.

Discriminant Analyses

Stepwise discriminant function analyses were also calculated using all 26 (sub)dimensions, attempting to predict hypnotizability in terms of low (0–4), medium (5–8), or high (9–12) hypnotizability. Prediction of susceptibility resulted in a 57.4, 46.1, and a 49.2% correct classification ratio for low, medium, and high susceptible subjects, respectively, during the eyes-closed condition.

In predicting susceptibility from the PCI (sub)dimensions during hypnosis, 72.7, 60.7, and 75.4% of the lows, mediums, and highs, respectively, were correctly predicted, while only 4.5% of the lows were falsely predicted to be highs, and only 1.8% of the highs to be lows. The overall successful classification ratio was 67.9%, double that predicted by chance alone.

In order to determine a cross-validated classification table for hypnosis, a stepwise discriminant analysis was performed on group 1 ($n = 140$) and used to predict membership of low, medium, or high susceptibility for group 2 ($n = 86$) using the classification function coefficients. Whereas 68% of the lows were successfully predicted, only 41% of the mediums and 44% of the highs were successfully predicted, for an overall classification ratio of 48%.

Discussion and Interpretation

The discriminant analyses, on cross-validation, did not support the usefulness of the PCI in predicting membership in low, medium, or high susceptible groups. Using regression analyses, however, over 50% of the variance of the Harvard Group Scale was correctly predicted from the PCI (sub)dimensions across all subjects. In addition, using only the significant PCI (sub)dimensions yielded a multiple R of .73 on group 1 subjects, that dropped to only .62 on cross-validation with group 2 subjects. [Validity coefficients, at least in industrial psychology research, usually only run between .30 and .60 (Jewell, 1985).]

Thus, 39% of the variance of the Harvard Group Scale group 2 subjects was correctly predicted from PCI regression coefficients from the group 1 subjects. These results suggest that the use of the PCI (sub)dimensions to predict hypnotizability, by multiple regression, may be appropriate for assessing the extent to which a hypnotic induction leads to significant phenomenological alterations that correlate with the Harvard Group Scale. Given the reluctance of current clinical hypnosis research to use standard assessment instruments (Wadden & Anderton, 1982), the present research supports the possible usefulness of a self-report inventory to map phenomenological correlates of being hypnotized (as assessed by the Harvard Scale).

STUDY 2

The previous section has suggested the possible usefulness of the PCI in the prediction of hypnotic susceptibility. In an attempt to replicate

the previous research, the PCI was given to a new subject pool to complete in reference to three stimulus conditions: a three-minute eyes-closed sitting quietly condition, a three-minute eyes-open sitting quietly period, and a three-minute interval within a hypnotic procedure (Pekala & Kumar, 1987).

It was predicted that the PCI, during hypnosis, would generate a multiple R similar to that obtained from previous research. Furthermore, cross-validation regression analyses (using the previous study's regression coefficients to predict the actual Harvard Scale scores of the present study and vice versa) would generate similar validity coefficients as were found in earlier research. The previous study also employed discriminant analyses, attempting to predict inclusion in low, medium, or high susceptibility groups. Although such analyses were less predictive of susceptibility than the regression analyses, the present study also attempted such analyses.

Research Design

The subjects, materials, and procedure for this study were the same as that reported for the second hypnosis study on trait-state effects associated with hypnosis (see Chapter 12). Subjects consisted of 434 undergraduates enrolled in introductory psychology classes at West Chester University. The Harvard Group Scale of Hypnotic Susceptibility, Form A (Shor & Orne, 1962) was used to assess hypnotic susceptibility, while the PCI was used to map phenomenological state.

Four hundred and thirty-four subjects experienced a three-minute sitting quietly period (the baseline condition) followed by a hypnotic induction with the Harvard Scale wherein was embedded a three-minute sitting quietly period. The PCI was completed retrospectively in reference to each of the three-minute periods.

Nature of the Results

PCI Preliminary Analyses

Although the initial subject pool consisted of 434 subjects, complete data (completion of all paper-and-pencil tests without errors or omissions) were available on 375 subjects (237 females and 138 males). This represented 86% of all subjects tested.

Each subject's responses to the PCI were then assessed for intra-individual reliability. Subjects having a marginal reliability index were eliminated. PCI (sub)dimension intensity scores were then computed for each subject for each condition by averaging those items that composed a given PCI (sub)dimensions for each subject.

Regression Analyses

Stepwise multiple regression equations were calculated for all 26 dimensions and subdimensions of the PCI, and then again only for PCI (sub)dimensions having statistically significant correlations with the Harvard Scale score. This was done for the eyes-closed and the hypnotic induction conditions to predict the Harvard Scale scores from the PCI (sub)dimensions. (The comparatively small sample for the eyes-open condition, $n = 84$, precluded regression analyses for this condition.)

The Eyes-Closed Condition. Using all (sub)dimensions of the PCI yielded a multiple R of .38 (R^2 of .14). Using only PCI (sub)dimensions having a significant correlation ($p < .05$) with the Harvard Scale score yielded an R of .36 (R^2 of .13). (Both were significant at $p < .001$.)

For cross-validation, the regression equation from the previous study (Pekala & Kumar, 1984) was used to predict the Harvard Scale scores of subjects using PCI intensity scores obtained in the present study. The predicted scores were then correlated with subjects' actual Harvard Scale scores in the present study. This resulted in an r of .27 ($p < .001$) when using all PCI (sub)dimensions and .22 ($p < .001$) when using only significant (sub)dimensions.

The subjects' actual Harvard Scale scores from the previous study were then predicted from PCI scores obtained in the previous study, but using the regression equation of the present study. This resulted in an r of .33 ($p < .001$) when using all PCI (sub)dimensions and an r of .30 ($p < .001$) when using only (sub)dimensions significant at the .05 level.

The Hypnosis Condition. Table 14.3 lists the results of the multiple regression analysis across all 26 (sub)dimensions during the hypnotic induction. The analysis generated a multiple R of .63 (R^2 of .40). Using only PCI (sub)dimensions correlating significantly ($p < .001$) with the Harvard Scale yielded a multiple R of .62 (R^2 of .39). (Table 14.3 also lists the simple correlations and the unstandardized regression coefficients using all 26 (sub)dimensions and only those significant at .001.)

For cross-validation, the regression coefficients during hypnosis from the previous study were used to predict the hypnotic susceptibility of the subjects of the present study. This was done by computing predicted Harvard Scale scores from PCI intensity scores obtained in the present study and correlating them with the present study's actual Har-

Table 14.3. PCI (Sub)Dimension Predictors of Hypnotic Susceptibility
(Assessed during Hypnosis) from Stepwise Multiple Regression:
Second Study[a]

Dimension	Multiple R	Multiple R^2	Change in R^2	B^b	B^c	r^d
Altered state	.55	.30	.304	.33	.31	.55**
Self-awareness	.582	.339	.034	−.28	−.27	−.49**
Altered time sense	.594	.352	.0137	.07	.13	.45**
Absorption	.604	.364	.0119	.20	.19	.32**
Volitional control	.609	.371	.0070	−.32	−.28	−.52**
Rationality	.613	.376	.0047	.26	.23	−.32**
Internal dialogue	.617	.380	.0043	−.12	−.11	−.24**
Altered experience	.620	.384	.0040	.49	.35	.50**
Memory	.622	.387	.0031	−.13	−.14	−.36**
Arousal	.624	.390	.0024	.14		−.10
Imagery amount	.626	.392	.0026	−.16		.02
Sexual excitement	.629	.396	.0035	.18		.01
Sadness	.631	.398	.0025	−.05		−.05
Fear	.6321	.399	.0013	.22		.04
Imagery vividness	.6328	.400	.0010	.09		−.18**
Joy	.6335	.401	.0008	−.08		.11*
Negative affect	.6341	.402	.0007	−.28		−.03
Altered body image	.6343	.402	.0003	−.06	−.07	.38**
Altered meaning	.6343	.402	.00004	−.04		.32**
Constant				4.29	4.51	

Simple correlations of (sub)dimensions not meeting inclusion criteria:

Love	.08
Anger	−.07
Altered perception	.39**
Attention direction	.09
Positive affect	.08
Visual imagery	−.08
Attention	.22**

[a]From Pekala & Kumar (1987). Reprinted with permission of the publisher.
[b]Unstandardized coefficients using all dimensions.
[c]Unstandardized coefficients using only dimensions significant at alpha < .001. [Used to compute the "hypnoidal state" or "predicted Harvard Group Scale" (pHGS) score.]
[d]$* = p < .05$; $** = p < .001$.

vard Scale scores. This yielded an r of .57 ($p < .001$) whether using either all PCI (sub)dimensions or only those significant at $p < .001$.

Predicting the Harvard Scale scores from the PCI scores of the previous study using the unstandardized regression coefficients of the present study yielded rs of .65 ($p < .001$), whether using all PCI (sub)dimensions or only those significant at $p < .001$.

Discriminant Analyses

The Eyes-Closed Condition. Stepwise discriminant function analyses (Nie *et al.*, 1975) were calculated using all 26 (sub)dimensions to predict low (Harvard Scale scores of 0–4), medium (5–7), or high (8–12) susceptibility. Prediction of susceptibility for the eyes-closed condition resulted in a 63%, 47%, and a 48% correct classification rate for low, medium, and high susceptible subjects, respectively. The overall successful classification rate was 52%.

To determine a cross-validated classification table, analyses were performed using the discriminant function classification equation of the previous study to predict membership for subjects in the present study and vice versa. This resulted in an overall success rate of 44% and 39%, respectively, for the eyes-closed conditions.

The Hypnosis Condition. Predicting susceptibility for the hypnotic condition from the PCI (sub)dimensions, 60%, 47%, and 60% of the lows, mediums, and highs, respectively, were correctly classified. The overall successful classification rate was 58%. To determine a cross-validated classification table, analyses were performed using the discriminant function classification equation of the previous study to predict membership for subjects in the present study and vice versa. This resulted in an overall success rate of 54% and 57%, respectively, for the hypnotic induction conditions.

Discussion and Interpretation

Regression Analyses during Hypnosis

Validity coefficients of .57 and .65 suggest that the PCI may serve as one means for assessing susceptibility when completed in reference to hypnotic procedures. Having subjects complete a self-report instrument in reference to a hypnotic or hypnoticlike condition may provide a means to assess the extent to which a hypnotic procedure induces a hypnotic "state" without having to administer an intrusive assessment procedure. Such an approach may be especially appropriate for use with groups of subjects. By dividing subjects into those with low, medium, and high predicted Harvard Scale scores, one could then compare various dependent variables as a function of these groups and also assess the extent to which the predicted scores give the same results as scores based on the actual Harvard Scale responses.

Other Results

On the other hand, a resulting overall successful classification rate of 54% to 57% using the PCI by discriminant analysis does not appear to be particularly useful in attempting to predict susceptibility (too many false negatives appear to be generated by the discriminant analyses). Nor does the use of regression analysis in reference to nonhypnotic conditions such as eyes closed sitting quietly, as Pearson *r* coefficients of .22 to .33 indicate.

THE ASSESSMENT OF HYPNOIDAL STATES: RATIONALE AND CLINICAL APPLICATION

The two studies just reviewed found certain dimensions of phenomenological experience, assessed by the PCI, that were moderately correlated with hypnotic susceptibility. The PCI was able to generate a validity coefficient of .65 (Pekala & Kumar, 1987) between the actual Harvard Group Scale scores of a group of subjects and their predicted Harvard Group Scale (pHGS) scores (based on a regression equation using the regression coefficients obtained from another group of subjects). An additional study (Forbes & Pekala, 1991) obtained a validity coefficient of .63 between the actual Harvard Scale scores of a new group of subjects (nursing students) and the aforementioned pHGS scores.

The regression equation (using the unstandardized coefficients listed in Table 14.3 for only (sub)dimensions significant at alpha < .001) is composed of the unstandardized regression coefficients of 10 of the 26 (sub)dimensions of the PCI; it generates a pHGS score that can theoretically vary between −.71 to 11.77, although it usually ranges between 1 and 9 ($M = 5.97 \pm 1.82$). The usefulness of this regression equation may lie in its ability to generate a pHGS score that can serve as a measure of the phenomenological state a person or group of people experience. In contrast to other hypnotic instruments, the PCI is a state instrument. Instead of measuring hypnotic ability, it gives a measure of that ability as manifested in terms of a short stimulus condition, that is, the "hypnotic" state associated with that condition.

The potential usefulness of the PCI may lie in its ability to generate unobtrusively a pHGS score that correlates with standardized, but more obtrusive, assessment instruments, like the Harvard Group Scale of Hypnotic Susceptibility (Shor & Orne, 1962) or the Stanford Hypnotic Susceptibility Scale (Weitzenhoffer & Hilgard, 1962). Hence, the PCI

"may provide a means for measuring hypnotic susceptibility rather unobtrusively across groups of subjects" (Pekala & Kumar, 1987, p. 64).
Whereas simple "1 to 10" depth scales give a subjective estimate of
hypnotic "depth," the PCI pHGS score gives an intensity measure of the
phenomenological experiences associated with what subjects of low,
medium, and high hypnotic susceptibility would report during hypnosis. Being a linear combination of ten (sub)dimensions of the PCI, it *may*
be a more stable measure of hypnotic state than linear depth scales,
since it is sensitive to intensity variations along ten dimensions of subjective experience associated with being hypnotized.

Hypnoidal States

The PCI can be used to generate *hypnoidal scores* (Pekala & Nagler,
1989) that allow one to obtain an estimate of the phenomenological
parameters associated with what subjects of varying hypnotic susceptibility would report during hypnosis. In other words, a low hypnoidal
score would represent the phenomenological experience of low hypnotically susceptible individuals during hypnosis, while a high hypnoidal
score would represent the phenomenological experience typical of high
susceptible individuals during hypnosis.

It is premature to label the state associated with a high pHGS score a
"hypnotic" state, however. It is unknown at this point if experiencing all
of the phenomenological parameters that would generate a high pHGS
score of 11.77 would be associated with a "deep" hypnotic state—the
state a person would be in should he or she be deeply hypnotized and
subsequently be able to demonstrate hypnotic effects such as a negative
visual hallucination or selective amnesia. In other words, although the
regression equation allows one to determine the average phenomenological parameters associated with being in a "deep" hypnotic state, it
does not follow that experiencing such phenomenological effects would
be associated with being able to experience classic hypnotic effects.

Hilgard (1977), writing concerning the hypnotic contract, reviewed
a study (Weitzenhoffer *et al.*, 1959) that reported that a "formal induction
procedure, beyond eye fixation, was unnecessary, provided expectation
of hypnosis was present" (1977, p. 225). What may be a necessary, but
not sufficient, variable in demonstrating hypnotic behavior is the
proviso that a hypnotic contract (expectation of hypnosis) is implied;
such a contract may be a sine qua non if hypnotic behavior is subsequently to occur. Having phenomenological experience consistent with
deep hypnosis is not equivalent, however, to entering into a contract for
hypnosis.

Hence it may be preferable to use the adjective, *hypnoidal*, and the concept, *hypnoidal state*, to refer to phenomenological experience congruent with what high susceptibles, on the average, would endorse during a hypnotic induction. Since a state is "any well-defined condition or property that can be recognized if it occurs again" (Ashby, 1963, p. 17), a hypnoidal state is herein defined as a state, defined by a regression equation using the PCI (Pekala & Kumar, 1987), that is associated with the endorsement of PCI (sub)dimension intensity effects by high susceptibles during a short (eyes-closed) sitting quietly interval during the induction procedure of the Harvard Group Scale.

To determine what would be a high score based on pHGS scores and to determine if the scores during hypnosis would be different from those during eyes closed (as a test of discriminant validity), the subjects from an earlier study (Pekala & Kumar, 1984) were divided into 13 groups, based on their score on the Harvard, and pHGS scores were computed using the regression equation obtained with the subjects from a second study (Pekala & Kumar, 1987). Paired *t*-tests were then computed comparing the eyes-closed condition against the hypnotic induction condition with the pHGS scores as the dependent variable. Averaged pHGS scores were significantly higher during hypnosis than eyes closed for all subjects obtaining a Harvard Scale score of 4 or above and the difference between pHGS scores for eyes closed and the hypnotic induction became greater the higher the actual Harvard Scale score. A

Table 14.4. Comparison between pHGS Scores during Hypnosis and Eyes Closed as a Function of Harvard Group Scale Score

Harvard score	*n*	Hypnosis		Eyes closed		*t*-value	Probability
		Mean	S.D.	Mean	S.D.		
0	7	3.10	1.26	4.60	0.91	3.42	.01
1	6	3.53	1.73	3.46	1.08	0.14	.89
2	3	2.63	1.98	2.96	1.36	0.37	.75
3	10	3.74	1.44	3.66	0.74	0.19	.86
4	14	5.04	1.45	4.12	0.96	2.33	.04
5	18	5.75	1.08	4.42	1.40	3.34	.004
6	14	6.31	1.66	5.01	1.82	2.13	.05
7	25	5.94	1.55	4.54	1.45	4.48	.001
8	24	6.50	1.14	4.23	0.88	9.31	.001
9	16	6.97	1.21	4.93	1.03	6.34	.001
10	14	7.29	1.17	4.50	0.69	8.52	.001
11	13	7.64	1.11	5.59	1.18	4.91	.001
12	9	7.18	0.58	5.44	1.56	3.11	.02

pHGS score of 7 and above was defined (albeit somewhat arbitrarily) as associated with a hypnoidal state, since high susceptibles (scores of 10 or above on the Harvard) averaged scores of above 7, and none of these groups had average scores during eyes closed of 7 or above. Table 14.4 lists these means for hypnosis and the eyes-closed condition as a function of Harvard Group Scale score. (A second study, Pekala & Forbes, 1988, yielded equivalent data concerning 7 as a cutoff point for high susceptibles during hypnosis.)

The PCI has recently been used to assess the hypnoidal effects associated with individual hypnotherapy, biofeedback training, standardized hypnotic assessments, and a baseline condition for various patients (Pekala & Nagler, 1989). The following section will report, in case study fashion, on hypnosis and biofeedback with two patients who completed the PCI in reference to their experience of these conditions.

Using the PCI to Assess Hypnoidal Effects in Individual Patients

Both patients were referred to the Biofeedback Clinic of a VA hospital. Besides participating in individual biofeedback training, they also had their hypnotic susceptibility assessed by the Harvard Group Scale. Hypnographs have been provided to allow the reader to compare the hypnoidal effects associated with various conditions experienced by the patients.

The Case of Tony

Tony was a 25-year-old white male admitted after overdosing on sleeping pills. He reported having chronic insomnia since age 13 when he began having nightmares. Tony's diagnoses included borderline personality with depressive features and mixed substance abuse (in remission).

Tony, during an initial intake interview, related that he was an only child. His mother wanted him to have some companionship, and so between the ages of 5 and 7, she procured a "big brother" for Tony. One night, however, the big brother raped Tony. He reported that he then became amnestic to the experience until approximately age 12 or 13. At that time Tony related that while watching TV he remembered the incident and began to reexperience the trauma.

Since that time he reported having nightmares approximately three times a week where he would dream of being raped, become extremely fearful and helpless, and be unable to go back to sleep for fear of reexperiencing the trauma. Tony discovered, however, that if he smoked marijuana he would not remember dreaming and hence could have a better night's sleep. Unfortunately, the marijuana seemed to lead to other drugs. He needed to kick his drug habit, but found out when he tried to do that, the nightmares would return.

Tony experienced four sessions of individual biofeedback training. He was able to reduce initial muscle tension levels from an baseline level of 12 microvolts down to approximately 1 to 2 microvolts (which was within normal limits). Although such training was helpful in reducing tension, it did not have an appreciable effect on his nightmares.

Tony was given the Harvard Group Scale and obtained a score of 10. Figure 14.1 depicts the hypnograph illustrating the hypnoidal effects associated with the stimulus conditions experienced by Tony, including the biofeedback training, a baseline condition, hypnosis and progressive relaxation. (The y-axis indicates the pHGS score using the regression equation mentioned previously in terms of a hypnoidal score from 0 to 10.) During a three-minute eyes-closed sitting quietly period embedded in the Harvard, Tony obtained a pHGS score of 8.4. Interestingly, immediately after the assessment session with the Harvard Scale, Tony said he felt "stoned" (what I felt to be a good prognostic indicator for subsequent hypnotherapy since marijuana was used by Tony to eliminate remembering his nightmares).

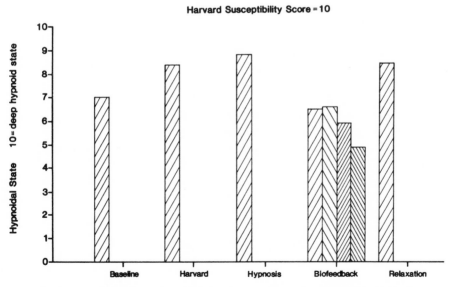

Figure 14.1. Predicted Harvard Group Scale scores: Tony. (From Pekala & Nagler, 1989. Reprinted with permission of the publisher.) (Sessions: ▨, 1; ▨, 2; ▨, 3; ▨, 4.)

During the baseline eyes-closed condition preceding the Harvard, Tony obtained a pHGS score of 7.0. Tony was seen for one session of individual ego-strengthening hypnosis during which time he was taught self-hypnosis and given suggestions: (1) to practice the self-hypnosis before going to bed, (2) to give himself suggestions to manipulate his dreams so that he would either be able to alter the dream sequence so as to not feel helpless or prevent the dream from occurring, and (3) to realize that he had suffered long enough and it was time for him to get on with his life without having to reexperience the past trauma. Completion of the self-report inventory during a two-minute period during the hypnosis (but before the aforementioned suggestions) indicated he obtained a pHGS score of 8.8. He was discharged before a second hypnosis session could be scheduled.

At six months he was contacted by letter and returned a postcard on which he wrote:

> I can't thank you enough for *stopping* my nightmares. I have not had a dream about what we have discussed since. Yes, I do still practice self-hypnosis, just the way you told me to do, and it works well. I feel better and work better now.

At a year and a half follow-up, Tony reported being nightmare-free and still practicing!

The Case of Karen

Karen was a 37-year-old white female referred to the Biofeedback Clinic for headaches. She suffered from left-sided pulsating migraine headaches several times a week, was having marital problems, and difficulty expressing anger. She originally came to the hospital due to depression. The psychologist treating her depression, who referred her to the clinic, indicated Karen would have short periods where she would not quite remember what she was doing, suggestive of mild dissociative episodes. Karen was verbally and physically abused as a child by her father and sexually abused by her uncle. She was extremely fearful of hypnosis. We had to make several appointments to get her involved in the hypnosis before she finally participated.

Karen began EMG biofeedback training and then moved into peripheral skin temperature (adrenergic sympathetic nervous system) training where she was able to raise her peripheral skin temperature from approximately 76°F to 96°F. For the hypnotic assessment, Karen obtained a Harvard Group Scale score of 10.

During a baseline condition of eyes closed, Karen obtained a pHGS

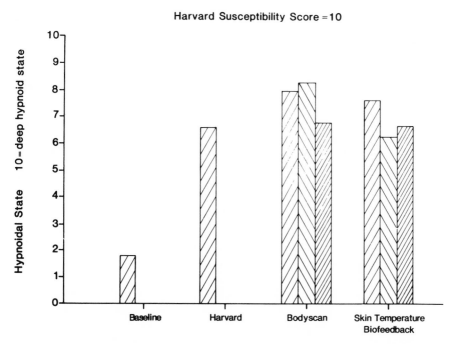

Figure 14.2. Predicted Harvard Group Scale scores: Karen. (Sessions: ▨, 1; ◩, 2; ▨, 3.)

score of 1.8, while during the Harvard she obtained a pHGS score of 6.6. During the "body scan" (progressive relaxation, but without the tensing) procedure, Karen reported experiencing subjective feelings similar to what she experienced during the hypnosis assessment (and obtained an average pHGS score of 7.7). She also had somewhat similar feelings during the skin temperature training, although she felt the temperature training to be qualitatively different from the "body scan" and the hypnosis. Figure 14.2 illustrates her pHGS scores for the Harvard assessment, a baseline comparison condition, the "body scan" relaxation procedure, and skin temperature biofeedback training.

As the biofeedback sessions continued, hypnotic suggestions were increasingly used in the sessions. During the latter biofeedback training sessions, she reported that the biofeedback training sessions appeared phenomenologically more similar to her experience during the Harvard assessment, and reported being able to put herself into hypnotic states on her own with increasing ease. At follow-up Karen reported only an occasional headache, although such headaches would become more frequent if she did not practice.

Discussion and Conclusions

The two cases discussed above suggest that the PCI appears to be able to furnish data on the hypnoidal states of these patients. For Tony, the hypnograph suggests possible equivalence between hypnosis and progressive relaxation, at least in terms of phenomenological experience. It also suggests a reason as to why the rape trauma may have been intruding into his dreams, that is, hypnoidal states may have been less than a rare occurrence. Tony obtained a phGS score of 7, indicative of a hypnoidal state, while just sitting quietly, and this may have allowed for dissociated affect to express itself during his dreams in ways not available to low susceptible subjects. For Karen the hypnograph illustrates how the body scan procedure generated high hypnoidal effects that were confirmed by her anecdotal self-reports.

In conclusion, although case study data do not allow one to assert external validity, the data do suggest the possible clinical usefulness of the PCI in generating phGS scores that may be important in assessing the hypnoidal states subjects, or more importantly, patients and clients, are experiencing during clinical hypnotic situations and related relaxation strategies, including biofeedback, progressive relaxation, and stress management techniques.

HYPNOIDAL EFFECTS ASSOCIATED WITH SEVERAL STRESS MANAGEMENT STRATEGIES

Given the usefulness of the PCI at assessing "hypnoidal states," it was wondered to what extent nonhypnotic conditions, such as progressive relaxation, would evince hypnotic effects. Hence it was decided to study hypnoidal effects obtained during four stimulus conditions: a baseline condition of eyes closed sitting quietly (of two minutes duration), a two-minute period following deep abdominal breathing, and a two-minute period embedded near the end of progressive relaxation instructions and the induction procedure of the Harvard Group Scale (reported in Pekala & Forbes, 1988).

Since research of indirect hypnotic techniques (Barber, 1977; Fricton & Roth, 1985) has been shown to yield hypnotic effects with resistant or low hypnotically susceptible individuals equivalent to that of direct hypnotic techniques, it was wondered to what extent progressive relaxation, an ostensible nonhypnotic technique, might be associated with hypnoidal effects. Although no prediction was made due to the dearth of data on the hypnoidal effects of progressive relaxation, the present study represents an attempt to measure such effects with progressive relaxation and also deep abdominal breathing.

Finally, it was hypothesized that the baseline condition of eyes closed would not be associated with hypnoidal effects, as was the case in previous research.

Research Design

Subjects consisted of 300 nursing students. The Harvard Group Scale of Hypnotic Susceptibility, Form A (Shor & Orne, 1962) was used to assess susceptibility, while the PCI was used to map phenomenological experience. The procedure for the following study is identical to that described in Chapter 12 (see Study 3, pp. 279–287).

Subjects experienced a baseline eyes-closed sitting quietly condition followed by a progressive relaxation routine during the first day of the study. On the second day of the study, they first experienced deep abdominal breathing and then hypnosis as induced by the Harvard Scale. In reference to two-minute sitting quietly periods embedded in each of the four conditions, subjects retrospectively completed the PCI.

Nature of the Results

Preliminary Analyses

After elimination of subjects with incomplete inventories, subjects were divided into four susceptibility groups, based on their scores on the Harvard Scale: lows (scores of 0 to 4, $n = 68$, $M = 2.24$), low-mediums (5–6, $n = 51$, $M = 5.53$), high-mediums (7–8, $n = 70$, $M = 7.56$), and highs (9–12, $n = 57$, $M = 9.74$). Using the regression equation obtained in earlier research (Pekala & Kumar, 1987), predicted Harvard Group Scale (pHGS) scores were computed for each subject for each stimulus condition.

Main Analyses

With (susceptibility) groups (low, low-medium, high-medium, and high) as the independent variable, a multivariate repeated-measures analysis of variance was performed with pHGS scores as the dependent variable and with repeated measures on conditions (eyes closed, breathing, progressive relaxation, and hypnosis).

The results yielded a significant main effect for groups [$F (3, 242) = 30.86$, $p < .001$] and conditions [$F (3, 240) = 135.6$, $p < .001$], and a significant interaction for groups and conditions [F (9, 716) = 9.47, $p <$ .001]. Figure 14.3 lists the interaction among susceptibility groups and conditions.

A variety of post hoc simple contrasts were then performed using the MGLH program of SYSTAT (Wilkinson, 1988b) which takes into account unequal sample numbers. Post hoc simple contrasts were first performed for Groups. [To offset inflation of alpha levels for the six comparisons, alpha was set at .008 using the Bonferroni (Kirk, 1968) adjustment procedure.] Significant differences were found between low and low-medium, low and high-medium, low and high, and low-medium and high subjects.

To determine the effects of session and order, post hoc contrasts were performed to test for significant main effects for sessions (first and second) and order (first and second conditions) and their interaction with groups and each other. (To offset inflation of alpha levels for these post hoc comparisons, alpha was set at .008.) The results yielded a significant main effect for order [F (1, 242) = 406.73, $p <$ .001], and significant interactions for groups by sessions [F (3, 242) = 12.45, $p <$

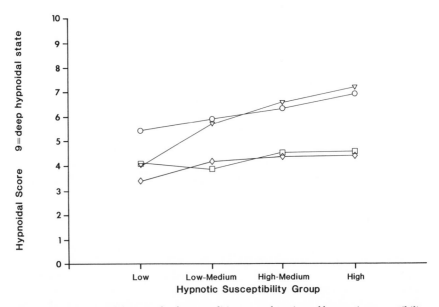

Figure 14.3. Hypnoidal scores for four conditions as a function of hypnotic susceptibility. (From Pekala & Forbes, 1988. Reprinted with permission of the publisher.) (□, Eyes closed; ○, progressive relaxation; ◇, deep abdominal breathing; ▽, hypnosis.)

.001] and groups by order [F (3, 242) = 13.10, $p < .001$]. The main effect for sessions, and the interactions between sessions, order, and groups were not significant.

Since the sessions main effect was not significant, simple contrasts were performed separately, assessing for differences between baseline and deep abdominal breathing, and progressive relaxation and hypnosis (the first and second conditions of each session) and their interaction with groups (alpha was set at .01). There was neither a significant main effect for the comparison between eyes closed and breathing [F (1, 242) = 2.68, $p < .10$], nor a significant interaction between these and groups [F (3, 242 = 3.83, $p < .02$] (see Figure 14.3).

For the progressive relaxation-hypnosis comparison, although there was not a significant main effect for conditions [F (1, 242) = 3.99, $p < .05$], there was a significant interaction between conditions and groups [F (3, 242 = 11.09, $p < .001$] (see Figure 14.3). Post hoc Newman-Keuls comparisons (alpha = .01) revealed that for progressive relaxation, lows reported significantly fewer hypnoidal effects ($M = 5.43$) than highs ($M = 6.91$). Low-mediums ($M = 5.89$) were also significantly different from highs.

For hypnosis, there were significant differences in hypnoidal scores between lows ($M = 4.05$) and low-mediums ($M = 5.73$), lows and high-mediums ($M = 6.59$), low-mediums and highs ($M = 7.17$), and lows and highs. Post hoc simple contrasts were also completed assessing for significant differences between progressive relaxation and hypnosis for the four groups (alpha was set at .01). Whereas the post hoc comparison between hypnosis and progressive relaxation was significant for lows [F (1, 242) = 30.43, $p < .001$], it was not for low-mediums [F (1, 242) = 0.17, $p < .70$], high-mediums [F (1, 242) = 6.86, $p < .02$], nor highs [F (1, 242) = 5.47, $p < .02$].

Discussion and Interpretation

Main Results

The results suggest that the hypnoidal effects a person reports, as assessed by the PCI, appear to be a function of both hypnotic susceptibility and stimulus condition. A significant main effect for susceptibility groups suggests that high susceptibles report greater hypnoidal effects than lows and low-mediums averaging across all stimulus conditions. Interestingly, for high susceptibles, progressive relaxation was not found to be significantly different from hypnosis in terms of reported hypnoidal effects, and yet progressive relaxation was found to be associated with greater hypnoidal effects for low susceptibles than hypnosis itself.

These results may have interesting sequelae for stress management techniques with individuals of varying susceptibility. They suggest that progressive relaxation and hypnosis may be relatively equivalent methods to induce hypnoidal effects for highs. In contrast, low hypnotically susceptible individuals appear to have greater hypnoidal effects during progressive relaxation than hypnosis, although those hypnoidal effects for lows were less than that obtained by highs during either hypnosis or progressive relaxation.

The data appear congruent with research that suggests that a direct hypnotic induction, such as that induced by the Harvard Group Scale, has distracting effects for low susceptibles (Kumar & Pekala, 1988, 1989), and yet indirect hypnotic techniques [i.e., techniques not defined as hypnosis to subjects and yet possibly hypnotic in nature (Barber, 1977; Fricton & Roth, 1985)], have been found to produce hypnotic effects that are not able to be achieved when using a technique labeled as hypnosis with low susceptibles. Progressive relaxation may be such an indirect hypnotic technique.

Other Results

The lack of a significant difference between eyes closed and deep abdominal breathing across all subjects suggests that deep breathing does not produce greater hypnoidal effects than eyes closed. The hypnoidal effects of progressive relaxation for lows ($M = 5.43$), although above that of hypnosis for lows ($M = 4.05$), is still significantly less than that obtained by highs during hypnosis ($M = 7.17$) and below the cutoff of 7.0 that can be used to define a hypnoidal state (Pekala & Nagler, 1989). This suggests that although low susceptible subjects do not enter a *hypnoidal state* (defined as a score of 7.0 or above), progressive relaxation does appear to generate greater *hypnoidal effects* than an actual hypnotic induction for lows. The nonsignificant (although approaching significance) difference in hypnoidal scores for highs during hypnosis ($M = 7.17$) versus progressive relaxation ($M = 6.91$) suggests small, but probably negligible differences, in hypnoidal effects for high susceptibles.

Although the sessions effect was not significant, it approached significance ($p < .02$). This may have been due to a trend toward a practice effect and/or due to hypnosis/breathing having greater hypnoidal effects than progressive relaxation/baseline. Future research will need to control for such influences by counterbalancing sessions.

Inferences and Conclusions

The present study suggests that progressive relaxation is associated with greater hypnoidal effects than hypnosis for low susceptibles, and phenomenological effects equivalent to hypnosis for high susceptibles. This suggests that high susceptibles may be experiencing hypnoidal effects during stress management techniques (like progressive relaxation) other than hypnosis, and hypnotic suggestions given during such techniques may be effective (as they are for highs during hypnosis). In contrast, low susceptibles may be more comfortable and may experience greater therapeutic effects, *if hypnoidal effects are found to be therapeutic*, during stress management conditions that are not labeled hypnotic, such as progressive relaxation, biofeedback, or indirect hypnotic techniques (Barber, 1977).

CONCLUDING REMARKS: THE NATURE OF TRANCE

The several studies reviewed in this chapter indicate that the PCI is able to generate a predicted Harvard Group Scale score that correlates rather well with the actual Harvard Group Scale score. Two additional studies (Forbes & Pekala, 1991; Kumar & Pekala, 1991) generated similar multiple regression coefficients and similar predicted Harvard Group Scale scores, based on the regression equation cited previously.

The clinical hypnosis literature is replete with the term "trance" (Brown & Fromm, 1986). Everyone seems to use the term and yet no one, to my knowledge, has been able to come up with a meaningful and quantifiable definition of the term. Although we are able to get people to estimate trance depth with scales like the North Carolina Scale (Tart, 1963) and the Extended North Carolina Scale (Tart, 1979), these scales do not take into the account the multidimensional nature of the hypnotic state.

The PCI gives the researcher a quantifiable measure of "trance." Using the previously mentioned regression equation, the PCI estimates hypnotic experience along ten dimensions of phenomenological experience, summing these dimensions for an estimate of the "hypnoidal state" of the individual (Pekala & Nagler, 1989).

One may object that there may be different "types" of trance and we should not limit ourselves to just one type, such as that obtained with a regression equation and the PCI. In support of the notion that there may be different types of trance, cluster analysis research with the PCI in reference to high hypnotically susceptible individuals indicates that there are probably at least two types of trance experience in reference to a sitting quietly period embedded in the Harvard Group Scale (Pekala, in press). Whereas one type of high susceptible reported greater alterations in awareness, little volitional control, rationality, and self-awareness, a second type reported less of the above alterations but much more vivid imagery and positive affect. The former was labeled the "classic" highs, while the latter, the "fantasy" highs. (Their icons were illustrated in Chapter 9.)

Yet, a general quantifiable measure of trance is needed so clinicians and researchers alike can begin to tie their theoretical notions to quantifiable data. The PCI can be used to generate a predicted Harvard Group Scale score that can be used to estimate how subjective experience during a given stimulus condition compares with how high hypnotically susceptible individuals (as measured by the Harvard) report experiencing hypnosis. By using it in reference to a standardized but short induction procedure (Pekala, 1991c), it may provide a briefly administered measure of susceptibility to determine whether the clinician should try more hypnotically assisted or biofeedback-assisted approaches to stress management (Pekala, 1985b; Wickramasekera, 1988).

The data presented in the present chapter and others suggest that the PCI can be an appropriately reliable and valid instrument for mapping subjective experience in general and hypnotic experience in particular. Because it can be given retrospectively in reference to a preceding stimulus condition, it represents a much less obtrusive means for quantifying trance than anything else currently available.

Will hypnosis researchers and clinicians continue to use terms like "trance" without trying to operationalize their definitions? Psychology has made the gains that it has over the last 70 years because of operational definition of its terms. One of the reasons hypnosis research has waxed and waned over the last 100 years may relate to the inability of its researchers to operationally define such terms as "trance" or "dissociation." This was echoed by Dr. Frankel in his invited address to the Society of Clinical and Experimental Hypnosis in St. Louis (Frankel, 1989) when he questioned if "dissociation" had become too common a term and no longer had any specific meaning.

Psychologists no longer eschew concepts like attention, consciousness, or schema, but are actively trying to operationalize these terms (Baars, 1988; McClelland & Rumelhart, 1988). When will hypnosis researchers do the same?

Assessing an Out-of-the-Body Experience with the PCI and the DAQ

INTRODUCTION

Although the Phenomenology of Consciousness Inventory (PCI) and the Dimensions of Attention Questionnaire (DAQ) have been used primarily to assess states of consciousness associated with hypnosis, stress management conditions, and baseline states like eyes open or closed sitting quietly, their potential is really much greater. Both the PCI and the DAQ were developed to be used with, and in assessing, the wide variety of altered states including, but not limited to, near-death experiences (NDEs), out-of-the-body experiences (OBEs), insight and concentrative meditation, drug intoxification states, shamanistic experiences, lucid dreaming, and the like.

In the paragraphs to follow, the use of the PCI and the DAQ to map an OBE associated with an NDE of a particular individual will be illustrated. It hopefully will demonstrate the utility of the PCI and the DAQ for mapping and assessing altered states of consciousness besides hypnosis, relaxation, and baseline conditions. (The following is based on a paper by Maitz & Pekala, 1991.)

THE NEAR-DEATH EXPERIENCE

The occurrence of NDEs have been recorded since ancient times. Locke and Shontz (1983) report that the earliest descriptive accounts of NDEs to appear in the scientific journals originated with the work of Noyes and Kletti (1972), while the first attempt to evaluate the phenomenon empirically was provided by Osis and Haraldsson in 1977.

Phenomenologically, an NDE is usually experienced as "an overwhelming feeling of peace and well-being, a sense that one's consciousness has separated from one's body, a perception of moving through a dark tunnel or void, an encounter with . . . 'a being of light,' a panoramic life review, an awareness of the presence of deceased loved ones, and a number of transcendental elements" (Ring & Franklin, 1981/82, p. 191). Thanks to the recent work of Moody (1975), Ring (1980), Gabbard and Twemlow (1986), and others, the occurrence of NDEs has been firmly established.

THE OUT-OF-THE-BODY EXPERIENCE

Several researchers have attempted to better understand one particular component of a near-death experience, the out-of-the-body experience. Gabbard and Twemlow (1986) suggest that the OBE is the "prototype of altered mind/body perception" (p. 352). They define the OBE as "an altered state of consciousness in which the subject feels that his mind or self-awareness is separated from his physical body and that his sense of self-awareness is more vivid and more real than a dream" (p. 352).

Menz (1984) reported six elements that appear common in OBEs associated with NDEs. The first is the ability of the person to hear themselves pronounced dead, often in conjunction with feelings of calm and peace. The second is hearing a loud noise, usually described as a "buzzing, roaring, singing, whistling," or music. The third element concerns moving through a dark tunnel or void, after which the person finds himself viewing his body from some point outside it. This is often followed by an encounter with a "being of light," typically described as some deity or a deceased loved one. The fifth common element includes a life review. Finally, many people report confronting a boundary or border that represents a "point of no return." The person then returns to their body, or is directed to go back by the "being of light." Not unlike the NDE, one of the more perplexing questions for researchers is "What is the nature of the OBE and what does it represent?"

PURPOSES

Careful descriptive accounts of OBEs have helped to differentiate an OBE from other altered states. It has been difficult, however, to apply rigid scientific methods to the study of OBEs, primarily because of measurement difficulties. Twemlow and Gabbard (1984) discussed the "need for careful, scientific, phenomenological appraisal of these experiences to offset rash speculation about its meaning and etiology" (p. 223). It would be useful to demonstrate empirically whether these OBE experiences do indeed represent an "altered state," and if so, what aspects of consciousness are altered. It would also be helpful to distinguish empirically between altered states associated with an OBE and other forms of altered consciousness.

Hence the purposes of the following cited study were threefold. The first was to attempt to determine empirically whether or not an OBE represents an "altered state." Second, an attempt was made to begin to quantify phenomenological changes that occur during an OBE. Third, these changes in consciousness were compared to the phenomenological experience of other altered states of consciousness. Since this study employs a single-subject, case study design, no specific hypotheses were made.

METHODOLOGY

Subject

The subject for this study was a 40-year-old Caucasian male whom we will call Barry. He was a patient admitted to a VA hospital with a diagnosis of posttraumatic stress disorder (PTSD). While in the hospital the patient related an NDE subsequent to a severe gunshot wound of the chest that occurred approximately 20 years ago while the patient was a soldier in Vietnam. He related that he had been pronounced clinically dead on the operating table. The subject reported an OBE that is consistent with the description of others (Ring & Franklin, 1981/82). Barry was referred to the Biofeedback Clinic of the hospital for treatment of anxiety and pain management.

Barry was offered an opportunity to participate in a hypnosis study associated with the clinic. The study was designed to assess phenomenological changes across various stimulus conditions including individual biofeedback training and hypnosis. The patient agreed to participate in both hypnosis and biofeedback. During the initial intake interview he acknowledged that he had experienced an OBE associated with an NDE. He reported that he was very disturbed by the experience. He indicated that he had only recently talked about the experience with his wife, and had never before admitted it to anyone except her. The experience had left him questioning his own sanity, and he had always felt the need to better understand the experience. The patient asked the interviewer to relive the experience under hypnosis in order to determine whether there were additional elements to his NDE/OBE experience that had been suppressed/repressed, and to better integrate the entire experience into his own conscious awareness.

Materials and Procedure

The PCI and the DAQ were used to map phenomenological experience. While in the hospital, the patient completed the PCI and DAQ (given together in one instrument as the PCI/DAQ) under several conditions, including eyes closed sitting quietly (baseline), a hypnotic assessment (using the Stanford scale; Weitzenhoffer & Hilgard, 1962), hypnosis (self-hypnosis during a hypnosis group), biofeedback, recollection of the OBE, and recollection of the OBE under hypnosis.

Barry obtained a Stanford susceptibility score of 6 (on a 0–12 scale), suggestive of a moderately hypnotizable individual. Previous to experiencing the Stanford scale, Barry sat quietly for two minutes. In reference to this two-minute sitting quietly period and also similar periods during all the other stimulus conditions (embedded in the hypnosis, biofeedback, etc.), Barry retrospectively completed the PCI/DAQ, Forms 1 or 2.

Recollection of the OBE during normal waking consciousness and under hypnosis (after a hypnotic regression to the NDE/OBE experience) both occurred after the Stanford assessment. For recollection of the OBE during normal waking consciousness, Barry completed the PCI/DAQ in reference to exactly what he remembered of the OBE experience. During this recollection, Barry reported moving through space and thought he encountered a "presence," with whom he had some sort of communication. He was not certain whether or not he actually "spoke" with this presence. The entire experience was accompanied by a sense of comfort and "peace."

During the hypnotic recollection of the OBE, which occurred while Barry was hypnotically regressed to his NDE experience, Barry reported relatively the same phenomenological experience that he had reported without the hypnosis. During the reexperiencing of the OBE under hypnosis, however, he more definitively reported a "being," which before the hypnotic regression he had only a vague and unsure recollection. He reported that he had actually communicated with the "presence."

After completion of the PCI/DAQ for the different stimulus conditions, the inventories were scored and PCI and DAQ intensity scores for the different (sub)dimensions of the inventories were computed. Hypnoidal scores (Pekala & Nagler, 1989) were also computed for each stimulus condition using the regression equation obtained from prior research (Pekala & Kumar, 1987). All completed inventories were found to be reliable.

RESULTS

Figure 15.1 represents the hypnograph of the hypnoidal effects as measured by both the PCI (as previously defined) and the DAQ (using the unstandardized coefficients of those DAQ dimensions significant at $p < .01$ of Table 8.3, page 152) in reference to the several stimulus conditions. (High hypnoidal effects, scores of 7 or above, represent what high susceptibles would report, on the average, during the hypnotic

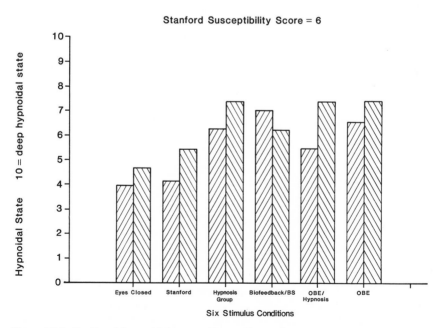

Figure 15.1. Predicted hypnoidal scores: Barry. (From Maitz & Pekala, 1989. Reprinted with permission of the publisher. ▨, pHGS scores/PCI; ▧, pHGS scores/DAQ.)

induction of the Harvard Scale.) As the reader can see, the degree of hypnoidal effects is similar during the recollection of the OBE during normal waking consciousness, the hypnotic regression back to the OBE, and the patient's state during a hypnotic session. It is also somewhat similar to the hypnoidal effects the patient achieved during biofeedback training. The graph demonstrates that these conditions are associated with greater hypnoidal effects than the baseline condition during which he sat quietly with his eyes closed and also during the (more experimental and less clinical) hypnosis assessment session with the Stanford.

Figure 15.2 illustrates the intensity levels of 12 dimensions of consciousness as measured by the PCI in reference to eyes closed, the OBE, and the experience of self-hypnosis during participation in a hypnosis group (the other stimulus conditions were not included so as not the "clutter" the graph). Although the hypnograph suggests similar hypnoidal effects between the OBE and hypnosis (as evinced during the hypnosis group), visual comparison of the PCI phenomenological intensity profiles between the OBE and hypnosis suggests differences in internal, absorbed attention and internal dialogue. During the OBE, in com-

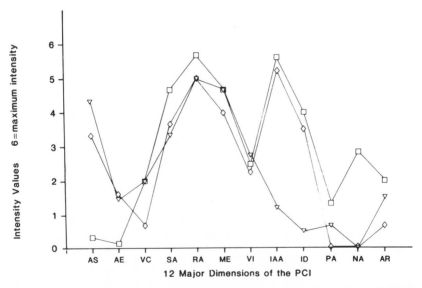

Figure 15.2. Phenomenological intensity profile using the PCI. (From Maitz & Pekala, 1989. □, Eyes closed; ◇, hypnosis group; ▽, OBE. Abbrev: AS, altered state; AE, altered experience; VC, volitional control; SA, self-awareness; RA, rationality; ME, memory; VI, vivid imagery; IAA, internal absorbed attention; ID, internal dialogue; PA, positive affect; NA, negative affect; AR, arousal.)

parison to the hypnosis condition and baseline, Barry reported a more externally oriented, nonabsorbed, attentional focus and much less internal dialogue (possibly because he was observing his environment and hence had less internal chatter). He also rated his OBE as more of an altered state of awareness than the self-hypnosis condition and the OBE reexperienced under hypnosis (not shown on the graph).

The DAQ more clearly demonstrates salient differences among these conditions. Figure 15.3 delineates the phenomenological intensity profile for these conditions for the dimensions of the DAQ. While the hypnosis and OBE conditions are very different from baseline, distinct differences are evident between the hypnosis condition and the OBE. In comparison to the self-hypnosis condition (and the OBE reexperienced upon hypnosis and not shown on the graph), the OBE was reported as localized as more out-of-the-body (a maximum score of 6 was obtained), while the hypnosis conditions were experienced as occurring "within" the body.

The DAQ indicated that the OBE, vis-à-vis the hypnosis condition,

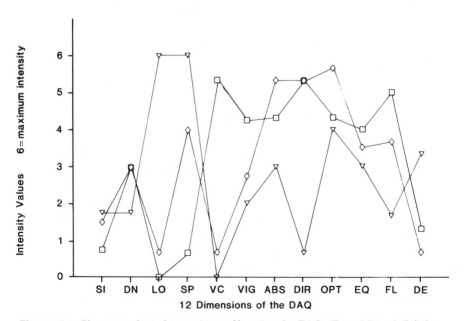

Figure 15.3. Phenomenological intensity profile using the DAQ. (From Maitz & Pekala, 1989. □, Eyes closed; ◇, hypnosis group; ▽, OBE. Abbrev: SI, simultaneity; DN, density; LO, locus; SP, spatiality; VC, volitional control; VIG, vigilance; ABS, absorption; DIR, direction; OPT, one-pointedness; EQ, equanimity; FL, flexibility; DE, detachment.)

was associated with greater perspicacity or spatiality (a spatial expansion of awareness), a direction of attention that was focused externally toward the environment as opposed to internally toward oneself, a less absorbed attentional focus but more attentional detachment.

DISCUSSION

Altered State and Hypnoidal Effects

The data suggest that Barry's OBE, which was associated with an NDE, does in fact represent an altered state of consciousness. According to the PCI phenomenological intensity profile, Barry rated it as a more altered state of consciousness than what he experienced during any of the other conditions, including those concerning hypnosis. His recollection of his phenomenological state during the OBE was somewhat similar to his reported phenomenological experience of hypnosis and biofeedback, in terms of the hypnoidal effects associated with those conditions as illustrated by the hypnograph. But, it is also clear from the hypnograph that his phenomenological state during all three conditions was very different from sitting quietly with eyes closed. Barry's out-of-the-body experience, then, can be described as an altered state of consciousness somewhat similar to the hypnoidal effects associated with hypnosis.

Phenomenological Intensity Effects

The study also allows us to begin to quantify elements of consciousness that are altered during an OBE as opposed to other altered states of consciousness, such as hypnosis. One salient difference is that during an OBE this particular individual experienced his "self" as being outside his body (his DAQ locus dimension score was a 6—the maximum obtainable). This is consistent with subjective reports alluded to earlier and supports the statement by Gabbard and Twemlow (1986) that the OBE subject experiences his self as outside the physical body.

Another interesting distinction is that during an OBE associated with an NDE, Barry's attention was clearly focused outward toward his environment. The subject related during his OBE that he was acutely aware of his "physical" surroundings (although his eyes were closed). He saw the physician "below" pronouncing him dead and then being revived. He was also aware of the "being" with whom he communicated and the physical form of the "young man" lying on the operating table. This is all consistent with his external attentional focus he reported on the DAQ and PCI, which is also different from the other stimulus conditions that he rated as more internally oriented.

Significance and Conclusions

This case study appears to provide quantifiable data to support earlier claims that an OBE, in conjunction with an NDE, represents an altered state of consciousness for this particular individual. It also provides quantifiable data on the particular changes in one subject's phenomenological field that occurred during an OBE and how these changes differ from other forms of altered states of consciousness. While many questions remain, the study does support the basic assumptions of the NDE/OBE experience reported in previous studies (Moody, 1975; Ring, 1980) in reference to this particular individual.

The above paragraphs offer a methodology for the study and quantification of OBEs associated with a near-death experience. It is possible to apply this methodology to other forms of OBEs as well. It may then become possible to identify quantifiable differences among these experiences that will help to further clarify the nature of the OBE and may help to explain those factors which determine its occurrence.

Consciousness

A Noetic-Behavioral Integration

AN INTEGRATION OF PHENOMENOLOGICAL DATA
WITH PSYCHOLOGICAL THEORY AND RESEARCH

The approach presented in this book is a psychophenomenological one. Subjective experience is retrospectively assessed according to questionnaires likes the PCI or the DAQ. That experience is then quantified according to various (sub)dimensions to yield intensity data for the various structures of consciousness or attention and pattern data as to how the various structures are differentially associated.

Although the aforementioned approach is *phenomenologically based*, it is *psychologically conceived*. The approach advocated in this book has communalities with what has been reviewed by the consciousness psychologists (Chapter 2) and the cognitive psychologists interested in consciousness (Chapter 3). Based on the theorizing of Tart (1975, 1977), Singer (cited in Zinberg, 1977), Silverman (1968), and others, various subsystems of consciousness were hypothesized to make up the "composition" of consciousness. Whereas the Phenomenology of Consciousness Inventory (PCI) tends to be comprehensive in assessing various general structures of consciousness, the Dimensions of Attention Questionnaire (DAQ) tends to be comprehensive in assessing the structures of attention (although the PCI also has two subdimensions devoted to attention).

These structures of consciousness can be conceptualized as general schemas of consciousness; representations of various processes of consciousness by which man re-presents his internal and external environment. Whereas certain of the PCI dimensions are schema concerning noema (visual imagery, internal dialogue, positive and negative affect), others are noeses (volitional control, attention, memory), to paraphrase the phenomenological tradition of Husserl (1913/72) and his followers.

The PCI and the DAQ dimensions or structures can easily be conceptualized as a set of processing units or processors representing a phenomenological parallel distributed processing (PDP) model of consciousness. The associations between dimensions that psygrams so well illustrate denote the pattern of connectivity (to use the PDP phrase), among the different phenomenological processors. And just as patterns of connectivity can be positive or negative, so the psygram vectors can also be positive or negative.

The psygram vectors do not indicate, however, the intensity or *valence* of the processors being activated. It is here that the PCI/DAQ (sub)dimension intensity ratings can be of value. By specifying not the pattern of connectivity between processors but rather the state of activation of the particular processor, phenomenological intensity profiles (pips) allow the states of activation of different processors to be quantified and visually displayed.

It is my opinion that both patterns of connectivity or association and levels of activation of processors are needed to quantify the configuration of a particular consciousness state at a particular time. The relationships between levels of activation and patterns of association may be quite complex and are probably dependent on the stimulus condition assessed and individual differences measures also. This is consistent with the theorizing of both Tart (1977) and Singer (cited in Zinberg, 1977) in regard to what is needed to quantify a state of consciousness. I would tend to agree with Tart, however, that patterns of association are probably of greater importance in defining a state of consciousness. Future research will be needed to unravel which of the two, or what combination of the two, are found to be most important for understanding states of consciousness.

The concept of state of consciousness as described and defined in this book is also consistent with the theorizing of the cognitive psychologists interested in consciousness. Mandler (1985) defines a state of consciousness as "the most general structures currently being activated by current concerns and environmental requirements" (p. 60). The psygram, when coded with the intensity values, illustrates which phenomenological structures are being activated in reference to a specific stimulus condition and also illustrates the patterns of association among subsystems.

Likewise, Izard (1977) defines ordinary states of consciousness as complexes of emotion, perception, and cognition that are joined by affective-cognitive structures due to neural and early-learned affective-cognitive experiences. The psygram device illustrates associations between the positive and negative affects and other systems such as rationality, volitional control, and memory. Although affect is not assumed to be primary, as it is in Izard's approach to consciousness, it is one of several major subsystems of consciousness thought to be of importance in understanding subjective experience. (Positive and negative affect account for two of the 12 major PCI dimensions.)

Altered states of consciousness, according to Izard, result from a radical change in interest and a collapse of the early-learned and well-engrained "affective-cognitive processing patterns." I would add that an altered state results in the radical change among various systems of consciousness that include not only affect and cognition, but also volition, attention, and memory, among others.

Many of the consciousness theorists, like Tart and Silverman, place attention/awareness in a crucial position in regard to understanding consciousness. So do the cognitive theorists such as Mandler (1985) and Baars (1988). For Mandler, consciousness is a construction in which the limited capacity of attention occupies a predominant position. Likewise, Baars's global workspace theory posits the global workspace as the "blackboard" for the parallel distributed system of recursive processors. Both theorists posit attention as the "regulator" of consciousness, "illuminating" the schema or parallel processors. The development of a separate instrument, like the DAQ, to map various facets of attention is consistent with the prominent position that attention/awareness occupies in the theorizing of the consciousness psychologists and the cognitive psychologists interested in consciousness. [A questionnaire to map various aspects of affection and cognition, called the Questionnaire on Affection and Cognition (QUAC) (Pekala, 1988a), has been developed. Although the data on which it is based have yet to be analyzed, it will allow for the "affective-cognitive processing patterns" of Izard to be more fully explored than would be possible with the PCI or the DAQ alone.]

AREAS OF FUTURE RESEARCH

Although little to date has been done in attempting to covary aspects of attention (via the DAQ) with various subsystems of consciousness (via the PCI), I believe that such an approach may yield very useful data on the relationships between various aspects of attention/awareness and other phenomenological systems of consciousness. Thus, although the attention dimension of consciousness of the PCI has been related to the other subsystems of consciousness of the PCI, the various dimensions of attention as mapped by the DAQ have not been systematically related to the various PCI (sub)dimensions. This is an area that may yield important data on the relationship between attention and consciousness in general.

Likewise, little to date has been done relating the data obtained with the PCI and the DAQ to behavioral, psychophysiological, and/or clinical variables. I have spent much of my time developing as comprehensive a phenomenological system as possible for mapping consciousness. That process has left little time for more traditional cognitive-behavioral, psychophysiological, or clinical approaches. Yet the payoff for the approach contained in this book will probably come in tying the phenomenological data obtained via the PCI, the DAQ, and other instruments to various aspects of human behavior, psychophysiology, and psychopathology.

As PDP models of consciousness assume more importance, it will become necessary to understand how these models represent and predict the nature of human subjective experience. Use of the PCI, the DAQ, and other, yet to be developed instruments will allow for the phenomenological quantification of human subjective experience. This, in turn, may allow for the operationalization and testing of PDP models from a phenomenological perspective.

Since the approach espoused in this book is a more structural, as opposed to a more functional, approach, it allows for a "snapshot" of the state of consciousness of an individual or group of individuals to be relatively specifically quantified. How different processing units behave in different stimulus conditions across differing types of subjects in terms of levels of activation and patterns of connectivity are questions that this approach will hopefully be able to help answer. Although no claim is made that what subjects phenomenologically report will be *exactly* what they do experience, this approach should be able to test PDP models in terms of subjects' reported experiences.

The recent development of sophisticated, PC-based "brain-mapping" devices that can record up to 20 EEG channels of information is another avenue of research whereby short stimulus intervals can be examined in terms of EEG parameters and retrospectively assessed in terms of PCI/DAQ inventories. By being able to specifically quantify both psychophysiological and phenomenological data, researchers will hopefully be better able to determine how subjective experience is related to EEG data from the various areas of the cerebral cortex.

The instruments described in this book are state instruments, as opposed to trait instruments, with which psychologists tend to be somewhat more familiar. State instruments allow for very discrete time periods to be assessed. The recent interest in state-specific memory (Rossi, 1986) looks at relationships between memory and affect in reference to discrete periods of time or "states." Instruments like the PCI or the DAQ may be able to provide a means to meticulously assess various aspects of cognition, affect, and memory in reference to short time intervals and thus provide useful data on the relationships between the various subsystems of consciousness and how they interact to produce state-specific effects.

Although I have rather comprehensively examined the nature of hypnosis from a phenomenological perspective, social-psychological aspects (Spanos & Chaves, 1989) of hypnosis have not been addressed to any great extent. Hence, how phenomenological experience is influenced by context effects (Council & Kirsch, 1989), expectancy (Kirsch, 1985), demand characteristics (Orne, 1962), and the like needs to be rigorously assessed. In addition, all the research to date on this approach has basically been done by myself and several collaborators. The results cited in this book need to be replicated by others. Only then will the data presented here have the necessary external validity to help enact the paradigm revolution (Kuhn, 1962) that I would like to see occur in psychology and the behavioral sciences in regard to phenomenological experience and consciousness.

Use of the PCI and DAQ may have important clinical implications. I have always been intrigued by Freud's genius in abandoning hypnosis for free association. By 1892 Freud realized that he could not hypnotize everyone and wanted another means to access the unconscious. Over the time period from 1892 to 1896 the method of free association was discovered, developed, and refined (Greenson, 1967).

It is my belief that Freud's method of free association, or the fundamental or basic rule as he called it (Freud, 1912), puts an individual in a hypnoidal state (Pekala & Nagler, 1989), and thus allows the person to access memories as one might with a more hypnotically explicit procedure (which, as indicated in this book, actually makes low susceptibles more distracted). Hence, it was Freud's genius to find a way to allow individuals to enter "hypnoidal states" by free association without having to use hypnosis, which then, as now, does not work for everyone. The PCI will allow for quantification of the phenomenological state associated with free association, and hence may provide a means to measure just how much of a "hypnoidal state" free association entails.

As Wadden and Anderton (1982) indicated, clinicians do not usually assess hypnotizability because of time constraints and the reactivity and obtrusiveness of standard assessment instruments. Although Spiegel's (1974) Hypnotic Induction Profile provides a briefly administered measure of hypnotizability, the use of the eye-roll sign as part of the induction procedure has not been empirically supported (Hilgard, 1982).

Research (Pekala, 1991c) is currently underway using a short form of the PCI (Pekala, 1988b), in conjunction with a short induction procedure and the eye catalepsy item from the Harvard Group Scale (Shor & Orne, 1962). Use of this one item from the Harvard Scale and the PCI (sub)dimensions has yielded a multiple R of .75 between hypnotizability, as measured by the Harvard Scale, and the PCI (sub)dimensions and the eye catalepsy item. Should this research hold up under cross-validation, the PCI hypnotic induction procedure (use of the PCI with a short hypnotic induction procedure) may provide a relatively quick (25 minutes) procedure for assessing hypnotizability that does not appear to have the drawbacks of more conventional instruments currently in use.

Although most of the research cited in this book is nomothetic (i.e., assessed across groups of individuals), the PCI, DAQ, and related instruments can also be used idiographically, as was described in Chapters 14 and 15 when data from single administrations of the PCI and the DAQ were described. Such case study approaches can be quite useful in trying to understand the subjective experiences of individual subjects in specific situations and may provide a means to better understand why people "behave" in particular situations as they do.

In addition to the above areas of research, the PCI, the DAQ, and related instruments need to be given in reference to many other types of altered states and various stimulus conditions besides those assessed and reported in this book. For example, what is the psychophenomenological nature, as assessed across single individuals or groups of subjects, of the OBE (Monroe, 1971), the NDE (Ring, 1980), the alcohol-intoxicated (Fishkin & Jones, 1978) and marijuana-intoxicated state (Anonymous, 1972), the various stages of the LSD experience (Grof, 1975, 1985), the lucid dream (LaBerge, 1985), mystical (Yogananda, 1974) or transcendental (Merrell-Wolff, 1973) experiences, or the orgasm (what William James regarded as the "common man's" altered state)? Does the procedure of therapeutic touch (Krieger, 1979) produce hypnoidal effects in the operator or subject, and to what extent if any are such hypnoidal effects responsible for the results obtained (Macrae, 1988)?

How do very deep hypnotic states (Tart, 1963) compare psychophenomenologically with the hypnotic experiences of the "hypnotic virtuoso" (Wilson & Barber, 1983), and to what extent if any do paranormal and parapsychological (Rao & Palmer, 1987; Zollschan et al., 1989) phenomena intercorrelate with alterations in psychophenomenological intensity and pattern parameters? Are subjects who score high on questionnaires assessing ESP experiences (Pekala *et al.*, in press) more prone to altered state experiences and can a quantification of phenomenological experiences during episodes of purported psi ability with such subjects map the psi-conducive state? How different phenomenologically is the "magical flight" of the shaman from that of "spirit possession" and how do these two types of altered states of consciousness covary with the use of hallucinogens, chanting and singing, fasting, and so on (Noll, 1989; Winkelman, 1989)? To what extent is the fire-walking ceremony, that is, walking over hot coals in one's bear feet (Robbins, 1986) associated with an altered state of consciousness (Pekala & Ersek, 1991)? And how do individual-differences measures, such as differences in absorption (Tellegen, 1981) or hypnotic susceptibility (Hilgard, 1977), moderate the nature of the subjective experiences mentioned above?

Does type of psychopathology have some relationship to the nature of psychophenomenology, and how does medication modulate the subjective experiences of depressed, anxious, or schizophrenic individuals? What is the phenomenological nature of the panic attack and how may it differ from an intense phobic experience, such as agoraphobia (Barlow, 1988)? Are there different types of depressive disorders that may be better differentiated phenomenologically than with current methods, and how does an agitated depression compare subjectively (via psygrams) with a more vegetative depression? Do different stress management techniques activate different phenomenological structures, such that a given technique may be more efficacious, provided there is a "match" between subject characteristics and stress management technique (Pekala & Forbes, 1990)?

These are just a few of the many, many questions that may be explored with the approach described in this book.

A NOETIC-BEHAVIORAL INTEGRATION

As argued in Chapter 1, the phenomena of consciousness are as legitimate data for the scientist as are gravity, sunlight, or the economy. Phenomenological data can be quantified, measured, and diagramed as can physical, social, or economic data. The result appears to be as valid and reliable an approach to understanding man as any of the physical or social sciences. It is interesting to note that psychology in the late 1800s was noetic in focus. As mentioned in the Introduction, consciousness or mind (the Greek word for mind is *nous*) formed the basis for its subject matter. With the publication of Watson's classic paper in 1913, psychology officially became behavioral. With the cognitive revolution of the 1960s and 1970s psychology became cognitive-behavioral. Psychology, however, must not become content to focus on the cognitive and behavioral aspects of human experience to the all but recent exclusion of other aspects of human experience such as affect, volition, and alterations in attention and consciousness. As Zajonc (1980) echoed a decade ago: "contemporary cognitive psychology simply ignores affect" (p. 152).

The work of Izard (1977) and the burgeoning research in state-specific memory (Rossi, 1986; Rossi & Cheek, 1988) have shown how important affect is to cognition and memory. Although progress has been made in incorporating affect into the study of such clinical phenomena as anxiety and panic (Barlow, 1988), much more research and theorizing including all aspects of subjective experience and altered state effects need to become part and parcel of the study of psychology, "cognitive" science, and psychopathology.

I believe the next revolution in psychology, mental health, and cognitive science (Gardner, 1985, 1987) will be a noetic-behavioral one from both a research and an applied perspective. This book may be considered a precursor to that revolution by showing that noetic aspects of human experience can be quantified and statistically assessed in a comprehensively reliable and valid manner. The psychophenomenological approach advocated in this book is such a beginning noetic-behavioral approach to human behavior and experience. It is not that behavior or cognition are not important, but rather that they are *incomplete* for a comprehensive understanding of the nature of man. Only an approach that considers both man's objective and subjective environments, his world and his psyche (in all of its various aspects, including, but not limited to: cognition, memory, affect, volition, awareness, attention, perception, altered states of awareness, etc.), will be able to do justice to that complexity we call *human*.

If a science of consciousness is to move beyond where astronomy was when Galileo turned his telescope on the moons of Jupiter, it must avoid sticking its head in the sand when trying to understand consciousness subjectively. Only then will the study of consciousness become as empirically, quantitatively, and theoretically based as psychology and cognitive science now are.

PCI Items as a Function of PCI (Sub)Dimension (Using Form 1 Items)

Left dipole	Right dipole

Positive affect

Joy

9. I felt ecstatic and joyful.

I felt no feelings of being ecstatic or joyful.

46. I experienced no feelings of ecstasy or extreme happiness beyond my usual feelings.

I felt feelings of ecstasy and extreme happiness.

Sexual excitement

5. I became aware of very intense sexual feelings.

I experienced no sexual feelings.

35. I was not aware of any sexual feelings.

I experienced very strong sexual feelings.

Love

20. I experienced no feelings of   I experienced very strong feelings
    love.   of love.

49. I felt intense feelings of loving-   I felt no feelings of loving-kindness.
    kindness.

Negative affect

Anger

14. I felt no emotions of rage   I felt enraged.
    whatsoever.

33. I felt very angry and upset.   I felt no feelings of being angry or
                                          upset.

Sadness

 7. I felt very, very sad.   I felt no feelings of sadness
                                          whatsoever.

31. I felt no feelings of unhappiness   I felt unhappy and dejected.
    or dejection.

Fear

16. I felt very frightened.   I felt no emotions of being
                                          frightened.

42. I felt no feelings of being scared   I felt very scared and afraid.
    or afraid.

Altered experience

Body image

11. My body ended at the   I felt my body greatly expanded
    boundary between the skin and   beyond the boundaries of my skin.
    the world.

26. My bodily feelings seemed to   My bodily feelings were confined to
    expand into the world around   the area within my skin.
    me.

51. I continually maintained a very strong sense of separation between myself and the environment.

I experienced intense unity with the world; the boundaries between me and the environment dissolved away.

Time sense

15. My perception of the flow of time changed drastically.

I noticed no changes in my perception of the flow of time.

30. Time seemed to greatly speed up or slow down.

Time was experienced with no changes in its rate of passage.

43. I felt no sense of timelessness; time flowed as I usually experience it.

Time stood still; there was no movement of time at all.

Perception

17. My perception of the world changed drastically.

I noticed no changes in my perception of the world.

29. The world around me became extremely different in color or form.

I noticed no changes in the color or form of the world around me.

39. I noticed no changes in the size, shape, or perspective of the objects in the world around me.

Objects in the world around me changed in size, shape, or perspective.

Meaning

4. I had an experience which I would label as very religious, spiritual, or transcendental.

I did not have any experience which I would label as religious, spiritual, or transcendental.

23. I had an experience of awe and reverence toward the world.

I had no experience of awe and reverence toward the world.

32. I experienced no profound insights besides my usual cognitive understanding of things.

I experienced very profound and enlightening insights of certain ideas or issues.

47. I experienced no sense of sacredness or deep meaning in existence beyond my usual feelings.

Existence became deeply sacred or meaningful.

Imagery

Amount

12. I experienced a great deal of visual imagery.

I experienced no visual imagery at all.

44. I experienced no or very few images.

My experience was made up almost completely of images.

Vividness

18. My visual imagery was so vivid and three-dimensional, it seemed real.

My visual imagery was so vague and diffuse, it was hard to get an image of anything.

48. My imagery was very vague and dim.

My imagery was as clear and vivid as objects in the real world.

Attention

Direction

8. My attention was completely directed toward my own internal subjective experience.

My attention was completely directed toward the world around me.

28. My attention was totally directed toward the environment around me.

My attention was totally directed toward my own internal subjective experience.

52. My attention was completely inner-directed.

My attention was completely outer-directed.

Absorption

1. I was forever distracted and unable to concentrate on anything.

I was able to concentrate quite well and was not distracted.

34. I was not distracted, but was able to be completely absorbed in what I was experiencing.

I was continually distracted by extraneous impressions or events.

Self-awareness

13. I was not aware of being aware of myself at all; I had no self-awareness.

I was very aware of being aware of myself; my self-awareness was intense.

27. I was continually conscious and well aware of myself.

I lost consciousness of myself.

50. I maintained a very strong sense of self-awareness the whole time.

I did not maintain a very strong sense of self-awareness at all.

Altered state of awareness

21. My state of consciousness was not any different or unusual from what it ordinarily is.

I felt in an extremely different and unusual state of consciousness.

40. My state of awareness was very different from what I usually experience.

My state of awareness was no different than usual.

53. My state of awareness was not unusual or different from what it ordinarily is.

I felt in an extraordinarily unusual and nonordinary state of awareness.

Internal dialogue

6. I was silently talking to myself a great deal.

I did not engage in any silent talking to myself.

45. I did not engage in any silent talking to myself.

I was silently talking to myself a great deal.

Rationality

2. My thinking was clear and understandable.

My thinking was unclear and not easy to understand.

24. Conceptually, my thinking was   Conceptually, my thinking was
    clear and distinct.   confused and muddled.

36. My thought processes were   My thought processes were rational
    nonrational and very hard to   and easy to comprehend.
    comprehend.

Volitional control

3. The thoughts and images I had   Images and thoughts popped into
   were under my control; I   my mind without my control.
   decided what I thought or
   imagined.

25. I had complete control over   I had no control over what I was
    what I was paying attention to.   paying attention to.

41. I relinquished control and   I was willfully controlling what I
    became receptive and passive to   was experiencing.
    what I was experiencing.

Memory

10. I cannot remember what I   I can remember just about
    experienced.   everything that I experienced.

22. I can recall nothing that   I can recall everything that
    happened to me.   happened to me.

38. My memory of the events I   My memory of the events I
    experienced is extremely clear   experienced is extremely blurred
    and vivid.   and hazy.

Arousal

19. The muscles of my body felt   The muscles of my body felt very
    very tense and tight.   loose and relaxed.

37. I felt no feelings of tension or   I felt tense and tight.
    tightness at all.

DAQ Items as a Function of DAQ Dimensions (Using Form 1 Items)

Left dipole	Right dipole

Flexibility

11. I felt my attention was very flexible; I could easily focus my attention on any thought, feeling, or sensation that came to my attention.

    My attention was not very flexible; I felt my mind kept dwelling on thoughts, feelings, and sensations that I could not get out of my mind.

19. I felt it very difficult to move and focus my attention; my mind kept returning to certain impressions.

    I was easily able to move, control, and focus my attention on whatever impressions that came into my mind.

30. My attention was not very flexible; I felt my mind kept dwelling on thoughts, feelings, and sensations that I could not get out of my mind.

    I felt my attention was very flexible; I could easily focus my attention on any thought, feeling, or sensation that came to my attention.

Equanimity

10. I was not equally attentive to every thought, feeling, sensation, etc., in my stream of consciousness; I focused on some impressions to the exclusion of others.

    I was equally attentive to every thought, feeling, sensation, etc., in my stream of consciousness.

23. I was not able to experience each and every sensation, feeling, or thought equally; I focused on some of them more than others.

    I was able to experience each sensation, feeling, or thought equally.

33. I was equally aware of all the different impressions and events that went through my mind; I did not dwell on some more than others.

    I was not equally aware of all the different impressions and events that went through my mind; I dwelled on some more than others.

37. I was equally attentive to every thought, feeling, sensation, etc., in my stream of consciousness.

    I was not equally attentive to every thought, feeling, sensation, etc., in my stream of consciousness; I focused on some impressions to the exclusion of others.

Detachment

12. I felt absorbed in my thoughts, feelings, and sensations.

    I felt very distant and detached from my thoughts, feelings, and sensations.

21. I felt very distant and detached from my thoughts, feelings, and sensations.

    I felt absorbed in my thoughts, feelings, and sensations.

32. I felt detached or distant from my thoughts, feelings, and sensations.

    I felt immersed and lost in my thoughts, feelings, and sensations.

Perspicacity

4. I felt a spatial expansion of my awareness: I felt like a sphere of

   I felt no spatial expansion of awareness; I did not feel like a

consciousness and I was simultaneously aware of everything within the sphere of consciousness.

sphere of consciousness and was not aware of everything simultaneously.

14. My attentional focus was not spatially expanded; my consciousness did not feel like a sphere of awareness illuminating everything within it.

My attentional focus was spatially expanded; my consciousness felt like a sphere of awareness illuminating everything within it.

26. My consciousness felt spatially expanded beyond my body so that I felt my awareness to be simultaneously everywhere.

My consciousness did not feel spatially expanded beyond my body; I did not feel my awareness to be simultaneously everywhere.

Locus

3. I felt my consciousness to be very much within my body.

I felt my consciousness to be "out of" and disconnected from my body.

15. I did not experience my consciousness to be outside of or separated from my physical body.

I actually experienced my consciousness to be outside of and separated from my physical body.

25. I felt my awareness completely separated and distant from my body.

I felt my awareness to be focused or centered within my body.

Direction

8. My attention was totally directed toward the environment around me.

My attention was totally directed toward my own internal subjective experience.

18. My attention was completely outer-directed.

My attention was completely inner-directed.

36. My attention was completely directed toward my own internal, subjective experience.

My attention was completely directed toward the world around me.

One-pointedness

9. My mind became one-pointed; I was able to focus on one thing to the exclusion of all others.

My mind was not one-pointed; many different impressions or thoughts intruded into my awareness.

22. I was able to easily and completely focus my mind on a single impression or event for as long as I wanted.

I found it impossible to focus my mind on a single impression or event for any length of time at all.

34. My attention was not focused on a single subjective event; many other events or impressions intruded into my attention.

My attention was focused on a single subjective event or impression to the exclusion of all other events.

Absorption

7. I became extremely distracted and was not able to become absorbed in what I was experiencing.

I was able to become so absorbed in what I was experiencing, I gave no notice to distracting events.

16. I became deeply absorbed in what I was attending to; I lost track of the world around me.

I did not become deeply absorbed in what I was attending to; I was extremely aware of the world around me.

29. I was not able to become absorbed in what I was experiencing; I was acutely aware of other things around me.

I became so deeply absorbed in what I was experiencing that I became oblivious (neglectful) to everything else around me.

Control

5. I felt I was willfully and actively controlling what I was attending to.

I stopped actively controlling what I was attending to and became passive and receptive to my experience.

17. I was able to "let go" and receptively experience whatever came to my attention.

I was actively involved in controlling what I was attending to.

28. I was actively involved in controlling what I was attending to.

I was able to "let go" and receptively experience whatever came to my attention.

Vigilance

6. I was not continually scanning and observing my attentional field for different-occurring events and impressions.

I was continually scanning and observing my attention field for different-occurring events and impressions.

24. I was constantly aware of and scanning my internal or external environment for any changes in that environment.

I did not scan or try to be constantly aware of my internal or external environment for any changes in that environment.

35. I was extremely vigilant and continually observant of everything in my attentional field.

I was not vigilant or continually observant of everything in my attentional field.

38. I was continually scanning and observing my attentional field for different-occurring events and impressions.

I was not continually scanning and observing my attentional field for different-occurring events and impressions.

Density

2. Too many thoughts, feelings, sensations, etc., kept rushing through my mind.

Not a single thought, feeling, sensation, etc., went through my mind.

13. My mind was in a state of "no thought"; I was not aware of a single thought, feeling, sensation, etc.

My mind was continually occupied; I was always aware of thoughts, feelings, sensations, etc.

27. My attentional field was completely empty of any sensations, feelings, or thoughts at all.

My attentional field felt "crowded" with many sensations, feelings, thoughts, etc.

39. My mind was continually occupied; I was always aware of thoughts, feelings, sensations, etc.

My mind was in a state of "no thought"; I was not aware of a single thought, feeling, sensation, etc.

Simultaneity

1. My attention was only focused on one subjective event at a time.

   My attention was focused on many subjective events simultaneously.

20. I was simultaneously aware of everything at once; I could perceive many subjective events simultaneously.

   I was not simultaneously aware of everything at once; I could not perceive many subjective events simultaneously.

31. I was aware of many sensations, thoughts, feelings, etc., simultaneously.

   I was aware of only one sensation, thought, feeling, etc., at a time.

40. I was not simultaneously aware of everything at once; I could not perceive many subjective events simultaneously.

   I was simultaneously aware of everything at once; I could perceive many subjective events simultaneously.

C

Item Numbers for Forms 1 and 2 of the Phenomenology of Consciousness Inventory

Dimension (subdimension)	PCI[a,b] Form 1	Form 2		Dimension (subdimension)	PCI Form 1	Form 2	
Positive affect				Attention			
Joy	9*	35*		Direction	8*	47*	R
	46	10			28	5	R
Sexual	5*	39*	R		52*	29*	
excitement	35	12	R	Absorption	1	33	
Love	20	36			34*	13*	
	49*	22*					
				Self-aware-	13	43	
				ness	27*	2*	
Negative affect					50*	25*	
Anger	14	32		Altered state	21	53	R
	33*	14*		of aware-	40*	18*	R
Sadness	7*	34*		ness	53	37	
	31	17					
Fear	16*	41*		Internal	6*	44*	R
	42	6		dialogue	45	20	R
Altered experience				Rationality	2*	45*	
Altered body image	11	46			24*	21*	
	26*	3*			36	30	
	51	24					
Altered time sense	15*	49*		Volitional control	3*	52*	
	30*	11*			25*	9*	
	43	31			41	27	
Altered perception	17*	50*		Memory	10	38	
	29*	19*			22	1	
	39	28			38*	26*	
Altered meaning	4*	51*		Arousal	19*	48*	
	23*	7*			37	15	
	32	23					
	47	16					
Imagery							
Amount	12*	42*	R				
	44	8	R				
Vividness	18*	40*					
	48	4					

[a]An asterisk (*) denotes time which must be reversed before dimension intensity scores are computed.
[b]Items followed by an "R" represent reliability item-pairs.

Item Numbers for Forms 1 and 2 of the Dimensions of Attention Questionnaire

Dimension	DAQ[a,b]				DAQ	
	Form 1	Form 2			Form 1	Form 2
Flexibility	11*	9*	R	One-	9*	12*
	19	29		pointedness	22*	22*
	30	14	R		34	31
Equanimity	10	8	R	Absorption	7	21
	23	23			16*	36*
	33*	34*			29	3
	37*	38*	R			
Detachment	12	7	R	Control	5*	11*
	21*	15*	R		17	24
	32*	28*			28*	32*
Perspicacity	4*	5*		Vigilance	6	33	R
	14	13			24*	10*
	26*	26*			35*	20*
					38*	39*	R
Locus	3	6		Density	2*	18*
	15	17			13	1	R
	25*	35*			27	30
					39*	40*	R
Direction	8	19		Simultaneity	1	25
	18	4			20*	16*	R
	36*	27*			31*	2*
					40	37	R

[a]An asterisk (*) denotes items which must be reversed before dimension intensity scores are computed.
[b]Items followed by an "R" represent reliability item-pairs.

E

Raw Score Conversion Tables for the PCI and the DAQ

PCI MAJOR DIMENSIONS[a]

Raw score	Percentile					Raw score	Percentile					Raw score	Percentile
6.00	100					6.00	100	93				6.00	100
5.75			99			5.75						5.75	
5.67		100				5.67	99	87				5.67	
5.50						5.50						5.50	
5.33	96	99		100		5.33	91	82				5.33	
5.25			100			5.25						5.25	
5.00	95	97		99	100	5.00	87	73	100	92	100	5.00	97
4.75					100	4.75		66	93		99	4.75	
4.67	94	96				4.67	76			89		4.67	
4.50			96			4.50		65	90		96	4.50	94
4.33	90	95		98		4.33	65			84		4.33	
4.25			99			4.25		60	85			4.25	
4.00	89	93	96	94		4.00	58	56	84	78	93	4.00	89
3.75			96			3.75		49				3.75	
3.67	84	88		91	95	3.67	49			72		3.67	
3.50					99	3.50		46	82		92	3.50	86
3.33	79	83	87			3.33	40	41		66		3.33	
3.25			98			3.25						3.25	
3.00	72	77	82	86	95	3.00	28	33		60	90	3.00	79

Table: Cumulative percentage distribution[a]

Scale	AS[b]	AE	VC	SA	RA	ME	VI	IAA	ID	PA	NA	AR
2.75		75	75					28				
2.67	64			80	80	89	23			53	86	
2.50		72	71					24	71			73
2.33	56			72	71	88	16			44	85	
2.25		60	59					20				
2.00	50	49	45	65	64	81	11	17	66	39	79	69
1.75		44	39					13				
1.67	47			53	56	70	7			31	73	
1.50		32	33					11	58			63
1.33	43			44	49	64	5			22	63	
1.25		21										
1.00	36	14	18	36	40	59	4	6	47	19	53	42
0.75		9										
0.67	24			26	31	41	2			12	47	
0.50		6						5	34			29
0.33	19			16	21	30	1			6	33	
0.25		2						3				
0.00	15	1	9	12	9	16		1	19	3	22	20

[a] Stimulus condition: eyes open sitting quietly (n = 110).
[b] AS, altered state of awareness; AE, altered experience; VC, volitional control; SA, self-awareness; RA, rationalty; ME, memory; VI, vivid imagery; IAA, inward, absorbed attention; ID, internal dialogue; PA, positive affect; NA, negative affect; AR, arousal.

PCI MINOR DIMENSIONS[a]

Raw score	Percentile							Raw score	Percentile						Raw score
6.00	100	100	100		100	100	100	6.00	100	100	100	100			6.00
5.75								5.75							5.75
5.67		97	99				92	5.67				91			5.67
5.50					84	89		5.50	94	94	93				5.50
5.33							88	5.33							5.33
5.25								5.25							5.25
5.00	99				76	82	82	5.00	88	92	92	82	100	100	5.00
4.75		96						4.75					97		4.75
4.67	92		98	100			73	4.67	72	84	87	73	95		4.67
4.50					65	64		4.50					92	99	4.50
4.33	89	91					61	4.33							4.33
4.25				99				4.25							4.25
4.00	86	88	96	98	56	55	56	4.00	59	80	82	67	86	98	4.00
3.75				97				3.75							3.75
3.67	82	82	94				49	3.67							3.67
3.50				95	48	40		3.50	50	69	76	59	86	93	3.50
3.33	76	70	91				41	3.33							3.33
3.25				90				3.25							3.25
3.00	65	63	86	84	44	30	34	3.00	39	63	68	47	83	89	3.00

370

Scale	ABI[b]	ATS	AP	AM	IA	IV	AD	AB	JY	SE	LO	AN	SD	FR
2.75				76										
2.67	50	51	83				20							
2.50				74	31	21		29	52	56	38	80	73	86
2.33	40	46	79				19							
2.25				67										
2.00	31	36	75	62	23	14	13	19	43	55	34	76	65	84
1.75				56										
1.67	26	31	68				11							
1.50				50	18	13		13	31	47	27	70	60	81
1.33	21	26	63				10							
1.25				45										
1.00	16	19	55	38	13	7	6	10	26	40	21	65	54	77
0.75				31										
0.67	9	14	45				3							
0.50				24	6	5		6	17	29	13	50	41	66
0.33	6	10	35				2							
0.25				19										
0.00	4	6	24	11	3	4		4	15	23	9	39	31	55

[a]Stimulus condition: eyes open sitting quietly ($n = 110$).

[b]ABI, altered body image; ATS, altered time sense; AP, altered perception; AM, altered meaning; IA, imagery amount; IV, imagery vividness; AD, attention direction; AB, absorption; JY, joy; SE, sexual excitement; LO, love; AN, anger; SD, sadness; FR, fear.

PCI MAJOR DIMENSIONS[a]

Raw score	Percentile						Raw score	Percentile						Raw score
6.00	100	100	100	100	100	100	6.00	100	100	100	100	100	100	6.00
5.75	99	99					5.75	93	82	84	96	98	99	5.75
5.67			89	92	83	63	5.67							5.67
5.50	97	98					5.50	88	72	78	93	97	96	5.50
5.33			81	85	73	49	5.33							5.33
5.25	94	96					5.25	84	63	70	91	95	94	5.25
5.00	91	94	74	77	63	36	5.00	79	56	62	85	94	92	5.00
4.75	90	92					4.75	69	49	53	77		90	4.75
4.67			67	69	54	26	4.67							4.67
4.50	87	91					4.50	59	45	48	72		86	4.50
4.33			61	58	43	21	4.33							4.33
4.25	81	87					4.25	52	39		67			4.25
4.00	77		52	45	38	15	4.00	43	34		61			4.00
3.75							3.75	35	30		52			3.75
3.67			41	34	33	11	3.67							3.67
3.50							3.50	27	27		49			3.50
3.33			35	30	27	8	3.33							3.33
3.25							3.25	22	22		45			3.25
3.00			28	22	20	5	3.00	18	19		38			3.00

372

	AS[b]	AE	VC	SA	RA	ME	VI	IAA	ID	PA	NA	AR
2.75		82										
2.67	70	78	22	18	17		15	13		32	91	
2.50	60	72	16	15	10		12	9	39	29	89	75
2.33		66					10	7		26	88	
2.25	52	63	12	10	7							
2.00	45	48				4	6	6	35	22	84	69
1.75		38					5					
1.67	36	33	8	6	4	3				17	78	
1.50		26							31	12	75	63
1.33	31	21	6	4	3		3	3		9	72	
1.25		20										
1.00	21	15	4	2	1	2	2	2	27	8	61	52
0.75		10									52	
0.67	16	9	3	1						7	49	
0.50		8							22	6	46	42
0.33	12	3	2							4	41	
0.25		2					1	1			37	
0.00		1	1		0	0			19	3	27	25

[a] Stimulus condition: eyes closed sitting quietly ($n = 233$).

[b] AS, altered state of awareness; AE, altered experience; VC, volitional control; SA, self-awareness; RA, rationality; ME, memory; VI, vivid imagery; IAA, inward absorbed attention; ID, internal dialogue; PA, positive affect; NA, negative affect; AR, arousal.

PCI MINOR DIMENSIONS[a]

Raw score	Percentile				Raw score	Percentile								Raw score
6.00	100	100			6.00	100	100	100	100	100	100	100	100	6.00
5.75	99				5.75									5.75
5.67					5.67	89								5.67
5.50	98	97	100		5.50		65	72	83	88	90	76	98	5.50
5.33					5.33	81								5.33
5.25					5.25									5.25
5.00	97	95	100	100	5.00	76	51	61	73	80	87	67	97	5.00
4.75	93	91			4.75	64								4.75
4.67					4.67									4.67
4.50	90	87	99		4.50	55	41	51	57	73	82	52	96	4.50
4.33					4.33									4.33
4.25					4.25									4.25
4.00	84	82	99	97	4.00	46	32	38	44	65	72	42	94	4.00
3.75	79	74	96	95	3.75									3.75
3.67					3.67	36								3.67
3.50	70	68	94	94	3.50	30	27	30	34	54	64	37	91	3.50
3.33					3.33									3.33
3.25			92		3.25									3.25
3.00	61	61	90	88	3.00	23	20	24	25	45	54	27	86	3.00

Scale	ABI[b]	ATS	AP	AM	IA	IV	AD	AB	JY	SE	LO	AN	SD	FR
2.75				84										
2.67	50	52	85											
2.50				82	13	16		17	35	45	20	82	82	91
2.33	40	45	82				18							
2.25				77										
2.00	32	41	76	71	9	14	11	10	25	37	15	76	75	90
1.75				62										
1.67	22	33	67				9							
1.50				53	8	7		7	21	33	13	71	70	85
1.33	18	29	60				6							
1.25				43										
1.00	15	22	55	36	5	4	4	5	14	29	9	61	60	81
0.75				31										
0.67	11	15	44				3							
0.50				21	3	3		3	11	24	8	55	50	73
0.33	7	11	34				2							
0.25				15										
0.00	5	8	24	12	2	2	1	2	9	21	6	45	39	63

[a]Stimulus condition: eyes closed sitting quietly (n = 233).
[b]ABI, altered body image; ATS, altered time sense; AP, altered perception; AM, altered meaning; IA, imagery amount; IV, imagery vividness; AD, attention direction; AB, absorption; JY, joy; SE, sexual excitement; LO, love; AN, anger; SD, sadness; FR, fear.

PCI MAJOR DIMENSIONS[a]

Raw score	Percentile						Raw score	Percentile						Raw score
6.00	100	100	100	100	100	100	6.00	100	100	100	100	100	100	6.00
5.75		100	99	93	92		5.75	99	97	99		100		5.75
5.67	85					86	5.67				94		98	5.67
5.50		94	98	90	88		5.50	97	90	98				5.50
5.33	80					80	5.33				91		97	5.33
5.25		93	97	87	82		5.25	95	86	97				5.25
5.00	72	90	96	82	77	74	5.00	94	80	96	87		95	5.00
4.75		89	95	79	72		4.75	91	69	95				4.75
4.67	65					67	4.67				83		93	4.67
4.50		85	92	74	70		4.50	89	61	94				4.50
4.33	59					59	4.33				78		89	4.33
4.25		84	89	68	61		4.25	88	55	92				4.25
4.00	52	77	88	63	55	53	4.00	87	50	91	72			4.00
3.75		71	83	58	49		3.75	85	44	89				3.75
3.67	43					46	3.67							3.67
3.50		67	80				3.50	80	36					3.50
3.33	37					40	3.33							3.33
3.25			79				3.25	78	30					3.25
3.00	31		72			35	3.00	74	23					3.00

376

	AS[b]	AE	VC	SA	RA	ME		VI	IAA	ID	PA	NA	AR	
2.75		63					2.75	69	18		84	96		2.75
2.67	25	58	60	48	40	28	2.67	64	15		82	96		2.67
2.50	19	52	50	40	35	23	2.50	57		65	78	95	82	2.50
2.33		44					2.33	52			75			2.33
2.25		39					2.25	47	10		73	92		2.25
2.00	16	32	41	33	31	21	2.00	38	8	61	68	90	76	2.00
1.75		24					1.75		7		62	89		1.75
1.67	14	21	34	23	24	16	1.67	32	6		61	85		1.67
1.50		16					1.50	26		53	59	82	69	1.50
1.33	12	14	28	15	20	11	1.33	21			56	80		1.33
1.25		13					1.25		5		53			1.25
1.00	11	10	22	12	16	9	1.00	13	4	48	47	72	58	1.00
0.75		7					0.75				36	64		0.75
0.67	10	6	17	10	10	5	0.67	10			34	61		0.67
0.50		5					0.50		2	37	31	58	49	0.50
0.33	9	3	9	5	7	3	0.33		1		26	53		0.33
0.25							0.25				24	50		0.25
0.00	5	1	5	1	3	1	0.00	5		26	14	40	34	0.00

[a]Stimulus condition: hypnotic induction via Harvard Scale (n = 210).
[b]AS, altered state of awareness; AE, altered experience; VC, volitional control; SA, self-awareness; RA, rationality; ME, memory; VI, vivid imagery; IAA, inward, absorbed attention; ID, internal dialogue; PA, positive affect; NA, negative affect; AR, arousal.

PCI MINOR DIMENSIONS[a]

Raw score	Percentile							Raw score	Percentile						Raw score	Percentile				
6.00	100	100	100	100	100	100	100	6.00	100	100	100	100	100	100	6.00	100					100
5.75	94	91						5.75							5.75						
5.67	90	88	98				90	5.67							5.67						
5.50			100		94	96	84	5.50						100	5.50						
5.33	88	81	97	99	91	92	76	5.33	99	99	98	94	90		5.33	98			99		99
5.25								5.25							5.25						
5.00	83	77	94	99	88	89	69	5.00	98	98	95	91	85		5.00	94	100		98		99
4.75	77							4.75							4.75						
4.67			98				61	4.67	94	96	94	90	83	76	4.67	100					98
4.50	77	73	93	98	85	84		4.50							4.50	98		99	96		
4.33			97				52	4.33	90	95	91	83	66		4.33	99			94		97
4.25			95					4.25							4.25						
4.00	75	66	92		80	80	44	4.00	97	95	94	90	80	85	4.00	90	99		94		97
3.75			93					3.75							3.75	99					
3.67	70	60	86	91	75	74	38	3.67	93	91	83	79	74		3.67	98		98	93		96
3.50								3.50							3.50	97					
3.33	62	51	82	89			28	3.33	85	89	76	66	28		3.33	98			91	95	95
3.25								3.25							3.25	95		96	86		
3.00	51	44	73	86				3.00							3.00	96	95				

	ABI[b]	ATS	AP	AM	IA	IV	AD	AB	JY	SE	LO	AN	SD	FR
2.75				80										
2.67							21							
2.50	41	36	65	77	66	61		43	77	83	63	90	90	91
2.33							16							
2.25	37	30	58	72			14							
2.00	30	24	53	67	56	50		26	71	80	57	88	85	87
1.75				64										
1.67							10							
1.50	22	15	45	55	46	42		16	58	76	51	85	81	83
1.33							9							
1.25	17	12	39	47										
1.00	12	10	31	41	39	32	7	11	45	74	40	80	75	79
0.75				36										
0.67							5							
0.50	6	7	25	25	26	20		8	36	67	33	74	67	69
0.33							3							
0.25			19	21										
0.00	4	6	12	15	13	11	2	3	27	59	24	68	59	61

[a] Stimulus condition: hypnotic induction (n = 210).

[b] ABI, altered body image; ATS, altered time sense; AP, altered perception; AM, altered meaning; IA, imagery amount; IV, imagery vividness; AD, attention direction; AB, absorption; JY, joy; SE, sexual excitement; LO, love; AN, anger; SD, sadness; FR, fear.

DAQ DIMENSIONS[a]

Raw score	Percentile					Raw score	Percentile				Raw score	Percentile	
6.00	100	100	100	100	100	6.00	100	100	100	98	6.00	100	100
5.75		98	99	98		5.75				97	5.75	98	96
5.67	94				85	5.67	97	95	89		5.67		
5.50		97	98	96		5.50				94	5.50	96	93
5.33	91				80	5.33	93	92	85		5.33		
5.25		96	96	94		5.25				92	5.25	95	87
5.00	85	94	94	93	75	5.00	90	86	80	91	5.00	92	77
4.75		91	92	87		4.75				88	4.75	91	68
4.67	76				65	4.67	87	78	73		4.67		
4.50		88	89	81		4.50				84	4.50	88	59
4.33	68				56	4.33	81	73	67		4.33		
4.25		87	85	75		4.25				78	4.25	81	48
4.00	61	83		66	50	4.00	78	63	62	72	4.00	76	39
3.75		80				3.75				64	3.75	69	27
3.67	50				40	3.67	70	53	52		3.67		
3.50		74				3.50				55	3.50	64	20
3.33	40				33	3.33	63	47	43		3.33		
3.25						3.25					3.25	61	14
3.00	36				22	3.00	59	40	35		3.00	51	9

	FL[b]	EQ	DT	PE	LO	DI	OP	AB	CO	VI	DN	SI
2.75		72								47		44
2.67	29		79	47	78	13	50	29	27			
2.50		65								38	5	33
2.33	23		76	40	74	10	43	23	22			
2.25		54								31	4	28
2.00	17	45	66	32	63	9	32	18	19	24	3	25
1.75		36								20		20
1.67	13		56	28	52	5	21	14	13			
1.50		30								13		15
1.33	10		46	22	45		16	9	11			
1.25		22								10	1	11
1.00	8	18	37	18	35	4	11	8	8	7		10
0.75		12								6		5
0.67	5		25	13	28	3	7	4	5			
0.50		7								4		4
0.33	4		20	10	22	2	4	3	4			
0.25		6										1
0.00	2	2	11	7	14		2	2	2	2		

[a] Stimulus condition: eyes closed sitting quietly (n = 246).
[b] FL, flexibility; EQ, equanimity; DT, detachment; PE, perspicacity; LO, locus; DI, direction; OP, one-pointedness; AB, absorption; CO, control; VI, vigilance; DN, density; SI, simultaneity.

DAQ DIMENSIONS[a]

Raw score	Percentile						Raw score	Percentile						Raw score
	100	100	100	100	100	100		100	100	100	100	100	100	
6.00	100	100	100	100	100	100	6.00	100	100	100	100	100	100	6.00
5.75		99					5.75					99		5.75
5.67	94		94	98	98	83	5.67	97	83	93	98		98	5.67
5.50							5.50							5.50
5.33	89			97	96	80	5.33		80	91		97	97	5.33
5.25							5.25							5.25
5.00	87	96	93	96	94	70	5.00	96	71	88	96	94	96	5.00
4.75		93		93			4.75				95	92	94	4.75
4.67	82		91		91	62	4.67	91	62	87				4.67
4.50	78	89	89	91	89	56	4.50	85	56	84	94	89	92	4.50
4.33		86					4.33				92	82	90	4.33
4.25							4.25							4.25
4.00	69	83	86	88	86	47	4.00	83	47	81	91	74	86	4.00
3.75		80		81	82	38	3.75	74	38	74	88	70	82	3.75
3.67	61		80				3.67							3.67
3.50		78			77	31	3.50	67	31	70				3.50
3.33	52	71	75	77			3.33	59	26		84	62	79	3.33
3.25							3.25				81	56	72	3.25
3.00	42	66	70	67	72	26	3.00			64	75	50	64	3.00

Scale	FL[b]	EQ	DT	PE	LO	DI	OP	AB	CO	VI	DN	SI
2.75										68	44	53
2.67	33	55	61	52	63	15	42	15	58	63	38	45
2.50	24	48	54	45	58	13	35	13	53	57	34	39
2.33		40	46	39	51	10	31	10	48	47	30	34
2.25										41	27	26
2.00	21	33	37	32	43	7	23		41	36	23	23
1.75		25						7	37	30	18	16
1.67	13									24	16	13
1.50	11	20	31	28	37	5	14	5	30	22	14	9
1.33		13								17	11	7
1.25										12	8	6
1.00	9	10	24	24	30		10		23	10	6	4
0.75		6						3				
0.67	7		15	18	24		7		19			
0.50		5										
0.33	4		12	14	20		3					
0.25												
0.00	2	3	9	11	15	2	2	2	13			
	FL[b]	EQ	DT	PE	LO	DI	OP	AB	CO	VI	DN	SI

[a] Stimulus condition: hypnosis induction via the Harvard Scale ($n = 246$).

[b] FL, flexibility; EQ, equanimity; DT, detachment; PE, perspicacity; LO, locus; DI, direction; OP, one-pointedness; AB, absorption; CO, control; VI, vigilance; DN, density; SI, simultaneity.

SYSTAT Programs

SYSTAT PROGRAM FOR CONVERTING THE PCI, FORM 1, INTO PCI INTENSITY AND RELIABILITY ITEMS

```
NOTE 'THIS COMMAND FILE IS CALLED PCI1.CMD; IT IS ON THE'
NOTE 'HARD DISK'
USE PCI1
NOTE 'THE DATA FILE IS ON THE HARD DISK AND IS CALLED:'
NOTE 'PCI1.SYS'
LET P1(09) = 6 − P1(09)
LET P1(05) = 6 − P1(05)
LET P1(49) = 6 − P1(49)
LET P1(33) = 6 − P1(33)
LET P1(07) = 6 − P1(07)
LET P1(16) = 6 − P1(16)
LET P1(26) = 6 − P1(26)
LET P1(15) = 6 − P1(15)
LET P1(30) = 6 − P1(30)
LET P1(17) = 6 − P1(17)
LET P1(29) = 6 − P1(29)
LET P1(04) = 6 − P1(04)
LET P1(23) = 6 − P1(23)
LET P1(12) = 6 − P1(12)
LET P1(18) = 6 − P1(18)
LET P1(08) = 6 − P1(08)
LET P1(52) = 6 − P1(52)
LET P1(34) = 6 − P1(34)
LET P1(27) = 6 − P1(27)
LET P1(50) = 6 − P1(50)
```

LET P1(40) = 6 − P1(40)
LET P1(06) = 6 − P1(06)
LET P1(02) = 6 − P1(02)
LET P1(24) = 6 − P1(24)
LET P1(03) = 6 − P1(03)
LET P1(25) = 6 − P1(25)
LET P1(38) = 6 − P1(38)
LET P1(19) = 6 − P1(19)
NOTE 'THE ABOVE STATEMENTS REVERSE ITEMS FOR THE PC1'
LET P1RELA = ABS(P1(05) − P1(35))
LET P1RELB = ABS(P1(12) − P1(44))
LET P1RELC = ABS(P1(08) − P1(28))
LET P1RELD = ABS(P1(21) − P1(40))
LET P1RELE = ABS(P1(06) − P1(45))
NOTE 'P1RELA THRU P1RELE REPRESENT THE 5 PAIRS OF'
NOTE 'RELIABILITY ITEMS'
LET P1PCI = (P1RELA + P1RELB + P1RELC + P1RELD + P1RELE)/5
NOTE 'P1PCI REPRESENTS THE RELIABILITY INDEX SCORE'
LET JY1   = (P1(09) + P1(46))/2
LET SE1   = (P1(05) + P1(35))/2
LET LO1   = (P1(20) + P1(49))/2
LET AN1   = (P1(14) + P1(33))/2
LET SD1   = (P1(07) + P1(31))/2
LET FE1   = (P1(16) + P1(42))/2
LET BI1   = (P1(11) + P1(26) + P1(51))/3
LET TS1   = (P1(15) + P1(30) + P1(43))/3
LET PE1   = (P1(17) + P1(39) + P1(29))/3
LET MN1 = (P1(04) + P1(23) + P1(32) + P1(47))/4
LET IA1   = (P1(12) + P1(44))/2
LET IV1   = (P1(18) + P1(48))/2
LET DR1   = (P1(08) + P1(52) + P1(28))/3
LET AB1   = (P1(01) + P1(34))/2
LET SA1   = (P1(13) + P1(27) + P1(50))/3
LET AS1   = (P1(21) + P1(40) + P1(53))/3
LET ID1   = (P1(06) + P1(45))/2
LET RA1   = (P1(02) + P1(24) + P1(36))/3
LET VC1   = (P1(03) + P1(25) + P1(41))/3
LET ME1   = (P1(10) + P1(22) + P1(38))/3
LET AR1   = (P1(19) + P1(37))/2
LET PA1   = (P1(09) + P1(46) + P1(05) + P1(35) + P1(20) + P1(49))/6
LET NA1   = (P1(14) + P1(33) + P1(07) + P1(31) + P1(16) + P1(42))/6
LET AE1   = (P1(11) + P1(26) + P1(51) + P1(15) + P1(30) + P1(43) + ,
P1(17) + P1(39) + P1(29) + P1(04) + P1(23) + P1(32) + P1(47))/13
LET IM1   = (P1(12) + P1(44) + P1(18) + P1(48))/4
LET AT1   = (P1(08) + P1(52) + P1(28) + P1(01) + P1(34))/5

NOTE 'JY1 THRU AT1 REPRESENT THE 26 (SUB)DIMENSIONS OF THE'
NOTE 'PC1, FORM1'
SAVE PCI1FNL
RUN

SYSTAT PROGRAM FOR CONVERTING THE PCI, FORM 2, INTO PCI INTENSITY AND RELIABILITY DATA

NOTE 'THIS COMMAND FILE IS CALLED PCI2.CMD; IT IS ON THE HARD'
NOTE 'DISK'
USE PCI2
NOTE 'THE DATA FILE IS ON THE HARD DISK AND IS CALLED:'
NOTE 'PCI2.SYS'
LET P2(35) = 6 − P2(35)
LET P2(39) = 6 − P2(39)
LET P2(22) = 6 − P2(22)
LET P2(14) = 6 − P2(14)
LET P2(34) = 6 − P2(34)
LET P2(41) = 6 − P2(41)
LET P2(03) = 6 − P2(03)
LET P2(49) = 6 − P2(49)
LET P2(11) = 6 − P2(11)
LET P2(50) = 6 − P2(50)
LET P2(19) = 6 − P2(19)
LET P2(51) = 6 − P2(51)
LET P2(07) = 6 − P2(07)
LET P2(42) = 6 − P2(42)
LET P2(40) = 6 − P2(40)
LET P2(47) = 6 − P2(47)
LET P2(29) = 6 − P2(29)
LET P2(13) = 6 − P2(13)
LET P2(02) = 6 − P2(02)
LET P2(25) = 6 − P2(25)
LET P2(18) = 6 − P2(18)
LET P2(44) = 6 − P2(44)
LET P2(45) = 6 − P2(45)
LET P2(21) = 6 − P2(21)
LET P2(52) = 6 − P2(52)
LET P2(09) = 6 − P2(09)
LET P2(26) = 6 − P2(26)
LET P2(48) = 6 − P2(48)
NOTE 'THE ABOVE STATEMENTS REVERSE ITEMS FOR THE PCI'
LET P2RELA = ABS(P2(39) − P2(12))
LET P2RELB = ABS(P2(42) − P2(08))

LET P2RELC = ABS(P2(47) − P2(05))
LET P2RELD = ABS(P2(53) − P2(18))
LET P2RELE = ABS(P2(44) − P2(20))
NOTE 'P2RELA THRU P2RELE REPRESENT THE 5 PAIRS OF RELIABILITY'
NOTE 'ITEMS'
LET P2PCI = (P2RELA + P2RELB + P2RELC + P2RELD + P2RELE)/5
NOTE 'P2PCI REPRESENTS THE RELIABILITY INDEX SCORE'
LET JY2 = (P2(35) + P2(10))/2
LET SE2 = (P2(39) + P2(12))/2
LET LO2 = (P2(36) + P2(22))/2
LET AN2 = (P2(32) + P2(14))/2
LET SD2 = (P2(34) + P2(17))/2
LET FE2 = (P2(41) + P2(06))/2
LET BI2 = (P2(46) + P2(03) + P2(24))/3
LET TS2 = (P2(49) + P2(11) + P2(31))/3
LET PE2 = (P2(50) + P2(28) + P2(19))/3
LET MN2 = (P2(51) + P2(07) + P2(23) + P2(16))/4
LET IA2 = (P2(42) + P2(08))/2
LET IV2 = (P2(40) + P2(04))/2
LET DR2 = (P2(47) + P2(29) + P2(05))/3
LET AB2 = (P2(33) + P2(13))/2
LET SA2 = (P2(43) + P2(02) + P2(25))/3
LET AS2 = (P2(53) + P2(18) + P2(37))/3
LET ID2 = (P2(44) + P2(20))/2)
LET RA2 = (P2(45) + P2(21) + P2(30))/3
LET VC2 = (P2(52) + P2(09) + P2(27))/3
LET ME2 = (P2(38) + P2(01) + P2(26))/3
LET AR2 = (P2(48) + P2(15))/2
LET PA2 = (P2(35) + P2(10) + P2(39) + P2(12) + P2(36) + P2(22))/6
LET NA2 = (P2(32) + P2(14) + P2(34) + P2(17) + P2(41) + P2(06))/6
LET AE2 = (P2(46) + P2(03) + P2(24) + P2(49) + P2(11) + P2(31) + ,
P2(50) + P2(28) + P2(19) + P2(51) + P2(07) + P2(23) + P2(16))/13
LET IM2 = (P2(42) + P2(08) + P2(40) + P2(04))/4
LET AT2 = (P2(47) + P2(29) + P2(05) + P2(33) + P2(13))/5
NOTE 'JY2 THRU AT2 REPRESENT THE 26 (SUB)DIMENSIONS OF THE'
NOTE 'PCI, FORM2'
SAVE PCI2FNL
RUN

SYSTAT PROGRAM FOR CONVERTING THE DAQ, FORM 1, INTO DAQ INTENSITY AND RELIABILITY ITEMS

NOTE 'THIS COMMAND FILE IS CALLED DAQ1.CMD; IT IS ON THE'
NOTE 'HARD DISK'
USE DAQ1

NOTE 'THE DATA FILE IS ON THE HARD DISK AND IS CALLED:'
NOTE 'DAQ1.SYS'
LET D1(11) = 6 − D1(11)
LET D1(37) = 6 − D1(37)
LET D1(33) = 6 − D1(33)
LET D1(21) = 6 − D1(21)
LET D1(32) = 6 − D1(32)
LET D1(04) = 6 − D1(04)
LET D1(26) = 6 − D1(26)
LET D1(25) = 6 − D1(25)
LET D1(36) = 6 − D1(36)
LET D1(09) = 6 − D1(09)
LET D1(22) = 6 − D1(22)
LET D1(16) = 6 − D1(16)
LET D1(05) = 6 − D1(05)
LET D1(28) = 6 − D1(28)
LET D1(38) = 6 − D1(38)
LET D1(24) = 6 − D1(24)
LET D1(35) = 6 − D1(35)
LET D1(02) = 6 − D1(02)
LET D1(39) = 6 − D1(39)
LET D1(20) = 6 − D1(20)
LET D1(31) = 6 − D1(31)
NOTE 'THE ABOVE STATEMENTS REVERSE ITEMS FOR THE DAQ'
LET D1RELA = ABS(D1(11) − D1(30))
LET D1RELB = ABS(D1(10) − D1(37))
LET D1RELC = ABS(D1(12) − D1(21))
LET D1RELD = ABS(D1(06) − D1(38))
LET D1RELE = ABS(D1(13) − D1(39))
LET D1RELF = ABS(D1(20) − D1(40))
NOTE 'D1RELA THRU D1RELF REPRESENT THE 6 PAIRS OF RELIABILITY'
NOTE 'ITEMS'
LET D1DAQ = (D1RELA + D1RELB + DIRELC + D1RELD + D1RELE +,
   D1RELF)/6
NOTE 'D1DAQ REPRESENTS THE RELIABILITY INDEX SCORE'
LET FL1   = (D1(11) + D1(19) + D1(30))/3
LET EQ1   = (D1(10) + D1(37) + D1(23) + D1(33))/4
LET DT1   = (D1(12) + D1(21) + D1(32))/3
LET PE1   = (D1(04) + D1(14) + D1(26))/3
LET LO1   = (D1(03) + D1(15) + D1(25))/3
LET DI1   = (D1(08) + D1(18) + D1(36))/3
LET ON1   = (D1(09) + D1(22) + D1(34))/3
LET AB1   = (D1(07) + D1(16) + D1(29))/3
LET CO1   = (D1(05) + D1(17) + D1(28))/3
LET VI1   = (D1(06) + D1(38) + D1(24) + D1(35))/4

```
LET DN1  = (D1(02) + D1(13) + D1(39) + D1(27))/4
LET SI1  = (D1(01) + D1(20) + D1(40) + D1(31))/4
NOTE 'FL1 THRU SI1 REPRESENT THE 12 DIMENSIONS OF THE DAQ,'
NOTE 'FORM 1'
SAVE DAQ1FNL
RUN
```

SYSTAT PROGRAM FOR CONVERTING THE DAQ, FORM 2, INTO DAQ INTENSITY AND RELIABILITY ITEMS

```
NOTE 'THIS COMMAND FILE IS CALLED DAQ2.CMD; IT IS ON THE'
NOTE 'HARD DISK'
USE DAQ2
NOTE 'THE DATA FILE IS ON THE HARD DISK AND IS CALLED:'
NOTE 'DAQ2.SYS'
LET D2(09) = 6 − D2(09)
LET D2(38) = 6 − D2(38)
LET D2(34) = 6 − D2(34)
LET D2(15) = 6 − D2(15)
LET D2(28) = 6 − D2(28)
LET D2(05) = 6 − D2(05)
LET D2(26) = 6 − D2(26)
LET D2(35) = 6 − D2(35)
LET D2(27) = 6 − D2(27)
LET D2(12) = 6 − D2(12)
LET D2(22) = 6 − D2(22)
LET D2(36) = 6 − D2(36)
LET D2(11) = 6 − D2(11)
LET D2(32) = 6 − D2(32)
LET D2(39) = 6 − D2(39)
LET D2(10) = 6 − D2(10)
LET D2(20) = 6 − D2(20)
LET D2(18) = 6 − D2(18)
LET D2(40) = 6 − D2(40)
LET D2(16) = 6 − D2(16)
LET D2(02) = 6 − D2(02)
LET D2RELA = ABS(D2(09) − D2(14))
LET D2RELB = ABS(D2(08) − D2(38))
LET D2RELC = ABS(D2(07) − D2(15))
LET D2RELD = ABS(D2(33) − D2(39))
LET D2RELE = ABS(D2(01) − D2(40))
LET D2RELF = ABS(D2(16) − D2(37))
NOTE 'D2RELA THRU D2RELF REPRESENT THE 6 PAIRS OF RELIABILITY'
NOTE 'ITEMS'
LET D2DAQ = (D2RELA + D2RELB + D2RELC + D2RELD + D2RELE +,
   D2RELF)/6
```

```
NOTE 'D2DAQ REPRESENTS THE RELIABILITY INDEX SCORE'
LET FL2  = (D2(09) + D2(29) + D2(14))/3
LET EQ2  = (D2(08) + D2(38) + D2(23) + D2(34))/4
LET DT2  = (D2(07) + D2(15) + D2(28))/3
LET PE2  = (D2(05) + D2(13) + D2(26))/3
LET LO2  = (D2(06) + D2(17) + D2(35))/3
LET DI2  = (D2(19) + D2(04) + D2(27))/3
LET ON2 = (D2(12) + D2(22) + D2(31))/3
LET AB2 = (D2(21) + D2(36) + D2(03))/3
LET CO2 = (D2(11) + D2(24) + D2(32))/3
LET VI2  = (D2(33) + D2(39) + D2(10) + D2(20))/4
LET DN2 = (D2(18) + D2(01) + D2(40) + D2(30))/4
LET SI2  = (D2(25) + D2(16) + D2(37) + D2(02))/4
NOTE 'FL2 THRU SI2 REPRESENT THE 12 DIMENSIONS OF THE DAQ,'
NOTE 'FORM 2'
SAVE DAQ2FNL
RUN
```

Jennrich Pattern Analysis Program Using APL*

*From Pekala & Kumar (1985). Reprinted with permission of the publisher.

```
        ∇JENN [□]∇
     ∇  CHI←X JENN Z                    M←60
[1]     N1←M                            N←60
[2]     N2←N
[3]     A←3 3ρX
[4]     B←⍉A
[5]     I←(⍳3)∘.=⍳3                     X←0 0 0    ,□
[6]     R1←(A+B)+I              □:
[7]     E←3 3ρZ                         .1 0 0    ,□
[8]     F←⍉E                   □:
[9]     R2←(E+F)+I                      .2 .3 0
[10]    NR1←N1×R1                       Z←0 0 0    ,□
[11]    NR2←N2×R2              □:
[12]    R←(NR1+NR2)÷(N1+N2)             .4 0 0    ,□
[13]    C←(N1×N2)÷(N1+N2)      □:
[14]    Z1←R1-R2                        .5 .6 0
[15]    RI←⌹R
[16]    ZZ←(C∘0.5)×(Z1+.×RI)
[17]    ZSQ←ZZ+.×ZZ
[18]    TR1←1 1⍉ZSQ                     X JENN Z
[19]    TR←+/TR1                  7.041605808
[20]    LCHI←0.5×TR
[21]    RIJ←R×RI
[22]    S←I+RIJ
[23]    SI←⌹S                           M←100
[24]    HD←1 1⍉ZZ                       N←100
[25]    VD←3 1ρHD                       X JENN Z
[26]    STEP1←SI+.×HD             11.73600968
[27]    RCHI←STEP1+.×VD
[28]    CHI←LCHI-RCHI
     ∇
```

References

Aaronson, B. S. (1972). Hypnosis, depth perception, and psychedelic experience. In C. T. Tart (Ed.), *Altered states of consciousness* (pp. 268–275). New York: John Wiley.

American Society of Clinical Hypnosis (1973). *A syllabus on hypnosis and a handbook of therapeutic suggestions.* Des Plaines, Illinois: American Society of Clinical Hypnosis Education and Research Foundation.

Andersen, P., & Andersson, S. A. (1968). *Physiological basis of the alpha rhythm.* New York: Appleton-Century-Crofts.

Anderson, J. R. (1976). *Language, memory, and thought.* Hillsdale, New Jersey: Lawrence Erlbaum.

Anderson, J. R. (1983). *The architecture of cognition.* Cambridge, Massachusetts: Harvard University Press.

Anderson, J. R., & Bower, G. H. (1973). *Human associative memory.* Washington, D.C.: Winston.

Angell, J. (1907). The province of functional psychology. *The Psychological Review, 14,* 61–91.

Anonymous (1972). The effects of marijuana on consciousness. In C. T. Tart (Ed.), *Altered states of consciousness* (pp. 343–364). New York: John Wiley.

Arbib, M. A. (1980). Perceptual structures and distributed motor control. In V. B. Brooks (Ed.), *Handbook of physiology,* vol. III. Bethesda, Maryland: The American Physiological Society.

Ashby, W. R. (1963). *An introduction to cybernetics.* New York: John Wiley.

Ashworth, P. (1976). Some notes on phenomenological approaches in psychology. *Bulletin of the British Psychological Society, 29,* 363–369.

Baars, B. J. (1983). Conscious contents provide the nervous system with coherent, global information. In R. J. Davidson, G. E. Schwartz, & D. Shapiro (Eds.), *Consciousness and self-regulation: Advances in research and theory,* vol. 3 (pp. 41–79). New York: Plenum Press.

Baars, B. J. (1985). Can involuntary slips reveal one's state of mind? With an addendum on the problem of conscious control of action. In T. M. Shlechter & M. P. Toglia (Eds.), *New directions in cognitive science* (pp. 242–261). Norwood, New Jersey: Ablex Publishing.

Baars, B. J. (1986). *The cognitive revolution in psychology.* New York: Guilford Press.

Baars, B. J. (1987). Global-workspace theory of consciousness: Evidence, theory, and some phylogenetic speculations. In G. Greenberg & E. Tobach (Eds.), *Cognition, language, and consciousness: Integrative levels* (pp. 209–236). Hillsdale, New Jersey: Lawrence Erlbaum.

Baars, B. J. (1988). *A cognitive theory of consciousness.* Cambridge, Massachusetts: Cambridge University Press.

Barber, J. (1977). Rapid induction analgesia: A clinical report. *American Journal of Clinical Hypnosis, 19,* 138–147.

Barber, T. X., & Calverly, D. S. (1966). Effects on recall of hypnotic induction, motivational suggestions, and suggested regression: A methodological and experimental analysis. *Journal of Abnormal Psychology, 71,* 169–180.

Barlow, D. H. (1988). *Anxiety and its disorders: The nature and treatment of anxiety and panic.* New York: Guilford Press.

Bartlett, F. C. (1932). *Remembering: A study in experimental and social psychology.* Cambridge, Massachusetts: Cambridge University Press.

Baruss, I. (1987). Metanalysis of definitions of consciousness. *Imagination, Cognition, and Personality, 6,* 321–329.

Battista, J. R. (1978). The science of consciousness. In K. S. Pope & J. L. Singer (Eds.), *The stream of consciousness: Scientific investigations into the flow of human experience* (pp. 55–90). New York: Plenum Press.

Bernstein, D. A., & Borkovec, T. D. (1973). *Progressive relaxation training: A manual for the helping professions.* Champaign, Illinois: Research Press.

Bieber, S. L. (1986). A hierarchical approach to multigroup factor invariance. *Journal of Classification, 3,* 113–134.

Blaney, P. H. (1986). Affect and memory: A review. *Psychological Bulletin, 99,* 229–246.

Bobrow, D. G., & Collins, A. (1975). *Representation and understanding.* New York: Academic Press.

Boring, E. G. (1929/50). *A history of experimental psychology.* New York: Appleton-Century-Crofts.

Boring, E. G. (1953). A history of introspection. *Psychological Bulletin, 50,* 176–189.

Bowers, K. S. (1981). Do the Stanford Scales tap the "classic suggestion effect?" *International Journal of Clinical and Experimental Hypnosis, 29,* 42–53.

Bowers, K. S. (1986). *The unconscious reconsidered.* Paper presented at the Western Canada Clinical Psychology Conference. University of Saskatchewan, Saskatchewan, Canada.

Bowers, K. S. & Meichenbaum, D. (Eds.) (1984). *The unconscious reconsidered.* New York: John Wiley.

Box, G. E. P. (1950). Problems in the analysis of growth and wear curves. *Biometrics, 6,* 362–389.

Bradburn, N., Rips, L., & Shevell, S. (1987). Answering autobiographical questions: The impact of memory and inference on surveys. *Science, 236,* 157–161.

Brentano, F. (1874/1925). *Psychologie vom empirischen standpunkt.* Leipzig, Germany: F. Meiner. (Original work published in 1925.)

Broadbent, D. E. (1958). *Perception and communication.* New York: Pergamon Press.

Brown, B. B. (1974). *New mind, new body.* New York: Harper & Row.

Brown, D. P., & Fromm, E. (1986). *Hypnotherapy and hypnoanalysis.* Hillsdale, New Jersey: Lawrence Erlbaum.

Bruner, J. (1957). On perceptual readiness. *Psychological Review, 64,* 123–152.

Cattell, R. B. (1930). The subjective character of cognition and the presentational development of perception. *British Journal of Psychology, Monographs, 14.*

Cleveland, W. S. (1985). *The elements of graphing data.* Monterey, California: Wadsworth Advanced Books.

Copleston, F. (1963). *A history of philosophy:* vol. IV: *Descartes to Leibniz.* New York: Doubleday and Company.

Council, J. R., & Kirsch, I. (1989). *Correlates or confounds: Suggestions for improved research methods.* Paper presented at the Annual Meeting of the Society for Clinical and Experimental Hypnosis, St. Louis, Missouri, November, 1989.

Crowder, R. G. (1976). *Principles of learning and memory.* Hillsdale, New Jersey: Lawrence Erlbaum.

Davidson, J. M., & Davidson, R. J. (Eds.) (1980). *The psychobiology of consciousness.* New York: Plenum Press.

De Groot, H. P., Gwynn, M. I., & Spanos, N. P. (1988). The effects of contextual information and gender on the prediction of hypnotic susceptibility. *Journal of Personality and Social Psychology, 54,* 1049–1053.

Deikman, A. J. (1966). Deautomatization and the mystical experience. *Psychiatry, 29,* 324–338.

Deikman, A. J. (1972). Experimental meditation. In C. T. Tart (Ed.), *Altered states of consciousness* (pp. 203–223). New York: John Wiley.

Descartes, R. (1641/1969). Meditations on the first philosophy. In R. Wolff (Ed.), *Ten great works of philosophy* (pp. 111–172). New York: New American Library. (Work first published in 1641.)

Diamond, S. J. (1976). Brain circuits for consciousness. *Brain, Behavior, and Evolution, 13,* 376–395.

Duncker, K. (1945). On problem solving. *Psychological Monographs, 58* (5, Whole No. 270).

Ericsson, K. A., & Simon, H. A. (1980). Verbal reports as data. *Psychological Review, 87,* 215–251.

Everitt, B. (1978). *Graphical techniques for multivariate data.* London, England: Heinemann Educational Books.

Eysenck, H. J. (1952). *Scientific study of personality.* New York: Macmillan.

Fabian, W. D., & Fishkin, S. M. (1981). A replicated study of self-reported changes in psychological absorption with marijuana intoxification. *Journal of Abnormal Psychology, 90,* 546–553.

Fehmi, L. (1978). EEG biofeedback, multichannel synchrony training, and attention. In A. Sugerman and R. E. Tarter (Eds.), *Expanding dimensions of consciousness* (pp. 155–182). New York: Springer.

Feuerstein, G. (1987). *Structures of consciousness: The genius of Jean Gebser—An introduction and critique.* Lower Lake, California: Integral Press.

Field, P. B. (1965). An inventory of hypnotic depth. *International Journal of Clinical and Experimental Hypnosis, 13,* 238–249.

Field, P. B., & Palmer, R. R. (1969). Factor analysis: Hypnosis Inventory. *International Journal of Clinical and Experimental Hypnosis, 17,* 50–61.

Finke, R. A., & MacDonald, H. (1978). Two personality measures relating hypnotic susceptibility to absorption. *International Journal of Clinical and Experimental Hypnosis, 26,* 78–83.

Fischer, R. (1971). A cartography of the ecstatic and meditative states. *Science, 174,* 897–904.

Fischer, R. (1978). Cartography of conscious states: Integration of East and West. In A. A. Sugerman & R. E. Tarter (Eds.), *Expanding dimensions of consciousness* (pp. 24–57). New York: Springer.

Fishkin, S. M., & Jones, B. M. (1978). Drugs and consciousness: An attentional model of consciousness with application to drug-related altered states, In A. A. Sugerman & R. E. Tarter (Eds.), *Expanding dimensions of consciousness* (pp. 273–298). New York: Springer.

Forbes, E., & Pekala, R. J. (1991). Predicting the hypnotic susceptibility of nursing students. Manuscript in preparation.

Frankel, V. (1989). *Hypnosis, hypnotizability, and clinical syndromes.* Invited address given at the Annual Meeting of the Society of Clinical and Experimental Hypnosis. St. Louis, Missouri, November, 1989.

Freud, S. (1912). The dynamics of transference. *Standard Edition, 12,* 97–108.

Fricton, J. R., & Roth, P. (1985). The effect of direct and indirect hypnotic suggestions for analgesia in high and low susceptible subjects. *American Journal of Clinical Hypnosis, 27,* 226–231.

Fried, R. (1987). *The hyperventilation syndrome: Research and clinical treatment.* Baltimore, Maryland: Johns Hopkins Press.

Fromm, E. (1979). Qua vadis hypnosis? Predictions of future trends in hypnosis research. In E. Fromm and R. E. Shor (Eds.), *Hypnosis: Developments in research and new perspectives* (pp. 687–703). New York: Aldine.

Fromm, E., Brown, D. P., Hurt, S. W., Oberlander, J. Z., Boxer, A. M., & Pfeifer, G. (1981). The phenomena and characteristics of self-hypnosis. *International Journal of Clinical and Experimental Hypnosis, 29,* 189–246.

Gabbard, G., & Twemlow, S. (1986). An overview of altered mind/body perception. *Bulletin of the Menninger Clinic, 50,* 351–366.

Gardner, H. (1985). *The mind's new science: A history of the cognitive revolution.* New York: Basic Books.

Gardner, H. (1987). Epilogue to the paperback edition. In H. Gardner, *The mind's new science: A history of the cognitive revolution* (pp. 393–400). New York: Basic Books.

Garner, W. R. (1974). *The processing of information and structure.* Hillsdale, New Jersey: Lawrence Erlbaum.

Gebser, J. (1986). *The ever present origin* (N. Barstad with A. Mickunas, Trans.). Athens: Ohio University Press.

Gellhorn, E., & Kiely, W. F. (1972). Mystical states of consciousness: Neurophysiological and chemical aspects. *Journal of Nervous and Mental Disease, 154,* 392–405.

Geschwind, N. (1979). Specializations of the human brain. *Scientific American, 241,* 180–201.

Gilman, L., & Rose, A. J. (1974). *APL: An interactive approach.* New York: John Wiley.

Goleman, D. (1977). *The varieties of the meditative experience.* New York: E. P. Dutton.

Greenfield, T. K. (1977). *Individual differences and mystical experience in response to three forms of meditation.* Unpublished doctoral dissertation, University of Michigan.

Greenson, R. R. (1967). *The technique and practice of psychoanalysis.* New York: International Universities Press.

Grof, S. (1975). *Realms of the human unconscious: Observations from LSD research.* New York: State University of New York Press.

Grof, S. (1985). *Beyond the brain: Birth, death, and transcendence in psychotherapy.* New York: State University of New York Press.

Guilford, J. P., & Fruchter, B. (1978). *Fundamental statistics in psychology and education* (6th ed.). New York: McGraw-Hill.

Gurwitsch, A. (1967). On the intentionality of consciousness. In J. J. Kockelmans (Ed.), *Phenomenology: The philosophy of Edmund Husserl and its interpretation* (pp. 118–136). New York: Doubleday.

Haber, R. N. (1974). Information processing. In E. C. Cartarette & M. P. Friedman (Eds.), *Handbook of perception,* vol. 1. *Historical and philosophical roots of perception* (pp. 313–333). New York: Academic Press.

Harman, R., McKim, R., Mogar, R., Fadiman, J., & Stolaroff, M. (1972). Psychedelic agents in creative problem-solving. In C. T. Tart (Ed.), *Altered states of consciousness* (pp. 455–472). New York: John Wiley.

Harrell, T. H., Chambless D. L., & Calhoun, J. F. (1981). Correlational relationships between self-statements and affective states. *Cognitive Therapy and Research, 5,* 159–173.

Hartigan, J. A. (1975). *Clustering algorithms.* New York: John Wiley.

Hathaway, S. R., & McKinley, J. C. (1948). *The Minnesota Multiphasic Personality Inventory.* New York: The Psychological Corporation.

Heidegger, M. (1927/62). *Being and time* (J. Macquarrie & E. Robinson, Trans.). New York: Harper and Row. (Original work published 1927.)

Helminiak, D. A. (1984). Consciousness as a subject matter. *Journal for the Theory of Social Behavior, 14,* 211–230.

Hilgard, E. R. (1965). *The experience of hypnosis.* New York: Harcourt Brace Jovanovich.

Hilgard, E. R. (1969). Altered states of consciousness. *Journal of Nervous and Mental Disease, 149,* 68–79.

Hilgard, E. R. (1975). Hypnosis. *Annual Review of Psychology, 26,* 19–44.

Hilgard, E. R. (1977). *Divided consciousness: Multiple controls in human thought and action.* New York: John Wiley.

Hilgard, E. R. (1980). Consciousness in contemporary psychology. *Annual Review of Psychology, 31,* 1–26.

Hilgard, E. R. (1982). Illusions: The eye-roll sign is related to hypnotizability. *Archives of General Psychiatry, 39,* 963–966.

Holt, R. R. (1964). Imagery: The return of the ostracized. *American Psychologist, 19,* 254–264.

Huba, G. J., Aneshensel, C. S., & Singer, J. L. (1981). Development of scales for three second-order factors of inner experience. *Multivariate Behavioral Research, 16,* 181–206.

Hunt, H. T., & Chefurka, C. M. (1976). A test of the psychedelic model of altered states of consciousness. *Archives of General Psychiatry, 33,* 867–876.

Hunter, J. E. (1977). *Cluster analysis: Reliability, construct validity, and the multiple indicator approach to measurement.* Paper presented at a workshop entitled "Advanced Statistics" given at the U.S. Civil Service Commission, Washington, D.C., March, 1977.

Hunter, J. E., & Cohen, S. H. (1971). *PACKAGE.* Unpublished manuscript. East Lansing: Michigan State University.

Hunter, J. E., & Gerbing, D. W. (1979). *Unidimensional measurement and confirmatory factor analysis.* East Lansing, Michigan: Institute for Research on Testing.

Hurlburt, R. T. (1980). Validation and correlation of thought sampling with retrospective measures. *Cognitive Therapy and Research, 4,* 235–238.

Husserl, E. (1913/72). *Ideas: General introduction to pure phenomenology.* New York: Collier.

Izard, C. E. (1977). *Human emotions.* New York: Plenum Press.

James, W. (1890/1950). *The principles of psychology.* New York: Dover Press.

James, W. (1902/58). *The varieties of religious experience.* New York: New American Library.

Jennrich, R. J. (1970). An asymptotic chi-square test for the equality of two correlation matrices. *Journal of the American Statistical Association, 65,* 904–912.

Jewell, L. N. (1985). *Contemporary industrial/organizational psychology.* New York: West Publishing.

Johnson, L. C. (1970). Psychophysiology for all states. *Psychophysiology, 6,* 904–912.

Johnson, L. S. (1979). Self-hypnosis: Behavioral and phenomenological comparisons with heterohypnosis. *International Journal of Clinical and Experimental Hypnosis, 27,* 240–264.

Jones, B., & Spanos, N. P. (1982). Suggestions for altered auditory sensitivity, the negative subject effect, and hypnotic susceptibility: A signal detection analysis. *Journal of Personality and Social Psychology, 43,* 637–647.

Joreskog, K. G., & Goldberger, A. S. (1972). Factor analysis by generalized least squares. *Psychometrika*, *37*, 243–260.

Kagan, J. (1972). Motives and development. *Journal of Personality and Social Psychology*, *22*, 51–66.

Kamiya, J. (1968). Conscious control of brain waves. *Psychology Today*, *1*, 56–60.

Kamiya, J. (1972). Operant control of EEG alpha rhythm and some of its reported effects on consciousness. In C. T. Tart (Ed.), *Altered states of consciousness* (pp. 519–529). New York: John Wiley.

Kelly, G. (1955). *The psychology of personal constructs*. New York: Norton Press.

Kendall, P. C., & Korgeski, G. P. (1979). Assessment and cognitive-behavioral interventions. *Cognitive Therapy and Research*, *3*, 1–21.

Keppel, G. (1973). *Design and analysis: A researcher's handbook*. Englewood Cliffs, New Jersey: Prentice-Hall.

Kihlstrom, J. F. (1984). Conscious, subconscious, unconscious: A cognitive perspective. In K. S. Bowers & D. Meichenbaum (Eds.), *The unconscious reconsidered* (pp. 149–211). New York: John Wiley.

Kihlstrom, J. F. (1987). The cognitive unconscious. *Science*, *237*, 1445–1452.

Kimble, G. A., & Garmezy, N. (1968). *Principles of general psychology* (3rd ed.). New York: Ronald Press.

Kintsch, W. (1974). *The representation of meaning in memory*. Hillsdale, New Jersey: Lawrence Erlbaum.

Kirk, R. E. (1968). *Experimental design: Procedures for the behavioral sciences*. Belmont, California: Brooks/Cole.

Kirsch, I. (1985). Response expectancy as a determinant of experience and behavior. *American Psychologist*, *40*, 1189–1202.

Klein, D. B. (1984). *The concept of consciousness—A survey*. Lincoln: University of Nebraska Press.

Klinger, E. (1971). *Structure and functions of fantasy*. New York: Wiley.

Klinger, E. (1978). Modes of normal conscious flow. In K. S. Pope & J. L. Singer (Eds.), *The stream of consciousness: Scientific investigations into the flow of human experience* (pp. 225–258). New York: Plenum Press.

Kluft, R. P. (1984). An introduction to multiple personality disorder. *American Journal of Clinical Hypnosis*, *14*, 19–24.

Knapp, T. J. (1986). The emergence of cognitive psychology in the latter half of the 20th century. In T. J. Knapp & L. C. Robertson (Eds.), *Approaches in cognition: Contrasts and controversies* (pp. 13–36). Hillsdale, New Jersey: Lawrence Erlbaum.

Kockelsman, J. J. (Ed.) (1967). *Phenomenology: The philosophy of Edmund Husserl and its interpretation*. New York: Doubleday.

Kohler, W. (1929). *Gestalt psychology*. New York: Liverright.

Krieger, D. (1979). *Therapeutic touch: How to use your hands to help and heal*. Englewood Cliffs, New Jersey: Prentice-Hall.

Kripke, D. F., & Sonnenshein, D. (1978). A biologic rhythm in waking fantasy. In K. S. Pope & J. L. Singer (Eds.), *The stream of consciousness: Scientific investigations into the flow of human experience* (pp. 321–334). New York: Plenum Press.

Krippner, S. (1972). Altered states of consciousness. In J. White (Ed.), *The highest state of consciousness* (pp. 1–5). New York: John Wiley.

Kroll, N. E. A., & Kellicut, M. H. (1972). Short-term recall as a function of covert rehearsal and of intervening task. *Journal of Verbal Learning and Verbal Behavior*, *11*, 196–204.

Kuhn, T. S. (1962). *The structure of scientific revolutions*. Chicago: University of Chicago Press.

Kukla, A. (1983). Toward a science of experience. *Journal of Mind and Behavior*, *4*, 231–246.

Kumar, V. K., & Pekala, R. J. (1988). Hypnotizability, absorption, and individual differences in phenomenological experience. *International Journal of Clinical and Experimental Hypnosis*, *36*, 80–88.

Kumar, V. K., & Pekala, R. J. (1989). Variations in phenomenological experience as a function of hypnosis and hypnotic susceptibility: A replication. *British Journal of Experimental and Clinical Hypnosis*, *6*,17–22.

Kumar, V. K., & Pekala, R. J. (1991). *The prediction of hypnotic susceptibility*. Manuscript in preparation.

LaBerge, S. (1985). *Lucid dreaming*. New York: Ballantine Books.

Lachman, R., Lachman, J. L., & Butterfield, E. C. (1979). *Cognitive psychology and information processing*. Hillsdale, New Jersey: Lawrence Erlbaum.

LaPointe, K., & Harrell, T. (1978). Thoughts and feelings: Correlational relationships and cross-situational consistency. *Cognitive Therapy and Research*, *2*, 311–322.

Lieberman, D. A. (1979). Behaviorism and the mind: A (limited) call for a return to introspection. *American Psychologist*, *34*, 319–333.

Lindsley, P. B. (1960). Attention, consciousness, sleep, and wakefulness. In J. Field (Ed.), *Handbook of physiology: A critical, comprehensive, presentation of physiology, knowledge, and concepts*, Section I: *Neurophysiology*, vol. III (pp. 1553–1593). Washington, D. C.: American Physiological Society.

Locke, J. (1690/1959). *An essay concerning human understanding*, vol. 1. New York: Dover Press.

Locke, T., & Shontz, F. (1983). Personality correlates of the near-death experience. *Journal of the American Society for Psychical Research*, *77*, 311–318.

Ludwig, A. H. (1972). Altered states of consciousness. In C. T. Tart (Ed.), *Altered states of consciousness* (pp. 11–24). New York: John Wiley.

Macrae, J. (1988). *Therapeutic touch: A practical guide*. New York: Knopf.

Mahoney, M. (1977). Cognitive therapy and research: A question of questions. *Cognitive Therapy and Research*, *1*, 5–16.

Maitz, E. A., & Pekala, R. J. (1991). Phenomenological quantification of an out-of-the-body experience associated with a near-death event. *OMEGA*, *22(3)*, 199–214.

Mandler, G. (1984). *Mind and body: Psychology of emotion and stress*. New York: W. W. Norton.

Mandler, G. (1985). *Consciousness: An essay in cognitive psychology*. Hillsdale, New Jersey: Lawrence Erlbaum.

Marcel, A. J. (1983). Conscious and unconscious perception: An approach to the relations between phenomenal experience and perceptual processes. *Cognitive Psychology*, *15*, 238–300.

Marsh, C. A. (1977). A framework for describing subjective states of consciousness. In N. E. Zinberg (Ed.), *Alternate states of consciousness* (pp. 121–144). New York: Free Press.

Maupin, E. W. (1972). Individual differences in response to a Zen meditation exercise. In C. T. Tart (Ed.), *Altered states of consciousness* (pp. 191- 202). New York: John Wiley.

McClelland, J. L., & Rumelhart, D. E. (1985). Distributed memory and the representation of general and specific information. *Journal of Experimental Psychology: General*, *114*, 159–188.

McClelland, J. L., & Rumelhart, D. E. (1988). *Explorations in parallel distributed processing: A handbook of models, programs, and exercises*. Cambridge, Massachusetts: MIT Press.

McClelland, J. L., Rumelhart, D. E., & the PDP Research Group (1986). *Parallel distributed processing*, vol. 2: *Psychological and behavioral models*. Cambridge, Massachusetts: MIT Press.

Meichenbaum, D., & Gilmore, J. B. (1984). The nature of unconscious processes: A cognitive-behavioral perspective. In K. S. Bowers & D. Meichenbaum (Eds.), *The unconscious reconsidered* (pp. 273–298). New York: John Wiley.

Menz, R. (1984). The denial of death and the out-of-the-body experience. *Journal of Religion and Health, 23,* 317–329.

Merrell-Wolff, F. (1973). *The philosophy of consciousness without an object: Reflections on the nature of transcendental consciousness.* New York: Julian Press.

Miller, G. A. (1951). *Language and communication.* New York: McGraw-Hill.

Miller, G. A., & Buckhout, R. (1973). *Psychology: The science of mental life* (2nd ed.). New York: Harper & Row.

Monroe, R. A. (1971). *Journeys out of the body.* New York: Doubleday.

Moody, R. (1975). *Life after life.* Georgia: Mockingbird Books.

Mountcastle, V. B. (1978). An organizing principle for cerebral function: The unit module and the distributed system. In G. M. Edelman & V. B. Mountcastle (Eds.), *The mindful brain* (pp. 7–50). Cambridge, Massachusetts: MIT Press.

Naranjo, C., & Ornstein, R. E. (1972). *On the psychology of meditation.* New York: Viking Press.

Natsoulas, T. (1978). Consciousness. *American Psychologist, 33,* 906–914.

Natsoulas, T. (1981). Basic problems of consciousness. *Journal of Personality and Social Psychology, 41,* 132–178.

Natsoulas, T. (1987). The six basic concepts of consciousness and William James's stream of thought. *Imagination, Cognition, and Personality, 6,* 289–319.

Neisser, U. (1967). *Cognitive psychology.* New York: Appleton-Century- Crofts.

Newell, A., & Simon, H. A. (1972). *Human problem solving.* Englewood Cliffs, New Jersey: Prentice-Hall.

Newell, A., Shaw, J. C., & Simon, H. A. (1958). Elements of a theory of human problem-solving. *Psychological Review, 65,* 151–166.

Nie, N. H., Hall, C. H., Jenkins, J. G., Steinbrenner, K., & Bent, D. H. (1975). *Statistical package for the social sciences* (2nd ed.). New York: McGraw-Hill.

Nin, A. (1978). *Delta of Venus: Erotica.* New York: Bantam.

Nisbett, R. E., & Wilson, T. D. (1977). Telling more than we can know: Verbal reports on mental processes. *Psychological Review, 84,* 231–259.

Noll, R. (1989). What has really been learned about shamanism? *Journal of Psychoactive Drugs, 21,* 47–50.

Norman, D. A., & Rumelhart, D. E. (1975). *Exploration in cognition.* San Francisco, California: W. H. Freeman.

Noyes, R., & Kletti, R. (1972). The experience of dying from falls. *OMEGA, 3,* 45–52.

Nulton, L., & Pekala, R. J. (1991). *A phenomenological comparison of several stress management strategies.* Manuscript in preparation.

Nunnally, J. C. (1967). *Psychometric theory.* New York: McGraw-Hill.

O'Grady, K. E. (1980). The absorption scale: A factor analytic assessment. *International Journal of Clinical and Experimental Hypnosis, 28,* 281–288.

Orne, M. T. (1959). The nature of hypnosis: Artifact and essence. *Journal of Abnormal and Social Psychology, 58,* 277–299.

Orne, M. T. (1962). On the social psychology of the psychological experiment: With particular reference to demand characteristics. *American Psychologist, 17,* 776–783.

Orne, M. T. (1971). The simulation of hypnosis: Why, how, and what it means. *International Journal of Clinical and Experimental Hypnosis, 19,* 183–210.

Orne, M. T. (1977). The construct of hypnosis: Implications of the definition for research and practice. *Annals of the New York Academy of Sciences, 296,* 14–33.

Orne, M. T., & Wilson, S. K. (1978). On the nature of alpha feedback training. In G. E.

Schwartz and D. Shapiro (Eds.), *Consciousness and self-regulation* (pp. 359–400). New York: Plenum Press.

Ornstein, R. E. (1972). *The psychology of consciousness.* San Francisco, California: W. H. Freeman.

Osis, K., & Haraldsson, S. (1977). *At the hour of death.* New York: Avon.

Osis, K., Bokert, E., & Carlson, M. L. (1973). Dimensions of the meditative experience. *Journal of Transpersonal Psychology, 5,* 109–135.

Oxford English Dictionary. (1933). Oxford, England: Oxford University Press.

Oxman, T. E., Rosenberg, S. D., Schnurr, P. P., Tucker, G. J., & Gala, G. (1988). The language of altered states. *The Journal of Nervous and Mental Disorders, 176,* 401–408.

Pahnke, W. H. (1972). Drugs and mysticism. In J. White (Ed.), *The highest state of consciousness* (pp. 257–277). New York: Plenum Press.

Palmer, S. E., & Kimchi, R. (1986). The information processing approach to cognition. In T. E. Knapp & L. C. Robertson (Eds.), *Approaches to cognition: Contrasts and controversies* (pp. 37–78). Hillsdale, New Jersey: Lawrence Erlbaum.

Parks, C. W., Klinger, E., & Perlmutter, M. (1988). Dimensions of thought as a function of age, gender, and task difficulty. *Imagination, Cognition, and Personality, 8,* 49–62.

Pekala, R. J. (1980). *An empirical-phenomenological approach for mapping consciousness and its various "states"* (Doctoral dissertation, Michigan State University, 1980). *44* (University Microfilm No. 82–02, 489.)

Pekala, R. J. (1982). *The Phenomenology of Consciousness Inventory.* Thorndale, Pennsylvania: Psychophenomenological Concepts. (Now published by Mid-Atlantic Educational Institute. See Pekala, 1991b.)

Pekala, R. J. (1985a). A psychophenomenological approach to mapping and diagraming states of consciousness. *Journal of Religion and Psychical Research, 8,* 199–214.

Pekala, R. J. (1985b). Biofeedback, hypnosis, and individual differences in cognitive style: When to do what to whom. *The Cognitive Behaviorist, 7,* 11–13.

Pekala, R. J. (1985c). *Mapping the structures and patterns of consciousness: User's manual for the Phenomenology of Consciousness Inventory (PCI).* Thorndale, Pennsylvania: Psychophenomenological Concepts (out of print).

Pekala, R. J. (1985d). *The Dimensions of Attention Questionnaire (DAQ).* Thorndale, Pennsylvania: Psychophenomenological Concepts. (Now published by Mid-Atlantic Educational Institute. See Pekala, 1991a.)

Pekala, R. J. (1987). The phenomenology of meditation. In M. West (Ed.), *The psychology of meditation* (pp. 59–80). London: Clarendon Press.

Pekala, R. J. (1988a). *Questionnaire on affection and cognition.* Unpublished psychological test. West Chester, Pennsylvania: Mid-Atlantic Educational Institute.

Pekala, R. J. (1988b). *The Phenomenology of Consciousness Inventory: Short Form (PCI:SF).* Unpublished psychological test. West Chester, Pennsylvania: Mid-Atlantic Educational Institute.

Pekala, R. J. (1989). *A cluster analysis of the phenomenology of individuals during hypnosis: Are there subclusters of very-low/low and very-high/high susceptible individuals.* Paper presented at the Annual Meeting of the Society for Clinical and Experimental Hypnosis, St. Louis, Missouri, November, 1989.

Pekala, R. J. (1991a). *The Dimensions of Attention Questionnaire (DAQ).* West Chester, Pennsylvania: Mid-Atlantic Educational Institute.

Pekala, R. J. (1991b). *The Phenomenology of Consciousness Inventory (PCI).* West Chester, Pennsylvania: Mid-Atlantic Educational Institute.

Pekala, R. J. (1991c). *Using a short form of the PCI to predict hypnotic susceptibility.* Manuscript in preparation.

Pekala, R. J. (in press). Hypnotic types: Evidence from a cluster analysis of phenomenal experience. *Contemporary Hypnosis.*

Pekala, R. J., & Bieber, S. L. (1990). Operationalizing pattern approaches to consciousness: An analysis of the phenomenological patterns of consciousness among individuals of differing susceptibility. *Imagination, Cognition, and Personality, 9,* 303–320.

Pekala, R. J., & Ersek, B. (1991). *States of consciousness associated with walking over hot coals (the firewalk): A preliminary study.* Study in progress.

Pekala, R. J., & Forbes, E. (1988). Hypnoidal effects associated with several stress management techniques. *Australian Journal of Clinical and Experimental Hypnosis, 16,* 121–132.

Pekala, R. J., & Forbes, E. (1990). Subjective effects associated with several stress management strategies: With reference to attention. *Journal of Behavioral Medicine, 16,* 39–44.

Pekala, R. J., & Kumar, V. K. (1984). Predicting hypnotic susceptibility by a self-report phenomenological state instrument. *American Journal of Clinical Hypnosis, 27,* 114–121.

Pekala, R. J., & Kumar, V. K. (1985). A short program for assessing the equality of two independent correlation matrices. *Educational and Psychological Measurement, 45,* 175–177.

Pekala, R. J., & Kumar, V. K. (1986). The differential organization of the structures of consciousness during hypnosis and a baseline condition. *Journal of Mind and Behavior, 7,* 515–539.

Pekala, R. J., & Kumar, V. K. (1987). Predicting hypnotic susceptibility via a self-report instrument: A replication. *American Journal of Clinical Hypnosis, 30,* 57–65.

Pekala, R. J., & Kumar, V. K. (1988). Phenomenological variations in attention across low, medium, and high hypnotically susceptible individuals. *Imagination, Cognition, and Personality, 7,* 303–314.

Pekala, R. J., & Kumar, V. K. (1989). Phenomenological patterns of consciousness during hypnosis: Relevance to cognition and individual differences. *Australian Journal of Clinical and Experimental Hypnosis, 17,* 1–20.

Pekala, R. J., & Levine, R. L. (1981). Mapping consciousness: Development of an empirical-phenomenological approach. *Imagination, Cognition, and Personality, 1,* 29–47.

Pekala, R. J., & Levine, R. L. (1982). Quantifying states of consciousness via an empirical-phenomenological approach. *Imagination, Cognition, and Personality, 2,* 51–71.

Pekala, R. J., & Nagler, R. (1989). The assessment of hypnoidal states: Rationale and clinical application. *American Journal of Clinical Hypnosis, 31,* 231–236.

Pekala, R. J., & Wenger, C. F. (1983). Retrospective phenomenological assessment: Mapping consciousness in reference to specific stimulus conditions. *Journal of Mind and Behavior, 4,* 247–274.

Pekala, R. J., Wenger, C. F., & Levine, R. L. (1985). Individual differences in phenomenological experience: States of consciousness as a function of absorption. *Journal of Personality and Social Psychology, 48,* 125–132.

Pekala, R. J., Steinberg, J., & Kumar, V. K. (1986). Measurement of phenomenological experience: Phenomenology of Consciousness Inventory. *Perceptual and Motor Skills, 63,* 983–989.

Pekala, R. J., Forbes, E., & Contrisciani, P. A. (1989). Assessing the phenomenological effects of several stress management strategies. *Imagination, Cognition, and Personality, 88,* 265–281.

Pekala, R. J., Hand, J., & Kumar, V. K. (1991). *Expectancy as a moderator and moderated variable in hypnosis: With reference to subjective experience.* Manuscript submitted for publication.

Pekala, R. J., Kumar, V. K., & Cummings, J. (in press). Types of hypnotically susceptible individuals and reported attitudes and experiences of the paranormal and the anomalous. *Journal of the American Society for Psychical Research.*

Piaget, J. (1962). *Play, dreams, and imitation in childhood*. New York: Norton.

Plotkin, W. B. (1979). The alpha experience revisited: Biofeedback in the transformation of psychological state. *Psychological Bulletin, 86*, 1132–1148.

Plutchik, R. (1962). *The emotions: Facts, theories, and a new model*. New York: Random House.

Plutchik, R. (1980). *Emotions: A psychoevolutionary synthesis*. New York: Harper & Row.

Pope, K. S. (1978). How gender, solitude, and posture influence the stream of consciousness. In K. S. Pope and J. L. Singer (Eds.), *The stream of consciousness: Scientific investigations into the flow of human experience* (pp. 259–298). New York: Plenum Press.

Pope, K. S., & Singer, J. L. (1978a). Regulation of the stream of consciousness: Toward a theory of ongoing thought. In G. E. Schwartz & D. Shapiro (Eds.), *Consciousness and self-regulation*, vol. 2 (pp. 101- 137). New York: Plenum Press.

Pope, K. S., & Singer, J. L. (Eds.) (1978b). *The stream of consciousness: Scientific investigations into the flow of human experience*. New York: Plenum Press.

Pribram, K. N. (1976). Problems concerning the structure of consciousness. In G. G. Globus, G. Maxwell, & I. Savodnik (Eds.), *Consciousness and the brain* (pp. 297–313). New York: Plenum Press.

Pribram, K. N., & McGuiness, D. (1975). Arousal, activation, and effort in the control of attention. *Psychological Review, 82*, 116–149.

Qualls, P. J., & Sheehan, P. W. (1981a). Imagery encouragement, absorption capacity, and relaxation during electromyograph biofeedback. *Journal of Personality and Social Psychology, 41*, 370–379.

Qualls, P. J., & Sheehan, P. W. (1981b). Role of the feedback signal in electromyograph biofeedback: The relevance of attention. *Journal of Experimental Psychology: General, 110*, 204–216.

Rabinowitz, A. (1975). Hostility measurement and its relationship to fantasy capacity. *Journal of Personality Assessment, 39*, 50–54.

Rachlin, H. (1974). Self-control. *Behaviorism, 2*, 94–107.

Ram Dass, B. (1974). *Be here now*. San Cristabel, New Mexico: Lama Foundation.

Rao, K. R., & Palmer, J. (1987). The anomaly called psi: Recent research and criticism. *Behavioral and Brain Sciences, 10*, 539–552.

Reise, S. P., & Hurlburt, R. T. (1988). The relations between dimensions of thought reported in two thought-sampling studies. *Imagination, Cognition, and Personality, 7*, 315–322.

Ring, K. (1980). *Life at death: A scientific investigation of the near-death experience*. New York: Coward, McCann, & Geoghegan.

Ring, K., & Franklin, S. (1981/82). Do suicide survivors report near-death experiences. *OMEGA, 12*, 191–208.

Robbins, A. (1986). *Unlimited power*. New York: Fawcett Columbine.

Robinson, D. N. (1979). *Systems of modern psychology: A critical sketch*. New York: Columbia University Press.

Rogers, T., & Craighead, W. (1977). Physiological responses to self-statements: The effects of statement valence and discrepancy. *Cognitive Therapy and Research, 1*, 99–119.

Rossi, E. L. (1986). *The psychobiology of mind-body healing: New concepts of therapeutic hypnosis*. New York: W. W. Norton.

Rossi, E. L., & Cheek, D. B. (1988). *Mind-body therapy: Ideodynamic healing in hypnosis*. New York: W. W. Norton.

Rumelhart, D. E., Hinton, G. E., & McClelland, J. L. (1986a). A general framework for parallel distributed processing. In D. E. Rumelhart, J. L. McClelland, & the PDP Research Group (Eds.), *Parallel distributed processing: Explorations in the microstructure of cognition*: vol. 1: *Foundations* (pp. 45–76). Cambridge, Massachusetts: MIT Press.

Rumelhart, D. E., McClelland, J. L., & the PDP Research Group (1986b). *Parallel distributed processing: Explorations in the microstructure of cognition*: vol. 1: *Foundations*. Cambridge, MA: MIT Press.

Rychlak, J. (1977). *The psychology of rigorous humanism*. New York: Wiley.

Rychlak, J. (1981). Logical learning theory: Proposition, corollaries, and research evidence. *Journal of Personality and Social Psychology, 40,* 731–749.

Sarbin, T. R., & Coe, W. C. (1972). *Hypnosis: A social psychological analysis of influence communication*. New York: Holt, Rinehart, & Winston.

Sartre, J. P. (1943/71). *Being and nothingness: An essay on phenomenological ontology* (H. Barnes, Trans.). New York: Simon & Schuster. (Original work published 1943.)

Savage, C. E. (1976). An old ghost in a new body. In G. G. Globus, G. Maxwell, & I. Savodnik (Eds.), *Consciousness and the brain* (pp. 125- 152). New York: Plenum Press.

Schank, R. C., & Abelson, R. P. (1977). *Scripts, plans, goals, and understanding*. Hillsdale, New Jersey: Lawrence Erlbaum.

Shannon, C. E., & Weaver, W. (1949). *The mathematical theory of communication*. Urbana: University of Illinois Press.

Shapiro, D. H. (1980). *Meditation: Self-regulation strategy and altered state of consciousness*. New York: Aldine.

Sharf, B., & Zamansky, H. S. (1963). Reduction in work-recognition threshold under hypnosis. *Perceptual and Motor Skills, 17,* 499–510.

Sheehan, P. W., & McConkey, K. M. (1982). *Hypnosis and experience: The exploration of phenomena and process*. Hillsdale, New Jersey: Lawrence Erlbaum.

Shor, R. E. (1959). Hypnosis and the concept of the generalized reality orientation. *American Journal of Psychotherapy, 13,* 582–622.

Shor, R. E. (1962). Three dimensions of hypnotic depth. *International Journal of Clinical and Experimental Hypnosis, 10,* 23–38.

Shor, R. E. (1979). A phenomenological method for the measurement of variables important to an understanding of the nature of hypnosis. In E. Fromm & R. E. Shor (Eds.), *Hypnosis: Developments in research and new perspectives* (2nd ed.) (pp. 105–135). New York: Aldine-Atherton.

Shor, R. E., & Orne, E. C. (1962). *The Harvard Group Scale of Hypnotic Susceptibility*. Palo Alto, California: Consulting Psychologists Press.

Shower, C., & Canter, N. (1985). Social cognition: A look at motivated strategies. *Annual Review of Psychology, 36,* 275–305.

Silverman, J. L. (1968). A paradigm for the study of altered states of consciousness. *British Journal of Psychology, 114,* 1201–1218.

Singer, J. L. (1966). *Daydreaming*. New York: Random House.

Singer, J. L. (1975). *The inner world of daydreaming*. New York: Harper & Row.

Singer, J. L. (1977). Ongoing thought: The normative baseline for altered states of consciousness. In N. E. Zinberg (Ed.), *Alternate states of consciousness* (pp. 89–120). New York: Free Press.

Singer, J. L. (1978). Experimental studies of daydreaming and the stream of consciousness. In K. S. Pope & J. L. Singer (Eds.), *The stream of consciousness: Scientific investigations into the flow of human experience* (pp. 187–223). New York: Plenum Press.

Singer, J. L. (1981). Towards the scientific study of imagination. *Imagination, Cognition, and Personality: The Scientific Study of Consciousness, 1,* 5–28.

Singer, J. L. (1984). The private personality. *Personality and Social Psychology Bulletin, 10,* 7–30.

Singer, J. L. (1985). The conscious and unconscious stream of thought. In D. Pines (Ed.), *Emerging syntheses in science* (pp. 95–120). Santa Fe, New Mexico: Santa Fe Institute.

Singer, J. L., & Antrobus, J. S. (1963). A factor-analytic study of daydreaming and conceptually-related cognitive and personality variables. *Perceptual and Motor Skills, Monograph Supplement* (3-V17).

Singer, J. L., & Antrobus, J. S. (1972). Daydreaming, imagery processes and personality: A normative study. In P. Sheehan (Ed.), *The function and nature of imagery*. New York: Academic Press.

Singer, J. L., & Kolligian, J., Jr. (1987). Personality: Developments in the study of private experience. *Annual Review of Psychology, 38*, 533–574.

Singer, J. L., & Pope, K. S. (1981). Daydreaming and imagery skills as predisposing capacities for self-hypnosis. *International Journal of Clinical and Experimental Hypnosis, 29*, 271–281.

Singer, J. L., & Rowe, R. R. (1962). An experimental study of some relationships between daydreaming and anxiety. *Journal of Consulting Psychology, 26*, 446–454.

Singer, J. L., & Salovey, P. (1985). *Organized knowledge structures in personality: Schemas, self-schemas, prototypes, and scripts. A review and research agenda*. Unpublished manuscript.

Singer, J. L., & Schonbar, R. (1961). Correlates of daydreaming: A dimension of self-awareness. *Journal of Consulting Psychology, 25*, 1–17.

Singer, J. L., & Singer, D. G. (1976). Imaginative play and pretending in early childhood: Some experimental approaches. In A. Davids (Ed.), *Child personality and psychotherapy: Current topics*, vol. 3 (pp. 69–112). New York: Wiley Interscience.

Singh, K. (1973). *The crown of life*. Delhi: Ruhani Satsang.

Skinner, B. F. (1974). *About behaviorism*. New York: Knoft.

Skinner, B. F. (1989). The origins of cognitive thought. *American Psychologist, 44*, 13–18.

Smith, E., & Miller, F. (1978). Limits on perception of cognitive processes: A reply to Nisbett and Wilson. *Psychological Review, 85*, 355–362.

Smith, J. (1978). Personality correlates of continuation and outcome in meditation and erect sitting controlled treatments. *Journal of Consulting and Clinical Psychology, 46*, 272–279.

Sokal, R. R., & Michener, C. D. (1958). A statistical method for evaluating systematic relationships. *University of Kansas Science Bulletin, 38*, 1409–1438.

Sokolov, E. N. (1963). *Perception and the orienting reflex*. New York: Macmillan.

Spanos, N. P., & Chaves, J. F. (1989). *Hypnosis: The cognitive-behavioral perspective*. Buffalo, New York: Prometheus Press.

Spanos, N. P., & McPeake, J. D. (1975). Involvement in everyday imaginative activities, attitudes toward hypnosis, and hypnotic susceptibility. *Journal of Personality and Social Psychology, 31*, 594–598.

Spence, K. W. (1957). The empirical basis and theoretical structure of psychology. *Philosophy of Science, 24*, 97–108.

Spiegel, H. (1974). *Manual for Hypnotic Induction Profile*. New York: Soni Medica.

Spoehr, K. T., & Lehmkuhle, S. W. (1982). *Visual information processing*. San Francisco, California: W. H. Freeman.

Starker, S., & Singer, J. L. (1975). Daydreaming and symptom patterns of psychiatric patients: A factor analytic study. *Journal of Abnormal Psychology, 84*, 567–570.

Steiger, J. H. (1980). Tests for comparing elements of a correlation matrix. *Psychological Bulletin, 87*, 245–251.

Strange, J. R. (1978). A search for the sources of the stream of consciousness. In K. S. Pope & J. L. Singer (Eds.), *The stream of consciousness: Scientific investigations into the flow of human experience* (pp. 9–29). New York: Plenum.

Tart, C. T. (1963). Hypnotic depth and basal skin resistance. *International Journal of Clinical and Experimental Hypnosis, 11*, 81–92.

Tart, C. T. (1969). *Altered states of consciousness*. New York: Wiley.

Tart, C. T. (1970). Self-report scales of hypnotic depth. *International Journal of Clinical and Experimental Hypnosis, 18*, 105–125.

Tart, C. T. (1971). *On being stoned: A psychological study of marijuana intoxification*. Palo Alto, California: Science and Behavior Books.

Tart, C. T. (1972). Scientific foundations for the study of altered states of consciousness. *Journal of Transpersonal Psychology*, *3*, 93–124.

Tart, C. T. (1975). *States of consciousness*. New York: Dutton.

Tart, C. T. (1977). Discrete states of consciousness. In P. R. Lee, R. E. Ornstein, D. Galin, A. Deikman, & C. T. Tart (Eds.), *Symposium on consciousness* (pp. 89–175). New York: Penguin.

Tart, C. T. (1979). Measuring the depth of an altered state of consciousness with particular reference to self-report scales of hypnotic depth. In E. Fromm & R. E. Shor (Eds.), *Hypnosis: Developments in research and new perspectives* (pp. 567–601). Hawthorne, New York: Aldine.

Tellegen, A. (1977). *The Multidimensional Personality Questionnaire*. Minneapolis, Minnesota: National Computing Systems.

Tellegen, A. (1979). On measures and conceptions of hypnosis. *American Journal of Clinical Hypnosis*, *21*, 219–236.

Tellegen, A. (1981). Practicing the two disciplines for relaxation and enlightenment: Comment on "Role of the feedback signal in electromyograph biofeedback: The relevance of attention" by Qualls and Sheehan. *Journal of Experimental Psychology: General*, *110*, 217- 226.

Tellegen, A., & Atkinson, G. (1974). Openness to absorbing and self- altering experiences ("absorption"), a trait related to hypnotic susceptibility. *Journal of Abnormal Psychology*, *83*, 268–277.

Thatcher, R. W., & John, E. R. (1977). *Foundations of cognitive processes*. Hillsdale, New Jersey: Lawrence Erlbaum.

Timm, N. H. (1975). *Multivariate analysis with applications in education and psychology*. Monterey, California: Brooks/Cole.

Titchener, E. B. (1898). The postulates of a structural psychology. *Philosophie Review*, *7*, 449–465.

Titchener, E. B. (1924). *Experimental psychology*. New York: Macmillan.

Tolman, E. C. (1927). A behaviorist's definition of consciousness. *Psychological Review*, *34*, 433–439.

Tomkins, S. S. (1962). *Affect, imagery, consciousness*: vol. 1. *The positive affects*. New York: Springer-Verlag.

Tomkins, S. S. (1963). *Affect, imagery, consciousness*: vol. 2. *The negative affects*. New York: Springer-Verlag.

Toulmin, S. (1982). The genealogy of "consciousness." In P. F. Secord (Ed.), *Explaining human behavior* (pp. 53–70). London: Sage Publications.

Tulving, E., & Donaldson, W. (1972). *Organization of memory*. New York: Academic.

Turk, D. C., & Salovey, P. (1985). Cognitive structures, cognitive processes, and cognitive-behavior modification: I. Client issues. *Cognitive therapy and research*, *9*, 1–17.

Twemlow, S., & Gabbard, G. (1984). The influence of demographic/psychological factors and pre-existing condition on the near-death experience. *OMEGA*, *15*, 223–235.

Valle, R. S., & King, M. (1978). An introduction to existential-phenomenological thought in psychology. In R. S. Valle & M. King (Eds.), *Existential phenomenological alternatives for psychology* (pp. 6–17). New York: Oxford University Press.

Vogel, G., Foulkes, D., & Trosman, H. (1972). Ego functions and dreaming during sleep onset. In C. T. Tart (Ed.), *Altered states of consciousness* (pp. 77–94). New York: John Wiley.

Wadden, T. A., & Anderton, C. H. (1982). The clinical use of hypnosis. *Psychological Bulletin*, *91*, 215–243.

Watson, J. B. (1913). Psychology as the behaviorist views it. *Psychological Review, 20,* 158–177.

Watson, J. B., & McDougall, W. (1929). *The battle of behaviorism.* New York: Norton.

Webster's Seventh New Collegiate Dictionary (1970). Springfield, Massachusetts: G. C. Merriam.

Weitzenhoffer, A. M. (1978). Hypnotism and altered states of consciousness. In A. A. Sugerman & R. E. Tarter (Eds.), *Expanding dimensions of consciousness* (pp. 183–225). New York: Springer.

Weitzenhoffer, A. M., & Hilgard, E. R. (1962). *The Stanford Hypnotic Susceptibility Scale, Form C.* Palo Alto, California: Consulting Psychologists Press.

Weitzenhoffer, A. M., Gough, P. B., & Landes, J. (1959). A study of the Braid effect: Hypnosis by visual fixation. *Journal of Psychology, 47,* 67–80.

Wharton, W. P. (1988). Imagery and the comprehension of college history texts: Free response measure. *Imagination, Cognition, and Personality, 7,* 323–333.

White, J. (Ed.) (1972). *The highest state of consciousness.* New York: Doubleday.

Wickramasekera, I. E. (1988). *Clinical behavioral medicine: Some concepts and procedures.* New York: Plenum Press.

Wilkinson, L. (1988a). *SYGRAPH.* Evanston, Illinois: SYSTAT.

Wilkinson, L. (1988b). *SYSTAT: The system for statistics.* Evanston, Illinois: SYSTAT.

Wilson, D. L. (1978). Brain mechanisms, consciousness, and introspection. In A. A Sugerman & R. E. Tarter (Eds.), *Expanding dimensions of consciousness* (pp. 3–23). New York: Springer.

Wilson, S. C., & Barber, T. X. (1983). The fantasy-prone personality: Implications for understanding imagery, hypnosis, and parapsychological phenomena. In A. A. Sheikh (Ed.), *Imagery: Current theory, research, and application* (pp. 340–387). New York: John Wiley.

Winkelman, M. (1989). A cross-cultural study of shamanistic healers. *Journal of Psychoactive Drugs, 21,* 17–24.

Winters, W. D., Ferror-Allado, T., Guzman-Flores, C., & Alavarex, M. (1972). The cataleptic state induced by ketamine: A review of the neuropharmacology of anesthesia. *Neuropharmacology, 11,* 313–316.

Wundt, W. (1897). *Outlines of psychology.* New York: Gustav E. Stechart.

Yanchar, R. J., & Johnson, H. J. (1981). Absorption and attitude towards hypnosis: A moderator analysis. *International Journal of Clinical and Experimental Hypnosis, 29,* 375–382.

Yogananda, P. (1974). *Autobiography of a yogi.* Los Angeles, California: Self-Realization Fellowship.

Zajonc, R. B. (1980). Feeling and thinking: Preferences need no inferences. *American Psychologist, 35,* 151–175.

Zajonc, R. B. (1984). On the primacy of affect. *American Psychologist, 39,* 117–123.

Zinberg, N. E. (1977). The study of consciousness states: Problems and progress. In N. E. Zinberg (Ed.), *Alternate states of consciousness* (pp. 1–36). New York: Free Press.

Zollschan, G. K., Schumaker, J. F., & Walsh, G. F. (Eds.) (1989). *Exploring the paranormal: Perspectives on belief and experience.* London: Prism Press.

Zuckerman, M., Persky, H., & Link, K. (1967). Relation of mood and hypnotizability: An illustration of the importance of the state versus trait distinction. *Journal of Consulting and Clinical Psychology, 31,* 464–470.

About the Author

Ronald J. Pekala, Ph.D., is a licensed psychologist in private practice in West Chester, Pennsylvania, and is co-director of the Biofeedback Clinic at the Veterans Administration Medical Center in Coatesville, Pennsylvania. Dr. Pekala specializes in using psychotherapy, biofeedback, and hypnosis in dealing with individuals suffering from stress-related, psychiatric, and psychophysiological disorders. Using a modified systems approach, he also works with couples and families.

Dr. Pekala is affiliated with several universities, where he teaches and does research, including Jefferson Medical College of Thomas Jefferson University, the Pennsylvania State University, West Chester University, and Immaculata College. For the past 15 years he has been involved in developing approaches to understanding and quantifying consciousness, its various states, and psychotherapeutic approaches based on his research and clinical practice. He has over 25 professional publications and has presented nationally on his theorizing and research concerning consciousness, psychotherapy, hypnosis, meditation, biofeedback, and psychotherapeutic approaches to health and healing.

Author Index

413

Subject Index